THE MOST TRUSTED NAME IN TRAVEL **FROMMER'S**

FROMMER'S

WASHINGTON, D.C.

8th Edition

Jess Moss and Kaeli Conforti

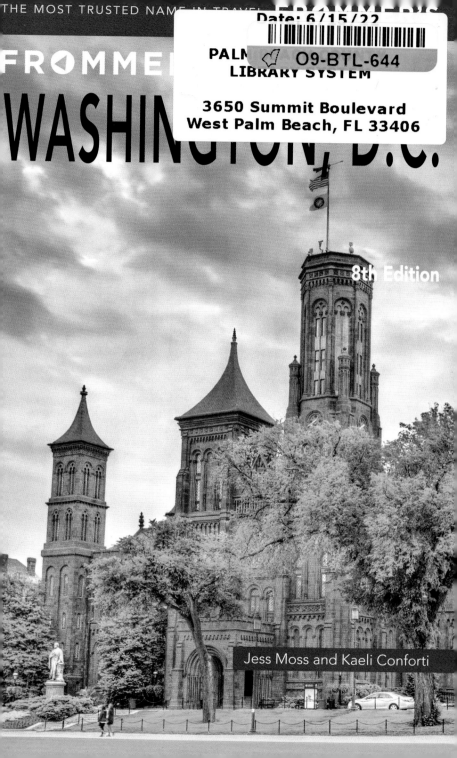

FROMMER'S STAR RATINGS SYSTEM

Every hotel, restaurant, and attraction listed in this guide has been ranked for quality and value. Here's what the stars mean:

★ Recommended
★★ Highly Recommended
★★★ A must! Don't miss!

AN IMPORTANT NOTE

The world is a dynamic place. Hotels change ownership, restaurants hike their prices, museums alter their opening hours, and buses and trains change their routings. And all of this can occur in the several months after our authors have visited, inspected, and written about these hotels, restaurants, museums, and transportation services. Though we have made valiant efforts to keep all our information fresh and up-to-date, some few changes can inevitably occur in the periods before a revised edition of this guidebook is published. So please bear with us if a tiny number of the details in this book have changed. Please also note that we have no responsibility or liability for any inaccuracy or errors or omissions, or for inconvenience, loss, damage, or expenses suffered by anyone as a result of assertions in this guide.

Previous page: The Smithsonian Institution Building, known as the "Castle."

This page: The Thomas Jefferson Memorial.

CONTENTS

1 THE BEST OF WASHINGTON, D.C. 1

2 WASHINGTON, D.C., IN CONTEXT 11

Washington, D.C., Today 11

The Making of the City 14

When to Go 22

3 SUGGESTED ITINERARIES & NEIGHBORHOODS 28

4 WHERE TO STAY 54

Getting the Best Deal 54

Capitol Hill 57

Capitol Riverfront 62

National Mall 64

Southwest Waterfront 65

Penn Quarter 66

Downtown 70

Adams Morgan 72

Dupont Circle 74

Foggy Bottom/West End 78

Georgetown 81

Shaw, 14th & U Street Corridors 83

Woodley Park 85

5 WHERE TO EAT 87

H Street Corridor 87

Capitol Hill & Barracks Row 93

Capitol Riverfront ("Navy Yard") 95

Southwest Waterfront 97

Downtown & Penn Quarter 99

Columbia Heights 105

14th & U Street Corridors 106

Adams Morgan 111

Dupont Circle 113

Foggy Bottom/West End 115

Georgetown 116

Woodley Park & Cleveland Park 120

6 EXPLORING WASHINGTON, D.C. 122

Capitol Hill 123

The National Mall & Memorial Parks 135

Southwest of the Mall 163

The White House Area 168

Penn Quarter 176

Dupont Circle 184

Foggy Bottom 186

U & 14th Street Corridors 187

Upper Northwest D.C.: Glover Park, Woodley Park & Cleveland Park 188

Georgetown 192

Northern Virginia 195

Parks 198

Especially for Kids 202

Outdoor Activities 204

7 SHOPPING 208

The Shopping Scene 208

Great Shopping Areas 208

Shopping A to Z 210

8 ENTERTAINMENT & NIGHTLIFE 221

The Performing Arts 221

The Bar Scene 228

The Club & Music Scene 231

The LGBTQ Scene 235

Spectator Sports 235

9 DAY TRIPS FROM D.C. 237

Mount Vernon 237

Old Town Alexandria 242

10 SELF-GUIDED WALKING TOURS 257

11 PLANNING YOUR TRIP 286

INDEX 308

ABOUT THE AUTHORS 318

The Kennedy Center for the Performing Arts viewed from the Potomac River.

A LOOK AT WASHINGTON, D.C.

For many visitors, a trip to Washington, D.C., isn't just a vacation. It's a pilgrimage of sorts. Schoolchildren are bused in by the hundreds of thousands and troop around the Mall in organized platoons as determined teachers feed them facts about the importance of what they're seeing. Veterans and their loved ones pay homage at memorials to fallen comrades. And ordinary citizens arrive in droves to see the monuments, museums, and historical sites of the most powerful city in the world. Where else, after all, are decisions made that affect not only the lives of every American but also the lives of people across the planet? The city was designed, from its very inception, to be a worthy place for pilgrimage, with its monuments, cultural archives, broad avenues, and impressive federal buildings and public spaces. But over the years, Washington has become even more multifaceted than the original planners could have envisioned. It's a highly cosmopolitan, multiracial, and wonderfully diverse city, thanks to its embassies (and their resident staff), large immigrant populations, and proud African American community. What follows is just a sampling of the remarkable sights you'll see and adventures you'll have in this engrossing capital.

View of the Washington Monument and Capitol Hill from the steps of the Lincoln Memorial.

Children play at the Albert Einstein memorial sculpture in front of the National Academy of Sciences building.

Artist Daniel Chester French's statue of Abraham Lincoln towers 19 feet inside the Lincoln Memorial.

The elaborate interior of the Library of Congress.

Looking up at the interior of the U.S. Capitol Building rotunda.

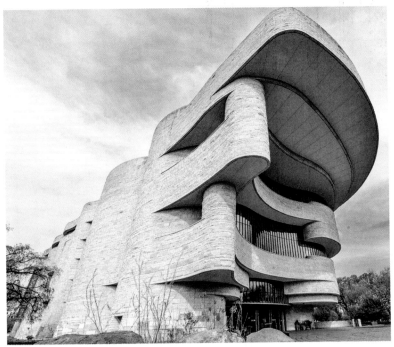

The National Museum of the American Indian.

Summertime "Jazz in the Garden" concerts are held on Friday evenings at the National Gallery of Art Sculpture Garden.

An installation at the Smithsonian Arts and Industries Building.

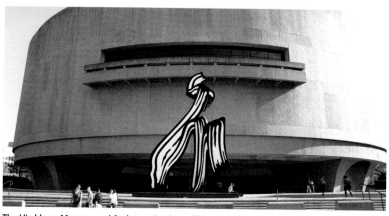

The Hirshhorn Museum and Sculpture Garden collection focuses on contemporary art.

An augmented reality exhibit at the Smithsonian's National Museum of Natural History.

District of Columbia War Memorial.

Chuck Berry's Gibson guitar is on display at the National Museum of African American History and Culture.

Le Diplomate on 14th Street in Logan Circle.

Adams Morgan is one of the District's most popular areas for nightlife.

Statue of Irish patriot Robert Emmet near the Irish Embassy.

A "panda-cam" watches the National Zoo's most beloved residents 24/7.

The Municipal Fish Market at The Wharf is the oldest continuously operating seafood market in the United States.

The Dupont Circle fountain is one of 18 Civil War memorials in the city.

Homes along the C&O Canal National Historical Park in Georgetown.

Penn Quarter Farmers Market.

The food hall at The Eastern Market.

An early evening stroll along Georgetown's waterfront.

Colorful row houses in Georgetown's Historical District.

Healy Hall on the main campus of Georgetown University.

The annual Capital Pride Parade takes place in June.

In 1912, Japan donated 3,020 ornamental cherry trees to Washington, D.C. Their blooms inspire the iconic yearly Cherry Blossom Festival.

The Citi Open Tennis Championship at the Rock Creek Park Tennis Center.

White House staff work in the handsome Eisenhower Executive Office Building.

The Petersen House, opposite Ford's Theatre, in which President Lincoln died on April 15, 1865.

DC JazzFest, held at the Wharf.

The African American Civil War Memorial.

NORTHERN VIRGINIA

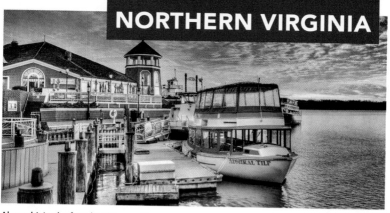

Alexandria's wharf on the Potomac River.

Outdoor dining in Old Town Alexandria.

More than one million people visit George Washington's home, Mount Vernon, yearly.

Brick row houses in Alexandria Old Town, Virginia.

The Tomb of the Unknown Soldier at Arlington National Cemetery.

A fully functioning distillery and gristmill are among the working exhibits at Mount Vernon.

THE BEST OF WASHINGTON, D.C.

by Jess Moss

The Georgetown University rowing team glides gracefully along the Potomac River as the sun paints the surface of the water. Museums open their doors and docents take their places. Jets take off from nearby Reagan National Airport and roar overhead. The Metro hums along its maze of tunnels and over the Potomac River. Chefs plot the day's menu in preparation for hungry D.C. restaurant-goers. Reporters gather at the White House to cover stories that will ripple across the country. All rub elbows from sunup to sundown in neighborhood coffee shops, in the halls of Congress, in waterfront restaurants, in Georgetown shops, in bars along 14th Street. Washington, D.C., is waking up.

But D.C.'s awakening is bigger than any one day. The city is coming into its own, becoming more than a haven of staunch politicos and white-marbled monuments. (Although it's still that, too.) Those who have power, those who want power, and those who are trying to change how power works are constantly shaping the here and now of Washington. A young generation is framing new neighborhoods, like the Wharf in Southwest, a formerly sleepy area abuzz with new restaurants, hotels, music halls, and nightlife, or Union Market, an epicenter for good food and artful retail. Avant-garde and "protest" art is making a statement on our streets and in our museums, giving volume to the city's often unheard voices. And, after a difficult stretch of pandemic shutdowns and political turmoil, the city is reemerging, a little tougher, more resilient, and ready to face what comes next.

Politics are here and will always be here in this "city of magnificent intentions," as Charles Dickens called it, but Washington is so much more. Each day is different. Things happen here that can happen nowhere else on earth. You're in the heartbeat of a nation, in a city that belongs to you. Make the most of it!

most unforgettable
WASHINGTON, D.C., EXPERIENCES

o **Viewing Washington Landmarks by Moonlight:** There is nothing as spectacular as the Lincoln Memorial illuminated at night, unless it's the sight of the White House, the Capitol, or the Washington Monument lit up after dark. Go via the Old Town Trolley or by bike on a Bike and Roll excursion; both operations offer narrated day and nighttime tours. See p. 300 and p. 302.

o **Waving to the White House:** It's one of the world's most famous addresses, and thanks to the recent removal of extra security fences, it's once again easy to catch a glimpse of the White House. You can view the President's residence and place of work from both sides of the building—the close-up view is of the North Portico, from Lafayette Park and Pennsylvania Ave. But the scene looking up the South Lawn from the Ellipse is arguably the more iconic of the two. Wondering if POTUS is home? The White House publishes a daily schedule that will give you a clue. And of course, if you have the opportunity to go *inside* and tour the building, take advantage. See p. 171.

o **Taking in a Show at the Historic Ford's Theatre:** It's memorable if not a bit eerie to see the Presidential Box where John Wilkes Booth shot President Abraham Lincoln on April 14, 1865, while the president watched the comedy "Our American Cousin." The renovated theater is still staging compelling productions today, and an attached museum holds surprisingly affecting exhibits on Lincoln's presidency and assassination, including the actual Deringer pistol used in the shooting. See p. 176.

The Lincoln Memorial and the Reflecting Pool.

○ **Perusing the Constitution:** Nowhere else in the U.S. can you see the original documents that grounded this nation in life, liberty, and the pursuit of happiness. The National Archives in Washington displays the Declaration of Independence, the Constitution of the United States, and the Bill of Rights behind glass. Sealed in scientifically advanced housing inside a low-lit marble rotunda designed to preserve the "Charters of Freedom," the documents are faded but still readable—and no less impressive when you consider their enormous impact on the beginnings of the United States. See p. 147.

○ **Visiting the U.S. Capitol or Supreme Court:** Washington is the capital of the United States, one of the world's greatest democracies, and it can be thrilling, inspiring, and just plain fun to see the inner workings of two of the three branches of government: the legislative branch in the U.S. Capitol building, and the judicial branch making decisions at the Supreme Court. Events in 2020 and 2021 affected tour schedules, so be sure to check for the latest info. See p. 123 and p. 132.

Visitors watch 4-year-old orangutan Redd and his mother, Batang, cross the O Line at the National Zoo in Washington, D.C.

THE best FAMILY EXPERIENCES

○ **Hanging Out at the National Zoo:** Make faces at the cute giant pandas, hear the mighty lion's roar, laugh at the playful monkeys, watch an elephant exercise, ride the solar-powered carousel. The National Zoo is essentially one big (163 acres!), family-friendly park, offering the chance to observe some 1,500 animals at play (or snoozing or eating). See p. 189.

○ **Ice Skating at the National Gallery:** The pond in the National Gallery of Art Sculpture Garden is transformed into an ice-skating rink in winter. Rent some skates and twirl around on the ice, admiring the sculptures as you go. Warm up with a hot chocolate at the garden's Pavilion Café. See p. 149.

○ **Getting the Wiggles Out at Rock Creek Park:** If you have little ones with lots of energy, then Rock Creek Park is for you. The Woodland Trail begins behind the Nature Center, while a quarter-mile, stroller-accessible Edge of the Woods trail leads from the Nature Center's front door. Inside the Nature Center itself are live turtles, fish, snakes, an active beehive, and a bird observation deck. The Planetarium offers scheduled daily shows, some for those under 5. See p. 199.

o **Riding a Roller Coaster, Piloting a Jet, and Other Adventuring:** Relax, parents. The Smithsonian's 19 museums and zoo have you covered. Kids will marvel at the suspended airplanes and astronaut and cosmonaut space suits, among 9,000 other artifacts, at the National Air and Space Museum. Or they can brave the simulated rides—inside a jet aircraft, a vintage airplane, or a spacecraft exploring the Milky Way. The National Museum of American History has cars, trains, and the interactive "Wegman's Wonderplace," designed exclusively for kids, where they can cook in a kid-sized Julia Childs' model kitchen, shop in a scaled-down market, and climb to their heart's content. Simulated adventures feel real in futuristic, high-speed race car and roller-coaster machines. *Note:* Height requirements and fees apply. See p. 145 and 153.

THE best FOOD

o **Best for a Special Occasion:** Dining at Georgetown's **1789 Restaurant** (p. 116) is about as old-school fine-dining Washington as you can get. The food is spectacular, the setting is refined, and the clientele is important. For something a little more contemporary, but no less memorable, treat yourself to the tasting menu at **Rose's Luxury** (p. 93). Each course is a delight, though the pork lychee salad course is in a class of its own. Since the best way to get a table at Rose's is to wait in line, if you really want to treat yourself, you can hire someone to do the waiting for you via TaskRabbit (www.taskrabbit.com) or Skip the Line (www.skipthelineus.com).

o **Best for Outdoor Dining:** These days, nearly everyone has outdoor dining, even if it's just a few two-tops on the sidewalk outside. But for a more established, weather-resistant open-air experience, head up to the 5th floor at The Wharf, where **La Vie** (p. 97) has a covered open-air terrace with monumental views. Nearly every other restaurant at The Wharf also has plenty of outdoor space. Another good option, also with waterfront views, is **The Point D.C.** (p. 96), down on Buzzard Point, whose retractable roof can keep things flexible, even during those sudden summer thunderstorms.

o **Best for Families:** It can be hard to get kids to sit still through dinner. At **Pinstripes** (p. 104) in Georgetown, the enormous Italian-American menu comes with plenty of bowling lanes and bocce courts to keep little ones entertained. Thin-crust, wood-fired pizzas fill you up at **Pizzeria Paradiso** (p. 114; with locations in Dupont Circle and M St. NW). More safe bets: chicken tenders and milkshakes at **Ted's Bulletin** (www.tedsbulletin.com; with locations on Capitol Hill and 14th St.); burgers and fries at **Good Stuff Eatery** (p. 95; with locations on Capitol Hill and Georgetown); or the lively, convenient **Hill Country Barbecue** (p. 100) in Penn Quarter for good ol' American barbecued chicken and mac and cheese.

o **Best for Regional Cuisine:** While Washington doesn't have its own cuisine per se, its central location in the Mid-Atlantic/Chesapeake Bay region gives it license to lay claim to the area's culinary specialties. And locals say nobody does Eastern Shore seafood better than Wharf restaurant **Rappahannock**

Oyster Bar (p. 98), the place to go for superb oysters, fresh from the waters off Virginia or Maryland. Try the briney Olde Salts from Chincoteague, Virginia, a personal favorite. The U-shaped seafood bar also serves up seafood classics like peel-and-eat shrimp steamed with Old Bay seasoning, clam chowder, and crab cakes.

o **Best All-Around for Fun and Food:** Oh, gosh, all sorts of D.C. restaurants satisfy this category, but Jose Andres' **Zaytinya** (Mediterranean tastes; p. 103) and **Jaleo** (Spanish tapas; p. 101) both offer imaginative and playful tasting menus. **Tiger Fork** (p. 111) in Shaw transports diners to a Hong Kong food market for crispy pork belly, soya chicken, and steamed rice noodles.

o **Best for a "Taste of Washington" Experience:** Real locals claim chicken and mumbo sauce, a bright orange sauce made by combining ketchup with a dash of BBQ and some sweet-and-sour sauce, as the hometown specialty. Find it at **Henry's Soul Café** (p. 112) on U Street NW. For some down-home fare, stop in at **Ben's Chili Bowl** (p. 109) and chat with the owners and your neighbor over a chili dog. The place is an institution, and you can stop by anytime—it's open for breakfast, lunch, and dinner.

o **Best for Vegetarians:** Fans flock to **Fancy Radish** (p. 90) for its rutabaga fondue, stuffed avocado with pickled cauliflower and spicy dan-dan noodles. **Beefsteak** (p. 116) is Chef Jose Andres' healthy and delicious salute to made-to-order vegetarian fast food. **Bombay Club** (p. 100) and **Rasika** (p. 101) are excellent choices for vegetarian-friendly Indian cuisine served in sophisticated surroundings.

Ben's Chili Bowl is a D.C. institution.

THE best THINGS TO DO FOR FREE IN WASHINGTON, D.C.

o **Take a Nature Hike:** Step into the nearly 2,000-acre **Rock Creek Park,** and within minutes you can find yourself surrounded by dense forest, worlds away from the busy sights and sounds of the capital city. There are over 30 miles of hiking trails throughout the park; some meander along the creek, others hoof it uphill for some elevation gain, and some are paved and easy for hikers of all ages. The park is managed by the National Park Service; access to all trails is free to the public. See p. 199.

o **People-Watch at Dupont Circle:** This traffic circle is also a park—an all-weather hangout for mondo-bizarre bike couriers, chess players, street musicians, and lovers. Sit and watch scenes of Washington life unfold around you—or join in the fun: The Circle is also the setting for outdoor yoga classes, sports screenings, and an annual snowball fight. See p. 276.

o **Attend a Millennium Stage Performance at the Kennedy Center:** Every evening at 6pm in its Grand Foyer, the Kennedy Center presents a free 1-hour concert performed by local up-and-coming, national, or international musicians. Purchase a cocktail from one of the Grand Foyer's bars near Millennium Stage and head through the glass doors to the terrace, where you can enjoy your drink and views of the Potomac River. Complimentary guided tours of the Kennedy Center are also available during the day. See p. 223.

o **Groove to the Sounds of Live Jazz in the Sculpture Garden:** On summery Friday evenings at the National Gallery of Art Sculpture Garden, you can dip your toes in the fountain pool and chill out to live jazz from 5 to 8pm. The jazz is free; the sandwiches, wine, and beer served in the Pavilion Café are not. See p. 150.

o **Pick a Museum, (Just About) Any Museum:** Because this is the U.S. capital, many of the museums are federal institutions, meaning admission is free. The National Gallery of Art, the U.S. Botanic Garden, and the Smithsonian's 19 Washington museums, from the National Air and Space Museum to its newest, the National Museum of African American History & Culture, are among many excellent choices. See chapter 6.

o **Watch Planes Take Off and Land at Gravelly Point:** Take the short drive to this waterfront park bordering Reagan National Airport, just minutes outside of D.C. Bring picnic eats and watch jet after jet descend and fly directly overhead. Not for the fainthearted! You can also see the planes from Hains Point, located on the other side of the Potomac River at the tip of East Potomac Park.

o **Attend an Event on the Mall:** Think of the National Mall as the nation's public square, where something is almost always going on—more than 3,500 events in a typical year, according to the National Park Service. There's the Kite Festival during cherry blossom season in the spring; the splendid Independence Day celebration every Fourth of July; special events reserved by individuals and random organizations that have obtained a permit, from weddings to speeches to religious gatherings; and walking tours, biking, Frisbee throwing, and assorted impromptu sports happenings year-round. See p. 135 for a calendar of annual events.

THE best NEIGHBORHOODS FOR GETTING LOST

o **Georgetown:** The truth is, you *want* to get lost in Georgetown, because it's the neighborhood's side streets that hold the history and centuries-old houses of this one-time Colonial tobacco port. Don't worry—Georgetown is so compact that you're never far from its main thoroughfares, M Street, and Wisconsin Avenue. For a backstreets tour of Georgetown, see p. 265.

o **Capitol Hill:** From the Library of Congress, walk east down Pennsylvania Ave. SE into the heart of one of the most storied neighborhoods in D.C. East of 2nd Street, blocks of large-scale government buildings fade into rows of beautifully restored 19th-century town houses. Coffee shops, restaurants, and stores frequented by resident Hill staffers abound. The historic Eastern Market (p. 129) lies just north of Pennsylvania Avenue; and fun and lively Barracks Row (p. 93) follows just south to the Washington Navy Yard, the oldest shore establishment of the U.S. Navy.

o **Old Town Alexandria:** Just a short distance from the District (by Metro, car, boat, or bike) is George Washington's Virginia hometown. On and off the beaten track are quaint cobblestone streets, boutiques and antiques stores, 18th-century architecture, and fine restaurants, many laying claim to the best crab cakes in town. See p. 242.

o **Dupont Circle:** Explore Dupont Circle's lovely side streets extending off Connecticut and Massachusetts avenues. You'll discover picturesque 19th-century town houses, small art galleries, historic museums, and actual residences (this is the Obama family's old neighborhood). Stroll Embassy Row (northward on Massachusetts Ave.) to view Beaux Arts mansions, many built by wealthy magnates during the Gilded Age. See p. 274.

THE best WAYS TO SEE WASHINGTON, D.C., LIKE A LOCAL

o **Shop at Eastern Market:** Capitol Hill is home to more than government buildings; it's a community of old town houses, antiques shops, and the venerable Eastern Market. Here, locals shop and barter every Saturday and Sunday for fresh produce, baked goods, and flea-market bargains, just as they've done for well over a century. *A must:* the blueberry pancakes at the Market Lunch counter. See p. 129.

o **Pub and Club It in D.C.'s Hot Spots:** Join Washington's footloose and fancy-free any night of the week (but especially Thurs–Sat) along 14th and U Streets, in Shaw, Adams Morgan, Capitol Riverfront, The Wharf (near southwest waterfront), Georgetown, Penn Quarter, and the H Street Corridor.

o **Go for a Jog on the National Mall:** Lace up your running shoes and race around the Mall at your own pace, admiring famous sights as you go. Your fellow runners will be buff military staff from the Pentagon, speed-walking members of Congress, and downtown workers doing their best to stave off the telltale pencil-pusher's paunch. It's about 2 miles from the foot of the Capitol to the Lincoln Memorial. See p. 150.

o **Attend a Hometown Game:** Take yourself out to a Washington Nationals baseball game at Nationals Park, drive to FedEx Field to root for Washington's NFL team along with its rabid fans, catch a Washington Wizards or Mystics basketball game at the downtown Capital One Arena, or hop the Metro to the new soccer stadium at Buzzard Point for a D.C. United match. To experience the true soul of the city, attend a Washington Capitals ice hockey match. Wear red. See p. 236.

o **Take in Some Live Music:** One of the best ways to feel at one with locals is by enjoying the live music scene together, not so much in large concert halls, but in smaller, seated venues such as **Blues Alley** (jazz and blues; p. 232) in Georgetown; the **Hamilton** (blues, rock, or country; p. 232) in the Penn Quarter; **The Anthem** (rock, country, pop; 901 Wharf St., SW; www.the anthemdc.com; ℂ **202/888-0020**) in the Southwest Wharf district; and **The Black Cat** (rock and independent; p. 233) on 14th Street. See p. 231.

Attending a hometown game at Nationals Park.

o **Sit at an Outdoor Cafe and Watch the Washington World Go By:** Locals watching locals. What better way to keep tabs on one another? The capital is full of seats offering front-row views of D.C. on parade. Here's a bunch: **Colada Shop** (p. 109), **Belga Café** (p. 93), **Café du Parc** (p. 70), **Fiola Mare** (p. 118), **Le Diplomate** (p. 107), and **Martin's Tavern** (p. 119).

THE best PLACES TO STAY

o **Best Historic Hotel:** The **Willard InterContinental** celebrates its 115th anniversary in 2021, and recently underwent a renovation. The original, smaller "City Hotel" existed here as early as 1816 before its name changed in 1906. The hotel has hosted nearly every U.S. president since Franklin Pierce was here in 1853. President Ulysses S. Grant liked to unwind with a cigar and brandy in the Willard lobby after a hard day in the Oval Office and is even said to have popularized the term "lobbyist" after so many locals would approach him there. Literary luminaries such as Mark Twain and Charles Dickens used to hang out in the Round Robin bar. See p. 70.

o **Best for Romance:** Its discreet service, intimate size, and exquisitely decorated guest rooms—and the fact that you need never leave the hotel for pampering or dining—makes **The Jefferson** (p. 74) perfect for a romantic rendezvous.

o **Best When You Have Business on Capitol Hill: Yotel Washington, D.C.** (p. 59) lies a short walk from the Capitol and offers a rooftop pool, a 24/7 fitness center, and an in-house power-dining spot, Art and Soul.

o **Best Bang for Your Buck:** Its great location near Georgetown, the White House, and the Metro and less than a mile from the National Mall, plus spacious studio and one-bedroom suites with kitchens, free Wi-Fi, and reasonable rates, make Foggy Bottom's **River Inn** (p. 80) one of the best values in town.

o **Best Views:** The **Hay-Adams** (p. 70) has such a great, unobstructed view of the White House that the Secret Service comes over regularly to do security sweeps of the place. Ask for a room on the H Street side of the hotel, on floors six through eight. Many of the guest rooms at the **Watergate** (p. 79) survey the Potomac River and the Georgetown waterfront, but the best view of all is from the hotel's Top of the Gate rooftop bar and lounge. Nearly half of the guest rooms in the **InterContinental Washington, D.C. – The Wharf** (p. 66), in the Southwest Waterfront neighborhood, capture a stunning view of the Washington Channel and East Potomac Park.

o **Best for Families:** The **Residence Inn DC/Capitol** (p. 65) is within walking distance of the National Mall, several Smithsonian museums, and the Metro. Breakfast is free; kids will love the indoor heated pool, while parents will appreciate its large, suite-style rooms with fully equipped kitchenettes. It's also pet-friendly if your family includes the four-legged variety.

THE best OFFBEAT EXPERIENCES

o **Join the Drum Circle at Meridian Hill Park:** Sunday afternoons, when the weather is right, Meridian Hill Park (p. 200) is the setting for an all-comers-welcome African drum circle. The tradition is 50 years old and dates from the tumultuous days of the 1960s, when activists sought a way to celebrate black liberation but also mourn the death of African-American leader Malcolm X. One drummer started, others gradually joined in, and over time the sonorous Sunday drum circle turned into a steady gig. The park is stunning, designed to resemble an Italian garden, complete with statuary, a cascading fountain, and landscaped grounds.

o **Explore Washington from an Unconventional Angle:** Yes, it's a graveyard, but Georgetown's **Oak Hill Cemetery** is also a handsome wooded and landscaped garden with a grand view of the city from its hillside perch. Here lie monuments for some of Washington's most illustrious residents, from the city's early days as well as recent years. See p. 271.

o **Play Street Hockey in Front of the White House:** Pennsylvania Avenue in front of the White House is closed to traffic, which makes it a perfect place for street hockey fanatics to show up Saturdays and Sundays at 10am. All you need are Rollerblades and a stick, although gloves and shin pads are also recommended. Go to www.white househockey.com for info.

Playing street hockey in front of the White House.

o **Visit the Barbie Pond:** All hail the Barbies. What started as a quirky front yard display outside a row house has become a neighborhood institution. **The Barbie Pond on Ave. Q** (1454½ Q St. NW, at 15th St. NW) displays elaborate scenes full of Barbie and Ken dolls representing holidays, TV shows and movies, or support for causes such as gay rights and environmentalism. You can follow the Barbies on Instagram at @barbie_pond_ave_q to see what the latest theme is. Just be sure to be respectful when here—take all the photos you want, but do not touch the dolls.

WASHINGTON, D.C., IN CONTEXT

by Jess Moss

The Federal City. The Nation's Capital. Hollywood for Ugly People. Chocolate City. A swamp. The DMV. Over the years, Washington, D.C., has garnered quite a few identities. Some pleasant; others not so much. Even Washingtonians have argued over what Washington, D.C., should really be called if it's ever granted its statehood. The New Columbia? Washington, Douglass Commonwealth?

Whatever nickname best describes D.C., you are bound to formulate your own after visiting. The city is that multi-hued and diverse. Sure, most visitors are here to see some of the country's most celebrated landmarks: the Washington Monument standing tall near the Lincoln Memorial, the stately U.S. Capitol Building staring down Pennsylvania Ave. toward the porticoed White House, the National Mall in all its shimmering green glory.

But Washington is not just a city of iconic sites. It's a dynamic metropolis full of life: marble-clad monuments providing a stately backdrop to a morning excursion on the Potomac River, a delicious meal at a Michelin-starred restaurant, a bike ride through Rock Creek Park on a beautiful fall day, a stroll past handsome embassies along Embassy Row, a tour of the Smithsonian's compelling National Museum of African American History & Culture, or a live jazz performance on a summer night in the Sculpture Garden of the National Gallery of Art.

This chapter, specifically, aims to put the story of Washington, D.C. into context beyond all of those monikers. It's also where we offer practical information on the best times to visit, the weather by season, and the city's most celebrated events.

WASHINGTON, D.C., TODAY

What Washington, D.C., was, is, and wants to be is constantly shifting. D.C. is both the capital of the United States and a city unto itself; therein lie its charms, but also a host of complications. Control of the city is the main issue. The District is a free-standing jurisdiction, but because it is a city with a federal rather than a state overseer, it has never been entitled to the same governmental powers as the states. Congress supervises the District's budget and legislation. Originally, Congress granted the city the authority to elect its own governance, but it rescinded that right when the District overspent its budget in attempts to improve its services and appearance after the Civil War. The White House then appointed three commissioners to oversee D.C.'s affairs.

It wasn't until a century later, in 1973, that the city regained the right to elect its own mayor and city council—although Congress still retains some control of the budget and can veto municipal legislation. The U.S. president appoints all D.C. judges and the Senate confirms them. District residents can vote in presidential primaries and elections and can elect a delegate to Congress, who introduces legislation and votes in committees but cannot vote on the House floor. This unique situation, in which residents of the District pay federal income taxes but don't have a vote in Congress, is a matter of great local concern. D.C. residents publicly protest the situation by displaying license plates bearing the inscription TAXATION WITHOUT REPRESENTATION. The proposed solution is to make D.C. a state, and calls for statehood have gained momentum in recent years, though it remains to be seen if the movement will gain enough traction in Congress to become reality.

Another wrinkle in this uncommon relationship is the fact that Washington's economy relies heavily on the presence of the federal government, which accounts for about 30% of all D.C. jobs, making it the city's second-largest employer. The city struggles toward political independence, although it recognizes the economic benefits of its position as the seat of the capital.

As you tour the city, you will see that Washington, D.C., is a remarkably resilient place. The combined pandemic, social justice protests, and political unrest of 2020 and 2021 have left a mark on the city's economy, as well as its collective memory. While the pandemic is not yet over at this writing, D.C. residents have largely adapted to life with mask mandates and shifting restrictions, and the vast majority are highly compliant—masking up, getting vaccinated, and staying home when told to do so.

Despite recent hardships, income here remains higher than the national average, residents are better educated than elsewhere, and the city has one of the highest rates of population growth in the nation, increasing nearly 15% in the last decade. Around 53% of the population is female, more than one-third are between the ages of 18 and 34, and the people are remarkably diverse: 46% African American, 46% white, 11% Hispanic, 5% Asian, 14% foreign-born, and 17% speaking a language other than English at home. The presence of embassies and the diplomatic community intensifies the international flavor.

One of the best ways to sample this global character is through the city's restaurant scene, which showcases an immense variety of international cuisines, from Ethiopian to Peruvian, as well as soul food and such regional specialties as oysters and crab (served soft-shell, hard-shell, soup, cake, you name it). The city's dining creds mount as critics from *Bon Appétit* magazine to the *New York Times* give high marks to the capital's restaurants. Eating out is a way of life here, whether simply for the pleasure of it or for business—the city's movers and shakers break bread at breakfast, lunch, and dinner.

Despite pandemic shutdowns, theaters, music venues, assorted historic and cultural attractions, hotels, brand-name stores, and homegrown boutiques abound, and Washingtonians make the most of their bounty. But whatever it is—exhibit, play, concert, or restaurant meal—it had better be good. As well-traveled, well-educated, and, let's face it, pretty demanding types, District dwellers have high standards.

It wasn't always this way. About 20 years ago, Washington wasn't as attractive. Tourists came to visit federal buildings and the city's memorials but stayed away from the dingy downtown and other off-the-Mall neighborhoods. The city had the potential for being so much more, and certain people—heroes, in my book—helped inspire action and brought about change themselves: Delegate Eleanor Holmes Norton, who fought (and continues to fight) steadfastly for D.C. statehood and economic revival and equality; former Mayor Anthony Williams, who rescued the District's budget when his predecessor, the notoriously mismanaging Mayor Marion Barry, brought the city to the brink of financial ruin; and the community-minded developers Abe and Irene Pollin, who used their own funds to finance the $200 million MCI sports center in the heart of town, spurring development all around it. Today, the popular arena (now known as Capital One Arena) anchors the utterly transformed Penn Quarter neighborhood.

"Revitalization" is too mild a word to describe the changes taking place in neighborhoods throughout the District. The city is literally reinventing itself. Look to the Capitol Riverfront neighborhood in southeast D.C. (locally known as "Navy Yard"), where a grand baseball stadium, Nationals Park, opened in March 2008, followed ever since by new restaurants and bars and hotels and housing; to the Columbia Heights enclave in upper northwest D.C., now a mélange of Latino culture, loft condominiums, and ethnic eateries; to historic Shaw, which has turned overnight from a quiet residential area into a trendy food and bar destination; and to the Southwest Waterfront, whose new Wharf complex of watersports and recreational activities, lodging, nightlife venues, shops, and eateries gives people plenty of reasons to come here, when they had few before. Add one more reason: Audi Field at Buzzard Point, the gorgeous stadium that debuted in 2018 as home base for D.C. United, the city's soccer team.

And more development is underway, including Capital Crossing, a mixed-use, 7-acre development between Union Station and Capital One Arena that actually adds 3 new city blocks, by way of its placement atop the I-395 Freeway! Meanwhile, the city's evergreens—the memorials and monuments, the historic neighborhoods, and the Smithsonian museums—remain unflaggingly popular.

But D.C. continues to have its share of problems, including crime, poverty, and lingering inequality. Some issues relate to the city's gentrification efforts, such as the displacement of residents from homes they can no longer afford in increasingly expensive neighborhoods. Mayor Muriel Bowser, who overwhelmingly won the 2018 election, continues to work hard to connect the city to its residents, as different as they may be, and to the politicians who reside here. Despite D.C.'s remarkable growth, many residents still struggle with access to all of those economic benefits, including healthcare, good schools, safe neighborhoods, adequate housing, and basic social services.

Diverse in demographics, residents are alike in loving their city, despite the issues it faces. Visitors seem to share this love, as statistics bear out: In a typical year, D.C. welcomes 24.6 million visitors a year, including 1.8 million from abroad.

THE MAKING OF THE CITY

As with many cities, Washington, D.C.'s past is written in its landscape. Behold the lustrous Potomac River, whose discovery by Captain John Smith in 1608 led to European settlement of this area. Take note of the city's layout: the 160-foot-wide avenues radiating from squares and circles, the sweeping vistas, the abundant parkland, all very much as Pierre Charles L'Enfant intended when he and Congress envisioned the "Federal District" in 1791. Look around and you will see the Washington Monument, the U.S. Capitol, the Lincoln Memorial, the White House, and other landmarks, their very prominence in the flat, central cityscape attesting to their significance in the formation of the nation's capital.

But Washington's history is very much a tale of two cities. Beyond the National Mall, the memorials, and the federal government buildings lies "D.C.," the municipality. Righteous politicians and others speak critically of "Washington"—shorthand, we understand, for all that is wrong with government. They should be more precise. With that snide repudiation, critics dismiss as well the particular locale in which the capital resides. It is a place of lively neighborhoods and vivid personalities, a vaunted arts-and-culture scene, international diversity, rich African-American heritage, uniquely Washingtonian attractions and people—the very citizens who built the capital in the first place and have kept it running ever since.

Early Days

The European settlers who arrived in 1608 weren't the region's first inhabitants, of course. Captain John Smith may have been the first European to discover this waterfront property of lush greenery and woodlands, but the Nacotchtank, Powhatan, and Piscataway tribes were way ahead of him. As Smith and company settled the area, they disrupted the American Indians' way of life and introduced European diseases. The Native Americans gradually were driven away or sold into slavery.

By 1751, immigrants had founded "George Town," named for the king of England and soon established as an important tobacco-shipping port. African Americans lived and worked here as well. Several houses from its early days still exist in modern-day Georgetown: The Old Stone House (p. 194) on M St. NW, a cabinetmaker's home built in 1765, is now operated by the National Park Service, and a few magnificent ship merchants' mansions still stand on

The Old Stone House, a woodworker's house built in the 1760s in Georgetown.

N and Prospect streets, though these are privately owned. The Vigilant Firehouse at 1066 Wisconsin Ave., NW., is the oldest surviving in the District. For a walking tour of Georgetown, see p. 265.

Birth of the Capital

After colonists in George Town and elsewhere in America rebelled against British rule, defeating the British in the American Revolution (1775–83), Congress, in quick succession, unanimously elected General George Washington as the first president of the United States, ratified a U.S. Constitution, and proposed that a city be designed and built to house the seat of government for the new nation and to function fully in commercial and cultural capacities. Much squabbling ensued. The North wanted the capital; the South wanted the capital. Alexander Hamilton, Thomas Jefferson, and James Madison hashed out a compromise, which resulted in the Residence Act of 1790, giving President George Washington the authority to choose his spot: The nation's capital would be "a site not exceeding 10 miles square" located on the Potomac. The South was happy, for this area was nominally in their region; Northern states were appeased by the stipulation that the South pay off the North's Revolutionary War debt, and by the city's location on the North–South border. Washington, District of Columbia, made its debut.

The only problem was that the city was not exactly presentable. The brave new country's capital was a tract of undeveloped wilderness, where pigs, goats, and cows roamed free, and habitable houses were few and far between. Thankfully, the city was granted the masterful 1791 plan of the gifted but temperamental French-born engineer, Pierre Charles L'Enfant. Slaves, free Blacks, and immigrants from Ireland, Scotland, and other countries worked to fulfill L'Enfant's remarkable vision, starting construction first on the White House in 1792 (making it the city's oldest federal structure) and months later the Capitol, the Treasury, and other buildings. (Read *The Great Decision: Jefferson, Adams, Marshall and the Battle for the Supreme Court,* by Cliff Sloan and David McKean, and *Empire of Mud: The Secret History of Washington, D.C.,* by J. D. Dickey, for excellent descriptions of the early days of the city.) Gradually, the nation's capital began to take shape, though too slowly perhaps for some. British novelist Anthony Trollope, visiting during the Civil War, declared Washington "the empire of King Mud."

The Early 1800s

Living in early "Washington City" was not for the faint-hearted. Functional roads went only to Maryland and the South, essentially stranding the city on its own. The roads that were in place, mainly Pennsylvania Avenue, were so full of potholes and tree stumps that carriages frequently overturned. Politicians "slipped into the gutter or stumbled against a bank of earth" walking home from the Capitol. L'Enfant's plans for the National Mall as a "grand and majestic avenue" were also derailed. The cofounder of the National Institute (the predecessor to the Smithsonian) described the Mall as "a magnificent Sahara of solitude and waste—appropriated as a cow pasture and frog pond...." To make matters worse, British forces stormed the city in August 1814 during the War of 1812 and torched the Capitol, the Library of Congress, and the White House before heading north to Baltimore. The city lay in tatters.

The Civil War & Reconstruction

During the Civil War, the capital became an armed camp and headquarters for the Union Army, overflowing with thousands of followers. Parks became campgrounds; churches, schools, and federal buildings—including the Capitol and the Patent Office (now the National Portrait Gallery)—became hospitals; and forts ringed the town. The population grew from 60,000 to 200,000, as soldiers, former slaves, merchants, and laborers converged on the scene. The streets were filled with the wounded, nursed by the likes of Louisa May Alcott and Walt Whitman, two of many making the rounds to aid ailing soldiers. In spite of everything, President Lincoln insisted that work on the Capitol continue. "If people see the Capitol going on, it is a sign we intend the Union shall go on," he said.

Lincoln himself kept on, sustained perhaps by his visits to St. John's Church, across from the White House. Lincoln attended evening services when he could, arriving alone after other churchgoers had entered and slipping out before the service was over. Then on the night of April 14, 1865, just as the war was dwindling down and Lincoln's vision for unity was being realized, the president was fatally shot while attending a play at Ford's Theatre (p. 176).

In the wake of the Civil War and President Lincoln's assassination, Congress took stock of the capital and saw a town worn out by years of war—awash

The inauguration of Abraham Lincoln in 1861 while construction of the U.S. Capitol continued.

with people but still lacking the most fundamental facilities. Indeed, the city was a mess. There was talk of moving the capital city elsewhere, perhaps to St. Louis or some other more centrally located city.

A rescue of sorts arrived in the person of public works leader Alexander "Boss" Shepherd, who initiated a "comprehensive plan of improvement" that at last incorporated the infrastructure so necessary to a functioning metropolis, including a streetcar system that allowed the District's overflowing population to move beyond city limits. Shepherd also established parks, constructed streets and bridges, and installed water and sewer systems and gas lighting, gradually nudging the nation's capital closer to showplace design. Notable accomplishments included the completion of the Washington Monument in 1884 (after 36 years) and the opening of the first Smithsonian Museum in 1881.

Washington Blossoms

With the streets paved and illuminated, the water running, streetcars and rail transportation operating, and other practical matters in place, Washington, D.C., was ready to address its appearance. In 1901, as if on cue, a senator from Michigan, James McMillan, persuaded his colleagues to appoint an advisory committee to develop designs for a more graceful city. With his own money, McMillan, a retired railroad mogul, sent a committee that included landscapist Frederick Law Olmsted (designer of New York's Central Park), sculptor Augustus Saint-Gaudens, and noted architects Daniel Burnham and Charles McKim to Europe for 7 weeks to study the landscaping and architecture of that continent's great capitals. "Make no little plans," Burnham counseled fellow members. "They have no magic to stir men's blood, and probably themselves will not be realized. Make big plans, aim high in hope and work, remembering that a noble and logical diagram once recorded will never die, but long after we are gone will be a living thing, asserting itself with ever growing insistency."

The committee implemented a beautification program that continued well into the 20th century. Other projects added further enhancements: A presidential Commission of Fine Arts, established in 1910, positioned monuments and fountains throughout the city; FDR's Works Progress Administration (WPA) erected public buildings embellished by artists. The legacy of these programs is on view today, in the Federal Triangle, the cherry trees along the Tidal Basin, the Lincoln Memorial, the Library of Congress, Union Station, East Potomac Park, Lafayette Square, and many other sights, each situated in its perfect spot in the city.

The American capital was coming into its own on the world stage, as well, emerging from the Great Depression, two world wars, and technological advancements in air and automobile travel as a strong, respected global power. More and more countries established embassies here, and the city's international population increased exponentially.

Black Broadway Sets the Stage

As the capital city blossomed, so did African-American culture. The many Blacks who had arrived in the city as slaves to help build the Capitol, the White House, and other fundamental structures of America's capital stayed on, later joined by those who came to fight during the Civil War, or to begin new lives after the war. From 1900 to 1960, Washington, D.C., became known as a hub of Black culture, education, and identity, centered on a stretch of U Street NW called "Black Broadway," where Cab Calloway, Duke Ellington, and Pearl Bailey often performed in speakeasies and theaters.

Many of these stars performed at the Howard Theatre, the first full-size theater devoted to black audiences and entertainers when it opened in 1910. Nearby Howard University, created in 1867, distinguished itself as the nation's most comprehensive center for higher education for blacks. (The reincarnated "U & 14th Street Corridors," or "New U," is now a diverse neighborhood of blacks, whites, Asians, and Latinos, and a top dining and nightlife destination.) The fact remained, however, that the city was a divided society, in which segregation and discrimination prevented blacks from achieving parity with whites.

The Civil Rights Era Ushers in a New Age

By the late 1950s, African Americans made up more than half of Washington's total population of 805,000, and their numbers continued to grow, reaching a peak of 70% in 1970, before beginning a steady decline that continues to this day. One hundred years or so after the passage of the 13th Amendment to the Constitution (abolishing slavery) and the 15th Amendment to the Constitution (outlawing the denial of voting rights based on race or color), African

Americans generally remained unequal members of society. Despite the best efforts and contributions of individuals—from abolitionist Frederick Douglass (p. 43), a major force in the human rights movement in the 19th century, to educator and civil rights leader Mary McLeod Bethune (p. 40), who served as an advisor to President Franklin Delano Roosevelt in the 1930s—the country, and this city, had a long way to go in terms of equal rights. (Read Edward P. Jones, the Pulitzer Prize–winning author whose short-story collections, Lost in the City and All Aunt Hagar's Children, will take you into D.C.'s black neighborhoods during the mid–20th century.) The tipping point may have come in 1954, when Thurgood Marshall (appointed the country's first Black Supreme Court justice in 1967) argued and won the Supreme Court case **Brown v. Board of Education of Topeka,** which denied the legality of segregation in America. This decision, amid a groundswell of frustration and anger over racial discrimination, helped spark the civil rights movement of the 1960s. On August 28, 1963, black and white Washingtonians were among the 250,000 who marched on Washington for jobs and freedom and listened to an impassioned Rev. Dr. Martin Luther King, Jr., deliver his stirring "I Have a Dream" speech on the steps of the Lincoln Memorial, where 41 years earlier, during the memorial's dedication ceremony, Black officials were required to sit separately from the white attendees.

The assassination of John F. Kennedy on November 22, 1963, added to a general sense of despair and tumult. On the day before his funeral, hundreds of thousands of mourners stood in line outside the Capitol all day and night to pay their respects to the president, who lay in state inside its Rotunda.

Then Martin Luther King, Jr., was assassinated on April 4, 1968, and all hell broke loose. For 3 days, angry, frustrated, and heartsick Blacks rioted, setting fire to and looting businesses and homes. Three neighborhoods in particular were decimated: Shaw's Seventh Street NW, the H Street Corridor in northeast D.C. (now known as the Atlas District), and the U & 14th Street Corridors. The corner of 14th and U Streets served as the flashpoint. Ben's Chili Bowl (p. 109) was ground zero and remained open throughout the riots to provide food and shelter to activists, firefighters, and public servants. Rehabilitation of these neighborhoods has been decades in the making.

As the 20th century progressed, civil rights demonstrations continued and led to Vietnam War protests, which in turn led to revelations about scandals, from President Nixon's

Martin Luther King, Jr., speaking at the March on Washington for Jobs and Freedom.

Watergate debacle to the late D.C. Mayor Marion Barry's drug and corruption problems to President Bill Clinton's sexual shenanigans.

Beyond the sordid headlines, the city itself was flourishing. A world-class subway system opened (though current Washingtonians may dispute this characterization), the Capital One Arena sports and concert venue transformed its aged downtown neighborhood into the immensely popular Penn Quarter, and arts-and-culture venues like the Kennedy Center and Shakespeare theaters came to worldwide attention, receiving much acclaim.

21st-Century Times

Having begun the 20th century as a backwater, Washington finished the century a sophisticated city, profoundly shaken but not paralyzed by the September 11, 2001, terrorist attacks. Barack Obama's landmark win as the first African-American president in 2008 lifted the country at a critical time, conveying an "all things are possible" perspective. But 2 full decades into the 21st century, the sense of American unity and fellowship that prevailed after the tragedy of 9/11, and the hopefulness that attended the election of President Obama, has been strained, done in by pervasive differences of political opinion coupled with an unwillingness to compromise. The Trump presidency divided Washington, with political appointees and supporters on one side and the overwhelming majority of D.C. residents on the other (only 5.4% of the city voted for Trump in 2020).

What this means for Washington, D.C., in its dual role as the nation's capital and as a culturally, historically, and socially integral city in its own right, is that the District has become even more of a focal point for the worries and dreams of the nation. Always a place for protests, the city continues to serve

President Kennedy lying in state in the Capitol Rotunda.

LITTLE-KNOWN facts

What's in a name? Many people—including Washington, District of Columbia, residents themselves—wonder how the city wound up with such an unwieldy name. Here's how: President Washington referred to the newly created capital as "the Federal City." City commissioners then chose the names "Washington" to honor the president and "Territory of Columbia" to designate the federal nature of the area. Columbia is the feminine form of Columbus, synonymous in those days with "America" and all it stood for—namely, liberty. In 1871, the capital was incorporated and officially became known as Washington, District of Columbia.

Green city: More than 27% of Washington, D.C., is national parkland, which makes the capital one of the "greenest" cities in the country. The biggest chunk is the 2,100-acre Rock Creek Park, the National Park Service's oldest natural urban park, founded in 1890.

Taking the measure of landmarks: The distance between the base of the Capitol, at one end of the National Mall, and the Lincoln Memorial, at the other, is nearly 2 miles. The circumference of the White House property, from Pennsylvania Avenue to Constitution Avenue and 15th Street to 17th Street, is about 1½ miles.

A global perspective: Every country that maintains diplomatic relations with the United States has an embassy in the nation's capital. There are more than 170 foreign embassies in D.C., mostly located along Massachusetts Avenue, known as Embassy Row, and other streets in the Dupont Circle neighborhood. Each May, the embassies open their doors to visitors during Passport DC in addition to holding events throughout the year.

in that regard, but now the demonstrations are often huge, starting with the Women's March on January 21, 2017, continuing with the inaugural March for Our Lives demonstration to end gun violence, ongoing climate change demonstrations, and the Black Lives Matter protests after the death of George Floyd in 2020—with more to come certainly in 2022 and beyond.

While the city embraces its identity as a stage for peaceful First Amendment exercise, things turned dark on January 6, 2021, when a crowd of rioters attacked the U.S. Capitol to try overturn President Joe Biden's election victory. It was the culmination of a trying year for Washingtonians, and the city is still very much healing from the combined impact of recent events. It's too soon to know how D.C. will emerge changed from this unprecedented time, but as security fences around the city begin to come down, offices and theaters and bars start to reopen, and visitors are once again filling hotels and museums, there's a renewed feeling of optimism around town.

History informs one's outlook, but so does the present. Look again at the Potomac River and think of Captain John Smith, but observe the Georgetown University crew teams rowing in unison across the surface of the water and water taxis traveling between Georgetown and Old Town Alexandria. As you traverse the city, admire L'Enfant's inspired design, but also enjoy the sight of office workers, artists and students, and people of every possible ethnic and national background making their way around town. Tour the impressive landmarks and remember their namesakes, but make time for D.C.'s home-grown attractions, whether a meal at a sidewalk cafe in Dupont Circle, jazz along U Street, a walking tour past Capitol Hill's old town houses, or a visit to a church where slaves or those original immigrants once worshiped.

2 | WHEN TO GO

The city's peak seasons generally coincide with two activities: the sessions of Congress, and springtime—beginning with the appearance of cherry blossoms. Specifically, from about the second week in September until Thanksgiving, and again from about mid-January to June (when Congress is "in"), hotels are full of guests whose business takes them to Capitol Hill or to conferences.

Mid-March through June is traditionally the most frenzied season, when families and school groups descend upon the city to see the cherry blossoms and bask in Washington's sensational spring. Hotel rooms are at a premium, and airfares tend to be higher. This is also the most popular season for protest marches, although in these tempestuous days, protests take place year-round.

If crowds turn you off, consider visiting Washington at the end of August or in early September, when Congress is still "out" and families have returned home to get their children back to school, or between Thanksgiving and mid-January, when Congress leaves again, and many people are busy with their own at-home holiday celebrations. Hotel rates are cheapest at this time, too, so check hotel websites for attractive packages.

If you're thinking of visiting in July or August, be forewarned: The weather is very hot and humid. Despite the heat, Independence Day (July 4) in the capital is a spectacular celebration. Summer is also the season for outdoor concerts, festivals, parades, and other events (see chapter 8 for performing-arts schedules). If you can deal with the heat, it's a good time to visit: Locals are on vacation elsewhere, so streets, subway trains, and attractions are somewhat less crowded. In addition, hotels tend to offer their best rates in July and August.

Weather

Season by season, here's what you can expect of the weather in Washington:

FALL This is our favorite season. The weather is often warm during the day—in fact, if you're here in early fall, it may seem entirely *too* warm. But it cools off, and even gets a bit crisp, at night. By late October, Washington has traded its famous greenery for the brilliant colors of fall foliage.

WINTER People like to say that Washington winters are mild—and sure, if you're from Minnesota, you'll find Washington warmer, no doubt. But D.C. winters can be unpredictable: bitter cold and windy one day, an ice storm the next, followed by a couple of days of sun and higher temperatures. It typically snows a few times, though it doesn't stick for long, though residents will readily remind you of the most recent "Snowpocalypse" or "Snowmageddon" blizzard that blanketed the city for days. In any event even a small amount of snow can shut down businesses in D.C. and can disrupt flights. *Best advice:* Check before you go and pack with all possibilities in mind.

SPRING   Early spring tends to be colder than most people expect. Cherry blossom season, late March to early April, can be iffy—and very often rainy and windy. As April slips into May, the weather usually mellows, and people's moods with it. Late spring is especially lovely, with mild temperatures and intermittent days of sunshine, flowers, and trees colorfully erupting in gardens and parks all over town. Washingtonians sweep outdoors to stroll the National Mall, relax on park benches, or laze away the afternoon at outdoor cafes.

SUMMER   Anyone who has ever spent July and August in D.C. will tell you how hot and steamy it can be. Though buildings are air-conditioned, many attractions, like the memorials and organized tours, are outdoors and unshaded, and the heat can quickly get to you. Make sure you stop frequently for drinks (vendors are plentiful), and wear a hat, sunglasses, and sunscreen.

Average Temperatures & Rainfall in Washington, D.C.

	JAN	FEB	MAR	APR	MAY	JUNE	JULY	AUG	SEPT	OCT	NOV	DEC
TEMP (°F)	44/29	47/31	57/39	68/48	76/58	85/67	89/72	87/71	80/64	69/52	59/42	48/34
TEMP (°C)	7/–2	8/–.6	13/3.9	20/9	24/14	29/19	32/22	30/22	27/18	21/11	15/6	9/–1
RAINFALL (in.)	2.46	2.41	3.02	3.41	4.14	5.04	4.41	3.12	3.66	3.89	2.58	3.50

Holidays

Banks, government offices, post offices, and many stores, restaurants, and museums are closed on the following legal national holidays: January 1 (New Year's Day), the third Monday in January (Martin Luther King, Jr., Day), the third Monday in February (Presidents' Day), the last Monday in May (Memorial Day), June 19 (Juneteenth), July 4 (Independence Day), the first Monday in September (Labor Day), the second Monday in October (Columbus Day/Indigenous People's Day), November 11 (Veterans Day/Armistice Day), the fourth Thursday in November (Thanksgiving Day), and December 25 (Christmas). In addition to these national holidays, the District of Columbia celebrates Emancipation Day on April 16; D.C. public schools and government offices and courts are closed but most everything else, including federal offices, are open. See below for details.

Washington, D.C., Calendar of Events

The capital's signature special event takes place every 4 years, when the winner of the presidential election is sworn in on Inauguration Day, January 20. Otherwise, the city's most popular annual events are the National Cherry Blossom Festival in spring, the Fourth of July celebration in summer, and the lighting of the National Christmas Tree in winter. But some sort of special activity occurs almost daily.

During the pandemic, most events have been cancelled, postponed, or modified to include virtual programming. The following events detail what you can expect at the city's biggest happenings if they do come back in person. For the latest schedules, check **www. washington.org**, **www.culturaltourismdc.org**, **www.dc.gov**, **www.washingtonpost.com**, and **https://washingtoncitypaper.com**. When you're in town, grab a copy of the *Washington Post* (or read it online), especially the Friday "Weekend" section, and/or a free copy of the weekly *Washington CityPaper* (or read it online).

The phone numbers below were accurate at press time, but these numbers change often. If the number you try doesn't get you the details you need, call **Destination D.C.** at ℂ **202/789-7000**.

Martin Luther King, Jr.'s Birthday. Events include a Martin Luther King Jr. Memorial peace walk, parade, and festival in Anacostia (www.mlkholidaydc.org); ongoing park-ranger talks about the civil rights hero at the **Martin Luther King Jr. National Memorial** (www.nps.gov/mlkm); and other commemorations of the slain leader's life at the **National Museum of African American History & Culture** (www.kennedy.si.edu), the **Kennedy Center** (www.kennedy-center.org), and elsewhere around town. The national holiday is marked on the third Monday in January; King's actual birthday is January 15. For more info, check the websites listed above, or call the **National Park Service** at ℭ **202/426-6841.**

Restaurant Week. Dining out at some of D.C.'s most popular restaurants becomes much more affordable during the city's biannual Restaurant Week, held in January and again in August. More than 100 restaurants citywide offer three-course, prix-fixe meals for brunch, lunch, and dinner, with brunch and lunch priced at $22 and dinner at $35 or $55. Visit www.ramw.org/restaurantweek for a list of participating restaurants. Call the restaurant directly to make a reservation, but call early—reservations fill up fast.

FEBRUARY

Black History Month. Every month is Black History Month at the **National Museum of African American History & Culture** (www.nmaahc.si.edu), but the NMAAHC and its fellow Smithsonian museums further highlight the contributions of African Americans to American life with special concerts, talks, films, discussions, and exhibits. Park rangers give black-history-related talks at the **Frederick Douglass House** (p. 43; www.nps.gov/frdo), the **MLK and Lincoln memorials,** and other National Park sites. For details, check the websites listed in the intro to this section and the Smithsonian Institution calendar at www.si.edu/Events.

Chinese New Year Celebration. A Friendship Archway, topped by 300 painted dragons and lighted at night, marks the entrance to Chinatown at 7th and H streets NW. The Chinese New Year celebration begins on the day of the first new moon of the new year, which might fall anywhere from late January to mid-February and continues for 14 or so days. Festivities center on the Friendship Archway and include a big parade throughout downtown, with firecrackers, dragon dancers, and live musical performances. The Smithsonian's Asian art museum, the **National Museum of Asian Art** (www.asia.si.edu), often hosts Chinese cooking and art demonstrations and performances on a day close to the official start of the new year. Get details at www.washington.org. Late January to early February.

Abraham Lincoln's Birthday. Expect quiet recognition of Lincoln's birthday at **Ford's Theatre** and its **Center for Education and Leadership,** an exploration of Lincoln's legacy in the time since his assassination (p. 177). The commemoration at the **Lincoln Memorial** usually includes a wreath-laying and a reading of the Gettysburg Address. For more details, check the websites listed in the intro to this section. February 12.

George Washington's Birthday/Presidents' Day. The city celebrates Washington's birthday in two ways: on the actual day, February 22, with a ceremony that takes place at the **Washington Monument;** and on the federal holiday, the third Monday in February, when schools and federal offices have the day off. The occasion also brings with it great sales at stores citywide. For information on the bigger celebrations held at **Mount Vernon** and in **Old Town Alexandria** on the third Monday in February, see chapter 9.

D.C. Fashion Week. This biannual event features designers from around the world. The weeklong extravaganza stages parties, runway shows, and trunk shows at citywide venues, sometimes including an international couture fashion show at an embassy. Most events are open to the public but may require a ticket. Call ℭ **202/600-9274** or visit www.dcfashionweek.org. Mid-February and mid-September.

MARCH

Women's History Month. Count on the Smithsonian to cover the subject to a fare-thee-well. For a schedule of Smithsonian events, visit www.si.edu/events. Be sure to check out the **Belmont-Paul Women's Equality National Monument**'s schedule of women's history events; visit www.nps.gov/bepa. The historic house is headquarters for the National Woman's Party and is a stop on "A Women's History Tour of Washington, D.C." (p. 40). For other events, check sites listed above in the section intro.

St. Patrick's Day Parade. This big, family-friendly parade on Constitution Avenue NW, from 7th to 17th streets, is complete with floats, bagpipes, marching bands, and the wearin' o' the green. For parade details, visit www.dcstpatsparade.com. The Sunday before March 17.

APRIL

National Cherry Blossom Festival. Strike up the band! 2022 marks the 110th anniversary of the city of Tokyo's gift of cherry trees to the city of Washington. This event is celebrated annually; if all goes well, the festival coincides with the blossoming of the nearly 3,800 Japanese cherry trees by the Tidal Basin, on Hains Point, and on the grounds of the Washington Monument. Events take place all over town and include the Blossom Kite Festival on the grounds of the Washington Monument; a Japanese Street Fair on Pennsylvania Avenue; "Petalpalooza," an outdoor celebration with fireworks, art activities, and live music at the Wharf on the Southwest Waterfront; special art exhibits; park-ranger-guided tours past the trees; and blossom-inspired menu specials around town. A grand parade winds down the festival, with floats, marching bands, celebrity guests, and more. Most events are free; exceptions include the Japanese Street Fair ($10 per ticket), and grandstand seating at the parade (from $20 per person). For details, go to www.nationalcherryblossom festival.org. March 20 to April 17, 2022.

White House Easter Egg Roll. A biggie for kids 13 and under, the annual White House Easter Egg Roll continues a practice begun in 1878. Entertainment on the White House South Lawn and the Ellipse traditionally includes appearances by cartoon characters, clowns, musicians (Idina Menzel and Ariana Grande are among those who have performed in the past), egg-decorating exhibitions, puppet and magic shows, an Easter egg hunt, and an egg-rolling contest. To get tickets, you must use the online lot-tery system, www.recreation.gov, up and running about 7 weeks before Easter Monday. For details, visit www.nps.gov/whho/plan yourvisit/easter-egg-roll.htm. Easter Monday 8am to 5pm.

Emancipation Day. On April 16, 1862, Pres. Abraham Lincoln signed the D.C. Compensated Emancipation Act, ending slavery in Washington, D.C., and freeing more than 3,000 slaves, reimbursing those who had legally owned them, and offering money to the newly freed women and men to help them emigrate. Lincoln issued this decree 8 months before the Emancipation Proclamation liberated slaves in the South. To mark the occasion, the D.C. government closes its public schools and government offices on the day itself, and throws a parade, concert, and fireworks show downtown either on the day or the weekend preceding the holiday. (Federal offices and all else stay open.) For details, visit https://emancipation.dc.gov. April 16.

Smithsonian Craft Show. Held in the National Building Museum (401 F St. NW), this juried show features one-of-a-kind, limited-edition crafts by more than 120 noted artists from all over the country. There's an entrance fee of $20 (or $17 in advance) per adult each day; it's free for children 12 and under. No strollers. For details, visit www.smithsoniancraftshow.org. Four days in mid- to late April.

MAY

Embassy Open Houses. If you're in D.C. in May, you may have the opportunity to tour embassies that participate in either or both the **Around the World Embassy Tour,** held on the first Saturday in May, and the **EU Open House,** held on the second Saturday in May. Go to www.culturaltourismdc.org and click on "Passport DC" for more information.

Washington National Cathedral Annual Flower Mart. Since 1939, the flower mart takes place on cathedral grounds, featuring displays of flowering plants and herbs, decorating demonstrations, ethnic food booths, children's rides and activities (including an antique carousel), costumed characters, puppet shows, tower climbs, and other entertainment. Free admission. For details, visit www.allhallowsguild.org. First Friday and Saturday in May, rain or shine.

Memorial Day. Ceremonies take place at **Arlington National Cemetery's Memorial Amphitheater** (p. 196) and the **Tomb of the Unknowns, at the National World War II** (p. 196) and **Vietnam Veterans memorials** (p. 160), at the **Women in Military Service for America Memorial,** and at the **U.S. Navy Memorial.** A National Memorial Day Parade marches down Constitution Avenue from the Capitol to the White House. On the Sunday before Memorial Day, the National Symphony Orchestra performs a free concert at 8pm on the West Lawn of the Capitol to honor the sacrifices of American servicemen and servicewomen. Last Monday in May.

JUNE

Capital Pride. Events celebrating D.C.'s large LGBTQ+ population take place throughout the month of June. Many are concentrated around the second weekend of the month, including a colorful parade down 17th Street NW in Dupont Circle, and a festival and dance party near the Capitol. You'll find parties all over town, especially in Dupont Circle, 14th and U Street NW, and Shaw. Go to www.capitalpride.org for more information. Early June.

Soldier places flags in Arlington National Cemetery for Memorial Day ceremonies.

DC Jazz Festival. The multi-day festival presents more than a range of musical performances in dozens of venues all over the city. Performers include both stars and up-and-comers, and some performances are free. www.dcjazzfest.org. Early to late June.

Smithsonian Folklife Festival. A major event celebrating both national and international traditions in music, crafts, food, games, concerts, and exhibits, staged between 4th and 7th streets on the National Mall. Each Folklife Festival showcases two or three cultures or themes. All events are free; most take place outdoors. To learn more, visit www.festival.si.edu, or check the listings in the *Washington Post.* Ten days in late June and early July, always including July 4.

JULY

Independence Day. There's no better place to be on the Fourth of July than in Washington, D.C. The all-day festivities include a massive National Independence Day Parade down **Constitution Avenue,** complete with lavish floats, marching groups, and military bands. A morning program in front of the National Archives includes military demonstrations, period music, and a reading of the Declaration of Independence. In the evening, the **National Symphony Orchestra** plays on the west steps of the **Capitol** with guest artists. And big-name entertainment precedes the fabulous fireworks display behind the Washington Monument. For details, go to www.july4thparade.com or www.nps.gov/subjects/nationalmall4th/fireworks.htm. July 4.

Citi Open. This week-long tennis tournament brings some of the top players from the WTA and ATP tours to D.C. for a series of nail-biting matches at the Rock Creek Park Tennis Center. www.citiopentennis.com. Late July to early August.

Capital Fringe Festival. Celebrating experimental theater in the tradition of the original Fringe Festival in Edinburgh, Scotland. Nearly 100 separate productions take place at multiple venues daily for 3 weeks or more, sometimes throughout the city and sometimes in one locale, like the Southwest Waterfront. Ticket prices range between $11 to $24; purchase at www.capitalfringe.org. Three weeks in mid- to late July.

AUGUST

Washington slows down in August, with Congress on recess and the weather driving many Washingtonians to flee to the beach. See Restaurant Week (January) and Citi Open (July).

SEPTEMBER

Labor Day Concert. The National Symphony Orchestra closes its summer season with a free performance on the West Lawn of the Capitol. Sunday before Labor Day (rain date: same day and time at Constitution Hall or the Kennedy Center).

Library of Congress National Book Festival. The Library of Congress sponsors this festival welcomes more than 100 established authors and their many fans. The festival includes readings, author signings (2021 authors included Roxane Gay, Kazuo Ishiguru, and Michael J. Fox), panel discussions, and general hoopla surrounding the love of books. Historically, the festival has taken place over 1 very long day; since the pandemic parts of it have gone virtual and are available all year. For details, visit www.loc.gov/bookfest. Festival is a Saturday in late August/early to mid-September.

H Street Festival. What started as a neighborhood block party has grown into a 150,000-participant festival along the H Street Corridor between 4th and 14th streets, NE. Expect to hear live music of different genres, catch youth performances, participate in interactive children's programs, and enjoy fashion, poetry, and arts programs throughout the 1-day festival. For details, visit www.hstreetfestival.org. Mid- to late September.

OCTOBER

Snallygaster. The biggest beer festival in the District features more than 400 beers from over 150 breweries. You'll find a mix of local brewers and small batch beers, cask ales, and experimental draughts. A $60 ticket gets you all you can drink, plus there are food trucks and live music. Go to www.snallygasterdc.com for tickets. Early October.

Marine Corps Marathon. A maximum of 30,000 may compete in this 26.2-mile race (one of the largest marathons in the United States). The start line is at a spot located between the Pentagon and Arlington Memorial Cemetery, and the course takes racers through Georgetown, through Rock Creek Park almost to the National Zoo, along the Potomac River, past memorials and museums on the National Mall, and so on, before reaching the finish line at the Marine Corps Memorial (the Iwo Jima statue). Participants must be 14 or older. Register online for the lottery system that determines entry in the marathon (entry fee is $45). A 1-mile kids' run is held the day before and is open to anyone ages 5 to 12. Registration is $20. For details, go to www.marinemarathon.com. Third or fourth Sunday in October.

NOVEMBER

Veterans Day. The nation's tribute to those who fought in wars to defend the United States, and to those who died doing so, takes place with a wreath-laying ceremony at 11am at the **Tomb of the Unknowns** in **Arlington National Cemetery,** followed by a memorial service in the **Amphitheater.** The president of the United States or a stand-in officiates, as a military band performs. Wreath-laying ceremonies also take place at other war memorials in the city. November 11.

DECEMBER

National Christmas Tree Lighting. At the northern end of the **Ellipse,** the president lights the National Christmas Tree to the accompaniment of orchestral and choral music, and big-name performers take the stage. The lighting ceremony inaugurates several weeks of holiday concerts performed mostly by local school and church choruses, afternoons and evenings on the Ellipse. (Brrrr!) The 17,000 tickets (3,000 seated, 14,000 standing) are free but required for the tree-lighting ceremony. (No tickets are required to attend the other holiday concerts.) To enter the lottery to try to score tickets, visit the website www.recreation.gov—the lottery opens in mid-October. For further details, visit www.thenationaltree.org. The tree-lighting ceremony takes place at 5pm in late November to early December. Following the ceremony, the tree stays lit until January 1.

SUGGESTED ITINERARIES & NEIGHBORHOODS

by Jess Moss

3

"Washington is a city of Southern charm and northern efficiency," John F. Kennedy famously declared. You'll certainly feel that way if you're caught up in the throng on the National Mall on a sunny day or waiting for a table at one of the city's hottest restaurants. The crowd is intense, and the wait can be long. There's so much to see here, and everyone has his or her own way of seeing it. This chapter lays out suggested itineraries to help make your Washington, D.C., trip as fun-filled and stress-free as possible. It includes a 3-day tour of the capital's iconic sites, plus three themed itineraries: one for families, another to explore women's history, and the third an African-American history tour. Follow them to the letter or adapt them for your own purposes—it's entirely up to you.

Prepare to be calm and flexible: Hours, entry requirements, and security measures are subject to change. Lines to enter public buildings can be lengthy; depending on the season and security clearance procedures, you'll need to enter many of the federal buildings. Reserve spots on tours whenever possible to avoid some of those waits. Most important, don't be afraid to ask questions. Tour guides, the National Park Service rangers, and the staff at all the museums know an awful lot; take advantage of their expertise.

Following the itineraries is an overview of D.C.'s neighborhoods. Among the most enjoyable activities in D.C. is exploring its neighborhoods on foot, so if you tire of crowded museums, choose a neighborhood and simply stroll. See chapter 10 for walking tours of a few standout neighborhoods.

Do your research ahead of time—many buildings are asking visitors to sign up in advance for a timed entry spot in order to limit crowds and maintain social distancing.

Some attractions, like the **National Museum of African American History & Culture** (p. 151), a trip to the top of the **Washington Monument** (p. 161),

and a tour of the **White House** (p. 171), have always been difficult to get tickets due to their popularity. Check the websites of all the sights you plan on hitting for tickets and current open hours. You may need to shuffle around the order of some of the stops on the following pages if your tickets require; that's fine!

ICONIC WASHINGTON, D.C., IN 1 DAY

If you have limited time in Washington, D.C., and would like to do a deep dive into several specific landmark attractions (rather than the rushed experience of many), then this is the itinerary for you. *Start: Metro on the Blue, Orange, or Silver Line to the Capitol South stop on Capitol Hill or on the Red Line to Union Station.*

1 The U.S. Capitol Building ★★★

This is Congress's "House," its cornerstone laid in 1793 by President George Washington. The Capitol was officially completed in 1826, but by 1850, Congress had grown and there was already need for expansion. In 1868, the larger building was finally finished and the impressive Statue of Freedom placed atop the dome. Head inside the Capitol Visitor Center to take the hour-long guided Capitol tour (highly recommended), armed with the timed passes you've ordered in advance online. If you've neglected to order these, you may well be in luck: Go to the "Visitors Without Reservations" walk-up line to see if any same-day passes are available—they usually are (I've put this to the test even at the busiest times of year). The Visitor Center is itself worth checking out. See. p. 123.

Walk around to the east side of the Capitol and just keep walking, or head south on First St. SE to return to the Capitol South Metro station, where you take a Blue, Orange, or Silver Line train to the L'Enfant Plaza stop. Exit at Maryland Ave. and 7th St. SW, walk down 7th St. SW to cross Independence Ave., and continue along 7th St., stopping midway to take in the:

2 National Mall ★★★

Stroll the long green promenade, buttressed end-to-end by the Capitol, where you started, and the Lincoln Memorial, westward in the distance, where you'll end up later today. Once you've had a chance to catch your breath, it's time to resume touring.

Iconic Washington, D.C.

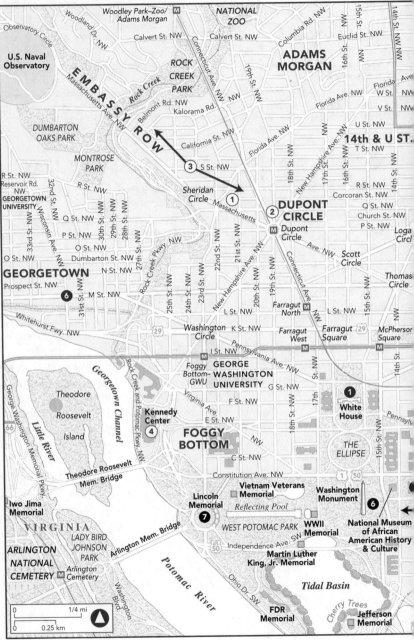

Woodley Park–Zoo/
Adams Morgan

NATIONAL
ZOO

Observatory Circle

Woodland Dr. NW

Calvert St. NW

Calvert St. NW

Columbia Rd. NW

Euclid St. NW

15th St. NW

14th St. NW NW

**U.S. Naval
Observatory**

EMBASSY ROW

Massachusetts Ave. NW

ROCK
CREEK
PARK

19th St. NW

**ADAMS
MORGAN**

16th St.

Florida Ave.

W St. NW

V St. NW

Rock Creek

Belmont Rd. NW

Kalorama Rd.

Connecticut Ave. NW

Florida Ave. NW

U St. NW

14th & U ST.

T St. NW

15th St. NW

DUMBARTON
OAKS PARK

MONTROSE
PARK

California St. NW

③ S St. NW

Florida Ave. NW

18th St. NW

17th St.

16th St. NW

R St. NW

R St. NW
Reservoir Rd.
NW

**GEORGETOWN
UNIVERSITY**

32nd St. NW

R St. NW

Q St. NW

P St. NW

O St. NW

30th St. NW

29th St. NW

28th St. NW

Sheridan
Circle

①

Massachusetts

②**DUPONT
CIRCLE**

Ⓜ Dupont
Circle

New Hampshire Ave. NW

Corcoran St. NW

R St. NW

Q St. NW

Church St. NW

P St. NW

Logan
Circle

Wisconsin Ave. NW

33rd St. NW

Dumbarton St. NW

27th St. NW

25th St. NW

24th St. NW

23rd St. NW

22nd St. NW

21st St. NW

20th St. NW

19th St. NW

Connecticut Ave. NW

Scott
Circle

Thomas
Circle

GEORGETOWN

Prospect St. NW

31st St. NW

⑥

N St. NW

M St. NW

Rock Creek Pkwy. NW

L St. NW

K St. NW

18th St. NW

17th St. NW

Farragut
North

Ⓜ

Farragut
West

L St. NW

Farragut
Square

29

McPherson
Square

14th St.

Whitehurst Fwy. NW

29

Washington
Circle

Pennsylvania Ave. NW

Ⓜ

Theodore
Roosevelt

Island

Georgetown Channel

Rock Creek and Potomac Pkwy. NW

I St. NW

Ⓜ

Foggy
Bottom–
GWU

**GEORGE
WASHINGTON
UNIVERSITY**

Virginia Ave.

G St. NW

F St. NW

E St. NW

St. NW

17th

Ⓜ

①

**White
House**

Pennsylv

George Washington Memorial Pkwy.

66

Little River

**Kennedy
Center**
④

**FOGGY
BOTTOM**

18th St.

THE
ELLIPSE

15th St. NW

Iwo Jima
Memorial

Theodore Roosevelt
Mem. Bridge

C St. NW

Constitution Ave. NW

**Lincoln
Memorial**
⑦

Vietnam Veterans
Memorial ■

Reflecting Pool

**Washington
Monument**

⑥

VIRGINIA

LADY BIRD
JOHNSON
PARK

Arlington Mem. Bridge

WEST POTOMAC PARK

WWII
Memorial

**National Museum
of African
American History
& Culture**

**ARLINGTON
NATIONAL
CEMETERY**

Arlington
Cemetery

Independence Ave. SW

50

**Martin Luther
King, Jr. Memorial**

Ⓜ

Washington Blvd.

Ohio Dr. SW

Potomac River

Tidal Basin

Cherry Trees

1/4 mi

0.25 km

**FDR
Memorial**

**Jefferson
Memorial** ■

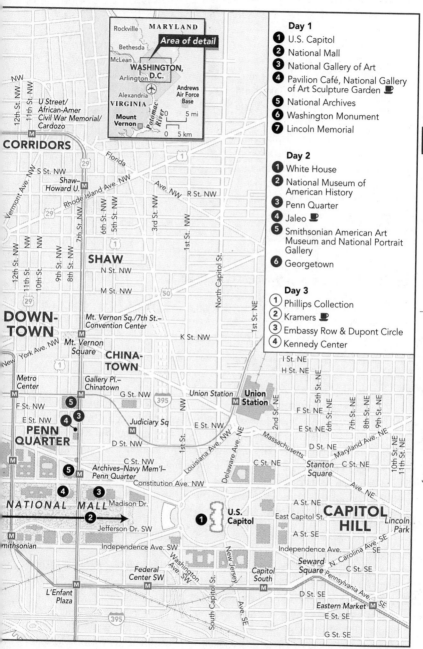

Day 1

1. U.S. Capitol
2. National Mall
3. National Gallery of Art
4. Pavilion Café, National Gallery of Art Sculpture Garden ☕
5. National Archives
6. Washington Monument
7. Lincoln Memorial

Day 2

1. White House
2. National Museum of American History
3. Penn Quarter
4. Jaleo ☕
5. Smithsonian American Art Museum and National Portrait Gallery
6. Georgetown

Day 3

1. Phillips Collection
2. Kramers ☕
3. Embassy Row & Dupont Circle
4. Kennedy Center

Continue across the Mall and cross Madison Dr. to enter the West Building of the:

3 National Gallery of Art ★★★

If you have time to visit only one of the city's free art museums, make it this one. The East Building showcases modern and contemporary art, while the West Building's galleries display European paintings and sculptures spanning the 13th to 19th centuries and American art. Don't leave without checking out the gallery's special exhibits, which are always superb. See p. 149.

Hall of the National Gallery of Art.

Exit the Gallery's West Building and cross 7th St. NW to the:

4 Pavilion Café at the National Gallery Sculpture Garden ☕

Order a quiche Lorrain or a pancetta flatbread and maybe a glass of rosé, and if the weather's pleasant, try to snag a seat at one of the outside tables. Be sure to wander through the entire garden to admire all 21 sculptures and a delightful mosaic by Chagall, one of the garden's newer pieces. See p. 150.

Exit the Sculpture Garden and proceed westward down the Mall, or hop a DC Circulator bus at Madison Dr. and 7th St. to reach the:

5 The National Archives ★★★

No trip to Washington is complete without a visit to this museum located just behind the Gallery of Art's Sculpture Garden. Here, the three "Charters of Freedom" reside: the Declaration of Independence, the Constitution, and the U.S. Bill of Rights, among other important historical documents, photos, and audio recordings. Housed behind glass in a low-lit rotunda, it can be a hushed, almost reverent, experience to read the documents in the Founding Fathers' own script. The gallery almost always has a special exhibit on view, too.

Exit the museum to Madison Dr. and cross 15th St. to reach the grounds of the:

6 Washington Monument ★★★

People often ask: Which is taller, the Washington Monument or the Capitol? The answer is the Washington Monument. The monument reopened in 2019 after an extensive renovation of its interior, including an elevator that delivers you to the observation tower and its panoramic views stretching for miles (20 miles on a clear day!). A ticket to enter the monument can be elusive in peak season; you'll need to reserve one in advance online. If tickets are gone for the day or the monument isn't open, you

Boats on the Tidal Basin and the Jefferson Memorial.

can still stand back and consider the fact that this 555-foot, 5⅛-inch-high obelisk, D.C.'s version of a skyscraper, is one of the world's tallest free-standing works of masonry. See p. 161.

Walk the rest of the way or hop the DC Circulator bus at the 15th St. and Madison Dr. stop to arrive at the:

7 Lincoln Memorial ★★★

Visit this templelike memorial to contemplate the inspiring life and spirit of the nation's 16th president. Citizens of the world surround you, reading aloud the words inscribed on its walls: "FOUR SCORE AND SEVEN YEARS AGO OUR FATHERS BROUGHT FORTH ON THIS CONTINENT A NEW NATION, CONCEIVED IN LIBERTY, AND DEDICATED TO THE PROPOSITION THAT ALL MEN ARE CREATED EQUAL..." Stand at the top of the memorial's steps to take in the sweeping view across the Reflecting Pool and green expanse of the National Mall. See p. 143.

ICONIC WASHINGTON, D.C., IN 2 DAYS

We've modified this second day to account for ongoing closures at major government buildings. If the Supreme Court, Library of Congress, and White House are back to running tours to the public, you may want to adjust this plan to slot in a tour of one of those oh-so-Washington experiences.

In the meantime, with a second day added onto your trip, you can take a photo in front of the White House, spend some time exploring a Smithsonian Museum, and get lost in Georgetown's historic side streets or shop the neighborhood's many boutiques. *Start: Metro on the Blue, Orange, or Silver Line to the Farragut West stop, or take the Red Line to the Farragut North stop and walk down to 1600 Pennsylvania Ave.*

1 The White House ★★★

A visit to the White House is a highlight of a trip to the nation's capital, even if you aren't able to go inside for a tour. I encourage you to admire its exterior view and consider the facts: Its cornerstone was laid in 1792, making the White House the capital's oldest federal building. It's been the residence of every president but George Washington (although the nation's second president, John Adams, lived here for only 4 months). The British torched the mansion in 1814, so what you see is the house rebuilt in 1817, using the original sandstone walls and interior brickwork. Consider following the "Strolling Around the White House" tour in chapter 10. See p. 171.

Return to the metro at Farragut West and take the train one stop on the Blue, Orange, or Silver lines to Federal Triangle. Alternately, from the White House you can walk east on Pennsylvania Ave., past the Treasury Building on your right, then take a right on 15th St. NW. Walk until you hit Constitution Ave.—you're back on the National Mall! This time you're heading to:

2 National Museum of American History ★★★

This museum has so much inside of it that it can be overwhelming, so it's best to pick and choose which exhibits interest you. My advice? Start with a walk through the Star-Spangled Banner gallery. As you move through the darkened gallery, you'll follow the story of the American Revolution's Battle of Baltimore and the enormous flag that was raised there, which inspired Francis Scott Key to write what became the U.S. national anthem. In the middle of the gallery, you'll see the banner itself, a delicate 200-year-old flag that has grown to mean so much to so many people. Prefer not to overdo it with the history? No problem; swap in any of the mega-museums down here instead: The National Museum of American History, National Gallery of Art, and National Air and Space Museum are all right here, plus more. See p. 153.

From the museum, walk east on Constitution to 7th St. NW. (Take a little detour through the National Gallery of Art's Sculpture Garden on your way.) From here walk north into:

3 Penn Quarter

This lively neighborhood just north of the National Mall is full of restaurants, bars, and assorted sightseeing attractions, all within a short walk of one another. Wander down to Pennsylvania Avenue and up 7th Street, the main arteries, and explore side streets. Then head to lunch at:

4 Jaleo 🍵

Washingtonians are proud to be the hometown of star chef and global humanitarian Jose Andres, and Jaleo is one of the best places to taste his work. The Spanish restaurant serves a wide range of tapas and other dishes inspired by Chef Andres's Spanish roots. See p. 101.

The Capitol.

Exit Jaleo and walk 1 block north on 7th St. to the:

5 Smithsonian American Art Museum & National Portrait Gallery ★★★

Nothing reveals the essence of the American spirit and character better than its art. Pop in here and look into the portraiture faces of America's presidents (and First Ladies—don't miss Michelle Obama's portrait on the third floor), its poets, its heroes, its historic figures, its celebrities. Study Georgia O'Keeffe's southwestern landscapes, and admire the creations from self-taught folk artists, from exquisite quilts to outlandish sculptures made of metallic foil and found objects. The enclosed Kogod Courtyard with its wavy, glass and steel roof is a work of art itself.

From here your next stop is Georgetown, on the west side of the city. The easiest way to get there is to hail a taxi or order a ride share. You can also walk north to Massachusetts Ave. and catch the D.C. Circulator bus's Georgetown to Union Station route. This will drop you at M St. and Wisconsin Ave., the heart of Georgetown:

6 Georgetown ★★★

Come for the shops and restaurants, stay for the historic homes, gardens, and picturesque side streets. You could spend all afternoon into evening here—and even later if you're up for some nightlife. The Georgetown walking tour in chapter 10 will give you a good taste of the neighborhood's character. From there, pick one of the many eateries that line M Street, Wisconsin Avenue, or the waterfront plaza at Washington Harbour.

ICONIC WASHINGTON, D.C., IN 3 DAYS

Time for some off-the-Mall attractions. Take in a beloved museum, explore a neighborhood, and get a taste of the city's international identity. *Start: Metro on the Red Line to reach Dupont Circle, exiting at Q St.*

1 Phillips Collection ★★

Tour this charming museum to view its growing collection ranging from French Impressionist to contemporary art, all housed in an 1897 mansion and its modern wings. Always keep an eye out for favorites, such as Renoir's *Luncheon of the Boating Party,* Jacob Lawrence's *Migration Series,* the gallery devoted to Mark Rothko's bold artworks, and, on display from time to time, *Night Baseball,* a painting by founder Duncan Phillips's wife, Marjorie Phillips. Book your entry tickets in advance online. See p. 185.

Turn right outside the museum, turn left onto Q St., NW, then right on Connecticut Ave.:

2 Kramers 🍽

Open early in the morning and late at night, this storied neighborhood eatery (with bookstore attached) serves a generous American menu (1517 Connecticut Ave., NW; www.kramers.com; 📞 202/387-3825).

Return to Q St., follow it to Massachusetts Ave. heading north to start your tour of:

3 Embassy Row & Dupont Circle

Stop in shops along Connecticut Avenue, and then follow side streets to discover boutiques, little art galleries, and quaint, century-old town houses. If you look carefully, you'll notice that some of these buildings are actually embassies or historic homes. The most evocative embassies lie on Massachusetts Avenue, west of Dupont Circle. Turn onto S Street NW and look for no. 2340 to see the house where President Woodrow Wilson lived after he left the White House (p. 171). A bit farther along Massachusetts Avenue, turn onto Belmont Road NW to find Barack and Michelle Obama's post-presidency digs, at no. 2446. Few embassies are open to the public; those that are limit their hours. For an in-depth tour of Dupont Circle and Embassy Row, take the self-guided walking tour outlined in chapter 10. See p. 274.

Walk, if you feel up to it, or take a taxi to the:

4 Kennedy Center ★★★

Head to the Kennedy Center for the 6pm nightly free concert in the Grand Foyer (part of the center's Millennium Stage program). See p. 223. At concert's end, proceed through the glass doors to the terrace overlooking Rock Creek Parkway and the Potomac River, and enjoy the view. You're a short walk around the bend of the river from Georgetown; why not head there next for dinner? See p. 116.

WASHINGTON, D.C., FOR FAMILIES

Here's a bold statement: Few if any other U.S. cities are truly as perfect for kids as D.C. From the countless museums that keep them entertained (and educated, too) to the vast expanse of the National Mall (perfect for letting off steam), Washington is made for families. *Start: The National Zoo.*

Washington, D.C., for Families

Map labels:

3rd St. NW
4th St. NW
Judiciary Sq
G St. NW
GAO
Gallery Pl–Chinatown
Verizon Center
5th St. NW
6th St. NW
E St. NW
D St. NW
C St. NW
National Gallery of Art East
National Gallery of Art West
Nat'l Museum of the American Indian
Federal Center SW
Madison Dr. NW
Nat'l Air and Space Museum
Constitution Ave. NW
Archives–Navy Mem'l/Penn Quarter
L'Enfant Plaza
7th St. NW
8th St. NW
Nat'l Portrait Gallery
U.S. Navy Memorial
Nat'l Archives
National Gallery of Art Sculpture Garden
Pennsylvania Ave.
NATIONAL MALL
Jefferson Dr. SW
Hirshhorn Museum
Arts & Industries Building
Hancock Park
D St. SW
9th St. NW
F St. NW
E St. NW
FBI
Dept. of Justice
Smithsonian Castle
Independence Ave. SW
National Museum of African Art
Freer Gallery
Sackler Gallery
10th St. SW
Metro Center
PENN QUARTER
G St. NW
10th St. NW
11th St. NW
Federal Triangle
FEDERAL TRIANGLE
Nat'l Museum of Natural History
Smithsonian
Department of Agriculture
To the National Zoo (see inset)
12th St. NW
Pennsylvania Ave. NW
Freedom Plaza
Pennsylvania Ave. NW
14th St. NW
15th St. NW
Commerce Dept.
White House Visitor Center
Constitution Ave. NW
National Museum of African American History & Culture
Washington Monument
Sylvan Theater
U.S. Holocaust Museum
Bureau of Engraving and Printing
Independence Ave. SW
Cherry Trees
Tidal Basin

Inset:

NATIONAL ZOO
Beach Dr. NW
Connecticut Ave. NW
Cathedral Ave. NW
Woodley Rd. NW
Woodley Park–Zoo/Adams Morgan
Calvert St.
1/4 mi
0.25 km

Legend:

1 National Zoo
2 Duke's Counter
3 National Mall
4 Tidal Basin
5 Café du Parc

1/4 mi
0.25 km

1 National Zoo ★★

The zoo opens early, so it's a good place to start your day—just remember to reserve your free tickets ahead of time! Certain children's exhibits (the Kids' Farm, the seasonal ZooTubing down Lion/Tiger Hill) lie at the very bottom of this large zoo, situated on a hill. Keep that part in mind as you explore the zoo, since it'll be all uphill—and quite a long hill it is—back to Connecticut Avenue. But you need not go all the way to the bottom of the hill, as pandas, a solar-powered carousel, a fab elephant exhibit, and nearly 2,700 other animals are on view elsewhere in the zoo. See p. 189.

Head across Connecticut Ave. to:

2 Duke's Counter 🍺

Located directly across the street from the National Zoo, this British gastropub has a little something for everyone, including a kids' menu with fish n' chips and a "Proper Cheeseburger." Open early to late. See p. 104.

Head down Connecticut Ave to the Woodley Park–Zoo Metro station and catch a Red Line train going in the Glenmont direction. Take the train to the Metro Center station, where you can transfer to the Orange, Blue, or Silver lines and travel 2 stops to the Smithsonian stop to reach the National Mall and two of the city's largest museums.

3 Pick a Museum

One of the best things about the Smithsonian museums' free entry is you can devote as much—or as little—time as you'd like to a visit. This is especially true if you're here with kids; you can spend hours exploring exhibits dedicated to young learners; or pop, see one thing, and leave before any meltdowns take place. That said, the museums are large and can be overwhelming, so your best bet is to choose one that interests your kiddos the most. Have a young history buff? The National Museum of American History (p. 153) has tons of kid-friendly activities, from the hands-on Wegmans Wonderplace to a 23-room dollhouse and simulator rides that make you feel like you're in a race car or rollercoaster. If there are fans of gems, bugs, or dinosaurs in your family, beeline it to the National Museum of Natural History. Activities here include a butterfly pavilion, tarantula feedings, mummies, gemstones, and the recently renovated Hall of Fossils, where you'll find an impressive T-Rex skeleton, among 700 other specimens. See p. 156.

Exit either museum on the south side to find yourself on the:

4 National Mall ★★★

It's not *actually* a giant playground but it might as well be. The nearly 2-mile-long grassy expanse has plenty of room to run around and burn off some steam. On breezy days, you may see people flying kites, especially around the base of the Washington Monument. If the classical Carousel outside the Smithsonian Castle is operating when you visit, it's a treat for the little (and not-so-little) ones. See p. 150.

Children riding the National Mall carousel.

Follow Independence Ave. on the south side of the Mall east, to where it intersects with Maine Ave. Cross over to reach the:

5 Tidal Basin

This tranquil inlet is famous for its cherry trees that blossom every spring, but it's also a great spot to putter around on a paddle boat. You can rent boats that seat up to four people (two paddlers plus two passengers), and life jackets are provided. In addition to the monuments to Jefferson and Martin Luther King, Jr. that sit on the shores of the Tidal Basin, you'll likely run into some curious ducks and geese on the water.

You must be starving! You can dine around the Mall in the Smithsonian's **museum cafes** or from the **food trucks** parked outside, but if your family has the energy, it's worth the short walk to get to your next stop. Cross the Mall to reach 14th St., then follow 14th St. north, past the U.S. Treasury building, to reach a classic Washington restaurant:

6 Old Ebbitt Grill ☕

Washington's first saloon is now a D.C. dining institution, with something for everyone—including kids. The children's menu features standbys like mac and cheese and mini cheese pizzas, while the full menu covers a mix of seafood and American grill classics. See p. 102.

The National Museum of African American History and Culture is a Smithsonian museum located on the National Mall.

A WOMEN'S HISTORY TOUR OF WASHINGTON, D.C.

"Remember the ladies," Abigail Adams famously advised her husband, John Adams, in 1776, when he was attending the Continental Congress and busy formulating his ideas about the new government. John Adams, who went on to become the second president of the United States in 1797, did his best. But that was a long time ago, and women have long acted as their own advocates. One day, perhaps, Americans might marvel that there was ever a time when a woman couldn't vote, own property, succeed in sports, run a large company, or become the president. In the meantime, let us now celebrate the achievements of women in many realms. Unfortunately, at least two of the city's main monuments to women, the Belmont-Paul Women's Equality National Monument, and the National Museum of Women in the Arts, will be closed for renovations through 2022 and possibly beyond. ***Start:*** *The Mary McLeod Bethune National Historic Site near the 14th St. Corridor.*

---

1 Mary McLeod Bethune National Historic Site

Mary McLeod Bethune bought this house not as a residence, but to serve as headquarters for the National Council for Negro Women. Although she did live here from 1943 to 1949, it is the sense of her professional rather than personal life that you absorb from the exhibits—which speak volumes. Look for a black-and-white photo of FDR's cabinet in the 1930s, and there you will see a panel of white men and, in their midst, a Black woman—Bethune, appointed as a national advisor to the president. The house is managed by the National Park Service; even when it's closed to the public, it's a worthwhile reminder of the accomplishments of this impressive woman. See p. 188.

It's about a 1-mile walk down 14th St., or you can take the 52 bus to the:

2 National Museum of African American History & Culture ★

African American women and their contributions to politics, academics, arts, and athletics are reflected throughout this impressive museum. The newest museum to the National Mall, it details the entire African American experience from slavery to modern times, so much of which features the contributions of women. Exhibits include Rosa Parks' handmade dress from 1955–56 and Althea Gibson's Wightman Cup blazer when she became the first African American Grand Slam tennis champion in 1957. Stories of lesser-known African American women, including Mae Reeves, who fashioned hats in Philadelphia for more than 50 years, are also on display. ***Note:*** You must reserve visitor passes before arriving. See p. 151.

A Women's History Tour of Washington, D.C.

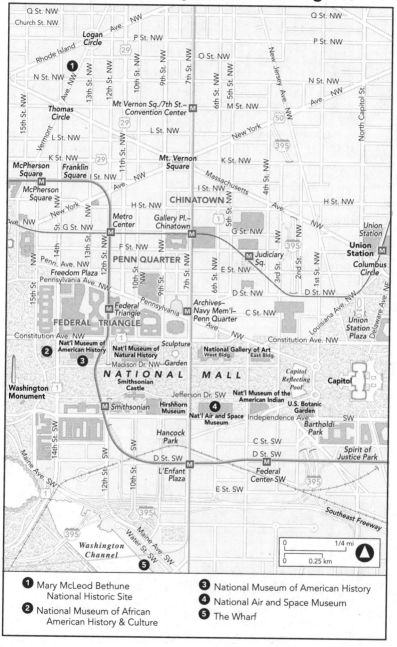

3

SUGGESTED ITINERARIES | A Women's History Tour of Washington, D.C.

1. Mary McLeod Bethune National Historic Site
2. National Museum of African American History & Culture
3. National Museum of American History
4. National Air and Space Museum
5. The Wharf

3 National Museum of American History ★★★

The most popular exhibit in the museum is the First Ladies exhibit, which gives First Ladies their due as strong and interesting people in their own right. Also don't miss Julia Child's Kitchen (in the "Food: Transforming the American Table 1950–2000" exhibit), a tribute to a different kind of icon; "Uniformed Women in the Great War," presenting the role of women in World War I; and the individual stories of ordinary women woven throughout the museum's exhibits, such as that of abolitionist Lucy Caldwell, who lived "Within These Walls," an occupant of the old Ipswich House on view, from 1836 to 1865. And the Star-Spangled Banner? The handiwork of a woman, or rather, several women: Mary Pickersgill and her daughter, nieces, and a maid. See p. 153.

Exit the museum on the National Mall side and walk diagonally across the Mall to the:

4 National Air and Space Museum ★★★

Throughout history, women pilots have played an integral part in aviation. But it wasn't until the 1970s that women gained full access to military and commercial cockpits, as well as the Space Shuttle. From Amelia Earhart's red Lockheed Vega (the one she flew solo across the Atlantic Ocean in 1932) to the clothes Sally Ride wore during her Space Shuttle mission aboard *Challenger* in June 1983, when she became the first U.S. woman in space, this museum honors the lasting legacy women have made in flight.

Exit the museum onto Independence Ave, heading east. Take a left on 7th St. SW to reach the L'Enfant Plaza Metro station. From here you'll board a Green Line train and take it one stop to the Waterfront:

5 The Wharf ★

The buzziest development in town is also home to a number of local women-owned businesses. Contrary to what the name suggests, Hank's Oyster Bar (p. 97) is owned by female chef Jamie Leeds, who has been growing her collection of eateries in the D.C. area for over a decade. Nearby, Chopsmith (p. 98) and Colada Shop (p. 109) also have women at the helm. On the shopping side, a number of stores here are women-owned and operated. Shop Made in DC is one of them and is a great stop for DC-inspired feminist gear, like "Madame Vice President" clothing and prints celebrating the late Ruth Bader Ginsberg.

AN AFRICAN-AMERICAN HISTORY TOUR OF WASHINGTON, D.C.

The story of African Americans in Washington, D.C., actually predates the founding of the capital, for African Americans were here from the get-go. Records show that blacks were living and working in Alexandria, Virginia, in its early days as a tobacco port. (And worshipping: See p. 273 for information about Georgetown's **Mount Zion United Methodist Church,** which celebrates its 205th year in 2021, making its worshippers the city's oldest black congregation.) In 1800, African Americans made up 29% of the District's roughly 14,000 residents, but 80% of them were enslaved. The capital's very design was plotted by self-taught mathematician/surveyor Benjamin Banneker, who in 1791 assisted Andrew Ellicott in mapping out Pierre L'Enfant's 10-square-mile territorial vision. Slaves built many of the capital's historic buildings, the White House and the U.S. Capitol among them. The population of African Americans in the capital, always significant, now stands at about 46%. This tour aims to shed some light on the local and national history of African Americans, from pre-Revolutionary War times to the present. *Start: Frederick Douglass National Historic Site in Anacostia.*

3

SUGGESTED ITINERARIES | An African-American History Tour of Washington, D.C.

1 Frederick Douglass National Historic Site (Cedar Hill) ★★

Douglass is best known for being an abolitionist, but his story doesn't stop there. After the Civil War, Douglass held a number of government positions, including U.S. Marshal, appointed by President Rutherford Hayes in 1877. His office was in the U.S. Capitol. He was 60. Douglass walked the 5 miles daily to and fro. You could make the same trek as Douglass, but actually, it's quite easy to get there: From Union Station, take the DC Circulator bus headed in the direction of Congress Heights

The Duke Ellington mural on U Street.

An African-American History Tour of Washington, D.C.

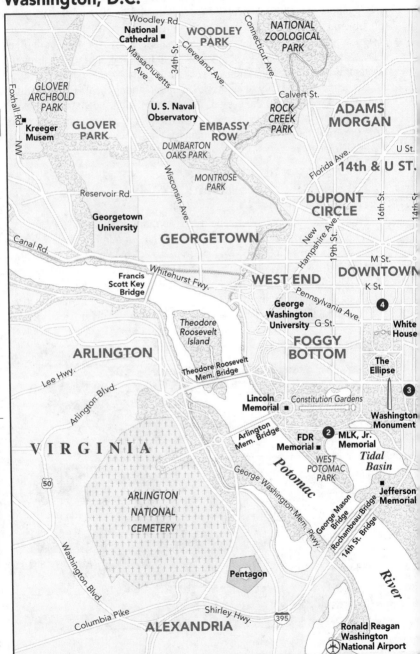

Woodley Rd.

National Cathedral ■

WOODLEY PARK

NATIONAL ZOOLOGICAL PARK

Massachusetts Ave.

34th St.

Cleveland Ave.

Connecticut Ave.

Calvert St.

GLOVER ARCHBOLD PARK

Foxhall Rd. NW

■ Kreeger Musem

GLOVER PARK

U. S. Naval Observatory

EMBASSY ROW

ROCK CREEK PARK

ADAMS MORGAN

DUMBARTON OAKS PARK

Florida Ave.

U St.

14th & U ST.

MONTROSE PARK

Wisconsin Ave.

DUPONT CIRCLE

16th St.

14th

Reservoir Rd.

Georgetown University

GEORGETOWN

New Hampshire Ave.

19th St.

M St.

Canal Rd.

Whitehurst Fwy.

WEST END

DOWNTOWN

Francis Scott Key Bridge

Pennsylvania Ave.

K St.

George Washington University

G St.

4

White House

Theodore Roosevelt Island

FOGGY BOTTOM

The Ellipse

ARLINGTON

Lee Hwy.

Theodore Roosevelt Mem. Bridge

3

Arlington Blvd.

Lincoln Memorial ■

Constitution Gardens

Washington Monument

VIRGINIA

Arlington Mem. Bridge

FDR Memorial ■

2 MLK, Jr. Memorial

Tidal Basin

50

George Washington Mem. Pkwy.

WEST POTOMAC PARK

Potomac

George Mason Bridge

Rochambeau Bridge

Jefferson Memorial ■

Washington Blvd.

ARLINGTON NATIONAL CEMETERY

14th St. Bridge

River

Pentagon

Columbia Pike

Shirley Hwy.

395

ALEXANDRIA

Ronald Reagan Washington ✈ National Airport

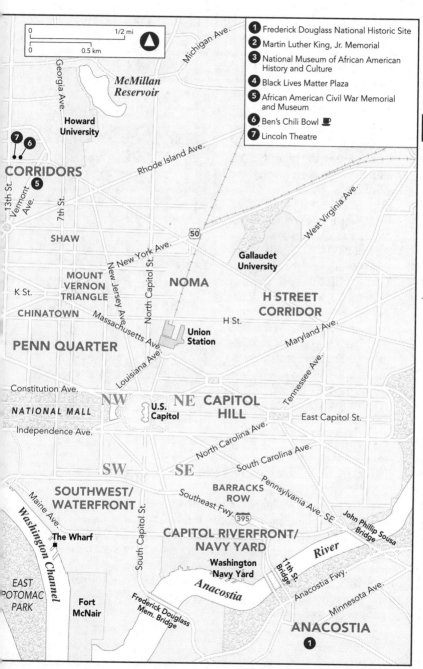

1. Frederick Douglass National Historic Site
2. Martin Luther King, Jr. Memorial
3. National Museum of African American History and Culture
4. Black Lives Matter Plaza
5. African American Civil War Memorial and Museum
6. Ben's Chili Bowl
7. Lincoln Theatre

3

SUGGESTED ITINERARIES | An African-American History Tour of Washington, D.C.

and travel 7 stops farther to the corner of W Street SE and Martin Luther King, Jr. Avenue SE, hop off and walk 4 blocks east to 14th and W streets SE. Easy-peasy. See p. 194.

From the house, simply reverse the steps listed above, picking up the DC Circulator at Martin Luther King Jr. Ave. SE and W St. SE, headed toward Congress Heights, and travel 1 stop to the Anacostia Metro station, where you catch the Green Line train to the L'Enfant Plaza Metro station. From here you can either exit and walk to your next stop, or switch to the Blue Line, travel to the Smithsonian station, exit to 12th St. SW, and walk along Independence Ave. until you reach the:

2 Martin Luther King, Jr. National Memorial ★★

In his 39 years, the Rev. Dr. Martin Luther King, Jr. helped found the Southern Christian Leadership Conference, wrote and delivered 2,500 speeches, organized massive protests and drives to register Black voters, won the Nobel Peace Prize, and led the August 28, 1963, historic March on Washington for Jobs and Freedom that helped convince Congress to pass the Civil Rights Act of 1964. The memorial at the northwest corner of the Tidal Basin has 15 quotes inscribed into the walls that attempt to define the man, including one that inspired the memorial's design: OUT OF THE MOUNTAIN OF DESPAIR, A STONE OF HOPE. See p. 145.

The Martin Luther King, Jr. National Memorial.

Cross Independence Ave. and walk northeast across the Washington Monument grounds until you reach a lane leading to the:

3 National Museum of African American History and Culture ★★★

You can't explore Washington's African American history without a visit to this moving museum dedicated to the topic. It can be hard to get tickets, so you'll need to plan ahead and reserve online before you arrive. You could spend an entire day here, following the story of the African American experience, from the slave trade up until present day culture. Even if you can't get in, take some time to marvel at the striking bronze facade, which was designed with shapes and features derived from African and African Diaspora influences. See p. 151.

From the museum, walk up 15th St. and take a left on H St. NW. Turn right at 16th St. to find yourself at:

4 Black Lives Matter Plaza

Born from the tragedy of the George Floyd murder and the subsequent civil justice protests, this massive street mural spells BLACK LIVES MATTER in large yellow letters that take up 2 city blocks outside of the White House. The Plaza is now a popular gathering place, as well as a place of reflection.

From the plaza, either catch a taxi or walk east along I St. NW until you reach 14th St. From here, get on the northbound Woodley Park–Adams Morgan DC Circulator Bus and ride it all the way to U St. NW. At U St., walk east about 5 blocks and take a right on Vermont Ave. to find:

5 African American Civil War Memorial and Museum

When you exit the Metro station at 10th Street, you'll exit to the plaza that holds the African American Civil War Memorial: *The Spirit of Freedom* sculpture portraying uniformed soldiers and a sailor on one side of the rounded pedestal, a family on the other side. The sculpture sits within a semicircular Wall of Honor, a series of stainless-steel plaques on which are engraved the names of 209,145 United States Colored Troops mustered into military service during the Civil War. Now cross Vermont Street to visit the African American Civil War Museum to view exhibits that tell the story of the slaves and freed blacks who fought in the Civil War.

When you leave the museum, walk 3 blocks westward on U St. until you reach 1213 U St.:

6 Ben's Chili Bowl 🍽

In the 1950s and '60s, the capital was a violent hotbed of civil rights activism. Ben's, around since 1958, was one establishment that somehow remained open during the tumultuous days of race riots and heartbreak following Dr. King's assassination in 1968. And it's still going strong. Famous for its half-smokes and chili fries, Ben's also serves decent vegetarian fare. See p. 109.

From here you need go no farther than right next door to view the historic:

7 Lincoln Theatre

The greater U Street neighborhood is a place for dining out, hanging out, and nightlife. But for decades, this area was predominantly a cultural and residential stronghold for African Americans, who had started to settle here after the Civil War. In the 1920s, '30s, and '40s, the popularity of jazz venues and their stars, like D.C.'s own Duke Ellington, led fans to dub the area "Black Broadway." The Lincoln Theatre, open since 1922, was at the center of it all, welcoming Duke Ellington, Pearl Bailey, Ella Fitzgerald, Billie Holliday, Cab Calloway, Louis Armstrong, and others to its stage. See a show if you're here at night.

Washington, D.C., at a Glance

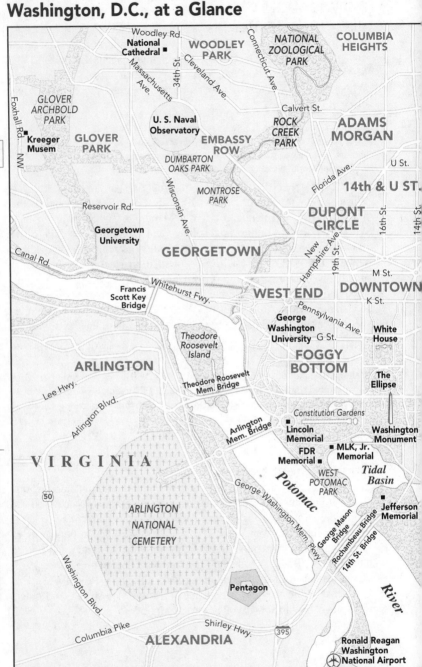

Woodley Rd.
National Cathedral
WOODLEY PARK
NATIONAL ZOOLOGICAL PARK
COLUMBIA HEIGHTS
34th St.
Massachusetts Ave.
Cleveland Ave.
Connecticut Ave.
GLOVER ARCHBOLD PARK
Calvert St.
ROCK CREEK PARK
ADAMS MORGAN
Foxhall Rd. NW
Kreeger Musem
GLOVER PARK
U. S. Naval Observatory
EMBASSY ROW
DUMBARTON OAKS PARK
Florida Ave.
U St.
14th & U ST.
Reservoir Rd.
Wisconsin Ave.
MONTROSE PARK
DUPONT CIRCLE
16th St.
14th St.
Georgetown University
GEORGETOWN
New Hampshire Ave.
19th St.
M St.
Canal Rd.
Whitehurst Fwy.
Francis Scott Key Bridge
WEST END
DOWNTOWN
K St.
Pennsylvania Ave.
Theodore Roosevelt Island
George Washington University
G St.
White House
ARLINGTON
Lee Hwy.
Theodore Roosevelt Mem. Bridge
FOGGY BOTTOM
The Ellipse
Arlington Blvd.
Constitution Gardens
Arlington Mem. Bridge
Lincoln Memorial
FDR Memorial
MLK, Jr. Memorial
Washington Monument
VIRGINIA
50
WEST POTOMAC PARK
Tidal Basin
Potomac
Jefferson Memorial
ARLINGTON NATIONAL CEMETERY
George Washington Mem. Pkwy.
George Mason Bridge
Rochambeau Bridge
14th St. Bridge
Washington Blvd.
Pentagon
River
Columbia Pike
Shirley Hwy.
395
ALEXANDRIA
Ronald Reagan Washington National Airport

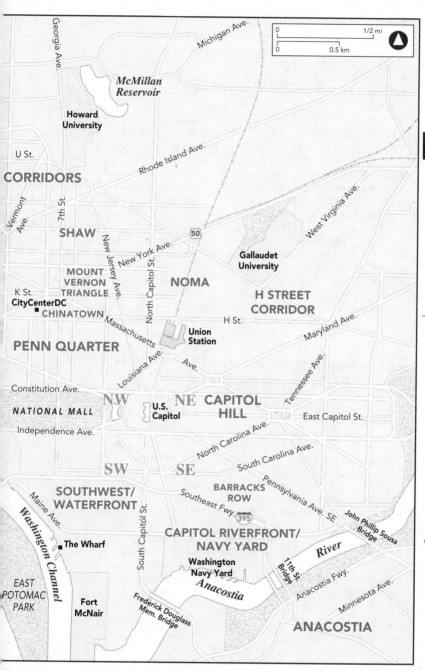

3

SUGGESTED ITINERARIES | An African-American History Tour of Washington, D.C.

Georgia Ave.

Michigan Ave.

0   1/2 mi
0   0.5 km

McMillan Reservoir

Howard University

U St.

CORRIDORS

Vermont Ave.

7th St.

Rhode Island Ave.

West Virginia Ave.

SHAW

50

New York Ave.

North Capitol St.

New Jersey Ave.

MOUNT VERNON TRIANGLE

NOMA

Gallaudet University

H STREET CORRIDOR

K St.

CityCenterDC

CHINATOWN

Massachusetts

H St.

Maryland Ave.

PENN QUARTER

Union Station

Louisiana Ave.

Ave.

Constitution Ave.

Tennessee Ave.

NATIONAL MALL

NW **NE** **CAPITOL HILL**

U.S. Capitol

East Capitol St.

Independence Ave.

North Carolina Ave.

SW **SE**

South Carolina Ave.

SOUTHWEST/ WATERFRONT

Maine Ave.

South Capitol St.

BARRACKS ROW

Southeast Fwy.

Pennsylvania Ave. SE

395

John Phillip Sousa Bridge

Washington Channel

The Wharf

CAPITOL RIVERFRONT/ NAVY YARD

Washington Navy Yard

Anacostia

11th St. Bridge

River

Anacostia Fwy.

EAST POTOMAC PARK

Fort McNair

Frederick Douglass Mem. Bridge

Minnesota Ave.

ANACOSTIA

The Neighborhoods in Brief

14th & U Street Corridors The diverse 14th Street NW and U Street neighborhood is rooted in black history and culture but is better known these days as a dining and nightlife destination. During its "Black Broadway" heyday in the first half of the 20th century, jazz and blues legends Duke Ellington, Louis Armstrong, and Cab Calloway performed at the Lincoln Theatre (p. 227) and other venues. Most folks flocking here at night now are the young and the restless in search of a hot new eatery or bar hangout.

Adams Morgan This bohemian-trendy, multi-ethnic neighborhood is crammed with shops, bars, clubs, and restaurants. Most everything is located on either 18th Street NW or Columbia Road NW. Parking is manageable during the day but difficult at night, especially on weekends (a parking garage on Champlain St., just off 18th St., helps a little). Luckily, you can easily walk to Adams Morgan from the Dupont Circle or Woodley Park Metro stop or take the bus or a taxi there. (Be alert in Adams Morgan at night and try to stick to the main streets: 18th St. and Columbia Rd.).

Anacostia When people talk about the Washington, D.C., that tourists never see, they're talking about neighborhoods like this; in fact, they're usually talking about Anacostia, specifically. Named for the river that separates it from "mainland" D.C., it's an old part of town, with little commercial development and mostly modest, often low-income housing. Anacostia does have three notable attractions: the Smithsonian's **Anacostia Community Museum** and the **Frederick Douglass National Historic Site** (see the African-American History Tour, above, and "Museums in Anacostia" box, p. 194); and the **Anacostia Riverwalk Trail** (p. 204), a popular walking and bicycling path that connects southwest and southeast neighborhoods fronting the Anacostia River. Also be alert if here, especially at night.

Barracks Row Barracks Row refers mainly to a single stretch of 8th Street SE, south of Pennsylvania Avenue SE, but also to side streets occupied by Marine Corps barracks since 1801. This southeastern subsection of Capitol Hill is known for its lineup of shops, casual bistros, and pubs. Its attractions continue to grow as a result of the 2008 opening of the Nationals baseball team's stadium, Nationals Park, half a mile away. In fact, the ballpark has spawned its own neighborhood, dubbed Capitol Riverfront (see below).

Capitol Hill Everyone's heard of "the Hill," the area crowned by the Capitol building. The term, in fact, refers to a large section of town, extending from the western side of the Capitol to the D.C. Armory going east, bounded by H Street to the north and the Southwest Freeway to the south. It contains not only this chief symbol of the nation's capital, but also the **Supreme Court Building,** the **Library of Congress,** the **Folger Shakespeare Library, Union Station,** and **Eastern Market.** Much of it is a quiet residential neighborhood of tree-lined streets, rows of Federal and Victorian town houses, and old churches. Restaurants keep increasing their numbers, with most located along Pennsylvania Avenue SE on the south side of the Capitol and near North Capitol Street NW on the north side of the Capitol—the north side, near Union Station, is where most of the hotels are, too. Keep to the well-lit, well-traveled streets at night, and don't walk alone—crime occurs more frequently in this neighborhood than in some other areas.

Capitol Riverfront/Navy Yard The opening of **Nationals Park** in 2008 spurred the development of this once-overlooked part of town. Known also as "Navy Yard" (that's the name of the subway stop here), the revitalized 500-acre neighborhood abuts 1½ miles of the Anacostia River. Besides the ballpark, the area has five hotels, tons of restaurants and bars, a brewery or two, the city's first winery, numerous shops, and public parks, trails, and docks. Much, much more to come.

Cleveland Park Cleveland Park, just north of Woodley Park, is a picturesque enclave of winding, tree-shaded streets dotted with charming old houses with wraparound porches. The streets extend off the main artery, Connecticut Avenue. With its own stop on the Red Line Metro system and a respectable number of good restaurants, Cleveland Park is worth visiting when you're near the zoo (just up the street) or seeking a good meal after a bike ride or stroll through nearby Rock Creek Park.

Columbia Heights Hispanic immigrants have long settled here but now are joined by millennials and others seeking more affordable housing. Here you'll find historic mansions, colorful town houses, Hispanic cultural attractions, the gorgeous **Meridian Hill Park** (p. 200), and loads of good ethnic restaurants. The neighborhood lies north of U Street to Quincy Street NW, and east of 16th Street to Georgia Avenue NW. In recent years crime has been on the increase in this area, so stay alert.

Downtown The area bounded roughly by 6th and 21st streets NW to the east and west, and M Street and Pennsylvania Avenue to the north and south, is a mix of the Federal Triangle's government office buildings; K Street, ground zero for the city's countless law and lobbying firms; Connecticut Avenue restaurants and shopping; historic hotels; the city's poshest small hotels; **Chinatown;** the huge Walter E. Washington Convention Center; and the White House. You'll also find the historic **Penn Quarter,** one of D.C.'s hottest locales, which has continued to flourish since the 1997 opening of the MCI Center, now renamed the **Capital One Arena** (sports and concerts; see p. 226). A number of off-the-Mall museums, such as the massive **National Building Museum** and the **Smithsonian's National Portrait Gallery** and **American Art Museum,** are here. Besides hip restaurants, boutique hotels, and nightclubs, the Penn Quarter claims ultra-trendy **CityCenterDC,** a mini-Manhattan of chic shops and restaurants.

Dupont Circle One of my favorite parts of town, Dupont Circle provides easy fun, day or night. It takes its name from the traffic circle minipark, where Massachusetts, New Hampshire, and Connecticut avenues converge. Washington's famous **Embassy Row** centers on Dupont Circle and refers to the parade of grand embassy mansions lining Massachusetts Avenue and its side streets (see walking tour; p. 274). The streets extending out from the circle are lively, with all-night bookstores, good restaurants, wonderful art galleries and art museums, hip nightspots, and Washingtonians at their loosest. Once the hub of D.C.'s LGBTQ community, the neighborhood continues to host the annual High Heel Drag Queen Race the Tuesday preceding Halloween and the Capital Pride Parade every June, despite the fact that LGBTQ residents live throughout the city now. The neighborhood has plenty of hotel choices, most of them moderately priced.

Foggy Bottom/West End The area west of the White House, south of Dupont Circle, and east of Georgetown encompasses both Foggy Bottom and the West End. Foggy Bottom, located below, or south, of Pennsylvania Avenue, was Washington's early industrial center. Its name comes from the foul fumes emitted in those days by a coal depot and gasworks, but its original name, Funkstown (for owner Jacob Funk), is perhaps even worse. There's nothing foul or funky about the area today. The West End edges north of Pennsylvania Avenue, booming with the latest big-name restaurants and new office buildings. Together, the overlapping Foggy Bottom and West End neighborhoods present a mix: the **Kennedy Center,** town house residences, George Washington University campus buildings, offices for the World Bank and the International Monetary Fund, State Department headquarters, small- and medium-size hotels, student bars, and several fine eateries, lining either side of Pennsylvania Avenue and its side streets.

Georgetown This historic community dates from Colonial times. It was a thriving tobacco port long before the District of Columbia was formed, and one of its attractions, the **Old Stone House,** dates from pre-Revolutionary days. Georgetown action centers on M Street and Wisconsin Avenue NW, where you'll find hundreds of boutiques, chic restaurants, and popular pubs. Detour from the main drags to relish the quiet, tree-lined streets of restored Colonial row houses, stroll the beautiful gardens of **Dumbarton Oaks,** and check out the **C&O Canal.** Georgetown is also home to **Georgetown**

University. (See chapter 10 for a walking tour of Georgetown.) The neighborhood gets pretty raucous on weekends.

Glover Park   Mostly a residential neighborhood, this section of town just above Georgetown and just south of the **Washington National Cathedral** is worth mentioning because of several good restaurants and bars located along its main stretch, Wisconsin Avenue NW. Located between the campuses of Georgetown and American universities, Glover Park has a large student presence.

H Street Corridor   This section of H Street, also known as the Atlas District, stretches between 4th and 14th streets, but centers on the 12th to 14th streets segment. Primarily known as a nightlife and restaurant destination, the neighborhood has lately sprouted a cafe and coffeehouse culture that attracts young entrepreneurs and locals during the day.

Mount Vernon Triangle   Yet another old neighborhood experiencing renewal, Mount Vernon lies east of the convention center, its boundary streets of New Jersey, Massachusetts, and New York avenues defining a perfectly shaped triangle. Within that triangle, trendy restaurants are starting to multiply.

The National Mall   This lovely, tree-lined stretch of open space between Constitution and Independence avenues, extending for nearly 2 miles from the foot of the Capitol to the steps of the Lincoln Memorial, is the hub of tourist attractions. It includes most of the Smithsonian Institution museums and several other notable sites. Tourists as well as natives—joggers, food vendors, kite flyers, and picnickers among them—traipse the 700-acre Mall. Hotels and restaurants are located beyond the Mall to the north, and, increasingly, south of the Mall across Independence Avenue all the way to the waterfront, thanks to intense development. The proper name for the entire parkland area is actually **National Mall and Memorial Parks,** which is how I refer to it in chapter 6.

NoMa   NoMa, as in "North of Massachusetts," is a curious mix of a neighborhood. Located east of downtown D.C. and directly north of Union Station, NoMa's got old residential streets of real character, but also major thoroughfares slicing through, which makes it not the most walkable of areas. Wide swaths of commuter and Amtrak train tracks form the neighborhood's eastern boundary. Except for the smattering of pleasant side streets, the place has an industrial look about it. And yet, NoMa won't be ignored, and here's why you shouldn't: You're close to Capitol Hill and Union Station; you have access to two Metro stations, bike stations, and a bike path; and the neighborhood has caught the eye of developers, who have built three hotels here in the last few years and more and more restaurants. If you're here on Capitol Hill business, this might be a good pick.

Northern Virginia   Across the Potomac River from the capital lies Northern Virginia and its close-in city/towns of Arlington and Old Town Alexandria. The Arlington Memorial Bridge leads directly from the Lincoln Memorial to Arlington National Cemetery, and beyond to Arlington and Alexandria (see chapter 9). Commuters travel back and forth daily between the District and Virginia.

Penn Quarter   This refers roughly to the part of downtown from 15th Street east to 6th Street, and Pennsylvania Avenue north to New York Avenue. See "Downtown," above.

Shaw   Located due north of the Penn Quarter, this historic district encompasses the area between 11th and 6th streets NW going west to east, and Massachusetts Avenue to U Street NW going south to north. Shaw remains largely a neighborhood of longstanding houses and old churches, even as it undergoes a renewal that started with the opening of the Walter E. Washington Convention Center in 2003. Shaw has been garnering a lot of attention lately for its hot new restaurants and bars, a city market, and interesting shops. Suddenly, Shaw is the place to go for the best dining in D.C., but it has also been experiencing an uptick in crime, so be aware as you walk around here, especially at night.

Southwest/Waterfront With the fall 2017 opening of the **Wharf,** the waterfront complex of eateries, shops, live music venues, bars, and outdoor recreation activities, this neighborhood has been transformed quite suddenly into an attractive, vital area of the city. As development goes on and new buildings go up, this stretch of waterfront continues as a working marina, with vendors selling fresh crabs and fish straight off their docked fishing barges. This is where locals and restaurateurs come to buy fresh seafood. The neighborhood is also home to the acclaimed **Arena Stage** (p. 222) and **Anthem** music hall (p. 226). Traffic congestion can be a problem, especially at night and in pleasant weather when people descend on the Wharf; even though it does have a large parking garage, take advantage of the many transportation alternatives to driving (p. 294).

Woodley Park Home to two large hotels, including the Omni Shoreham (p. 85), Woodley Park is mainly a pretty residential neighborhood. Its biggest attractions are the **National Zoo, Rock Creek Park,** good restaurants, and some antiques stores.

WHERE TO STAY

by Kaeli Conforti

ourism continues to break records in D.C., and new hotels of all kinds are popping up fast, including an increasingly diverse selection of bed-and-breakfasts, "pod" hotels (with tiny but functional guest rooms and low rates), high-end hostels, historic gems, properties beckoning to business travelers, hotels catering to families, and accommodations appealing to millennials.

4

This chapter describes properties in different neighborhoods and the features that make them uniquely recommendable. Among them are the posh **Hay-Adams** (p. 70) with its view of the White House; the **Capitol Hill Hotel** (p. 58), the only hotel truly located on "The Hill"; **The Ven at Embassy Row** (p. 77), situated among embassies and elegant residential town houses; and the **Hampton Inn & Suites Washington DC–Navy Yard** (p. 63), where baseball fans can watch the action at Nationals Park from its rooftop lounge. And coming soon: The environmentally conscious hub for counterculture and creatives, **Mob Hotel** (www.mobhotel.com). The stylish Paris-based chain is expected to launch its first U.S. outpost in 2023 in Union Market.

GETTING THE BEST DEAL

Want the secret for getting the best hotel deal ever in Washington, D.C.? Come to town when Congress is out of session or when cherry blossom season is over, in the blazing-hot days of July or August and during the icy cold days of (a non-inauguration-year) January or February. Don't try to negotiate a good deal for late March or early April in peak cherry blossom season; hotel reservationists will laugh at you, I've heard them. Do, however, book online whenever possible (see the box on p. 57 for more on that) and consider these money-saving tips:

o Check out hotels that are **located away from big events taking place** while you are visiting the capital. For example, during cherry blossom season, stick to properties in Georgetown, upper Dupont Circle, Woodley Park, or places that are a few miles from Downtown and the National Mall.

o **Visit on a weekend.** Hotels looking to fill rooms vacated by weekday business travelers lower their rates and might even be

As a result of Covid-19, many hotels have made adjustments to help travelers feel safer and more at home during these uncertain times. In many cases, that means hotels are making it easier for guests to check-in via app, kiosk, email, and other contactless methods, or stepping up the cleaning of commonly used spaces, elevators, door handles, and public bathrooms. You might see more hand sanitizer around the lobby than usual or signs requiring masks or social distancing in the fitness center. Some hotels have removed in-room mini-bars (which you can usually request for a fee), while others have cut back on the number of times housekeepers visit during your stay. Many have adopted more flexible booking and cancellation policies just in case. As always, it helps to be flexible and check the website before arrival.

willing to negotiate further for weekend arrivals. Sundays usually have the lowest nightly rates.

- **Ask about special rates or other discounts.** You may qualify for substantial corporate, government, student, military, senior, trade union, or other discounts. Members of the **National Trust for Historic Preservation** (www.savingplaces.org) get up to 30% off stays at the Trust's affiliated Historic Hotels of America. Washington, D.C. has 14 National Trust properties, including The Georgetown Inn and the Riggs Washington, DC.
- **Look into group or long-stay discounts.** If you come to D.C. as part of a large group, you should be able to negotiate a bargain rate because the hotel can then guarantee occupancy in a number of rooms. Likewise, if you're planning a long stay (of at least 5 days), you might qualify for a discount. As a general rule, expect 1 night free after a 7-night stay.
- **Book directly with the hotel whenever possible,** as it's easier to make changes and for them to keep you updated should anything change on their end, especially nowadays. Major hotel chains like Hyatt, Marriott, Hilton, and IHG, among others, offer special discounts for travelers booking directly through their websites instead of through a third party.
- **Consider enrolling in hotel loyalty programs.** Joining a loyalty program is free and often grants access to discounts, upgrades, and other perks. You can also accumulate points . . . allows you to save up a certain number per stay (these vary by program) to redeem for free nights and other benefits later on.
- **Check out deals listed in the "DC Hotel Deals" tab on the Destination DC tourism board website** (www.washington.org/hotel-deals; ℭ **202/789-7000**). In 2021, for instance, The Watergate Hotel offered a discount of up to 25% for bookings made at least 14 days in advance.
- **Subscribe to e-mail alerts and follow all your favorite hotel brands on social media.** Alerts from your favorite hotels or booking sites can keep you informed of special deals—so can following their social media accounts.
- **Even if you haven't gotten the best deal possible on your room rate, you can still save money on incidental costs.** D.C. hotels charge unbelievable rates for overnight parking—more than $50 a night at some hotels, plus an

WHAT YOU'LL really PAY

The prices given in this chapter are based on searches of both third-party discount sites and the hotels' own web-sites; they're the lowest average rates and the highest ones, for both double rooms and suites. At most hotels, you probably won't pay the top rate unless you visit in the spring, especially during cherry blossom season from late March through mid-April, as high season typi-cally happens March through July and in October during conventions. Rates vary are listed as a general guideline only.

It's important to note that when the tim-ing is right, it's possible to obtain a room at an expensive property for the same rate as a more moderate one. And if you're persistent, or book at the last minute, you might get a steal. Or you could end up paying through the nose, especially if you're visiting during a special event.

Four things to keep in mind: (1) Quoted discount rates almost never include the hefty 14.95% hotel sales tax. (2) Some hotels also tack on a "guest amenity fee" to your daily room rate when you book your reservation. Not all hotels charge this, but for those that do—like the Capitol Hill Hotel (p. 59) and The Kimpton George Hotel (p. 59)—the fee is not optional. Also known as a "resort fee" or "amenity fee," it can be substantial (Kimpton's is $25 plus tax) and covers services you may not even be interested in, like premium Wi-Fi and long-distance phone calls. (3) Parking fees listed in this chapter are per night and include in-and-out privileges unless otherwise noted. Consider taking public transportation, as these fees can really add up. (4) Finally, the word "double" refers to the number of people in the room, not the size of the bed; most hotels charge one rate, regardless of whether one or two people occupy the room.

18% tax—so if you can avoid driving (and using the mini-bar) you can save yourself quite a bit of money. D.C.'s hotel sales tax is a whopping 14.95%, merchandise sales tax is 5.75%, and the food and beverage tax is 10%, all of which can rapidly increase the cost of a room.

Consider Alternative Accommodations

These alternatives to traditional hotels are another smart way to save:

o **Stay in a hostel.** I've listed a few good ones in this chapter that qualify as high-end hostels or "poshtels," complete with artistic designs, plenty of freebies, spacious common areas, and fun activities to help you bond with your fellow travelers while saving you more money per night.

o **Go the vacation rental route: Airbnb, VRBO,** and **FlipKey.com,** among others, match people looking for a place to stay with locals interested in renting out space in their home, or sometimes entire apartments or homes, often for far less than you might pay at a hotel. According to the website **Inside Airbnb** (www.insideairbnb.com), Washington, D.C. has roughly 9,300 active listings, with more than 70% of them being for entire houses or apartments.

o **Consider house swapping or house/pet sitting. HomeExchange** (www. homeexchange.com) and **HomeLink International** (www.homelink.org) offer thousands of would-be swaps worldwide, while sites like **Trusted**

Housesitters (www.trustedhousesitters.com) hook you up with hosts looking for people to watch their pets at home while they're away. Membership fees apply but pay for themselves if you do a few each year.

o **Check in with the tourism board, Destination DC** (www.washington.org; ✆ 202/789-7000). View lists of new hotels online or call and ask for the names of any **new** or **about-to-open hotels.** Up-and-coming hotels may have more affordable rooms for the simple reason that few people know about them.

o **Stay outside the city.** You'll find lower lodging prices in Arlington, Virginia, and its location directly across the Potomac River from D.C. offers easy access to the city. Each of Arlington's close-in "urban villages"—Rosslyn, Crystal City, Pentagon City, Ballston, Clarendon, and Courthouse—has a Metro stop connecting you to D.C. Rosslyn, is the most convenient, and some of its hotels even offer spectacular views of the river and capital.

CAPITOL HILL

For proximity to the U.S. Capitol, Supreme Court, Library of Congress, and other Capitol Hill attractions, the hotels in this section can't be beat. Union Station (where you'll find both the Amtrak station and the Metro stop) is a short walk from all four hotels listed, providing easy access to the rest of the city.

Best for: Travelers who have business at the Capitol and tourists whose priority is visiting the Capitol Hill neighborhood while staying within easy reach of other D.C. attractions.

USING THE internet or apps FOR HOTEL DISCOUNTS

It's not impossible to get a good deal by calling a hotel, but you're more likely to snag a discount online or by using an app. Here are some strategies:

1. **Browse extreme discounts on sites where you reserve or bid for lodgings without knowing which hotel you'll get.** Priceline.com and Hotwire.com can be real money-savers, particularly if you're booking within a week of travel. Both feature major chains, so it's unlikely you'll book a dump.

2. **Review discounts on the hotel's website.** As we said above, hotels generally give the lowest rates to those who book through their sites. But you'll only have access to truly deep discounts by being part of a loyalty program, so join the club—it's free to sign up anyway.

3. **Use the right hotel search engine.** They're not all created equal, as we at Frommers.com discovered after testing the top 20 sites in 20 cities around the globe. **Booking.com** listed the lowest rates for hotels in the city center and in the under $200 range 16 out of 20 times—the best record, by far, of all the sites we tested. Listings on Booking.com also included all taxes and fees in the initial results (not all do, which can make for a frustrating shopping experience). For top-end properties, again in the city center, both Priceline.com and HotelsCombined.com came up with the best rates.

Drawbacks: These streets are in the thick of things during the day; not so much at night.

Moderate

Capitol Hill Hotel ★   This hotel's foremost distinction is its unbeatable location: It is the only hotel in the city actually *on* Capitol Hill (on the House side), occupying two buildings on a residential street lined with old town houses. Neighbors include the Library of Congress, the Capitol Building complex, and the Supreme Court; just a block away is Pennsylvania Avenue SE's stretch of fun bars and restaurants. Guest rooms are comfortably furnished, with pleasing touches like L'Occitane products in the bathroom and accent pillows embossed with the D.C. skyline on beds and sofas. Rooms in the west wing have kitchenettes; rooms in the east wing have full kitchens. Some suites have pullout sofas. All rooms are spacious, ranging in size from 320 to 510 square feet. Best room? The northwest corner suite on the fifth floor of the west wing, which has a partial view of the Capitol Building and the Library of Congress. Each morning in the east wing breakfast room, an ample continental breakfast of baked goods, yogurt, oatmeal, breakfast sandwiches, cereals, and fruit is laid out. A grab-and-go coffee station is available in the west wing library for guests as well. Other pluses include a well-equipped gym and a tiny gift shop featuring items like chocolates decorated with cherry blossoms, the Capitol Building, and other iconic images of D.C. A daily amenities fee of $25 plus tax applies.

200 C St. SE (at 2nd St.). www.capitolhillhotel-dc.com. *©* **202/360-4736.** 153 units. Doubles from $142–$306, plus a daily $25 amenities fee. Extra person $25 for rollaway only. Children 12 and under stay free. Parking $50 including tax. Metro: Union Station. Pets accepted ($150 fee per pet). **Amenities:** Business center, fitness center, Wi-Fi (free).

Hyatt Regency Washington on Capitol Hill ★   Travelers can't go wrong with this venerable hotel set within sight of the U.S. Capitol Building and National Mall, and just 3 blocks from Union Station. Business travelers will love the sleek, soaring atrium lobby with communal tables and 24/7 business center, while families will love the skylit indoor pool. Standard guest rooms range from 290 to 354 square feet (suites go up to 1,480 square feet), with contemporary finishes like sleek silver lamps, mod carpeting, and spacious worktables. Bathrooms are exceptionally spacious for a D.C. hotel. **Article One American Grill** offers an extensive continental breakfast, free for guests, with an omelet bar, flaky pastries, and fresh fruit, as well as a decent dinner. Next door, **Article One Lounge & Bar** is best for a quick bite, cocktails, craft beer, and for sports fans catching the big game on the massive jumbotron. For the best views and largest space, ask for a king corner room facing south. For the quietest rooms, request one on the upper floors facing First Street NW.

400 New Jersey Ave., NW (btw. D and E sts.). www.washingtondc.regency.hyatt.com. © **202/737-1234.** 838 units, with 31 suites. Doubles from $117–$297, suites from $237–$469, plus daily $20 amenities fee. Parking $62 plus tax. No pets allowed, only service dogs. Metro: Union Station. **Amenities:** Restaurant, bar, fitness center, pool, Wi-Fi (free).

Kimpton George Hotel ★★

This is the best hotel closest to the Capitol. Celebrities often stay here despite its location not being the hot spot of, say, a Penn Quarter or Georgetown property. The sumptuously comfortable 270-square-foot guest rooms have a touch of whimsy, with parchment and ink-stylized graphics of George Washington's inaugural address on the wallpaper, and accent pillows based on GW's notable uniform. The Capitol is a pleasant 10-minute walk away, and the hotel's restaurant, **Bistro Bis,** is a favorite among locals and visitors alike. If you're traveling with infants, ask about the hotel's partnership with 4Moms, which lets you reserve seats, tubs, and other baby gear to use during your stay.

15 E St. NW (at N. Capitol St.). www.hotelgeorge.com. © **800/546-8331** or 202/347-4200. 139 units. Doubles from $162–$323, suites from $476–$578, plus a $25 daily amenities fee, which includes a $10 electric scooter and rideshare credit per day, premium Wi-Fi, and a hosted evening wine hour. Children 17 and under stay free. Parking $49 plus tax, eco-friendly hybrid vehicles save $10. Metro: Union Station. Pets accepted (free, no restrictions). **Amenities:** Restaurant, bar, children's amenity program, fitness center with Peloton bike, Wi-Fi (free).

Yotel Washington, D.C. ★

This stylish and futuristic hotel (formerly the Liaison Capitol Hill) reopened in 2020 as a Yotel, the U.K.-based brand's 10th property in the U.S. Aviation enthusiasts take note, as its theme is a first-class flight. Rooms are referred to as first-class and premium cabins, while the lobby is reminiscent of a high-end airport lounge and guests are able to check in via kiosks at "Mission Control" (there's still a check-in desk available in the lobby for those who prefer to take a more traditional route). Inside each room (or, cabin), high-tech features are the main focus, with smart beds that become couches with the touch of a button, and a funky mood-lighting system designed to help you personalize your space. There's complimentary coffee on every floor, while **Art and Soul** is the hotel's full-service restaurant and a popular spot for Congressional events (so keep your eyes peeled for famous faces). Stop by during the summer for live music during the week. Head up to **Deck 11,** one the largest rooftop pool and bar decks in D.C., for incredible views of the Capitol Building and surrounding neighborhood. Groups of up to four people can splurge on a posh poolside cabana rental ($600 for the day).

415 New Jersey Ave. NW (btw. D St. NW and E St. NW). www.yotel.com/en/hotels/yotel-washington-dc. © **202/638-1616.** 337 units. Doubles from $119–$314, plus a $25 amenities fee per night. Parking $50 with tax (no in-and-out privileges). No pets except service dogs; let them know in advance. Metro: Union Station. **Amenities:** Restaurant, rooftop pool and bar, fitness center, self-service check-in kiosks, Wi-Fi (free).

Washington, D.C., Hotels

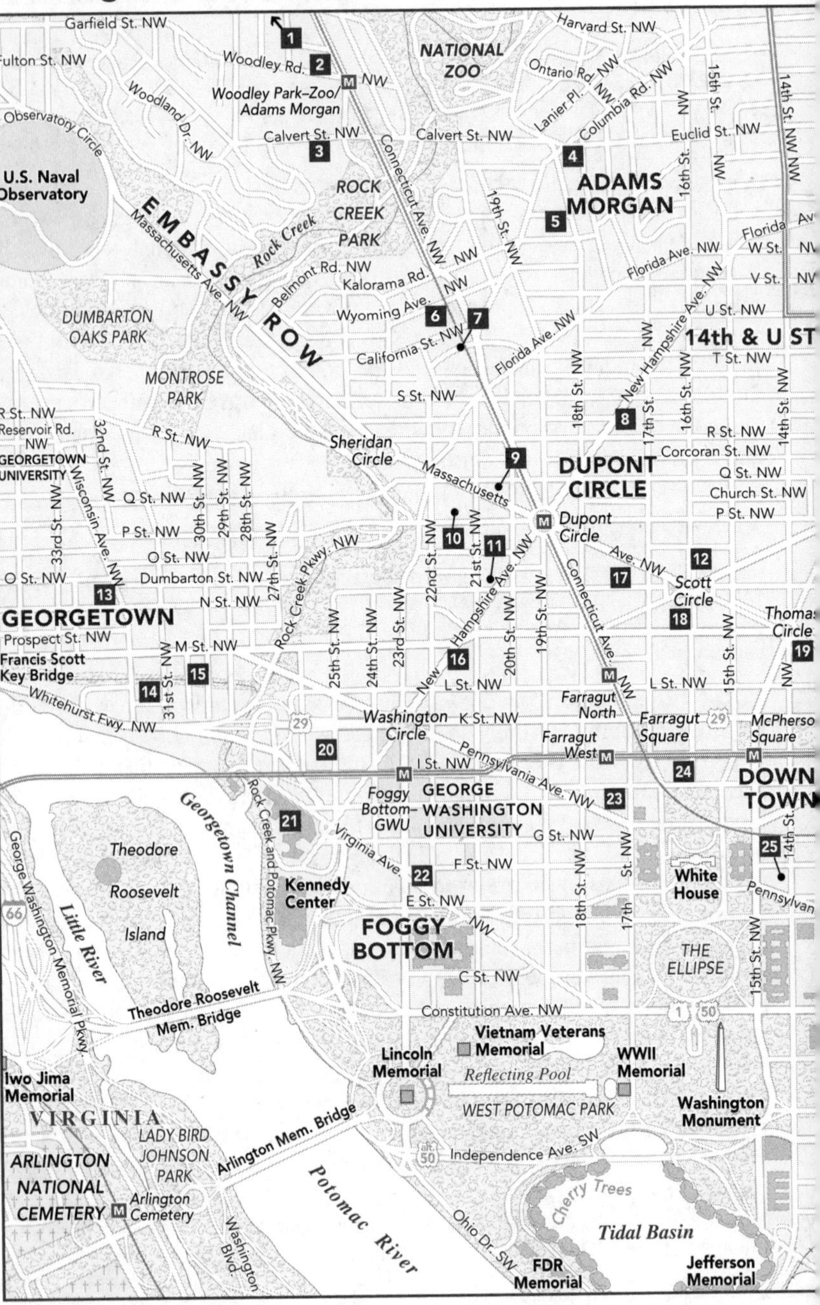

Garfield St. NW
Fulton St. NW
Woodley Rd. **1**
Woodley Rd. **2**
NATIONAL ZOO
Harvard St. NW
Woodland Dr. NW
Woodley Park–Zoo/ Adams Morgan
Ontario Rd. NW
Calvert St. NW **3**
Calvert St. NW
Observatory Circle
Lanier Pl. NW
Columbia Rd. NW
Euclid St. NW
U.S. Naval Observatory
ROCK CREEK PARK
ADAMS MORGAN **4**
5
EMBASSY ROW
Massachusetts Ave. NW
Rock Creek
Belmont Rd. NW
Kalorama Rd. NW
Wyoming Ave. NW **6** **7**
California St. NW
Florida Ave. NW
Florida Av
W St. NV
V St. NV
U St. NW
DUMBARTON OAKS PARK
MONTROSE PARK
S St. NW
14th & U ST
T St. NW
Sheridan Circle
Massachusetts
8
R St. NW
Corcoran St. NW
Q St. NW
Church St. NW
P St. NW
R St. NW
Reservoir Rd. NW
GEORGETOWN UNIVERSITY
R St. NW
Q St. NW
P St. NW
O St. NW
Dumbarton St. NW
N St. NW
9
DUPONT CIRCLE
Dupont Circle
10 **11**
17
12
Scott Circle
18
Thomas Circle
19
GEORGETOWN **13**
Prospect St. NW
M St. NW
15
16
L St. NW
L St. NW
Francis Scott Key Bridge
14
Whitehurst Fwy. NW
Washington Circle
K St. NW
Farragut North
Farragut Square
McPherson Square
20
Pennsylvania Ave. NW
Farragut West
24
I St. NW
Foggy Bottom-GWU
GEORGE WASHINGTON UNIVERSITY
23
DOWN TOWN
21
Virginia Ave.
G St. NW
25
Theodore Roosevelt Island
Kennedy Center
22
F St. NW
E St. NW
White House
Pennsylvan
Little River
FOGGY BOTTOM
C St. NW
THE ELLIPSE
Theodore Roosevelt Mem. Bridge
Constitution Ave. NW
Iwo Jima Memorial
VIRGINIA
LADY BIRD JOHNSON PARK
Lincoln Memorial
Vietnam Veterans Memorial
Reflecting Pool
WEST POTOMAC PARK
WWII Memorial
Washington Monument
ARLINGTON NATIONAL CEMETERY
Arlington Cemetery
Arlington Mem. Bridge
Independence Ave. SW
Cherry Trees
Potomac River
Ohio Dr. SW
Tidal Basin
FDR Memorial
Jefferson Memorial

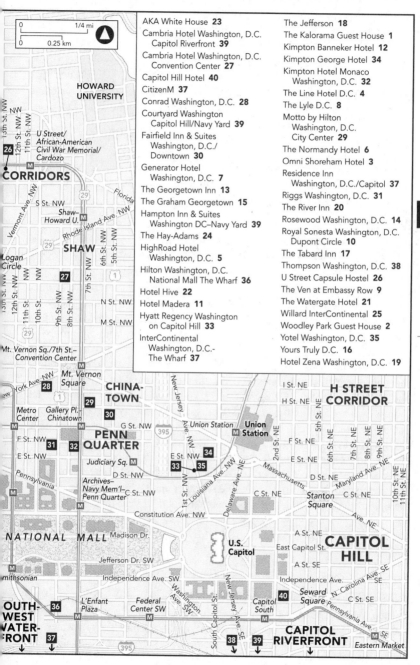

AKA White House **23**
Cambria Hotel Washington, D.C. Capitol Riverfront **39**
Cambria Hotel Washington, D.C. Convention Center **27**
Capitol Hill Hotel **40**
CitizenM **37**
Conrad Washington, D.C. **28**
Courtyard Washington Capitol Hill/Navy Yard **39**
Fairfield Inn & Suites Washington, D.C./ Downtown **30**
Generator Hotel Washington, D.C. **7**
The Georgetown Inn **13**
The Graham Georgetown **15**
Hampton Inn & Suites Washington DC–Navy Yard **39**
The Hay-Adams **24**
HighRoad Hotel Washington, D.C. **5**
Hilton Washington, D.C. National Mall The Wharf **36**
Hotel Hive **22**
Hotel Madera **11**
Hyatt Regency Washington on Capitol Hill **33**
InterContinental Washington, D.C.- The Wharf **37**

The Jefferson **18**
The Kalorama Guest House **1**
Kimpton Banneker Hotel **12**
Kimpton George Hotel **34**
Kimpton Hotel Monaco Washington, D.C. **32**
The Line Hotel D.C. **4**
The Lyle D.C. **8**
Motto by Hilton Washington, D.C. City Center **29**
The Normandy Hotel **6**
Omni Shoreham Hotel **3**
Residence Inn Washington, D.C./Capitol **37**
Riggs Washington, D.C. **31**
The River Inn **20**
Rosewood Washington, D.C. **14**
Royal Sonesta Washington, D.C. Dupont Circle **10**
The Tabard Inn **17**
Thompson Washington, D.C. **38**
U Street Capsule Hostel **26**
The Ven at Embassy Row **9**
The Watergate Hotel **21**
Willard InterContinental **25**
Woodley Park Guest House **2**
Yotel Washington, D.C. **35**
Yours Truly D.C. **16**
Hotel Zena Washington, D.C. **19**

HOWARD UNIVERSITY

U Street/ African-American Civil War Memorial/ Cardozo
26

CORRIDORS

S St. NW

Shaw–Howard U.

Florida

Rhode Island Ave. NW

SHAW

Vermont Ave. NW

13th St. NW
12th St. NW
11th St. NW

Logan Circle

13th St.
12th St.
11th St.
10th St.
9th St. NW
8th St.
7th St. NW
6th St. NW
5th St. NW

27

N St. NW.

M St. NW.

Mt. Vernon Sq./7th St.–Convention Center

Mt. Vernon Square
28

New York Ave. NW

CHINA-TOWN
29

30

New Jersey Ave. NW

I St. NE
H St. NE

H STREET CORRIDOR

5th St. NE

Metro Center
Gallery Pl.–Chinatown

G St. NW

Union Station
Union Station

F St. NE

6th St. NE
7th St. NE
8th St. NE
9th St. NE

PENN QUARTER

F St. NW

E St. NW

31 **32**

Judiciary Sq.

E St. NW
34

E St. NE

10th St. NE
11th St. NE

Pennsylvania

Archives–Navy Mem'l–Penn Quarter

D St. NW

33 **35**

D St. NE

Maryland Ave. NE

D St. NE

C St. NW

Louisiana Ave. NW

C St. NE

Stanton Square
C St. NE

2nd St. NE

Massachusetts

Delaware Ave. NE

Ave. NE

Constitution Ave. NW

NATIONAL MALL
Madison Dr.

U.S. Capitol

CAPITOL HILL

A St. NE

Jefferson Dr. SW

East Capitol St.

A St. SE

Smithsonian

Independence Ave. SW

Independence Ave.

N. Carolina Ave. SE

Seward Square
C St. SE

SOUTH-WEST WATER-FRONT

L'Enfant Plaza
36

Federal Center SW

Washington Ave. SW

Capitol South
40

Pennsylvania Ave.

New Jersey Ave. SE

South Capitol St.

37

38 **39**

CAPITOL RIVERFRONT

Eastern Market

SE

395

0   1/4 mi
0   0.25 km

29
29
29

61

CAPITOL RIVERFRONT

About 1 mile south of the U.S. Capitol Building, this southeast riverside enclave development has been going full throttle ever since the 2008 opening of the Washington Nationals' baseball stadium, Nationals Park. (The Southwest Waterfront lies due west of the Capitol Riverfront, just one Metro stop away on the Green Line.) The Courtyard by Marriott Capitol Hill/Navy Yard, the sole hotel here for a decade, now has several rivals, including the Hampton Inn & Suites Washington DC-Navy Yard, Thompson Washington, D.C., and the Cambria Hotel Washington, D.C., Capitol Riverfront.

Best for: Those with business on Capitol Hill or visitors who want to experience a young and vibrant waterfront neighborhood located just south, but within easy reach, of the city's core. And during baseball season, Nats fans!

Drawbacks: Sights and sounds of construction will continue here for many years to come. Crime is also a concern in these parts.

Moderate

Cambria Hotel Washington, D.C., Capitol Riverfront ★   If you're planning on visiting D.C. for a baseball game at Nationals Park or a soccer game at Audi Field, this new Cambria's location—and prices—can't be beat. Opened in 2021, the building blends nods of nostalgia (you'll see original details from the rowhouse that once stood here as well as photography, in-room murals, and books about the neighborhood that harken back to the city's past) with a look toward the future and new technology, with an impressive movie-screen effect near the elevator and in-room Bluetooth capabilities so you can stream music through the bathroom mirror. At an average of 550 feet, rooms here are among the most spacious in the city, ideal for families or anyone working remotely. Choose from 77 king rooms and 70 double queen rooms, each with an expansive desk workspace and plenty of room to spread out and relax after a long day of sightseeing. Pick up some snacks in the grab-and-go **Marketplace** in the lobby, or enjoy breakfast, dinner, or happy hour at **RowHouse Restaurant & Bar,** which has comfort foods like steaks and burgers on the menu. Visit **Perch SW,** the rooftop bar and lounge, where you can sip your suds by a firepit in chillier weather and take in stunning views of the Potomac and Capitol Riverfront neighborhood all year long.

69 Q St. SW (btw. First St. SW and Half St. SW). www.cambriadccapitolriverfront.com. ℂ **202/220-8400.** 154 units. Doubles from $122–$251, suites from $237–$399. Valet parking $43 plus tax. Up to two pets per room accepted (free). Metro: Navy Yard/Ballpark. **Amenities:** Restaurant, two bars (one on the rooftop), grab-and-go marketplace, fitness center, complimentary bikes, yoga mats available upon request, Wi-Fi (free).

Courtyard Washington Capitol Hill/Navy Yard ★   When this hotel opened in 2006, its guests probably felt like outliers in nowheresville. The Capitol Riverfront neighborhood now includes Nationals Park, a waterfront walkway, scores of restaurants, pubs, and breweries, an award-winning public park that stages Friday-night concerts in summer and festivals year-round, and a trapeze school, to boot. Glance northward on New Jersey Avenue and you'll spot the Capitol Building preening just a mile away.

Most rooms here have king beds and a sofa bed, and about 50 rooms have two queen beds. There are 12 spacious suites. For a lovely view of the river, ask for a corner king room at the L Street and New Jersey Avenue corner of the hotel—note that these rooms have a king bed but no pullout sofa. Other pluses: The Metro stop is just across the street; the market and fitness center are available 24 hours, the pool is open daily from 7am–10pm; and the lobby is a sea of media pods, rounded banquettes with individual TVs, and power outlets.

140 L St. SE (at New Jersey Ave.). www.marriott.com/hotels/travel/wasny-courtyard-washington-capitol-hill-navy-yard. © **202/479-0027.** 204 units. Doubles from $161–$313, suites from $209–$361. Limited parking $47 plus tax. One pet per room under 60 lb. allowed ($150 nonrefundable fee). Metro: Navy Yard/Ballpark. **Amenities:** Restaurant, bar, laundry, fitness center, Wi-Fi (free).

Hampton Inn & Suites Washington DC–Navy Yard ★

Baseball fans, this is your hotel. Situated directly across the street from Nationals Park, this reliable chain hotel is a great base if you're in town for a Nats game. Otherwise, guests (and locals) can enjoy views of home plate, first base, and the pitcher's mound, as well as cocktails and bar fare, from the rooftop **Top of the Yard** lounge. Here, panoramic vistas take in the Anacostia River, as well as the Washington Monument and U.S. Capitol Building in the distance.

Year-round reasons to stay at here are its location in the increasingly popular Capitol Riverfront/Navy Yard area and its smart amenities and furnishings, from ergonomic desk chairs to a contemporary decor of dark woods and leather and metal accents. Hampton Inn's signature features are also on hand: the complimentary hot breakfast with eggs, sausage or bacon, and waffles; to-go breakfast bags for those in a hurry; and a 24-hour **Pavilion Pantry** market.

1265 First St. SE (at N St.). www.hilton.com/en/hotels/wasnyhx-hampton-suites-washington-dc-navy-yard. © **800/HAMPTON** (426-7866) or 202/800-1000. 168 units. Doubles from $126–$241, suites from $143–$303. Parking $55 plus tax. Pets under 50 lb. allowed (free). Metro: Navy Yard/Ballpark. **Amenities:** Rooftop bar, grab-and-go market, complimentary breakfast and to-go bags, fitness center, laundry, Wi-Fi (free).

Thompson Washington, D.C. ★★

The only hotel in The Yards, a 500-acre riverfront development of restaurants, apartments, a winery, and shops next to Nationals Park, Thompson Washington, D.C., is a boutique hotel offering 225 rooms with 17 suites, a massive meeting space, a seafood restaurant, and a picturesque rooftop bar. The Hyatt property, which opened in 2020, reflects the neighborhood's industrial nautical history with its weathered wood, brick, and glass design. Rooms feature rich emerald and ivory tones and soft, curving tables and furniture meant to evoke a ship's cabin. Oversized windows in most rooms overlook the river or ballpark. Restauranteur Danny Meyer opened **Maialino Mare,** featuring an Italian-centric menu of seafood, and pasta. For a 360-degree view of the waterfront and city, head upstairs to the 6,000-square-foot rooftop bar **Anchovy Social,** which offers classic cocktails and small plates.

221 Tingey St. SE (at 3rd St.). www.hyatt.com/en-US/hotel/washington-dc/thompson-washington-dc/iadth. ℰ **855/949-1949.** 225 units. Doubles from $136–$228, suites from $312–$499, plus daily $25 amenities fee. Parking $55 including tax. One pet under 75 lb. allowed per room (free). Metro: Navy Yard/Ballpark. **Amenities:** Restaurant, bar, fitness center, Wi-Fi (free).

NATIONAL MALL

Several neighborhoods bordering the National Mall are less than a mile away, including Penn Quarter to the north and Capitol Hill to the east. Closest is the area immediately to the south, across Independence Avenue. The streets in this southwest quadrant of the city have long been home to government buildings and old residences, joined gradually over the last 15 years or so by a smattering of hotels and other developments. In addition to the Smithsonian museums and other National Mall sites, area attractions include the International Spy Museum, the U.S. National Holocaust Memorial Museum, and the Museum of the Bible. Best of all, affordable family-oriented properties predominate.

Best for: Travelers who want to be as close as possible to the National Mall, as well as within easy reach of Capitol Hill.

Drawbacks: Busy during the day, these streets are quiet at night, so you'll need to travel elsewhere in the city for restaurants, nightlife, and urban liveliness. Be aware that passenger and freight trains run on tracks that lie close to all the hotels in this neighborhood, so ask for a room away from the train-track side of the hotel for maximum quiet.

Expensive

Hilton Washington, D.C., National Mall The Wharf ★★   Luxury and practicality abound in this hotel, and it's location can't be beat: within walking distance to the White House and The Wharf, facing the International Spy Museum, and on top of L'Enfant Metro station (with an elevator that takes you directly to the Metro platform). All rooms are spacious, bright, and modern, with one or two king platform beds, floor-to-ceiling windows, plank flooring, and a 65-inch HDTV. Families will love the large suites, which come with a dining table, sofa bed, and guest powder room. View the monuments from the heated outdoor pool on the 12th floor which also sports cabanas, fire pits, and cozy lounge seating. Other pluses: expansive fitness and business centers, and a nifty Grab & Go Market, available 24/7.

480 L'Enfant Plaza. SW (at 9th St.). www.hilton.com/en/hotels/dcaephh-hilton-washington-dc-national-mall-the-wharf. ℰ **800/445-8667** or 202/484-1000. 367 units. Doubles from $207–$344. Parking $55 including tax. Metro: L'Enfant Plaza. **Amenities:** Restaurant, bar, onsite Starbucks Café, fitness center, outdoor pool, solarium, Wi-Fi (free).

Moderate

CitizenM ★★   Not so long ago, Washington, D.C., hotels were all beige: off-white walls, tan furniture, brown carpeting, you get the idea. Now,

European brands are opening bright, modern, and sleek properties stateside like CitizenM, from the Dutch hospitality brand known for its "affordable luxury." The entrance is more living room than lobby, designed in Amsterdam and packed with iconic mid-century-esque furniture, bold pillows, books, and eye-popping art. Check in via app or at one of the self-check-in kiosks, then head to your "MoodPad" room. All abodes are tech-equipped, so you can turn off the lights, change the color of your room, adjust the temperature, and lower the blinds without getting out of bed. **CanteenM** provides grab-and-go bites and counter service from Chef Jess, a local female-owned business, while on the 12th floor, **CloudM** boasts a large rooftop lounge and bar. The property also features an open workspace with iMacs, and a fitness and yoga studio.

550 School St., SW (at 6th St. SW). www.citizenm.com/hotels/united-states/washington-dc/washington-dc-capitol-hotel. © **202/747-2145.** 252 units. Doubles from $107–$329. Metro: L'Enfant Plaza or Federal Center SW. **Amenities:** Rooftop bar, grab-and-go eatery, fitness center, Wi-Fi (free).

Residence Inn Washington, DC/Capitol ★ It's no accident that this Residence Inn is located within walking distance of the National Museum of the American Indian. Four Native American tribes are 49% owners of the hotel, which made it the first multi-tribal partnership with non-tribal partners on land off a reservation when it first opened in 2005. Although certain features such as the sandstone walls in the lobby and artwork throughout hint at its Native American heritage, the hotel is otherwise similar to standard Residence Inns. All rooms are spacious studio, one-bedroom, or two-bedroom suites equipped with full kitchens. Guest rooms and the lobby have a modern look, think chaise lounges and stainless-steel accessories, and amenities like 52-inch flatscreen TVs with access to Netflix and Hulu. The hotel lies close to a train track, so ask for a room on the other side if you desire a quiet stay.

333 E St. SW (at 4th St.). www.marriott.com/wascp. © **202/484-8280.** 233 units. Studios from $187–$237. Rates include hot breakfast. Parking $53 plus tax. Metro: Federal Center SW or L'Enfant Plaza. Pets accepted ($150 nonrefundable fee). **Amenities:** Fitness center, indoor pool, Wi-Fi (free).

SOUTHWEST WATERFRONT

Arena Stage, boating activities, and fish markets have long been the main reasons anyone, out-of-towner or local, might visit this southern D.C. neighborhood located along the Washington Channel. The debut of **The Wharf** complex in 2017 reinvented the quarter overnight, adding more reasons to visit: live music venues, restaurants and bars, tons of watersports and other outdoor recreational activities, shops, and hotels, all strewn along the picturesque waterfront. In spring, summer, and fall, day and night, the place is lively. In winter, however, the neighborhood can seem quiet and out of the way. But you're less than a mile south of the National Mall and a free daily shuttle travels continuously, connecting The Wharf, Metro stations, and the National Mall. Water taxis travel the waterfront, taking you to and from Georgetown, Old Town Alexandria in Virginia, and National Harbor in

Maryland. All three of the Wharf hotels overlook the lovely Washington Channel and **East Potomac Park** (p. 199), which, for 2 weeks in spring, is full of blossoming cherry trees. **Hyatt House Washington, D.C./The Wharf** (www.hyatt.com/en-US/hotel/washington-dc/hyatt-house-washington-dc-the-wharf/wasxs) is recommended for extended stays since some of its suites are equipped with full kitchens. **Canopy by Hilton Washington, D.C./The Wharf** (www.hilton.com/en/hotels/dcacupy-canopy-washington-dc-the-wharf), the Hilton brand's "lifestyle" lodging, offers complimentary artisanal breakfast and bikes with a lively mix of pop-up shops, nightly tastings, and filtered spring water stations on each floor. The InterContinental is the largest and most interesting (see more details below).

Best for: Those who prefer water views and activities over city vibes, and for anyone who wants to experience one of D.C.'s trendiest neighborhoods.

Drawbacks: The Wharf's location, between Maine Avenue and the waterfront, limits its access, which can create traffic nightmares when there's a lot going on in the city and at The Wharf itself. Insufficient and/or poorly placed signage can make travel confusing; be sure to get precise directions from your hotel.

Expensive

InterContinental Washington, D.C. – The Wharf ★★   All Inter-Continental guest rooms measure at least 340 square feet, while onsite amenities are a cut above, including its new, modern Vietnamese restaurant, **Moon Rabbit;** spiffy bars; the fully equipped and waterfront-facing fitness center; and **The Wharf Spa by L'Occitane Spa.** Its lively, light-filled living-room-like lobby opens directly onto the Wharf's wide strand of a walkway and the waterfront, blending pleasantly into the scene; the hotel also operates a seasonal open-air "watering hole" across this strand, so you can enjoy a drink as you people-watch. One very practical feature off the lobby is a real-time monitor displaying arrivals and departures of shuttles, Metro trains, jitneys, and other modes of transportation. Rooms on the sides and at the rear of the hotel view Maine Avenue, buildings, and passageways. Waterfront rooms with balconies are best. Prices vary by time of year so you may luck out with lower rates for off-season dates.

801 Wharf St. SW (at 7th St.). www.wharfintercontinentaldc.com. ✆**800/424-6835.** 278 units, including 33 suites. Doubles from $183–$453, suites from $408–$902. Children 17 and under stay free. Parking $58 with tax. Pets up to 40 lb. accepted ($75 fee). Metro: Waterfront or L'Enfant Plaza. **Amenities:** Restaurant, 4 bars, seasonal pool and rooftop bar, expansive fitness center, full-service spa, Wi-Fi (free).

PENN QUARTER

At the center of the city is this hot locale, jam-packed with restaurants, bars, museums, theaters, the Capital One Arena, and the posh CityCenterDC shopping arcade. Hotels include modern venues catering to convention crowds and historic properties switched up for luxury-loving fun-seekers.

Best for: Those who love being in the center of the action, within easy reach of downtown offices, the convention center, and Capitol Hill. Likewise,

Penn Quarter is a prime home base for tourists, with attractions within its boundaries and the National Mall just across Pennsylvania Avenue.

Drawbacks: Crowded sidewalks and noisy traffic can be annoying—and sometimes even overwhelming.

Expensive

Conrad Washington, D.C. ★★ Just north of the busiest blocks of Penn Quarter and set within CityCenterDC (the city's sparkling new hub of shops, restaurants, and condos), you'll find this all-glass hotel, which opened in 2019. Rooms are spacious—from 416 to 465 square feet—with either two queen beds or one king bed. All have floor-to-ceiling windows, marble bathrooms, and calming white and cream interiors. Book a premium corner king room with views stretching down New York Avenue. Guests who book rooms on the 10th floor have access to the **Sakura Club,** a lounge that offers meals made to order by a private chef, complimentary beer and wine, and a dedicated concierge. "Top Chef" alums Bryan and Michael Voltaggio anchor the hotel's seafood-centric restaurant **Estuary,** focused on the flavors of Chesapeake Bay. **Summit,** its swanky rooftop bar and terrace, offers unobstructed views of the Capitol Building, Washington Monument, and in the distance, the Potomac River. The hotel's ground level features 30,000 square feet of luxury retail space, which now includes a Tiffany & Co.

950 New York Ave. NW (at 10 St. NW). www.conradwashingtondc.com. ℂ **202/844-5900.** 360 units. Doubles from $264–$487, suites from $318–$546. Parking $60 plus tax. Pets accepted ($75 fee). Metro: Gallery Place–Chinatown. **Amenities:** Restaurant, rooftop bar, fitness center, Wi-Fi (free).

Riggs Washington, D.C. ★★★ For more than 160 years, Riggs National Bank billed itself as "the most important bank in the most important city in the world." More than 20 U.S. presidents (from Lincoln to Nixon) have banked

family-friendly HOTELS

Kimpton Banneker Hotel ★★★
(p. 75) Little ones receive cookies and milk, as well as treats like board games and tiny telescopes in honor of Benjamin Banneker, the African American author, astronomer, and mathematician the hotel is named for. Also available are inspirational children's books full of positive messages and affirmations, like "I Am Confident, Brave & Beautiful: A Coloring Book for Girls," "Little Feminist," "I Promise" by LeBron James, and "Superheroes Are Everywhere" by VP Kamala Harris.

Omni Shoreham Hotel ★★★
(p. 85) With two pools (including a kiddie pool), loads of lawn out back to run around on (and Rock Creek Park beyond that), the National Zoo up the street, and the Woodley Park–Zoo–Adams Morgan Metro nearby, the Omni is one of the best hotels in town for families. It sweetens the deal with a backpack filled with games that your child can wear when you set off sightseeing and cookies and milk left in the room at turndown the first night. The hotel sometimes partners with the National Zoo for special packages including a furry stuffed animal and Zoo backpack.

there, but financial scandals eventually spelled its demise in 2004. The national branch building on the National Register of Historic Places reopened in 2020 as the swanky Riggs Washington, D.C., offering 181 guest rooms and suites, an expansive restaurant, and a lounge and rooftop event space. Rooms echo the building's historic design, with Italian marble bathrooms and bespoke artwork. You'll also find the two-bedroom Riggs Suite in the original bank boardroom and four "First Lady" suites inspired by Ida McKinley, Ida Van Buren, Louisa Adams, and Caroline Harrison. **Café Riggs** anchors the main floor of the hotel and offers round-the-clock dining. **Silver Lyan,** the hotel's cocktail bar on the lower level, contains a secret room in the original bank vault just for private groups.

900 F St. NW (at 9th St). www.riggsdc.com. © **202/638-1800.** 181 units. Doubles from $224–$429, suites from $509–$747. Children 15 and under stay free. Parking $55 plus tax. Pets up to 35 lb. accepted ($100 fee per stay). Metro: Metro Center or Gallery Place–Chinatown. **Amenities:** Restaurant, bar, fitness center, complimentary bikes, Wi-Fi (free).

Moderate

Kimpton Hotel Monaco Washington, D.C. ★★ For deluxe accommodations in a terrific location, you can't beat Hotel Monaco. When it was completed in 1866, this historic, four-story marble building served as a general post office and tariff building for an area that was a developing mishmash of big government and small-town buildings. Today, it's one of the city's top hotels, located near the Smithsonian Museum of American Art, National Portrait Gallery, and trendy restaurants such as **Succotash.**

The hotel has an "elegance-meets-bold" design. Note the playful architectural details in each guest room, like a 5-foot lion's head medallion above the bed and the night table resembling the top of a Corinthian column, as well as eye-catching features in the lobby/living room, with Murano glass chandeliers, brilliant green walls, and modern art on display. Guest rooms average 400 square feet, with vaulted ceilings, long windows, and vibrant hues of bronze, plum, champagne, and royal blue. Ask for an F Street or 7th Street–facing Monte Carlo room (525 sq. ft.) for the best views, or a first-floor room if quiet is preferred (some guests call this "the basement," because it is nearly subterranean). The hotel restaurant, **Dirty Habit DC,** gets good reviews for its take on global cuisine, and for its bars in the atrium and courtyard.

700 F St. NW (at 7th St.). www.monaco-dc.com. © **800/649-1202** or 202/628-7177. 184 units. Doubles from $189–$340, suites from $387–$452, plus $25 daily amenities fee. Children 17 and under stay free. Rates include free morning coffee, an evening wine hour, and complimentary bikes. Self-parking $38, valet parking $55 plus tax. All pets stay free (no restrictions, supplies provided). Metro: Gallery Place–Chinatown. **Amenities:** Restaurant, bar, children's amenity program, fitness center, Wi-Fi (free when you join the IHG Rewards program).

Inexpensive

Fairfield Inn & Suites Washington, D.C./Downtown ★ You're really in the thick of things at this hotel, situated on a busy Chinatown street in bustling Penn Quarter, a block north of the Capital One Arena, and surrounded by hip eateries. But this is an old neighborhood, too: The bells of St. Mary Mother of God, the 1890 Catholic church across 5th Street, peal from 7am to—don't worry—9pm. And if you walk down H Street to no. 604, you'll notice a plaque on the facade of what is now the Wok and Roll restaurant, identifying the structure as Mary Surratt's Boarding House—she conspired here with John Wilkes Booth to assassinate President Lincoln. The property plays up the Chinatown connection, with the color red and Chinese symbols predominating in furnishings. Most spacious are 10th-floor rooms and corner suites ending in "24." Fifth Street–facing rooms offer nice city views. Executive king rooms have pullout sofas. Suites and double-queen rooms have mini-fridges, which are available upon request in king and executive king rooms. Guests also like the availability of a coin-operated washer/dryer, same-day dry-cleaning service (for a fee), and the complimentary hot breakfast buffet. Downstairs, the **Irish Channel Restaurant and Pub** serves casual pub fare and bar snacks in front of a big TV screen.

500 H St. NW (at 5th St.). www.marriott.com/hotels/travel/wasfc-fairfield-inn-and-suites-washington-dc-downtown. © **202/289-5959.** 198 units, including 9 suites. Doubles from $99–$369, suites from $129–$439. Children 17 and under stay free. One pet allowed per room ($75 fee). Parking $49 plus tax. Metro: Gallery Place–Chinatown. **Amenities:** Restaurant, bar, fitness center, Wi-Fi (free).

Motto by Hilton Washington, D.C., City Center ★

Originally opened in 2017 as the Pod DC Hotel, the property was converted to the Motto by Hilton in 2020. It's inexpensive and centrally located, but also small and so efficient it borders on uncomfortable if you're used to spreading out on vacation. Still, it's a worthy contender for business or young travelers who want to be in the heart of the action without having to pay a lot of money to do so. As befits its Penn Quarter locale, Motto is lively from the jump, welcoming you into an open space that serves as both lobby and the hotel's **Crimson Diner and Coffee Bar.** Of-the-moment music plays, as guests check in at the little reception counter or chill on one of the teal-colored barstools. Downstairs is the **Crimson Whiskey Bar,** while the **Crimson View** rooftop bar offers views of the city and the Washington Monument, and—a rarity for D.C. hotels—the capability to stay open year-round. Guest rooms are all the same tiny size, 149 square feet, but you can choose from full bed, queen bed, or bunk bed options. Everything fits just so, the frosted bathroom door sliding to close and space left beneath the bed for luggage storage. Despite the allure of bunk beds, I wouldn't recommend the hotel to families unless your children are old enough to stay alone in a room (there are no connecting rooms) but solo travelers, millennials, and thrifty types? Go for it.

627 H St. NW (7th St.). www.hilton.com/en/hotels/wasuaua-motto-washington-dc-city-center. © **202/847-4444.** 245 units. Doubles from $129–$399. No on-site parking; reserve space in advance at a partner garage from $26 per 24 hrs. Children under 18 stay free. No pets; service animals only. Metro: Gallery Place–Chinatown. **Amenities:** Restaurant, two bars (one on the rooftop), fitness center, Wi-Fi (free).

DOWNTOWN

Think of the White House as center stage, with an array of hotels, law and lobbyist office buildings, and restaurants at its feet. Several historic hotels, as well as contemporary, more affordable properties, are among the best options.

Best for: Travelers interested in a central location that's less raucous than Penn Quarter at night. Also, those doing business with the executive branch or at one of the law, lobbying, or association offices that line K Street.

Drawbacks: Urban sounds like traffic, construction, and garbage collection may be part of the experience.

Expensive

The Hay-Adams ★★★   This 92-year-old hotel's tagline, "Where nothing is overlooked but the White House," would be corny were it not true. The Hay-Adams is known not only for its sublime service but for being the only hotel with such straight-on views of the White House, best seen from rooms on the top floors, six through eight. (You can also see Lafayette Square, the Washington Monument, and the Jefferson Memorial.) Views elsewhere are of historic **St. John's Episcopal Church** and downtown buildings, and in a way, the views determine the rates. Similarly sized at about 385 square feet, guest rooms are furnished with creamy white and tan toile fabrics, European linens, and marble bathrooms. Interior designs that were here when Amelia Earhart stayed in 1928—intricate plaster moldings, walnut wainscoting, and high ceilings—are still in place. One thing that was not here then was the **Off the Record** bar, a regular hangout for the press and politicos. The hotel's restaurant, **The Lafayette,** is one of the most elegant in the capital, with chandeliers white-linen-topped tables and contemporary American cuisine taken to new heights by French chef Nicolas Legret.

800 16th St. (at H St.). www.hayadams.com. ℰ **800/853-6807** or 202/638-6600. 145 units. Doubles from $359–$629, suites from $959–$1,229. Third person $30. Children 17 and under stay free. Valet parking $62 plus tax. Dogs up to 25 lb. allowed (free but you'll be charged for dog-sitting if you leave your dog alone in the room). Metro: Farragut West. **Amenities:** Restaurant, bar, bikes, fitness center, Wi-Fi (free).

View of the White House from the Federal Suite of the Hay-Adams.

Willard InterContinental ★★★   The guest list at this historic hotel, which celebrates its 115th anniversary in 2021, has always included illustrious figures. President Abraham Lincoln actually lived here for 10 days in 1861 before moving into the White House, 1 block away. Dr. Martin Luther King, Jr. sat in its lobby in August 1963 finishing his historic "I Have a Dream" speech

The Willard InterContinental Hotel.

before delivering it from the steps of the Lincoln Memorial. The Willard has also hosted foreign dignitaries, like Japan's first delegation to the U.S., which included three Samurai ambassadors and their entourage of 74 in 1860.

The spacious guest rooms, are elegantly decorated with dark wood furnishings; shades of blue, cream, and gold; and comfortable extras like a velvet armchair and ottoman. Ask for courtyard-facing rooms for quiet, or Pennsylvania Avenue–facing rooms for views of the Washington Monument, the Lincoln Memorial, and the Jefferson Memorial (the higher your floor, the better the sights). Expansive oval suites offer the best views from floor-to-ceiling windows that sweep down Pennsylvania Avenue.

But you're here as much for the history and ambience as for a place to sleep. Enjoy a cocktail at the **Round Robin Bar,** expertly mixed by bartender Jim Hewes as he tells tales about Willard guests, from Charles Dickens to Bill Clinton. Stroll through the lobby and admire its mosaic floor, marble columns, and ornate ceiling, then tour the history gallery filled with memorabilia, like a copy of Lincoln's hotel bill. Varied events—afternoon tea, Kentucky Derby Day soirées, Christmas tree viewing and caroling throughout December— attract as many locals as hotel guests. Finally, stop by **Café du Parc** and sit on the terrace if possible, to savor the views and lovely French brasserie flavors of *boeuf bourguignon* and *croque monsieur.*

1401 Pennsylvania Ave. NW (at 14th St.). www.washington.intercontinental.com. ✆ **800/ 424-6835** or 202/628-9100. 335 units. Doubles from $213–$503, suites from $352–$650. Parking $59 plus tax. Dogs up to 40 lb. accepted ($200 nonrefundable cleaning fee). Metro: Metro Center. **Amenities:** Brasserie with seasonal terrace, bar, seasonal afternoon tea in Peacock Alley, health club with sauna, fitness center, onsite spa, Wi-Fi (free).

Travelers who plan to visit for a week or longer should know about the centrally located **AKA White House ★★★** apartments and hotel, 1710 H St. NW (www.stayaka.com/aka-white-house; ℰ 202/904-2500). The D.C. location is one of 10 AKA properties (others are in NYC, LA, Philadelphia, and London), all of which offer luxuriously furnished one- and two-bedroom apartments. AKA can offer tremendous value, especially if your timing is right. Check the website to see the property's appointments and amenities, including fully equipped kitchens, stylish decor, free Wi-Fi, an on-site fitness center, and laundry services. K Street law offices, the White House, the Renwick Gallery, and excellent restaurants, such as **Founding Farmers** (p. 115), are just some of the property's notable neighbors. Note that while AKA serves mainly as an extended-stay property, it also accommodates visitors for shorter stays as availability allows.

ADAMS MORGAN

Inns, hostels, and BNBs are far more common than hotels in Adams Morgan (AdMo). Just one hotel, **The Line DC,** lies in this neighborhood's boundaries. **The Normandy Hotel,** technically situated next door in Kalorama, where the Obamas live, is also listed here, as it's a 5-minute walk from AdMo proper.

Best for: Travelers who want to stay in a 24-hour neighborhood with a quirkier, artsier, and grittier vibe than Downtown.

Drawbacks: The closest Metro stops (Dupont Circle and Woodley Park) are each about half a mile away, though buses and Circulator shuttles are available.

Moderate

The Line Hotel D.C. ★★★   If you want to be charmed, intrigued, and wowed, book a room here. The Line Hotel occupies a former church, which was built in 1912 at the crest of the hill that defines the Adams Morgan neighborhood, now the crossroads of 18th St. NW. and Columbia Road. Its architecture is Neoclassical Revival style—in other words, it's temple-like with colossal columns framing the grand entrance.

A renovation transformed the church interior into a spectacular gallery of a lobby. The hotel employed local artists and designers to create an imaginative decor throughout, incorporating found objects and original features of the church as much as possible. In the lobby, for example, the enormous chandelier was sculpted by a local artist from brass pieces of the church's pipe organ. The talent behind the onsite restaurant/bar/coffee shop **No Goodbyes** are locals, too, but with national acclaim: Spike Gjerde (A Rake's Progress) and Erik Bruner-Yang (Brothers and Sisters). The hotel's radio station, Full Service Radio, broadcasting news about the city from the lobby.

Guest rooms are located in the U-shaped, eight-floor annex at the rear of the structure. They measure 300 square feet or larger, and each is outfitted with hand-hewn oak floors, brass beds, copper accessories, and whimsical original

Entrance to The Line Hotel DC.

artworks. About one-third of the rooms capture a glimpse of the Washington Monument; all have long windows that bring in lots of light.

1770 Euclid St. NW (at Columbia Rd.). www.thelinehoteldc.com. © **202/588-0525.** 220 units. Doubles from $153–$305, suites from $449–$739. Extra person $25. Children 12 and under stay free. Parking $60 including tax. Pets allowed (free, no restrictions). Metro: Woodley Park or Dupont Circle. **Amenities:** Restaurant, fitness center, Wi-Fi (free).

The Normandy Hotel ★★   This six-floor boutique hotel has plenty of pretty, Parisian charm. The Normandy lies on a tree-shaded street lined with embassies; not surprisingly, the clientele here is an international mix. You're a peaceful detour only minutes away, by foot, from the heart of the Dupont Circle, Adams Morgan, and Woodley Park neighborhoods. The Normandy's 75 rooms range in size, measuring between 210 and 352 square feet, and each makes good use of the space with cleverly designed and positioned furnishings: long, skinny desks; nifty little reading lamps with stems you can twist out of the walls just so; and compact Nespresso coffee machines and glass-fronted fridges placed out of the way. Front-facing rooms overlook tranquil Wyoming Avenue, while those at the back survey the courtyard. Three first-floor rooms open to a private garden terrace. Also on the first level is the parquet-floored lounge, with little sofas, armchairs, and a fireplace. The Normandy is perfect for couples and solo travelers, but a larger hotel might be a better choice for groups, large families, and those who crave lots of space.

2118 Wyoming Ave. NW (at Connecticut Ave.). www.thenormandydc.com. © **202/483-1350.** 75 units. Doubles from $170–$264. Limited parking $40 plus tax. Pets (dogs only) $25 per night. Metro: Dupont Circle. **Amenities:** Complimentary fitness passes to nearby Washington Sports Club, limo and town car service available upon request, Wi-Fi (free).

Inexpensive

HighRoad Hotel Washington, D.C. ★   This stunning boutique hotel, located in a restored Victorian mansion in the heart of Adams Morgan, began as one of D.C.'s first upscale hostels back in 2016 and after a series of renovations reopened in spring 2022 as HighRoad Hotel Washington, D.C. The property embodies everything you love about staying in hostels—the ability to meet fellow travelers in common spaces and have a comfortable bed to crawl back into after a night out on the town—adding posh features like luxury linens and towels, memory foam mattresses, customized bunk beds with built-in stairs (not ladders like you'll see in other hostels), complimentary Wi-Fi, and free access to Netflix and Hulu in the common room. Private rooms (similar to what you'd find in a budget hotel) and three-person dorms each measure 150 square feet, while six-bunk dorm rooms are 250 square feet and a cut above your average hostel, with hand-crafted pod beds featuring blackout curtains, headrests, reading lights, power outlets, and, as its website states, "all the hooks you could ever need." Curl up by the fireplace with a book from the in-house library. Best of all, its Adams Morgan location puts you within stumbling distance of some of the best bars, restaurants, and nightlife in the city.

1804 Belmont Rd. NW (at 18th St. NW) www.highroadhotel.com. ✆ **202/735-3622.** 40 units, including 30 private rooms with private bathrooms and 10 dorm-style rooms with either 3 or 6 bunk beds. Dorms (mixed or female-only) from $29–$39. Private rooms from $120–$220. No onsite parking; use the local garage across the street (from $20). Pets allowed in private rooms only (free). Must be 18 or older to stay in private rooms, children can stay with parents in private rooms only. Metro: 15-minute walk from Dupont Circle or take the DC Circulator bus from U St./Cardozo or Woodley Park/Zoo/Adams Morgan. **Amenities:** Front yard terrace; laundry room; fireplace; complimentary coffee, TV, Netflix, and Hulu in the common room; Wi-Fi (free).

DUPONT CIRCLE

This neighborhood of town houses, beautiful embassies, bistro restaurants, art galleries, and bars is home to more hotels than any other part of the city. Boutique hotels reign supreme, though several chains have outposts here, too.

Best for: Travelers who love a city scene minus the office buildings. Also, for LGBTQ visitors, since Dupont Circle is a major hub of activity and culture.

Drawbacks: If you have business on Capitol Hill or in Penn Quarter, this might not be your first choice since there are plenty of closer options.

Expensive

The Jefferson ★★★   If you can afford to, stay at the Jefferson, which I consider to be D.C.'s best hotel. If you don't plan to stay here, at least stop by **Quill** ★★★ (p. 230), the hotel's delightful bar. Located slightly off the beaten track about a half-mile north of the White House, The Jefferson exudes the ambience of a country-house hotel. Decor throughout pays homage to Thomas Jefferson in all his passions, from Quill's display of 18th-century maps tracing the oenophile's journeys through the wine regions of France, to guest-room fabrics imprinted with architectural and agricultural scenes of Monticello. A handful of rooms offer glimpses of the Washington Monument a mile away, while others look to the White House at the end of 16th Street; none, alas, capture the sight of the Jefferson Memorial a bit beyond. The hotel's dining options include the sublime and intimate Michelin-starred **Plume** restaurant, which serves seasonal menus inspired by the harvest from Thomas Jefferson's kitchen gardens at Monticello. In addition to **Quill,** the elegant cocktail bar and lounge, skylit **Greenhouse** restaurant is also quite lovely.

1200 16th St. NW (at M St.). www.jeffersondc.com. © **202/448-2300.** 99 units. Doubles from $497–$614, suites from $755–$1,243. Children 18 and under stay free. Valet parking $55 with tax. Dogs up to 50 lb. accepted ($50 fee includes pet supplies, on request). Metro: Farragut North. **Amenities:** 2 restaurants, bar, children's amenities, fitness center with Peloton bikes, spa with massages and facials, iPad in each room, Wi-Fi (free).

Moderate

Hotel Madera ★ Following an extensive 1-year renovation, Hotel Madera (formerly Kimpton Hotel Madera) reopened in 2021 as a luxury boutique property flaunting its newly decorated and well-appointed rooms. They're spacious enough (most measure 360–450 square feet), with balconies in 36 rooms adding 60 more square feet, a valuable perk in a time where fresh air and outdoor space are so revered. For those looking to stay active, the hotel sports a shiny new fitness center with Peloton bikes, Matrix treadmills, free weights, and a rowing machine, among other equipment. You'll find water dispensers and bags of pre-packaged ice in the hallway, and bottles and mini-fridges in each room (there's also an in-room pour-over coffee set-up with La Colombe coffee and tea sachets). Kids receive ice cream or cookies at check-in, while those traveling with fur-babies can borrow pet beds, bowls, and treats. Downstairs, **Firefly** offers New American and Southern cuisine with a modern twist, with sticky mango chicken wings and Peking duck tacos on the menu as appetizers, and steak and truffle fries, burgers, and crab cakes available as entrées. Dinner happens Wed–Sat from 4–10pm, while weekend brunch (featuring items like kimchi pork hash, brioche French toast, and chicken and waffles) is from 10am–3pm. The restaurant and bar also play host to activities like mixology classes and a Drag Happy Hour that's a hit with visitors and locals alike (check the website for events).

1310 New Hampshire Avenue NW (at N St. NW). www.hotelmadera.com. © **844/781-1152.** 81 units. Doubles from $145–$298, studios from $185–$387, plus a $25 daily amenities fee. Valet parking $50 plus tax. Pets allowed (free, no restrictions). Metro: Dupont Circle. **Amenities:** Restaurant, bar, fitness center with Peloton bikes, Wi-Fi (free).

Kimpton Banneker Hotel ★ Formerly the Kimpton Rouge Hotel, this stylish property reopened in 2021 as the Kimpton Banneker; it's named for Benjamin Banneker, the African American mathematician, astronomer, and scholar known for building the first wooden clock in North America in 1753, creating one of the first Almanacs in 1791, and speaking out about injustice and slavery—he famously penned a letter to President Thomas Jefferson about such topics at the time and received a response praising his many achievements. Today, everything in the hotel, from the directional signage found on each floor to the tiny telescopes handed out to younger guests (p. 67) honors his legacy and the spirit and culture of neighboring Washingtonians, through evocative artwork created by local artists on display in the lobby and throughout the hotel's public spaces. Rooms are bright and cozy, measuring between 385 and 495 square feet, with signature Kimpton features like in-room yoga mats, evening wine hour from 5 to 6pm, special welcome amenities for loyalty program members, and downloadable self-guided tours of the neighborhood. Enjoy modern French cuisine at **Le Sel**, a traditional Parisian-style bistro, and take in the views and vibes at **Lady Bird,** an indoor/outdoor rooftop bar and lounge. Admire the spectacular mural behind the bar area, hand-painted by local artist Meg Biram, then enjoy views of 16th Street and the White House from your perfect perch above the city. The hotel's centralized location also puts you within walking distance of Dupont Circle, a funky and chic part of town worth checking out on any trip to Washington, D.C. (p. 274).

1315 16th St. NW (at O St.). www.thebanneker.com. © **202/234-6399** or 800/994-4654. 144 units. Doubles from $155–$357, suites from $324–$519. Valet parking $50 plus tax, black car service upon request. Children 17 and under stay free and receive a special welcome amenity. Pets allowed (free). Metro: Dupont Circle or Farragut North (12-minute walk). **Amenities:** Restaurant, rooftop bar, fitness center with Peloton bikes, free bikes, complimentary car service within a 1-mile radius, Wi-Fi (free).

The Lyle D.C. ★   Part of the prestigious Lore Group, a British brand known for minimalist, artsy, and stylish boutique hotels (Riggs Washington, D.C also falls under its umbrella; p. 67), the hotel reopened in 2021 following a 1-year closure. It's all about the details here, from spaces highlighting art deco styles to hand-painted antiques that were hand-picked by the hotel designer. Guest rooms measure 240–395 square feet, depending on whether you book one with a kitchenette, while the apartment-like Lyle Suite offers 875 square feet of space and can be connected with adjoining rooms to create your own two- or three-bedroom private sanctuary. The décor is simple yet elegant, with natural materials and neutral tones that make the exquisite burl wood head-board really stand out when you enter the room. The hotel is pet friendly and front desk staff are happy to point out their favorite neighborhood dog parks. Exercise enthusiasts will love the spacious fitness center, which has Peloton bikes and a separate area that serves as a yoga or barre studio in addition to your standard hotel gym equipment. Sign up for the Lyle Loyalty program to receive special discounts and perks like guaranteed late checkout and compli-mentary welcome drinks. Onsite restaurant and bar **Lyle's** is open for break-fast, brunch, and dinner, serving New American food and cocktails like apricot sours, smoked Moscow mules, and a refreshing spritz made with grapefruit, vodka, Sauvignon Blanc, and elderflower.

1731 New Hampshire Ave. NW (at Riggs Pl. NW). www.lyledc.com. © **202/964-6750.** 196 units. Doubles from $149–$333. Parking $64 plus tax. Pets allowed (dogs only, $100 nonrefundable deposit). Metro: Dupont Circle. **Amenities:** Restaurant, bar, fitness center, laundry, Wi-Fi (free).

Royal Sonesta Washington, D.C. Dupont Circle ★★

Originally opened in 2006 as Kimpton's Hotel Palomar, the hotel was transformed into a Royal Sonesta in 2020. Studio rooms are 500 square feet, decorated with bright colors, mod lamps, and bold geometric prints. If you're visiting in the summer, don't miss the chance to sit around the outdoor courtyard pool, which whisks guests away from the sounds of the city. Check the website for deals and packages, which can help you save money if you're staying over weekends, discounted parking, or if you belong to the brand's Sonesta Travel Pass loyalty program; **Certo!** Is the hotel's acclaimed Italian restaurant, serving handcrafted pastas with fresh ingredients. The hotel is just 2 blocks from Dupont Circle.

2121 P St. NW (between 21st St. NW and 22nd St. NW). www.sonesta.com/us/district-columbia/washington/royal-sonesta-washington-dc-dupont-circle. ☏ **202/448-1800.** 335 units. Doubles from $188–$369, suites from $242–$429, plus $25 daily guest amenities fee. Children 17 and under stay free. Rates include evening wine (5–6pm). Parking $49 plus tax. Pets allowed (free). Metro: Dupont Circle. **Amenities:** Restaurant, bar, swimming pool (seasonal), electric car charging stations, fitness center, bikes, Wi-Fi (free).

The Ven at Embassy Row ★

Many D.C. hotels claim to be an urban oasis or the ultimate place for an urban retreat, but this one actually means it. Against all odds, the former Embassy Row Hotel completed its transition to a Marriott Tribute Portfolio Hotel during the pandemic and successfully opened as The Ven at Embassy Row in 2021. Located near the Dupont Circle Metro station, you're within walking or Metro distance of everything D.C. has to offer, yet the tranquil setting and ninth-floor rooftop pool (the only one in Dupont Circle) make you feel as if you've entered a different world entirely. If you happen to be here during the warmer months, also known as "rooftop season," Epic Yoga sessions are available poolside. Four times a day, you can catch an impressive digital light installation of the Northern Lights and guided meditation session, designed to help you feel as peaceful as possible during your stay. If you need more relaxation, try some pour over tea, provided by a partnership with Valley Brook Tea, with customized tea sachets featuring oils from plants and flowers native to the countries of nearby embassies. Rooms average 240 square feet and are quite stylish, blending modern and traditional features, with subtle color palates and sophisticated antiques. Onsite marketplace **The Exchange** offers ethically sourced goods from local vendors, while full-service restaurant **Fred & Stilla,** serves a variety of breakfast and dinner dishes inspired by the countries of its neighboring embassies, namely those of China, Finland, Costa Rica, Poland, Laos, Nigeria, Greece, Lebanon, Italy, Canada, Mexico, Kenya, and Japan.

2015 Massachusetts Ave. NW (btw. 20th St. NW and 21st St. NW), www.marriott.com/hotels/travel/wastx-the-ven-at-embassy-row-washington-dc-a-tribute-portfolio-hotel. ☏ **202/265-1600.** 231 units. Doubles from $162–$324, plus a $28 daily amenities fee. Parking $48 with tax. One dog per room up to 50 lb accepted (free). Metro: Dupont Circle. **Amenities:** Restaurant, bar, grab-and-go marketplace, fitness center, pool, seasonal Epic Yoga sessions, $28 food and beverage credit and Wi-Fi (included in the $28 daily amenities fee).

Inexpensive

Generator Hotel Washington, D.C. ★   Trendy European-style boutiques have infiltrated the D.C. hotel scene, and the new Generator is no exception. Opened in 2020, this hostel-meets-hotel offers both private rooms and shared accommodations, which guests can rent by the room or by the bed. The hotel's restaurants, terrace lounge, and rooftop bar are chic, laidback spaces perfect for collaborating on work projects while discussing the news of the day. Rooms feature reimagined political portraits from the 18th, 19th, and 20th centuries—for instance, a portrait of Thomas Jefferson overlaid with a woman's manicured hands. Generator D.C. also houses an outdoor pool on the second floor as well as a fitness center. Its nifty centralized location near Kalorama also puts you a 10-minute walk from both the Dupont Circle and Adams Morgan neighborhoods.

1900 Connecticut Ave. NW (at Leroy Place NW and T St. NW). www.staygenerator.com/hostels/washington-dc. 𝄐 **202/332-9300.** 148 units. Private rooms $90-$324; beds in shared rooms (female-only or mixed) $35-$55; suites from $273. Parking $40 plus tax. Pets accepted with a $30 fee, plus a $250 deposit. Metro: Dupont Circle. **Amenities:** Restaurant, bar, pool, fitness center, laundry, Wi-Fi (free).

The Tabard Inn ★   Fans of quaintness and quirks—and I am one of them—will continue to find them throughout the three joined 19th-century town houses that make up The Tabard Inn. Nooks, bay windows, exposed brick, vibrantly hued walls (shades of purple, chartreuse, or periwinkle, for instance), flea-market finds, and antiques are some of the characteristics of individual guest rooms—and no TVs. Quaintness also means a certain creakiness throughout. There is no elevator, which may pose a challenge to those trudging upstairs with (or without) luggage to lodging on the third or fourth floor. That, and narrow hallways, may make a stay here challenging for travelers with disabilities.

The Tabard Inn is a beloved institution to locals, who flock to its charming Michelin award-winning **restaurant** (p. 114) and the adjoining paneled lounge.

1739 N St. NW (btw. 17th and 18th sts.). www.tabardinn.com. 𝄐 **202/785-1277.** 35 units, 27 with private bathroom (6 with shower only). Doubles from $130–$260, suites from $160–$320, includes $10 meal voucher per guest. Nearby parking $26 plus tax per night. Children welcome, ages 4 and up are considered adults. Small and confined dogs allowed ($100 fee). Metro: Dupont Circle. **Amenities:** Restaurant, bar, Wi-Fi (free).

FOGGY BOTTOM/WEST END

This section of town is halfway between the White House and Georgetown; Foggy Bottom lies south of Pennsylvania Avenue, with the West End just above it. Together, the neighborhoods are home to town house–lined streets, George Washington University, International Monetary Fund offices, World Bank headquarters, and lodging options ranging from upscale to budget-friendly.

Best for: Parents visiting their kids at GW, international business travelers, and those who desire proximity to the Kennedy Center, also located here.

Drawbacks: Around 12,000 undergraduate students attend GW and sometimes make their presence known throughout the Foggy Bottom neighborhood in ways you'd rather they wouldn't. On the flip side, the West End might seem too quiet if you like being where the action is.

Expensive

The Watergate Hotel ★★★   This latest iteration of the Watergate Hotel opened in 2016, is an "unapologetically luxurious" property, complete with a wellness floor (spa, fitness center, and a pool), highly stylized modern decor (heavy on the metalwork, streamlined furnishings, and lots of curvy artwork suggesting the wavy shape of the Watergate building), and the best rooftop bar and lounge in the city—come winter, the rooftop features a synthetic skating rink, a bar serving boozy cocoa, and comfy seating around fire pits. The hotel lies within the six-building Watergate complex of condos, shops, and offices, one of which made the name Watergate famous when five men working for the Nixon presidential campaign were arrested on June 17, 1972, while breaking into and attempting to bug the Democratic National Committee headquarters. Next door to the complex is the Kennedy Center, while the nearby Thompson Boat Center rents bikes, kayaks, canoes, rowboats, and stand-up paddleboards. Cross Rock Creek Parkway to stroll the lovely waterfront—you'll reach the Lincoln Memorial if you walk south and Georgetown 5 minutes away in the other direction. Guest rooms have mini-fridges and spa-like marble bathrooms; suites feature deep soaking tubs. Some 117 rooms have balconies, many with views of the Potomac River and Georgetown. The Watergate Hotel is posh but also comfortable, the service impeccable, and its Potomac River front perch unique in the city.

2650 Virginia Ave. NW (at Rock Creek Pkwy.). www.thewatergatehotel.com. ℂ **844/617-1972** or 202/827-1600. 336 units, including 34 suites. Doubles from $181–$368, suites from $400–$831, plus a daily "Urban Resort" fee of $33.34 with tax. Children under 16 stay free (extra guests over 16 are $50). Parking $52 with tax. Pets up to 50 lb. ($100 per stay, up to two pets). Metro: Foggy Bottom. **Amenities:** Restaurant; 3 bars, fitness center, indoor pool (open 6am–9pm), bike rental, spa, sauna, steam room, Jacuzzi, Wi-Fi (free).

A "Diplomat" room at the sleek Watergate Hotel.

Moderate

The River Inn ★★   Nestled among quaint town houses on a quiet side street a short walk from the Kennedy Center, Georgetown, the White House, and the Foggy Bottom Metro station, the River Inn is a comfortable refuge for all sorts except rabble-rousers. Most of the units in the all-suite property are studios, in which the bedroom and living room are combined; 33 units are one-bedrooms, which are roomier and include either a king-size bed or two double beds, as well as a second TV in the separate bedroom. All guest rooms provide a full kitchen, bed with pillowtop mattress, cushy armchair, a sleeper sofa, and a sophisticated decor. Upper-floor suites offer views of the Potomac River and two rooms, numbers. 702 and 802, catch sight of the Washington Monument (these are always in demand, so seldom available). Complimentary bikes, self-serve laundry facilities, a "stock-the-fridge" program that allows guests to have groceries from Trader Joe's waiting for them, and an especially gracious staff are among the pluses that keep The River Inn steeped in bookings from happy repeat customers. Note that **DISH Drinks** is currently closed but complimentary coffee is available in the lounge from 7am–3pm and you can purchase canned cocktails in the lobby bar.

924 25th St. NW (btw. K and I sts.). www.theriverinn.com. ℭ **202/337-7600.** 125 units. Doubles from $126–$310. Children 17 and under stay free. Parking $50 plus tax. Pets accepted (free). Metro: Foggy Bottom. **Amenities:** Restaurant, bar, free bikes, fitness center, cribs available upon request, Wi-Fi (free).

Yours Truly D.C. ★★   2020, Yours Truly D.C. is proving to be a strong contender among D.C.'s many boutique hotels. The building's history as a former hospital (which allows for larger elevators, rooms, and suites) certainly helps it stand out, as do unique touches like a Ping Pong room and an outpost of popular Orlando vinyl shop, El Donut Shop, which can both be found in the lobby—guests are also welcome to borrow a record player and a collection of curated vinyl to listen to during their stay. Feeding the cozy living room vibe are the dozens of couches and comfy chairs that make up **Mercy Me,** a "Sorta South American" café and weekend brunch destination by day, and a bar, restaurant, and all-around cool neighborhood hangout spot by night (there's plenty of seating on the outdoor patio areas as well). It's also home to some of the most innovative cocktails you'll find in the city—try the smoky South Paw Manhattan and thank me later—brought to you by Micah Wilder and his talented team (he's also behind the cocktail menu at Chaplin's and Zeppelin in Shaw, p. 229). The hotel gym is equipped with Peloton bikes, rowing machines, treadmills, a boxing bag, and a battling rope, while guests have access to a personal trainer and daily workouts written up on the chalkboard. Rooms are warm and colorful, measuring 200–360 square feet (suites are a spacious 365–600 square feet and can be connected up to a three-bedroom 1,500-square-foot suite). Expect 65-inch Smart TVs, mini-fridges, concrete floors covered in vintage-style rugs, and a nifty app to address any needs that should arise during your stay.

1143 New Hampshire Ave. NW (at M St. NW). www.yourstrulydc.com. ☎ **202/775-0800.** 355 units. Doubles from $128–$264, suites from $208–$339, plus a $30 daily amenities fee. Parking $60 plus tax. Pets accepted (free). Metro: Dupont Circle. **Amenities:** Restaurant, bar, Ping Pong room, fitness center with Peloton bikes, Wi-Fi (free).

Inexpensive

Hotel Hive ★★ Hotel Hive was D.C.'s first micro hotel when it opened in 2017 and it is adorable, from its tagline, "Buzz More. Spend Less" to the individual decorative elements that cleverly maximize the use of space. Guest rooms average 150 square feet. Most have queen beds, some have bunk beds, and all come with a private bathroom. Pocket doors, cubbies beneath platform beds, and built-in nightstands and plasma-screen TVs help create an uncluttered feel. Hexagonal outlines suggesting hives crop up in carpet designs, headboard fabrics, and in bathroom amenities bearing the special Hotel Hive logo. On the first floor, the hotel's cool bar occupies the space and beyond, joining up with **&Pizza,** a local favorite restaurant; on the rooftop terrace, the hive area is incorporated into a seasonal cocktail lounge with views of the Lincoln Memorial. On all other levels, the turret holds the best rooms in the house, with six windowed walls letting in lots of light, and connecting, if desired, to the bunk-bed room next door: Voilà! Instant suite. Although the budget rates and small rooms may speak most to millennials, families should consider it, too, as the location is pretty sweet: at the edge of the GWU campus, close to the Foggy Bottom Metro station, up the street from the Kennedy Center, and within walking distance of the National Mall. There's no parking, but the website directs you to nearby garages where you can reserve a spot in advance. Note that rooms above the bar or basement can be noisy.

2224 F St. NW (at Virginia Ave.). www.hotelhive.com/washington-d-c. ☎ **202/849-8499.** 83 units. Doubles from $79–$344. Children 5 and under stay free. Pets accepted (free). Metro: Foggy Bottom. **Amenities:** Restaurant, bar, seasonal rooftop, Wi-Fi (free).

GEORGETOWN

Bustling day and night with shoppers and tourists, Georgetown's handful of hotels ranges from the city's most sublime accommodations to one that offers good value, especially for families.

Best for: Shopaholics; tourists; and parents, students, and academics visiting Georgetown University.

Drawbacks: Crowds throng sidewalks and cars snarl traffic daily. College kids and 20-somethings party hearty here nightly, especially on weekends.

Expensive

The Graham Georgetown ★★ Named for the inventor of the telephone, Alexander Graham Bell, who once lived and worked nearby, the seven-story hotel holds 57 rooms, nearly half of them deluxe guest rooms. The rest are suites, either junior or full, and all come with a king bed, while King suites have an extra-large pullout sofa in the adjacent living room. Each unit is stylishly decorated in shades of grays, whites, and pale blues, with white, tufted-leather headboards on beds made up in Irish linens. The pretty bathrooms feature white marbled floors and walls, Mexican accent tiles, and Molton Brown amenities. On the lower level lies the **Alex Craft Cocktail Cellar & Speakeasy,** while the Rooftop Lounge wraps offers one of the best views in town of Georgetown and the surrounding D.C. cityscape. It attracts a sea of scene-seeking Washingtonians, so reserving a spot is a must. Wear something trendy, as there is a business or resort casual dress code.

1075 Thomas Jefferson St. NW (just below M St.). www.thegrahamgeorgetown.com. ℱ **202/337-0900.** 57 units. Doubles from $184–$379, suites from $208–$409. Extra person $25. Children 17 and under stay free. Parking $50 plus tax. Metro: Foggy Bottom. Small pets accepted ($100 cleaning fee). **Amenities:** Restaurant, rooftop bar, Wi-Fi (free).

Rosewood Washington, D.C. ★★   The Rosewood is unabashedly luxurious and, after a recent refresh, even more fit for the discerning traveler. Want to tour a museum after hours? Done. Craving a personal shopping experience in Georgetown after the shops have closed? Also done. Staff are on hand 24/7 to cater to your every whim. Some of the Rosewood's 55 rooms overlook the C&O canal, as do the bar and the seasonal outdoor terrace. Six 1,000-foot townhouses were added to the property in 2019, each with a well-appointed kitchen and bathroom and furnished with curated works of art created by local artists and photographers. A **rooftop lounge** includes a fitness center, indoor/outdoor relaxation pool, and views of Georgetown, the Kennedy Center, the Potomac River, and the Washington Monument. **CUT by Wolfgang Puck** is the Rosewood's restaurant, a steakhouse with regional influences.

1050 31st St. NW (at Waters Alley NW). www.rosewoodhotels.com/washington-dc. ℱ **202/617-2400.** 55 units, including 12 suites and 6 townhouses. Doubles from $497–$600, suites from $925–$1,070. Parking $54 with tax. Pets 50 lb. and under allowed ($100 nonrefundable fee). Metro: Foggy Bottom. **Amenities:** Restaurant, 2 bars, babysitting, children's programs, rooftop pool, in-spa services, Wi-Fi (free).

Moderate

The Georgetown Inn ★   It's been a tough time for Georgetown hotels, with standard go-to properties like Georgetown Suites closing up shop in 2020. Through it all, The Georgetown Inn has continued to weather the storm, renovate, and remain a sophisticated icon since it opened in 1962. Famous past guests include George Burns, Robert Stack, astronaut Gordon Cooper, and the Duke and Duchess of Windsor, among other pop stars and members of the Hollywood elite. The hotel is a proud member of the National Trust for Historic Preservation's Historic Hotels of America. A 20-minute walk from the Foggy Bottom/GWU Metro station, the Inn puts you in the center of all the action in Georgetown, one of the most charming and historic parts of the city. When you've finished strolling its storied cobblestone streets, wander down for a walk by the Waterfront and join the locals as they picnic in the grass.

Back at the Inn, elegantly decorated rooms range from 250 to a spacious 575 square feet, with luxury linens, plush pillows, and thick duvets atop pillow-top mattresses. Guests receive complimentary issues of The Washington Post each day, water bottles upon arrival (yoga mats are also available), as well as free access to the nearby Washington Sports Club. The new **1310 Kitchen & Bar,** operating under the creative direction of Chef Jenn Crovato, serves dishes created with locally sourced ingredients. Jenn's chicken pot pie and the Peruvian chicken thighs are popular choices; save room for dessert, as options include Mississippi mud pie, rum cake, peach cobbler, and key lime ice cream sandwiches.

1310 Wisconsin Ave. NW. (at N St. NW). www.georgetowninn.com. ℂ **202/333-8900.** 96 units. Doubles from $202–$339. Parking $41.30 with tax. No pets. Metro: 20-minute walk from Foggy Bottom/GWU Metro station. **Amenities:** Restaurant, bar, free access to the nearby Washington Sports Club; yoga mats; Wi-Fi (free).

SHAW, 14TH & U STREET CORRIDORS

Shaw is home to several hotels, including the city's largest, with 1,175 rooms and 49 suites: the Marriott Marquis Washington, D.C., adjacent to the Walter E. Washington Convention Center. Only one hotel, the Cambria Hotel Washington, D.C., Convention Center, is located in the heart of this historic neighborhood; others along 14th Street and U Street keep guests close to buzzy restaurants and bars on busy corridors located just outside Shaw's borders.

Best for: Travelers who are attending a conference or event at the convention center or are visiting nearby Howard University. And for folks who enjoy an urban residential feel but prefer to be within walking distance of nighttime attractions over sightseeing venues.

Drawbacks: The city's major attractions, from Capitol Hill to the National Mall, are at least a mile away. There's also a lot of construction going on, so be prepared for building sights and sounds and road obstructions. For hotels closer to the 14th & U Street Corridors, sometimes it seems (and sounds like) the party never ends, especially on hot summer nights, when rooftop venues fill up.

Moderate

Hotel Zena Washington, D.C. ★★   The conversation at check-in is all about the really good restaurants nearby, such as Le Diplomate (p. 107) and Doi Moi, but there are plenty of other reasons to stay here: spacious guest rooms (double rooms run 250 to 325 sq. ft), a rooftop pool and bar, and the newness of the property, which opened in late 2020. You're meant to hang out in the uber-modern lobby (think "The Jetsons"), with its pool table, clusters of chairs and sofas, and full bar. The hotel is committed to female empowerment, and you'll see that in the many portraits of famous females, including an enormous one of Ruth Bader Ginsburg. Guest rooms are inviting, featuring pillow-top mattresses, subdued hues, mod-furniture, expansive desks, enormous 55-inch smart TVs, large marble bathrooms with luxury bath amenities (some with unique cocoon spiral showers), mini-fridges, and blackout shades. Its restaurant **Figleaf Bar & Lounge** offers small bites throughout the day.

1155 14th St. NW. www.viceroyhotelsandresorts.com/zena. © **877/544-0606** or 202/737-1200. 191 units. Doubles from $191–$399, suites from $395–$779. Parking $50 plus tax. Metro: McPherson Square. **Amenities:** Restaurant, bar, seasonal rooftop pool, fitness center, valet parking, laundry, Wi-Fi (free).

Inexpensive

Cambria Hotel Washington, D.C., Convention Center ★★ In
this old neighborhood of historic churches, colorful town homes, and corner shops, the modern, glass-fronted 10-story Cambria Hotel stands out. Two blocks away is the convention center, and on surrounding streets, scores of new and well-reviewed restaurants (p. 106), with U Street clubs and Howard University a few blocks north. From the rooftop patio, you'll have grand views of the area, as well as the Capitol Building and the Washington Monument in the distance. Ask for an O Street–side room, or best of all, a corner king overlooking both 9th and O Streets, the higher up the better. Of the 182 suites, 168 are studio suites with an abbreviated partition and worktable separating the bedroom from the living room, which sports a sleeper sofa. The remaining 14 suites are one-bedrooms. The hotel restaurant, **Social Circle,** is open for breakfast and dinner, but you really shouldn't miss the many excellent restaurants within walking distance.

899 O St. NW (at 9th St.). www.cambriadc.com. © **202/299-1188.** 182 units. Suites from $160–$439. Extra person (beyond 4) $20. Children 18 and under stay free. Parking $45 with tax. No pets allowed. Metro: Mt. Vernon Sq./7th St./Convention Center. **Amenities:** Restaurant, bar, fitness center, self-serve laundry, rooftop patio and fire pit, Wi-Fi (free).

U Street Hostel ★ Fans of hostels, rejoice! D.C. visitors have yet another affordable accommodation option, this time along the bustling U Street Corridor in Cardozo (just outside Shaw's boundaries). Opened in 2019, this is the city's first pod-style hostel, featuring a mix of traditional private rooms with bunkbeds and shared dorms with capsule beds—they're comfortable enough, with USB charging ports, worktables, vents, lights, and plenty of privacy, but the lack of space might not be appealing to some. For a bit more room and your own bathroom with a shower, spring for one of the five private rooms, which have two bunk beds each, instead. Prices are reasonable, too, with beds in one of the six shared capsule rooms starting at $27 to $49 a night and private rooms hovering in the $45 to $100 a night range (depending on the time of year). Note that unlike other hostels, there are no lockers in any of the shared rooms. You'll need to keep your luggage in a locked storage area by the front desk, but this also means there's less noise in your room—and no hapless hostel mates waking everyone up by turning on all the lights, crunching every plastic bag and zipping every zipper as they pack frantically at 3am. The location (steps from the U St. Metro) and other perks like contactless check-in via app and email (your smartphone is your key) are a

real plus. It's a great option for travelers looking for a fun and memorable place to stay, mingle with their fellow travelers, and get to know one of D.C.'s thriving local communities.

1931 13th. NW. www.ustreethostel.com. ☏ **202/892-1122.** 11 rooms, 72 beds total. $27–$49 per bed; private rooms from $45–$100. No parking or pets. Metro: U Street/African-Amer Civil War Memorial/Cardozo. **Amenities:** Spacious common areas, Wi-Fi (free).

WOODLEY PARK

This Connecticut Avenue–centered upper northwest enclave is a residential neighborhood featuring family-owned stores and restaurants, proximity to Rock Creek Park and the National Zoo, and one of Washington's biggest hotels.

Best for: Families who prefer a tamer, home-away-from-home experience near Rock Creek Park and the National Zoo. Travelers interested in lodging that's nightlife-adjacent (Adams Morgan is a 15-minute stroll to the east). Groups requiring a large hotel without convention center ambience.

Drawbacks: This area may be a little too quiet for some, especially at night.

Moderate

Omni Shoreham Hotel ★★★ Stepping into the enormous lobby really does make it feel like you've arrived at a resort—maybe it's the towering ceiling, chandeliers, and sheer expanse of it leading through the dining room, out the French doors to the terrace, and the acres of landscaped lawns, all backing up to Rock Creek Park. Truly, one of the pleasures of staying here is exploring the premises. Inspect the muraled scenes of Monticello in the Palladian Ballroom or check out the Diplomat Ballroom, modeled after the East Room of the White House. Built in 1930 as a hotel and apartment building, the guest rooms are of varying sizes and shapes. For the best views and quiet, ask for a park-view room at the back, preferably with a balcony. Join Omni's loyalty program, which gets you perks like complimentary Wi-Fi, morning-beverage room service, pressing service, and a shoeshine on subsequent stays at Omni hotels. The hotel attracts groups, thanks to its size (11 acres, 834 rooms, 24 meeting rooms, and several ballrooms), but families love it, too, for its large seasonal pool, children's amenities (p. 67), its on-site restaurants, and for its proximity to Rock Creek Park and the National Zoo. Open seasonally, **The Pool Bar** offers small bites (think sandwiches, salads, and burgers) with a side of creative cocktails, wine, or beer), while **Robert's Restaurant** is the place to go for breakfast, dinner, or a nightcap after a long day of sightseeing.

2500 Calvert St. NW (near Connecticut Ave.). www.omnihotels.com/hotels/washington-dc-shoreham. ☏ **202/234-0700.** 834 units. Doubles from $126–$382, suites from $252–$495. Extra person $20. Children 12 and under stay free. Parking $55 with tax. Up to 2 pets under 25 lb. per room ($150 nonrefundable cleaning fee and $75 nightly deposit). Metro: Woodley Park–Zoo. **Amenities:** 2 restaurants, seasonal pool and bar, bike rentals, children's amenities, fitness center, spa services, Wi-Fi (free with loyalty program).

Moderate

The Kalorama Guest House ★ On the outside, the rambling redbrick house blends right in among the large townhouses in this residential neighborhood. Yet on the inside, it's a whole different world of luxury and sophistication. Built in 1910, The Kalorama Guest House has seen it all, changing owners in 2021 and undergoing intense renovations highlighting a more modern style and design featuring exposed brick walls and hardwood floors. A luxury rooftop space, provides guests with 2,000-square-feet to stretch out and enjoy views of the city. In terms of service and amenities, think of it as a cross between a Japanese ryokan and an old-world European guest house experience, where relaxation is key (unwind in peace, as there are no TVs in any of the guest rooms). The price includes breakfast and beverages—as long as the ingredients are on-hand, guest are free to order whatever they want. You're also in a great area, with the National Zoo, good restaurants, Rock Creek Park, and the Woodley Park–Zoo Metro stop a short walk away.

2700 Cathedral Ave. NW (off Connecticut Ave.). www.kaloramaguesthouse.com. © **410/ 533-2000.** 12 units. Doubles from $179–$399. Rates include breakfast (to order) and complimentary beverages. Children 6 and older only. Free parking. No pets allowed. Metro: Woodley Park–Zoo. **Amenities:** Luxury rooftop space, laundry, Wi-Fi (free).

Woodley Park Guest House ★ This charming 10-room B&B offers clean, comfortable, and cozy lodging; inexpensive rates; a super location; and personable staff. Special features of this 1906 guest house include a wicker-furnished, tree-shaded front porch; exposed, century-old brick walls; beautiful antiques; gorgeous Oriental rugs, and original art, most of which was created by former guests. Innkeepers Laura and Raymond Saba are friendly, generous hosts, offering a delightful blend of Lebanese and native-Washingtonian hospitality. Breakfast is a real treat, with healthy items like homemade granola, fresh fruit, organic honey yogurt and breads, farm-fresh eggs, waffles, pancakes, steel-cut oats, and quiches from the nearby 350 Bakery. Midday snacks are also included. The Woodley Park-Zoo Metro stop, good restaurants, Rock Creek Park, and the National Zoo are all within a very short walk. Note: The B&B has no TVs.

2647 Woodley Rd. NW (off Connecticut Ave.). www.woodleyparkguesthouse.com. © **202/667-0218.** 10 units. Doubles from $170–$275. 2-night minimum preferred; call directly to book 1-night stays. No pets. Children 8 and older only. Limited parking $20. Metro: Woodley Park–Zoo. **Amenities:** Wi-Fi (free).

WHERE TO EAT

by Jess Moss

S hould you have any doubts about the quality—or even existence—of a worthy dining scene in the nation's capital, consider the fact that more than 130 restaurants in D.C. are on the coveted Michelin star list—23 restaurants earned stars in 2021 alone. *Bon Appétit* magazine named Washington, D.C., its "Restaurant City of the Year" in 2016. Plus, the city's restaurants, chefs, sommeliers, and other top pros in the trade regularly show up on the vaunted James Beard Foundation Awards lists (the Oscars for excellence in championing American cuisine).

So that's settled. Now comes the two-fold tricky part: how to choose where you want to eat from a world's choice of options, and then score a table. Washingtonians dine out a lot. *A lot.* Wheeler-dealers and socializing urbanistas fill restaurants throughout the city, from the newly bustling waterfront communities to hot-hot-hot Shaw (see box, p. 110) to Barracks Row on Capitol Hill and old reliable chestnuts near the White House. Be sure to make a reservation, and soon.

Of course, the past 2 years haven't been easy for Washington restaurants; many closed for at least some time during Covid shutdowns—some temporarily, and sadly some for good. For those that have persevered, the pandemic has changed D.C.'s restaurant scene in two major ways: outdoor dining and take-out are now both permanent fixtures. The latter is good news for visitors; if you can't snag a table at Rasika or Anju, you can pick up your dinner and create a picnic or hotel feast.

What hasn't changed? Good, and sometimes great, restaurants are open in every neighborhood, and this chapter leads you to a range of possibilities, spanning diverse cuisines, budget considerations, even trendiness (some of the best restaurants have been around for a while).

H STREET CORRIDOR
Moderate

Cane ★★ CARIBBEAN Welcome to eating in Washington. No two restaurants are the same and you don't have to travel far for genuine international dishes. Ready to begin? Start here, at Cane. Chef Peter Prime and his sister/co-owner Jeanine Prime bring all of the

Washington, D.C., Restaurants

U.S. Naval
Observatory

Observatory Circle

Woodland Dr. NW

Woodley Park–Zoo/
Adams Morgan

M 2

1

Calvert St. NW

Calvert St. NW

NATIONAL
ZOO 3

Columbia Rd. NW

Euclid St. NW

ROCK
CREEK
PARK

4 5

Belmont

ADAMS
MORGAN

33

31

Florida Ave.

W St. NW

V St. NW

DUMBARTON
OAKS PARK

6

Belmont Rd. NW

Kalorama Rd.

California St. NW

Florida Ave. NW

U St. NW

14th & U ST

MONTROSE
PARK

R St. NW

R St. NW

S St. NW

18

19

T St. NW

30

32

Wisconsin Ave. NW

32nd St. NW

R St. NW

Q St. NW

P St. NW

O St. NW

Sheridan
Circle

Massachusetts

17

DUPONT
CIRCLE

29

Corcoran St. NW

Q St. NW

Church St. NW

P St. NW

34

8

7

Dumbarton St. NW

30th St. NW

29th St. NW

28th St. NW

20

21

Dupont
Circle

M

28

35

GEORGETOWN

9

10

N St. NW

Scott
Circle

Thomas
Circle

Prospect St. NW

M St. NW

27th St. NW

Rock Creek Pkwy. NW

25th St. NW

24th St. NW

23rd St. NW

22nd St. NW

21st St. NW

New Hampshire Ave. NW

20th St. NW

19th St. NW

Connecticut Ave. NW

27

12

11

13

14

15

31st St. NW

Whitehurst Fwy. NW

L St. NW

22

Farragut
North

M

L St. NW

Farragut
Sq.

McPherson
Square

16

Washington
Circle

K St. NW

Pennsylvania Ave. NW

Farragut
West

M

26

Georgetown Channel

Rock Creek and Potomac Pkwy. NW

I St. NW

Foggy
Bottom–
GWU

M 23

24

GEORGE
WASHINGTON
UNIVERSITY

G St. NW

F St. NW

25

White
House

36

Pennsylvan

Theodore
Roosevelt
Island

Little
River

Kennedy
Center

Virginia Ave.

E St. NW

NW

FOGGY
BOTTOM

THE
ELLIPSE

Washington
Monument

Theodore Roosevelt
Mem. Bridge

George Washington Memorial Pkwy.

C St. NW

Constitution Ave. NW

Vietnam Veterans
Memorial

Lincoln
Memorial

Reflecting Pool

WWII
Memorial

VIRGINIA

ARLINGTON
NATIONAL
CEMETERY

LADY BIRD
JOHNSON
PARK

Arlington Mem. Bridge

Arlington
Cemetery

M

WEST POTOMAC PARK

Independence Ave. SW

Potomac River

Washington Blvd.

Ohio Dr. SW

Tidal Basin

Cherry Trees

FDR
Memorial

Jefferson
Memorial

0   1/4 mi
0   0.25 km

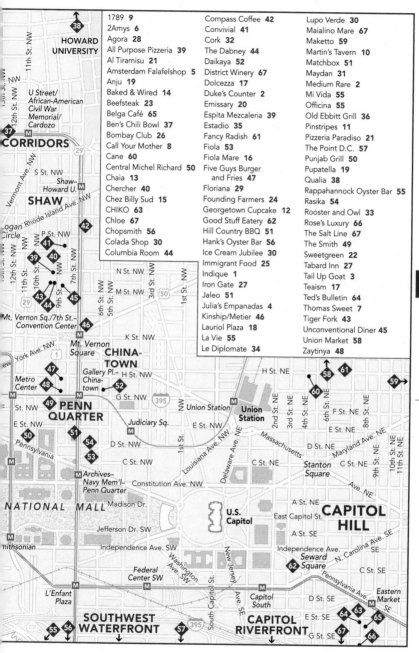

1789 **9**
2Amys **6**
Agora **28**
All Purpose Pizzeria **39**
Al Tiramisu **21**
Amsterdam Falafelshop **5**
Anju **19**
Baked & Wired **14**
Beefsteak **23**
Belga Café **65**
Ben's Chili Bowl **37**
Bombay Club **26**
Call Your Mother **8**
Cane **60**
Central Michel Richard **50**
Chaia **13**
Chercher **40**
Chez Billy Sud **15**
CHIKO **63**
Chloe **67**
Chopsmith **56**
Colada Shop **30**
Columbia Room **44**

Compass Coffee **42**
Convivial **41**
Cork **32**
The Dabney **44**
Daikaya **52**
District Winery **67**
Dolcezza **17**
Duke's Counter **2**
Emissary **20**
Espita Mezcaleria **39**
Estadio **35**
Fancy Radish **61**
Fiola **53**
Fiola Mare **16**
Five Guys Burger
  and Fries **47**
Floriana **29**
Founding Farmers **24**
Georgetown Cupcake **12**
Good Stuff Eatery **62**
Hank's Oyster Bar **56**
Hill Country BBQ **51**
Ice Cream Jubilee **30**
Immigrant Food **25**
Indique **1**
Iron Gate **27**
Jaleo **51**
Julia's Empanadas **4**
Kinship/Metier **46**
Lauriol Plaza **18**
La Vie **55**
Le Diplomate **34**

Lupo Verde **30**
Maialino Mare **67**
Maketto **59**
Martin's Tavern **10**
Matchbox **51**
Maydan **31**
Medium Rare **2**
Mi Vida **55**
Officina **55**
Old Ebbitt Grill **36**
Pinstripes **11**
Pizzeria Paradiso **21**
The Point D.C. **57**
Punjab Grill **50**
Pupatella **19**
Qualia **38**
Rappahannock Oyster Bar **55**
Rasika **54**
Rooster and Owl **33**
Rose's Luxury **66**
The Salt Line **67**
The Smith **49**
Sweetgreen **22**
Tabard Inn **27**
Tail Up Goat **3**
Teaism **17**
Ted's Bulletin **64**
Thomas Sweet **7**
Tiger Fork **43**
Unconventional Diner **45**
Union Market **58**
Zaytinya **48**

flavors from their native Trinidad and Tobago upbringing to D.C. in this tiny, reservation-less Caribbean dining room on H Street. Dishes blend Africa, India, Spain, France, and beyond, and drinks infuse rum from the West Indies. It's an authentic experience to say the least. Dine on apps like doubles, a type of street food, which is frybread, rolled and stuffed with curried chickpeas and spicy relish. (Don't miss the painting on the wall depicting former President Barack Obama eating a double during a state visit). Or jerk wings marinated for 12 hours and pimento smoked. Main dishes include a grilled oxtail and whole snapper deep fried and served with pickled chilis and coconut lime rice. The tiffin boxes—"omnivore" or "herbivore" containers filled with curries and Indian bread—are magical. Rum punch with a sweet lime juice and *mauby,* a concoction made from steeping a Caribbean bark, round out the bar menu.

403 H St. NE (at 4th St.). www.cane-dc.com. © **202/675-2011.** No reservations but waitlist available online. Main courses $12–$29. Mon–Thurs 5pm–9pm; Fri-Sat 5pm–10pm. Takeout and outdoor dining available. Metro: Union Station, then walk, take a taxi, or ride the streetcar.

Fancy Radish ★ VEGETARIAN   The greater Washington, D.C., area has become a hotbed for vegetarians, and based on the number of restaurants catering to plant-based eaters that have opened recently, it shows. But even non-vegetarians find this restaurant a treat. James Beard Award nominees Rich Landau and Kate Jacoby opened this "vegetable restaurant" in 2018, and it's been a hit since for presenting veggies in new and interesting ways, and for keeping texture in its dishes. No mushy green stuff here. A recent dinner started with stuffed avocado filled with pickled cauliflower in a crispy "rice" shell, and a rutabaga fondue served with hot pretzel bread and pickled veggies, followed by spicy dan-dan noodles tossed in a red chili sesame sauce and topped with five-spice mushrooms. Also perfect: the chermoula tofu, plated beautifully with a smear of eggplant puree and olives. Try the natural wines or craft sodas, like the Dr. Beet with beet and orange or the paradise falls with club soda, ginger and lime. With its gin, strawberry, yuzu and aquafaba foam, the Foam It In tastes like summer. Delicious and fresh.

600 H St. NE (at 7th St.). www.fancyradishdc.com. © **202/675-8341.** Reservations accepted for dinner. Main courses $13–$19. Wed–Sat 5pm–10pm. Takeout available. Metro: Union Station, then walk, take a taxi, or ride the streetcar.

Maketto ★★ CAMBODIAN/TAIWANESE   Stop by Maketto during the day and you'll find locals seated at tables and counters throughout the

the patio SCENE

If there's one good thing that's come out of the pandemic, it's that outdoor dining has become a fixture at restaurants across the city. Yes, you'll now see people eating al fresco even in the swampy heat of summer and the cold and wind of winter. Patios have popped up in unlikely places: parking lots, alleyways, sidewalks. Lanes of traffic or even whole streets have been transformed into "streateries," with restaurant tables spilling out onto the asphalt.

Throughout this chapter we've noted which restaurants have outdoor dining; these days most of them do. But if open-air meals are your top priority, head to these spots:

17th Street NW in the Dupont Circle neighborhood is a mini corridor dotted with restaurants and gay bars, many of which have ample outdoor dining options. One of the best bets is **Agora** (1527 17th St. NW; agorarestaurants.net; ✆ **202/332-6767**), which serves shareable Mediterranean *mezze* dishes under an open-sided permanent awning which will keep you dry in the rain. Other standouts with outdoor seating on this strip include **Floriana Restaurant** (1602 17th St. NW; www.florianarestaurant.com; ✆ **202/667-5937**), which in addition to fresh pastas and Italian fare, is known for its eye-catching political displays, such as its giant Christmas tree celebrating Vice President Kamala Harris; and an outpost of **Hank's Oyster Bar** (p. 97).

A short walk from 17th Street, **Lauriol Plaza** (1835 18th St. NW; www.lauriolplaza.com; ✆ **202/387-0035**) has turned the back lot formerly used for valet parking into a massive tented dining space. The restaurant has been a neighborhood fixture forever, and while its generous plates of Latin American food are reason enough to come, the main draw for many are the pitchers of frozen swirled margaritas.

Another neighborhood with ample al fresco dining is **The Wharf** on the Southwest Waterfront. Most restaurants have outdoor setups here, and some, like **La Vie** (p. 97), are on upper-level floors so have unobstructed views of the water (just keep in mind that you'll pay for these views in your menu prices). **Hank's Oyster Bar** (p. 97) has a large outdoor setup here, as do modern Mexican restaurant **Mi Vida** (98 District Square SW; mividamexico.com; ✆ **202/516-4656**), Italian trattoria and market **Officina** (1120 Maine Ave. SW; www.officinadc.com; ✆ **202/747-5222**) and Irish hangout **Kirwin's on the Wharf** (749 Wharf St. SW; www.kirwansonthewharf.com; ✆ **202/554-3818**).

Navy Yard has revitalized the Anacostia River waterfront around Nationals Park, bringing in a slew of outdoor-centric dining options (many with water views). Large canvas canopies cover a patio full of tables overlooking the river at **District Winery** (385 Water St. SE; districtwinery.com; ✆ **202/484-9210**), which carries a tasty menu of charcuterie, fresh salads, crispy soy glazed chicken wings and more. (Plus, wine!) Right near the stadium, **The Salt Line** (79 Potomac Ave. SE; thesaltline.com; ✆ **202/506-2368**) and **All Purpose Pizzeria** (79 Potomac Ave. SE; allpurposedc.com; ✆ **202/629-1894**) both have huge patios and are popular pre- and post-game stops for oysters and pizza, respectively.

Part of the new development around Buzzard Point, not far from Audi Field, Seafood restaurant **The Point D.C.** (2100 2nd St. SW; www.thepointdc.com; ✆ **202/948-2522**) has one of the best outdoor setups I've seen in the city. A massive deck overlooks the confluence of the Potomac and Anacostia rivers, and a retractable roof keeps you covered if the weather starts to turn.

place—in the downstairs restaurant, the upstairs cafe, the open kitchen, the courtyard, and the roof deck—typing away on laptops, a cup of coffee and a sticky bun within reach. (All the baking is done in-house.) They look like they live here, and that's the idea. But Maketto is first and foremost a restaurant, one of several operated by Chef Erik Bruner-Yang, including Brothers and Sisters at the **Line Hotel** (p. 72) in Adams Morgan. And the food is delish: steamed pork *bao* (doughy bun filled with shredded pork in hoisin sauce), crispy dumplings with braised beef, flash-fried broccoli with peanuts, and a crispy sweet and spicy version of Taiwanese fried chicken, served atop bread. Maketto grows livelier as the day progresses—this is the nightlife-happy Atlas District, remember. ***Other things to note:*** Maketto sells men's contemporary fashion (p. 214) and stages assorted events, from pop-up shops to yoga classes.

1351 H St. NE (btw. 12th and 13th sts.). www.maketto1351.com. ✆ **202/838-9972.** Reservations accepted for dinner. Restaurant $6–$12 lunch items, $6–$34 dinner items (most items under $16), $4–$15 dim sum. Cafe: Most items $2–$6. Mon–Thurs 7am–10pm; Fri–Sat 7am–11pm; Sun 7am–5pm. Takeout and outdoor dining available. Metro: Union Station, then walk, take a taxi, or ride the streetcar.

union **MARKET**

Where can you sample savory Indian crepes one minute, poke bowls the next, and finish with delicious doughnuts and homemade gelato? It's all found in **Union Market** (1309 5th St. SE; https://unionmarketdc.com). This vibrant, historic market and the streets that surround it are an all-in-one hotspot for eating, drinking, and shopping. Wander among the nearly 40 vendor stalls and you may feel as though you're on a foodie world tour. This is also a great one-stop-shop to try some of D.C.'s local culinary faves, like **Al Volo** (osteriaalvolo.com) and **Lucky Buns** (www.luckybuns.com). Sample the craft-roasted **Blue Bottle Coffee** (www.bluebottlecoffee.com) and bread from **Pluma by Bluebird,** then head over to **Shouk** (shouk.com) for modern Israeli street food. Italian eatery **Masseria** (1340 4th St. NE; www.masseria-dc.com; ✆ **202/608-1330**), one of the only free-standing restaurants in Union Market, stands out for its elegant Italian menu in a country-chic setting. Shops include **District Cutlery** (www.districtcutlery.com), a chef's knife shop; the lifestyle/homegoods shop **Salt & Sundry** (www.shopsaltandsundry.com);

and **Three Littles** (https://threelittles.co), selling children's goods, heirlooms and toys. It's an eclectic mix and worthy of a stop for the tastes alone.

La Cosecha (http://lacosechadc.com), a 20,000-square-foot contemporary market celebrating Latin American culture, opened in Union Market in 2019, adding at least six new food vendors. Among them is **El Cielo** (www.elcielorestaurant.com), from Colombian chef Juan Manuel "Juanma" Barrientos, which recently became the first Colombian restaurant to receive a Michelin star; **Las Gemelas** (lasgemelasdc.co), a chic coastal-inspired Mexican kitchen and a sister taqueria; and **Serenata** (www.serenatadc.com), a "Latino cocktail experience" with an all-day menu of small bites. Coffee lovers should head to **Café Unido** (cafeunido.com), which specializes in Panamanian beans, including Geisha, the world's most expensive type of coffee.

Union Market is open daily 8am to 9pm, though individual businesses' hours may vary (Metro: NoMa-Gallaudet/New York Ave., just a few blocks north of H Street Corridor).

CAPITOL HILL & BARRACKS ROW

Along with the recommendations below, for solid diner fare and lively local color, I recommend **Pete's Diner and Carryout** at 212 2nd St. SE (btw. Independence and Pennsylvania aves. in Capitol Hill), and for an insider's experience, **Market Lunch** inside Eastern Market (p. 129).

Expensive

Rose's Luxury ★★★ AMERICAN   Critics declared this quirky little labor of love in Barracks Row one of D.C.'s best restaurants almost as soon as it opened in 2013. America's "best new restaurant" (*Bon Appétit* magazine 2014), and "Best Chef in the Mid-Atlantic" (2016 James Beard Foundation Award) are among the many accolades both the restaurant and its chef/owner Aaron Silverman have received. Its success comes down to endearing service, an eclectic decor of antiques and pretty fabrics and china, and a simple menu of unexpected taste combinations. The menu changes frequently; currently it features a "choose your own adventure" approach, where the table orders two sharable dishes per guest. Keep an eye out for favorites like the pork sausage, habañero, and lychee salad. Rose's opens up reservations on the first of the month for dates in the following month (so Sept. reservations are released on Aug. 1). They go quickly so mark your calendar and head to the website. If you can't get a reservation, it's still worth it to walk in and wait. Give the receptionist your cellphone number, then head upstairs to the cute bar for a drink, or wander 8th Street until the restaurant calls to say your table is ready. Rose's siblings, the luxe **Pineapple and Pearls** right next door, and the precious and affordable **Little Pearl** one street over, also accept reservations.

717 8th St. SE (btw. G and I sts.). www.rosesluxury.com. ✆ **202/580-8889.** Small plates $10–$18. Mon–Thurs 5:30–10pm. Fri-Sat 5–10pm. Outdoor dining available. Metro: Eastern Market.

Moderate

Belga Café ★ BELGIAN   Open since 2004, Belga Café claims to be "the original Belgian restaurant in D.C.," and helmed by a true Bruge-native as chef, it offers a vibe and menu that rivals the old country. Come for dinner and try the wild mushroom waffle with pecorino cream and mushroom sauce. The mussel pots (seven varieties to choose from) are big enough to share and arrive with tasty *frites* and the traditional mayonnaise side. Brunching in D.C. is a competitive sport, so don't show up to Belga's storied weekend brunch without a reservation. You'll be glad you did, with dishes like a Belgian omelet stuffed with lobster, shrimp, crab, and calamari and topped with a tomato-bisque sauce, and waffles "like you've never seen before." A hearty menu of classic Belgian beers is also available.

514 8 St. SE (btw. E and G sts). www.belgacafe.com. ✆ **202/544-0100.** Reservations accepted. Main courses $3–$13 breakfast, $13–$22 brunch, $13–$27 lunch, $18–$38 dinner. Lunch Tues–Fri noon–3pm; Brunch Sat–Sun 10am–3pm; Dinner Sun–Thurs 5pm–9:30pm, Fri–Sat 5–10pm. Takeout and outdoor dining available. Metro: Eastern Market.

Ted's Bulletin ★ AMERICAN   Ted's Bulletin calls itself a family restaurant, and it is, but many of the "children" who come here are in their 20s and 30s and they're drinking milkshakes laced with coconut rum or maybe vodka and Kahlúa. So, it can get rowdy. What you'll enjoy, besides the retro decor, is the well-done comfort-food menu: grilled cheese, tomato soup, fried chicken, mac and cheese, barbecued chicken, chili, sloppy joes, and breakfast items (which are served all day). Ted's Tarts (a homemade Pop-Tart), available in a variety of flavors, are a favorite. Ted's Bulletin has another District location at 1818 14th St. NW (⟲ 202/265-8337), in the U & 14th Street Corridors.

505 8th St. SE (at E St.). www.tedsbulletin.com. ⟲ **202/544-8337.** Reservations accepted. Main courses $13–$20 breakfast; $16–$29 lunch/supper (most items under $20). Sun–Thurs 7am–10pm; Fri–Sat 7am–11pm. Takeout and outdoor dining available. Metro: Eastern Market.

Inexpensive

CHIKO ★ CHINESE/KOREAN   Almost overnight, this little restaurant transformed from a hot dog shop into one of the city's best "fast-casual" spots for Asian fare. Co-chefs Danny Lee and Scott Drewno (together as the Fried Rice Collective) opened this hit eatery in 2017, and soon drew a following for dishes like orange-ish chicken with candied mandarins, crispy chicken spring rolls, and wok-blistered Chinese broccoli and kimchi stew. Grab a seat at the reservation-only chef's counter, offering a $55 tasting menu. Big name chefs guest star at its Chiko After Dark series featuring late-night dishes and drinks. Another CHIKO location is in Dupont Circle at 2029 P St. NW (⟲ 202/331-3040).

423 8th St. SE (btw. D and E sts.). www.mychiko.com. ⟲ **202/558-9934.** Reservations only for chef's counter. Dinner $8–$18. Tasting menu $55. Daily 5–9pm. Takeout and outdoor dining available. Metro: Eastern Market.

Pastries at Ted's Bulletin Family Restaurant.

Good Stuff Eatery ★ AMERICAN   Spike Mendelsohn shot to fame as a *Top Chef* contestant and remains renowned thanks to the scrumptiousness of his burgers, fries, and shakes. The Prez Burger (with applewood bacon, onion marmalade, Roquefort cheese, and horseradish mayo sauce) is still the most popular item on the menu, according to the staff; the toasted marshmallow milkshake will always be the #1 milkshake, to my mind. *Warning:* Good Stuff Eatery is always jumping, with people in line on the first floor and filling upstairs and outdoor patio tables. The line moves fast, and table turnover is fairly quick, but just the same, you might consider getting the burgers to go, as so many do. The pizza place next door, **We, The Pizza** (www.wethepizza. com; *© 202/544-4008*), is also run by the Mendelsohn family. Other Good Stuff Eatery locations are in Georgetown at 3291 M St. NW (*© 202/337-4663*) and at Reagan National Airport (Terminal B).

303 Pennsylvania Ave. SE (at 3rd St.). www.goodstuffeatery.com. *© 202/543-8222.* Reservations not accepted. Burgers $7–$8; milkshakes $6; salads $8–$12. Takeout and outdoor dining available. Mon–Sat 11am–10pm. Metro: Capitol South.

CAPITOL RIVERFRONT ("NAVY YARD")

This neighborhood bustles with Washington Nationals fervor in baseball season (the ballpark is here), waterfront fun when weather permits, and restaurant and bar crowds year-round. Among your many choices are these keepers.

Moderate

Chloe ★★ AMERICAN   This glass-enclosed bistro sits at the corner of 4th and Tingey streets right across the road from Bluejacket Brewery (p. 228). Weekdays, this part of town is a workaday world; it's one of the most densely populated residential neighborhoods but isn't always on tourists' radar, unless they're heading to a baseball game. Nighttime and weekends are really when the restaurant, like the rest of the neighborhood, comes alive. Happy hour's a crush, as is weekend brunch. Dinner's the winner, with favorite dishes including roasted cod with tastes of coconut, curry, and ginger; hangar steak with crispy onions and chimichurri; and brussels sprouts and burrata with roast squash and apples. The cuisine is multi-culti American, drawing from diverse cuisines, New Orleans to India, Vietnamese to Lebanese. This, you might say, is what America tastes like.

1331 4th St. SE (at Tingey St.). www.restaurantchloe.com. *© 202/313-7007.* Reservations recommended. Main courses $5–$15 brunch, $14–$33 dinner. Sun 11am–9pm; Mon–Thurs 5pm–10pm; Fri 5pm–11pm; Sat 11am–11pm. Takeout and outdoor dining available. Metro: Navy Yard/Ballpark (M St. and New Jersey Ave. exit).

Maialino Mare ★★ ITALIAN   As its name implies, the focus of this blue checker–tabled trattoria in the new Thompson Hotel is on seafood pastas and fish. Early favorites include the ruby red shrimp in fettucine with a butter lemon sauce and the sweet little neck clams sautéed in white wine and garlic. Don't discount its meat offerings though: Roman-style braised chicken thighs are peppered to perfection and malfatto pasta with braised suckling pig and arugula is, well, amazing. Maialino means "little pig" in Italian so if you're up for it, order the slow roasted suckling pig for two ($74). You won't be disappointed. Be sure to save room for the tiramisu. As with most hotel restaurants, it's also open for breakfast and lunch.

221 Tingey St. SE (in the Thompson Hotel). www.maialinomare.com. ☏ **202/508-5249.** Main courses $5–$30 breakfast, $6–$39 brunch; $18–$22 lunch; $19–$26 dinner. Mon–Thurs 7–10am, noon–2pm, 5–10pm; Fri 7–10am, noon–2pm, 5–10:30pm; Sat–Sun 8am–2:30pm; 5–10:30pm. Takeout and outdoor dining available. Metro: Navy Yard/Ballpark (M and Half sts. exit).

The Point D.C. ★★ SEAFOOD Many Washingtonians haven't even made it to this newly redeveloped nook of the city yet, but if waterfront views and outdoor dining are your thing, put The Point on your dining agenda. The coastal eatery opened in 2021 in the Buzzard Point neighborhood, near D.C.'s soccer stadium, **Audi Field** (p. 236). The first thing you'll notice is how much space there is over here: A massive waterfront patio and even more cavernous interior make distanced dining pretty easy. The restaurant is perched near the confluence of the Potomac and Anacostia rivers, which results in more wide-open water views than you get elsewhere on the rivers; watch sailboats float past or try to spot Alexandria, VA in the distance. The menu covers the seafood bases, with local must-haves like Maryland blue crab cakes and locally sourced oysters in season, plus some fun experiments like the warm donuts filled with creamy crab dip, and fish and meats cooked over a 12-foot-long wood fire grill. It gets crowded here on weekends, but if you're able to score an outdoor seat around sunset you're in for a treat.

2100 2nd St. SW. thepointdc.com. ☏ **202/948-2522.** Reservations recommended. Lunch: $12–$22. Dinner min courses $18–$48. Mon–Tues 5–11pm; Wed–Thurs 11:30am–11pm; Fri–Sat 11:30am–midnight; Sun 11:30am–11pm. Outdoor dining available. Metro: Waterfront station, then take the 74 Bus from M St. & 4th St. SW.

The Salt Line ★ SEAFOOD This restaurant stands out among the growing number of good ones in the neighborhood for two reasons: its unimpeded view of the Anacostia River—especially from the outdoor bar areas, which bump up against a wide-planked boardwalk—and for the fresh seasonal seafood, with lobster rolls, crispy-skin rockfish, and oysters taking center stage. The menu also includes items like a summer salad for vegetarians and smash burger for carnivores. Delicious desserts are made in-house (as are the breads). Wash down your meal with the restaurant's potent cocktails, some of which have delightfully New England-y names like the "Caper Codder G&T." Come on Friday between noon and 4pm for "Happy Afternoon," with drink specials and half-price oysters.

79 Potomac Ave. SE (at First St.). www.thesaltline.com. ☏ **202/506-2368.** Main courses $27–$32 brunch and dinner. Mon–Thurs 4pm–midnight, Fri noon–midnight, Sat–Sun 11am–midnight; nightly 4:30–10:30pm; weekdays raw bar and outdoor bar 3pm to closing. Hours change with the seasons, the Nationals home-game schedule, and sundry other reasons; check website for the latest information. Outdoor dining available. Metro: Navy Yard/Ballpark (M and Half sts. exit).

SOUTHWEST WATERFRONT

The Wharf complex's waterfront location is its main attraction, but one that poses logistical challenges for anyone driving here. Traffic jams up on Maine Avenue, the primary route leading to the Wharf and its parking garages. If you can, use one of the many alternative transportation options, which include the Metro, the DC Circulator bus, water taxis, and a shuttle that loops continuously between the Wharf and the L'Enfant Plaza Metro station. If you must drive, take care to read the section "Getting Here" posted on the Wharf's website, www.wharfdc.com, as well as specific instructions provided by the restaurant to which you're headed.

Expensive

La Vie ★★ MEDITERRANEAN/SEAFOOD   Craving some eye candy? Sweeping views of the river and Jefferson Memorial aren't the only visual treats at this fifth-floor Wharf hotspot. The décor is elegant and playful, providing a tempting Instagram backdrop in every direction—colorful faux flowers and chrome baubles cascade from ceilings and a floral wall runs along the entire patio. Photo ops continue as the food is served: a recent meal started with perfectly grilled octopus; followed by roasted halibut served with roasted brussels sprouts, curried onion labneh, and chives; and ravioli stuffed with ricotta, parmesan, mozzarella, and mascarpone. Whatever you order, do not leave without trying the cotton candy baked Alaska, a blue beehive of sugary cloud that's lit on fire and burned down to reveal a sweet treat inside. La Vie also does a popular and swanky brunch ($55); reserve one of the dining cabanas and chow down on as many small plates as you wish, plus an entrée.

88 District Square SW, 5th floor (at 9th St. SW). www.lavie-dc.com. (C) **202/560-5501.** Reservations recommended. Main courses $27–$69. Brunch: $55. Mon–Thurs 5–10pm; Fri 5–11pm; Sat. brunch 10am–3pm, dinner 5–11pm; Sun brunch 10am–3pm, dinner 5–10pm. Outdoor dining available. Metro: Waterfront.

Moderate

Hank's Oyster Bar ★★ SEAFOOD   Around since 2005, Hank's just keeps getting better and better. Chef/owner Jamie Leeds now has three Oyster Bars, with the original at Dupont Circle (1624 Q St. NW; (C) **202/462-4265**) and this one at the Wharf the newest...*and* the largest: The restaurant can seat nearly 200 people. Like every other Wharf venue, Hank's capitalizes on its waterfront location, with windows opening to covered patios on two sides, giving patrons, inside and out, great views of wharf activity and the parade of people passing by. The place always feels festive, and the food is always great; I'm particularly fond of the crab cake, the po'boys, and just about anything with oyster in the name. Hank's other Oyster Bar is in Old Town Alexandria, at 1026 King St. ((C) **703/739-4265**).

701 Wharf St. SW (at 7th St.). www.hanksoysterbar.com. (C) **202/817-3055.** Reservations accepted. Small plates $10–$18; large plates $20–$36. Dinner Tues–Thurs and Sun 3pm–9pm, Fri–Sat 3pm–10pm; Brunch Fri–Sun 11am–2:45pm. Outdoor dining available. Metro: Waterfront.

Outdoor dining at Hank's Oyster Bar.

Rappahannock Oyster Bar ★★ SEAFOOD   As you may have noticed by now, seafood, particularly oysters, are kind of a big deal here in D.C. Cousins Travis and Ryan Croxton opened this branch of their popular bivalve bar in 2018 in a historic oyster-shucking shed across from the bustling Maine Avenue Fish Market, the oldest fish market in the U.S. The inside is tight, with only 27 bar seats surrounded by accordion-style folding doors. The 90-seat dining patio is my preference—it's much airier but only open in seasonal weather. But you're really there for the oysters, right? Try the sweet and buttery Rappahannock River oysters or the briny Rochambeau from Virginia. Oyster chowder, crab cakes, and crispy whole fish round out the menu. Rappahannock's other location is in Union Market (1309 5th St. NE; ℭ **202/544-4702**).

1150 Maine Ave. SW (at the Fish Market). www.rroysters.com. ℭ **202/484-0572.** Reservations not accepted. Small plates $8–$19; oysters $2.50 each; entrees $17–$36. Sun–Thurs 11:30am–8pm; Fri–Sat 11:30am–10pm. Takeout and outdoor dining available. Metro: Waterfront.

Inexpensive

Chopsmith ★ SALAD   A $16 takeout salad may not sound like a deal, but compared to most of the other dining options at The Wharf, it's a good bet if you're on a budget. Chopsmith focuses on fresh and healthy eats, like salads, bowls, and sandwiches. Veggies feature heavily on the menu and range from signature recipes like the Wharf Louis, a medley of greens, tomatoes, cucumbers topped with lump crab, shrimp and hard-boiled egg, to premade antipasto and pasta salads to design-your-own mixtures a la **Sweetgreen** (p. 120). Unlike many fast-casual salad shops, Chopsmith also has a full breakfast menu (breakfast burritos, sammies, and omelets) as well as beer and wine. There's some banquette seating in the sleekly designed café, but I prefer to take my food to go and sit on the District Pier to watch the water taxis come and go while I eat.

11 District Sq SW. www.chopsmith.com. ℭ **202/554-5400.** Reservations not accepted. $12–$19. Mon–Sat 8:30am–8:30pm; Sun 8:30am–8pm. Takeout. Metro: Waterfront.

DOWNTOWN & PENN QUARTER

In addition to the restaurants below, I highly recommend **Café du Parc** in the Willard Hotel (see p. 70 for info on the restaurant and lodging) for an elegant breakfast near the Mall and White House.

Expensive

Central Michel Richard ★★ FRENCH BISTRO   The ebullient spirit of chef Michel Richard lives on at Central, though the brilliant Richard died in 2016. His namesake restaurant continues to win high marks for both food and ambience. A great downtown location on Pennsylvania Avenue, a generous bar, a menu that speaks to both French and American cultures (puffy gougères, fried chicken, mussels in white wine with frites, a lobster burger, mushroom Bolognese), and voilà! Central is It. The dining room can be loud, but the commotion signifies the happy time that most are enjoying. *Tip:* For best value, dine at the bar or on the patio for weekday happy hour 3:30 to 6:30pm, and enjoy some delicious deals from the bar menu, such as French fries for $8 and a plate of three sliders for $15.

1001 Pennsylvania Ave. NW (at 11th St.). www.centralmichelrichard.com. *©* **202/626-0015.** Main courses $20–$36 lunch & dinner. Tues–Thurs 11:30am–8:30pm, Fri–Sat 11:30am–9:30pm. Outdoor dining available. Metro: Metro Center (12th and F sts. exit).

Fiola ★★★ ITALIAN   For a splash-out D.C. dining experience, book a table at this local favorite and enjoy inventive Italian cuisine and a lively atmosphere. With its wide swath of bar at the front, white banquettes, and modern art, the dining room has a glamorous, head-turning, New York feel, maybe informed by chef Fabio Trabocchi's stint there not so long ago. The menu is Italian-meets-Washington, as dishes and flavors from Italy are married with seasonal ingredients from the nearby Chancellors Rock Farm, and other local producers. The menu changes based on what's in season; recent hits included the "Crabbing in Sicily," a Chesapeake blue crab dome served with smoked steelhead roe, pappa al pomodoro, and Sicilian red prawn essence; or the tortellini with hen brodo and egg yolk bottarga; or—you get the idea: festive dining. Also consider Trabocchi's swank Italian seafood eatery, **Fiola Mare** (p. 118), at Georgetown's waterfront.

601 Pennsylvania Ave. NW (entrance on Indiana Ave., btw. 6th and 7th sts.). www.fioladc.com. *©* **202/525-1402.** Reservations recommended. Dinner a la carte main courses $38–$58; dinner prix-fixe menus $150. Tues–Sat 5–9pm. Takeout and outdoor dining available. Takeout and outdoor dining available. Metro: Archives–Navy Memorial or Gallery Place/Chinatown (7th and F sts. exit).

Punjab Grill ★★ INDIAN   Care for caviar with your *naan?* Or gold leaf with your lamb? Everything at this 4700-square-foot restaurant is decadent. A 40-foot slab of chiseled pink sandstone lines the wall while mother-of-pearl inlay composes the bar counter. Dine in the *Sheesh Mahal,* or palace of mirrors, a private dining room where 150,000 tiny mosaic mirrors carpet the walls floor to ceiling. Dishes are no less artful. The chicken tikka is served in a crisp noodle bowl and topped with lehsuni. King salmon rests on a bed of quinoa *bhel* among dollops of apricot murabba glaze. The "Pandora's Box" smoked rum cocktail comes nestled in a treasure chest that swirls with steam as you open it. The place is meant to look like the home of a rich Indian ruler, and from start to finish, you might even feel a little royal at the end too.

427 11th St. NW (at E St). www.punjabgrilldc.com. © **202/813-3004.** Reservations recommended. Dinner small plates $10-$40; main courses $12-$48. Wed–Sat 5–10pm; Sun brunch 11am–2:30pm, dinner 5–9pm. Takeout and outdoor dining available. Metro: Archives–Navy Memorial or Metro Center (12th and F sts. exit).

Moderate

Bombay Club ★★ INDIAN   Located across Lafayette Square from the White House, Bombay Club has been a favorite of one administration after the other (and the reporters who cover them) since it opened in 1988. This was Ashok Bajaj's first restaurant in D.C., and though he has added a slew of well-reviewed dining rooms since, most notably **Rasika** (see below), Bombay Club is special, a gracious veteran appealing to everyone. A pianist plays nightly in the dining room, which is decorated in hues of pale pink and yellow. You don't have to be from India to appreciate the cuisine (although the Indians I know say it is the real thing). Among the popular dishes are the sweet corn and pea samosa, a savory snack served with banana-raisin chutney; the chicken *tikka makhani,* prepared with tomato, garlic, fenugreek, and ginger; dal makhani, a black lentil dish that is cooked for 16 hours; and Bengali fish curry, served with eggplant and spices. Speaking of spice, if you like things hot, try the green chili chicken. To sample an assortment of tastes, order a house *thali.*

815 Connecticut Ave. NW (H St.). www.bombayclubdc.com. © **202/659-3727.** Reservations recommended. Main courses $20–$34. Mon–Fri lunch 11:30am–2:30pm; Mon–Thurs 5–9:30pm; Fri–Sat 5–10pm. Takeout and outdoor dining available. Metro: Farragut West (17th St. exit).

Hill Country Barbecue Market ★★ BARBECUE   Enter Hill Country Barbecue and you leave official Washington at the door. It's just not possible to cleave to lofty attitudes and politicking when Jumpin' Jupiter or some such band are playing up a storm, as you make your way through a mess of dry-rubbed Texas barbecued ribs ("smoked low and slow over Texas oak"), skillet corn bread, and sweet potato bourbon mash. Meats are priced by weight, from $6.25 per half-pound of barbeque chicken to $18 per pound of brisket; sides range in price from $4.95 for a standard serving of coleslaw to $11 for a large serving of mac and cheese. You place your order upstairs in the cafeteria/kitchen, and then carry it to your seat, either in the large dining room adjoining the cafeteria or to your table downstairs. I recommend the downstairs. That's where the lively **Boots Bar** is; it's also the stage for bands and Hill Country's famed Live Band Karaoke on Wednesday nights. Toss back a few Lone Stars, grab a friend, and see if you can wow the crowd with your voice. Families, however, will want to stay upstairs.

410 7th St. NW (at D St.). www.hillcountry/dc.com. © **202/556-2050.** Reservations recommended for downstairs. Main courses $6–$33. Sun–Thurs noon–9pm; Fri–Sat noon–10pm. Metro: Archives–Navy Memorial or Gallery Place–Chinatown (7th and F sts. exit).

Jaleo ★★★ SPANISH   Jaleo, at age 28, is now ancient in terms of restaurant years, but sure doesn't act it…or look it. A creative redesign added artwork by contemporary Spanish artists, foosball tables with chairs made from Vespa scooter seats, "love tables" closed off by metal curtains, and other whimsical touches, even in the restrooms, where photographed faces smile up at you from the floor. Chef extraordinaire José Andrés is 28 years older as well, and in that time has grown into a culinary and personal phenomenon, with restaurants here (**Zaytinya**, p. 103; **Oyamel, China Chilcano, Beefsteak,** p. 116; **Spanish Diner, minibar by José Andrés**), and elsewhere, and a number of cookbooks. Not to mention his humanitarian work fighting world hunger through his non-profit, World Central Kitchen. During the coronavirus pandemic last year, Andres actually closed his D.C. restaurants to the general public and reopened some of them as community kitchens for anyone in need during the outbreak. But it all started here at Jaleo, when Andrés introduced his version of Spanish tapas to the capital. Andrés and his staff may fiddle with the menu of some 60 individual small plates, but you always know you're enjoying the best tapas in the city (some say in the country). Look for fried dates wrapped in bacon and served with an apple-mustard sauce; mini-burgers made from acorn-fed, black-footed Iberico pigs; and roasted sweet onions, pine nuts, and Valdeón blue cheese. Be adventurous.

480 7th St. NW (at E St.). www.jaleo.com. ℂ **202/628-7949.** Reservations recommended. Tapas $4–$25 (most $10–$16), "big plates" and paellas $40–$55; tasting menus $35 (Tour de España), $55 (Jaleo Classics), $70 (the Jaleo Experience), $95 (José's Way); Sun–Thurs 11:30am–10pm; Fri–Sat 11:30am–11pm; Sat 10am–midnight. Takeout and outdoor dining available. Metro: Archives–Navy Memorial or Gallery Place–Chinatown (7th and F sts. exit).

Matchbox ★ PIZZA/AMERICAN   Named for the narrow, three-story-tall matchbox-resembling space the eatery first inhabited, Matchbox was immediately so popular that it soon expanded to this Chinatown location and added many other Matchboxes throughout the area, including one on Barracks Row (521 8th St. SE). Locals love the thin-crust pizzas cooked in 900°F wood-fired brick ovens (try the fire + smoke with smoked gouda and chipotle purée), the appetizer of mini burgers on toasted brioche topped with onion "straws" (skinny fried onion strands), the fried chicken Cobb salad, and entrees like the pan-seared salmon. Saturday and Sunday bottomless brunch are big, too.

750 E St. NW (btw. 7th and 8th sts.). www.matchboxrestaurants.com. ℂ **202/289-4441.** Reservations accepted. Main courses $18–$32; pizzas and sandwiches $11–$23; brunch $9–$16. Mon–Thurs 11:30am–19pm; Fri–Sat 11am–10pm; Sun 11am–9pm. Metro: Gallery Place–Chinatown (H and 7th sts. exit).

Rasika ★★★ INDIAN   Rasika serves exquisite modern Indian food in an intimate, softly lit, shimmering champagne-hued setting, frequented by a who's who in the capital and the world beyond. Little wonder that Chef Vikram Sunderam took home the prestigious James Beard Foundation award for Best Chef, Mid-Atlantic region, in 2014. Rasika's specialties are griddle, open barbecue, tandoori, and regional dishes. The *palak chaat* (crisped spinach in a yogurt sauce), black cod with honey, duck vindaloo, and tandoori salmon are among the most popular items. Intrigued? Better make a reservation now (tables are bookable up to 90 days in advance). You can dine in the bar/lounge without advance reservations, but that, too, is usually pretty full—and the seating is too low for comfortable eating. Rasika has a sister eatery in the West End, at 1190 New Hampshire Ave. NW (www.rasikarestaurant.com/westend; 🕿 **202/466-2500**), a larger location with a similar menu and just as popular as the Penn Quarter Rasika.

633 D St. NW (btw. 6th and 7th sts.). www.rasikarestaurant.com. 🕿 **202/637-1222.** Reservations recommended. Main courses $19–$36; pre-theater menu $37. Mon–Fri 11:30am–2:30pm; Mon–Thurs 5–10pm; Fri–Sat 5–10:30pm. Lounge stays open throughout the day serving light meals. Takeout and outdoor dining available. Metro: Archives–Navy Memorial or Gallery Place/Verizon Center (7th and F sts. exit).

Old Ebbitt Grill ★ AMERICAN   It's midnight and you're starving. Where you gonna go? Or maybe you want a taste of the capital's regional dishes and a dash of insider culture. Who brings that to the table? It's the Ebbitt.

It's comforting to have a conveniently located place that's nearly always open, with four capacious bars and a menu that's known for its untrendy dishes, like burgers, trout Parmesan, and the hearty house pasta, which is stuffed with spinach, mortadella ham, and three cheeses and baked in a cream sauce. Oysters are the standout, among the best and freshest in town. (The bivalves are discounted during the daily Oyster Happy Hour; check website for times as it varies day by day.)

Old Ebbitt has been around since 1856, first in another nearby location, and here since 1983. Some furnishings date from the early days, giving the place an old-fashioned air. Popular as the restaurant is among tourists, Ebbitt also draws attorneys from neighboring law firms, politicos visiting the White House a block away, and other downtown regulars, for power meals at breakfast, lunch, and dinner, and drinks late in the evening. If you're looking for more of an inside-D.C. experience, stop by.

675 15th St. NW (btw. F and G sts.). www.ebbitt.com. 🕿 **202/347-4800.** Reservations recommended. Main courses brunch $11–$22; lunch, dinner, and late night $14–$27. Mon–Thurs 11am–midnight; Fri 11am–1am; Sat 10am; Sun 10am–midnight. Takeout available. Metro: Metro Center (13th and F sts. exit).

The Smith ★ AMERICAN   It can get loud here—very loud—but this casual American brasserie is a fun and delicious experience, and a solid for good service. Specialties at this New York City offshoot include mac and cheese, ricotta gnocchi with truffle cream, and the signature Smith burger on a brioche bun with bacon shallot marmalade. You can dine in the bar/restaurant without reservations, but expect a wait—it's always packed, especially weekend nights. Locals also come here for the brunch, often jammed with millennials and downtown regulars. Try the shrimp and grits or vanilla bean

French toast. The Smith has a second D.C. location in the U Street Corridor (1314 U St. NW; ✆ **202/250-3900**).

901 F St. NW (at 9th St.). www.thesmithrestaurant.com. ✆ **202/868-4900**. Reservations recommended. Main courses $11–$19 breakfast, $12–$39 lunch/dinner. Mon–Fri 11:30am–9pm; Sat–Sun 1am–9pm. Takeout and outdoor dining available. Metro: Gallery Place–Chinatown (9th St. exit) or Metro Center.

Zaytinya ★★ GREEK/TURKISH/LEBANESSE When it opened in 2002, Zaytinya, with its full-on, authentic, and wide-ranging tastes of the Middle East, Greece, and Turkey, was quite the culinary adventure for Washingtonians. (Crispy brussels sprouts with coriander seed, barberries, and garlic, oh my! Olive-oil ice cream. How interesting!) But Washington was a different place then. Nineteen years, national acclaim, and a boom of restaurant openings later, Zaytinya is an old friend. Those brussels sprouts are a favorite among the dishes that appear on the four-page menu, which, in truth, has barely changed over the years. It consists primarily of *mezze* (small plates), Mediterranean small dishes, although some entrees appear as well. Other signature dishes include scallops in yogurt and dill sauce; roasted cauliflower with sultanas, caper berries, and pine-nut purée; spanakopita with house-made filo; and *kibbeh nayeh* (Lebanese-style veal tartare with bulgur wheat, radishes, mint, and pita chips). Zaytinya is enormous, seating 230 in the attractive dining rooms, another 52 on stools at the bar, and 65 outside on the patio. Best way to enjoy Zaytinya? Bring a crowd and order an array of mezze. Instant party!

701 9th St. NW (at G St.). www.zaytinya.com. ✆ **202/638-0800**. Reservations recommended. Mezze items $6–$20 (most are under $15); lunch sandwiches $11–$15; brunch items $8.50–$15. Mon–Thurs 11:30am–10pm; Fri 11:30am–11pm; Sat 11am–11 pm; Sun 11:30am–10pm. Takeout and outdoor dining available. Metro: Gallery Place–Chinatown (9th St. exit).

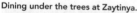

Dining under the trees at Zaytinya.

Inexpensive

Daikaya ★ JAPANESE This restaurant is an upstairs/downstairs affair—two different places with two separate entrances—but both offer authentic Japanese specialties. Downstairs is the tiny ramen noodle house, serving the city's best ramen in a 40-seat, sparsely decorated joint that lets you concentrate on slurping up one of five broths, meat-based or vegetable, filled with aged wheat noodles and topped with a bouquet of briefly stir-fried garnishes. On the second floor, which you reach via an outside staircase, is the larger *izakaya,* or Japanese tavern. The decorative woodwork and Japanese fabrics in this dimly lit bar and grill lend an exotic feel, which tastes from the menu only amplify. You might try grilled avocado with fresh wasabi, spicy tuna with

family-friendly **DINING SPOTS**

Most restaurants welcome families, starting, most likely, with the one in your hotel. Cafes at sightseeing attractions are always a safe bet, and so are these:

2Amy's (3715 Macomb St., NW; www.2amyspizza.com; ✆ **202/885-5700**) When you're craving pizza, it's hard to go wrong with this longtime Neapolitan pizzeria. No dedicated children's dishes here, but it's bright, loud and boasts a wide menu from the traditional tomato and cheese pie to the more adventurous Etna 2.0 with fried eggplant, parsley, and pine nuts. Just a few blocks from the National Cathedral, there's a large covered outdoor patio here; it's the perfect stop if you find yourself north of downtown.

Duke's Counter (3000 Connecticut Ave. NW, Suite J; http://dukescounter.com; ✆ **202/733-4808**) This London-inspired pub is located directly across the street from the National Zoo. Duke's kids' menu features mac and cheese, fish and chips, a "proper hamburger," a cheese toasty (grilled cheese), and other items, each $10 to $12. Sit inside its laidback dining room or outside on picnic tables.

Old Ebbitt Grill (p. 102) Well, first of all, Ebbitt's layout is incredibly kid-friendly: booths and nooks and lots of strategically placed plants, which all work to contain outbursts of any sort. Then there's the children's menu, which offers the usual pizza and mac and cheese, plus sometimes includes other fare like fish and grilled chicken breast, each priced at $6.99, which includes one choice from a list of drinks/sweets/sides. Finally, there's the location: 2 blocks from the White House and a short walk from the National Mall, it's a convenient pit stop.

Pinstripes (1064 Wisconsin Ave. NW; pinstripes.com/georgetown-washington; ✆ **202/625-6500**) Your kids can bowl or play bocce here while you enjoy a meal. (It's best to make a reservation for a lane.) The kids' menu includes a starter, entrée, dessert, and beverage, all for $10. Sunday brunch is free for kids under 5.

Ted's Bulletin (p. 110) This boisterous, laidback place in the Barracks Row section of Capitol Hill (and its twin at 1818 14th St. NW) welcomes children of all ages with a retro menu of comfort food, such as grilled cheese, Pop-Tarts (called "Ted's Tarts"), mac and cheese, and tomato soup. Breakfast is served all day, so that might decide things right there. But the kids' menu offers seven choices, PB&J to buttered pasta, each priced at $5.99. Or how about this: thick and creamy milkshakes ($8.99) in awesome flavors like Oreo and S'mores? There's always a lot going on here, so you never have to worry about your children being too noisy.

crispy rice, miso salmon with endives and citrus dressing, or the Wagyu beef tartare. Both upstairs and downstairs are always busy and noisy.

705 6th St. NW (at G St.). www.daikaya.com. ℂ **202/589-1600.** Reservations accepted for the upstairs *izakaya*. Ramen $14–17; Japanese small-plate items $7–$20. Ramen noodle house Wed–Thurs 5–10pm, Fri–Sun 11:30am–10pm. Upstairs *izakaya* Wed–Sun 5–10pm. Takeout and outdoor dining available. Metro: Gallery Place (H St./Chinatown exit).

Five Guys Burgers and Fries ★ AMERICAN   Five Guys is taking over the world! Yeah, I know it's a chain, but it's our chain, a family operation that got started in Arlington 34 years ago. You've got various iterations of hamburgers, all of which come in two sizes; assorted hot dogs; a BLT; a veggie sandwich; a grilled cheese; and your choice of regular or Cajun-style fries. One immediate difference between Five Guys and most other popular burgeries, like D.C.'s Good Stuff Eatery (p. 95), is the absence of a "magic sauce." You do get to add as many as 15 toppings, grilled onions to tomatoes, for free. D.C. currently has nine Five Guys, including this Penn Quarter/Chinatown location.

808 H St. NW (at 9th St.). www.fiveguys.com. ℂ **202/393-2900.** Burgers $6–$10; fries $4–$7. Daily 10am–10pm. Takeout available. Metro: Gallery Place (H St./Chinatown exit).

Immigrant Food ★ GLOBAL   Just 1 block from the White House, the location alone makes this place a gem; it's one of few affordable non-chain dining options in the vicinity. But convenience isn't the only feel-good factor here. The "cause-casual" restaurant celebrates and advocates for immigrants in the U.S.—there are cooking classes, cultural events, and an "engagement menu" which serves up ways to donate and support immigrant groups. On the food menu, Chef Enrique Limardo serves up dishes that mix flavors from cuisines around the world, like the banh mi sandwich with adobo chicken, pina colada pancakes with pineapples and coconut, and the "Madam VP's Heritage Bowl" which mixes Indian and Jamaican flavors in a curried chicken stew over rice. It's like the American melting pot, in meal form. There's a second location in **Union Market.**

1701 Pennsylvania Ave. NW. www.immigrantfood.com. ℂ **202/888-0760.** Mains: $10–$15. Tues–Sun, brunch 11am–3pm, dinner 4:30–8pm. Takeout and outdoor dining available. Metro: Farragut West (18th & I St. exit).

COLUMBIA HEIGHTS

This diverse and largely residential neighborhood north of the 14th and U Street hub has a large immigrant population, which makes it one of the best places in the city to try international cuisines. In addition to the restaurants below, taste Filipino fare at **Bad Saint** (www.badsaintdc.com), Cuban cuisine at **Mi Cuba Café** (micubacafe.com), and Laotian dishes at **Thip Khao** (www.thipkhao.com).

Expensive

Rooster and Owl ★★ NEW AMERICAN   From its name alone, you may expect all poultry at this edgy Michelin-starred restaurant in DC's Columbia Heights neighborhood, just north of bustling U Street. Instead, husband-and-wife duo chef Yuan and Carey Tang make veggies the star here. The menu (a prix-fixe four-course affair for $75 per person) changes frequently but a recent star is the Carolina-style barbeque whole carrots with cornbread ice cream. Don't deny yourself the amuse bouche—citrusy pineapple buns with butter. And what's with the name you ask? General manager and front-of-house lead Carey is the early-rising "rooster" and chef Yuan is the night "owl." Aha!

2436 14th St. NW (at Chapin St.). www.roosterowl.com. ☏ 202/813-3976. Dinner $75 per person; $35 beverage pairing; $55 wine pairing. Tues-Sat 5pm. Outdoor dining available. Metro: U St./Cardozo then 10 min. walk uphill, Bus 52 or 54, or taxi ride.

Moderate

Makan ★★★ MALAYSIAN   How's this for bad timing? Makan had been open for just 1 week before all restaurants in Washington, D.C., were forced to close in March 2020 because of the Covid-19 pandemic. Many neighboring eateries never reopened their doors. But Makan has not only survived—it's thriving, a testament to the extraordinarily high quality of the food.

The cuisine is Malaysian, a complex blending of influences from all the cultures on and near the Malay Peninsula: Chinese, Thai, Indian, Indonesian, Filipino, and Bornean. Middle Eastern spices brought in by Arab traders and contributions from Portuguese, Dutch, and British travelers are also part of the mix.

At Makan, that melding translates into tables laden with vindaloo curries, satays (broiled meats with peanut dipping sauce), rice noodles with Chinese sausages, and crisply fried chicken sided with salted egg yolks and pickled chili peppers. Vegetarians have many choices, including comforting *kerisik,* which is dry shredded coconut pounded with fresh coconut into patties and fried, before being placed in a tangy coconut curry.

Chef/owner James Wozniuk scours markets up and down the East Coast to find the fresh pandan leaves, bilimbi (a sour fruit), dried Malaysian anchovies, and other spices and produce that go into his dishes.

Two warnings: Take your server seriously if she tells you the dish is spicy. A few of the plates here will burn your tongue off.

And be sure to get two servings of the *sago,* a vegan dessert that mixes coconut cream with tapioca and palm sugar into a dish so well-balanced and refreshing you won't want to share (plus, the portion is on the small side).

3400 11th St. NW. www.makanrestaurant.com. ☏ 202/730-2295. Dinner $14–$25. Tues-Fri 5–10pm, Sat-Sun 11am–10pm. Takeout and outdoor dining available. Metro: Columbia Heights, then a 7-min. walk.

14TH & U STREET CORRIDORS

Some of the city's trendiest restaurants and bars are right here, along 14th Street and its side streets in particular. Many don't take reservations, so you'll need to be in the right mood to go with the flow (and maybe wait a bit for dinner).

Expensive

Estadio ★★ SPANISH   For Spanish tapas in the city, it would be easy to go to José Andrés' Jaleo (p. 101), but while delicious, it lacks a certain ambience that Estadio excels at—that rustic, traditional Spanish vibe you might find in a tucked-away restaurant in Madrid. Estadio is small, and features 19th-century Spanish tile, Spanish marble, and reclaimed timber tables in a terra-cotta-hued dining room. The food adheres to traditional tastes, too. Try the wide assortment of Spanish *quesos* and *embutidos* (charcuterie). The dinner menu changes seasonally but might include roasted baby chorizos or garlicky shrimp ajillo. Estadio also overlooks busy 14th Street, making it perfect for people-watching, day or night.

1520 14th St. NW (at Church St.). http://estadio-dc.com. ℂ **202/319-1404.** Reservations recommended. Tapas $4.50–$16; cheese plates $5–$27; charcuterie plates $9–$22. Mon–Thurs 5–10pm; Fri 11:30am–2pm, 5–11pm; Sat 11am–2pm, 5–11pm; Sun 11am–2pm, 5–9pm. Takeout and outdoor dining available. Metro: U St./Cardozo (13th St. exit).

Le Diplomate ★★ FRENCH Le Diplomate looks the part of a Parisian brasserie, right down to the red banquettes, large mirrors, zinc-topped bar, little lace curtains, and windows opening to the sidewalk. And it tastes the part, too, with its menu of Gallic staples, from escargots and steak frites to trout amandine and crème brûlée. And the bread! Le Dip's house-made baguettes, cranberry walnut boules, multigrain boules, and brioches are said to be the best breads in the city. It's popular among the brunch crowd, as well as date-nighters. From time to time Le Dip makes local headlines when the who's who of Washington dine here—like President Joe Biden and Vice President Kamala Harris.

1601 14th St. NW (at Q St.). www.lediplomatedc.com. ℂ **202/332-3333.** Reservations recommended. Main courses $14–$35 lunch and brunch; $20–$59 dinner (most around $30). Mon–Thurs 12pm–11pm; Fri 12pm–midnight; Sat 9:30am–midnight; Sun 9:30am–11pm. Takeout and outdoor dining available. Metro: U St./Cardozo (13th St. exit).

Moderate

Chercher Ethiopian Restaurant ★★ ETHIOPIAN The greater Washington, D.C. area is said to have the largest Ethiopian immigrant community in America, so it makes sense that Ethiopian cuisine has found a place for itself in D.C.'s expansive dining scene. If you're already a fan of Ethiopian food or are curious to try it, D.C. is the place. And Chercher, named for the mountainous region of Ethiopia known for its beef and vegetables, remains among the best. Ethiopian expats I've met routinely rave that Chercher is as close to their grandmother's home cooking as one can get in the city. Vegetarians, especially, love the vegan platter: yellow and black lentils, sautéed beets, greens, salad, yogurt, and sautéed cabbage. The special *kitfo* (beef) mixed with Chercher's homemade cottage cheese, herbal butter, cardamom, and *mitmita* (chili powder), can be ordered raw, medium, or well done, and arrives with more than enough *injera* (flat Ethiopian bread). Chercher also operates a second location in the Maryland suburb of Bethesda.

1334 9th St. NW (at O St.). www.chercherrestaurant.com. ℂ **202/299-9703.** Small plates $9–$12; large plates $13–$18; main courses $13–$20. Mon–Thurs 1pm–10pm; Fri–Sun noon–10pm. Takeout available. Metro: Mount Vernon Sq./7th St.

Cork Wine Bar & Market ★ AMERICAN   If I lived in this neighborhood, I would probably hang out here all the time. Upstairs is the cozy, 60-seat wine bar, with 250 bottles on offer (most from small producers) and a whopping 50 wines by the glass. The menu features about 20 small dishes nightly, half cold, half hot, all meant to be shared. Plates of cheeses and charcuterie; braised kale with pecorino; duck confit with sour cherry and endive salad; and French fries tossed with parsley, garlic, and lemon are all recommended. On the first floor is a market and a 20-seat all-day cafe. You can shop for bottles of wine and gourmet food items here, and then settle in at the cafe to enjoy something from the menu of freshly prepared sandwiches and salads, quiches, spreads, and baked goods, or else take everything to go.

1805 14th St. NW (btw. S and T sts.). www.corkdc.com. © **202/265-2675.** Reservations accepted. Cafe and brunch items $7–$17; dinner small plates $7–$20. Cafe/market: Tues–Thurs open 2pm; Fri–Sun open noon. Wine bar: Sat–Sun brunch at 11am; dinner nightly 5:30pm–midnight. Takeout and outdoor dining available. Metro: U St./Cardozo (13th St. exit).

Lupo Verde Cucina and Bar ★★ ITALIAN   It's easy to fall in love with Lupo Verde before you even look at the menu. Set in an old row house on busy 14th Street, the restaurant transports you to a rustic Italian osteria, from its leafy patio strung with twinkling cafe lights to its two floors of warmly lit exposed-brick dining rooms to the bottles of wine stashed in nooks reaching up to the ceiling. But you can't eat ambiance, so let's talk about the food. Pasta lovers: this is the place for you. The house-made pastas are cooked to the perfect degree of al dente. Try the cacio e pepe—it rivals those in Rome; simple and not too heavy—or the gemelli al Lupo ragu, an original recipe from when the restaurant opened in 2014. Rounding out the menu are a large assortment of antipasti, like grilled octopus, burrata, and fried artichokes, salads, and meat and seafood dishes, like pork saltimbocca or a whole, deboned fish. Top it off with Italian style dessert (tiramisu is a favorite), or selection of cheeses from the mini on-site cheese shop and salumeria. Lupo Verde has another location near Glover Park, as well as a recently opened pizza shop, **Lupo Pizzeria** (1908 1st St. NW; www.lupopizzeriadc.com; © **202/506-6137**), right next to the restaurant on 14th Street.

1401 T St. NW (at 14th St.). www.lupoverdedc.com. © **202/827-4752.** Reservations accepted. Lunch items $13–$24; dinner mains $24–$45. Lunch Tues–Fri 11am–3pm; Brunch Sat–Sun 10:30am–3:30pm; Dinner nightly 5pm–11pm. Takeout and outdoor dining available. Metro: U St./Cardozo.

Maydan ★★★ MIDDLE EASTERN/NORTH AFRICAN   I opened the unmarked, dusky-blue arched door, stepping into a dimly lit antechamber leading to Maydan, and it pulled me in. That's how it felt. Past an enormous open-fire hearth sending delicious smells of roasting meats and smoky spices wafting through the two-level atrium, past the surrounding tables and prep area I went. Artful Islamic shapes flourished in wooden screens and tabletops, and lights dangled from long wooden beaded cords. I settled in, sipped a glass of crisp sauvignon blanc, scooped up the creamy hummus and fatoosh salad with flatbread hot from the clay oven, and munched on chunks of roasted barramundi smeared with *zhough,* a spicy condiment tasting of cilantro and cumin.

Open since late 2017, Maydan shot to everyone's immediate attention, listed by both *Food & Wine* and *GQ* as one of the top new restaurants in America. Michelin also recognized it in 2020 with a star. Its name, appropriately, means "gathering place." And that's just what Maydan does—it gathers you in and makes you feel at home. And, as I discovered that evening, the food is scrumptious. If I could recommend only one restaurant for you to go to, this is the one. But first you have to find it! Be sure to read the directions to Maydan on its website, and then look for that dusky-blue door.

1346 Florida Ave. NW (at 14th St.). www.maydandc.com. ⓒ **202/370-3696.** Reservations recommended. Small plates $6–$22; large plates start at $35. Sun 5–10pm; Mon–Sat 5–11pm; bar open until midnight weekdays (until 1am Fri–Sat). Takeout and outdoor dining available. Metro: U St./Cardozo (13th St. exit).

Inexpensive

Ben's Chili Bowl ★ AMERICAN   Ben's opened in 1958 and it looks like it, with its old-fashioned storefront, Formica counters, and red barstools. Its staying power is impressive enough, but Ben's history is also compelling: When riots broke out throughout the city following the assassination of Dr. Martin Luther King, Jr., in April 1968, Ben's stayed open to serve police officers, firefighters, and anyone who needed sustenance, even as surrounding establishments closed or were destroyed.

On that basis alone, a visit to Ben's is warranted. You'll find yourself among a cross-section of locals: by day, workers from nearby municipal office buildings, students, and shoppers; by night, nightclubbers, cops, and neighborhood regulars. Often, it seems that everyone knows everyone else, including the Ali family, who own Ben's. Walls are hung with photographs that cover the history of the city and of Ben's and include snapshots of the many celebrities who've dined here, from President Obama to Mary J. Blige.

Folks go to Ben's for the homey ambience, and for the ultra-cheap and usually tasty food. Most famous is the half-smoke sandwich, a ¼-pound, half-beef, half-pork smoked sausage, served inside a warm bun and, if you so desire, smothered with mustard, chopped onions, and a spicy chili sauce. Vegetarians take note: Ben's has a few veggie-friendly options, like the vegetarian chili. There are locations now at Nationals Park, in the Atlas District, at National Airport and at Capital One Arena.

1213 U St. NW (btw. 12th and 13th sts.). www.benschilibowl.com. ⓒ **202/667-0058.** Reservations not accepted. Main courses $4–$10. No credit cards (there's an ATM here). Mon–Thurs 7am–2:30am; Fri–Sat 7am–4am; Sun 11am–midnight. Takeout available. Metro: U St./Cardozo (13th St. exit).

Colada Shop ★ CUBAN   This tiny shop has a big personality. Lively Cuban music splashes out to the patio; in fair weather, the window-front opens upward, creating an alfresco counter space for chatting. Munching diners sit on stools across from one another, inside and outside. The spirit is exuberant,

DINNER? DRINKS? shaw-thing

Visit Shaw by day and you'll likely encounter conference-goers (the convention center lies within its northwest D.C. boundaries), residents, and people who work here. Few tourists, little hustle-bustle. Except for the **African American Civil War Memorial and Museum** (p. 187) and the **Mary McLeod Bethune Council House** (closed for renovation through 2022), and the smattering of retail shops on or near U Street NW, there are no notable daytime attractions worth a detour from the sites awaiting you on the Mall and elsewhere. I invite you instead to visit Shaw in the evening, to dine, perchance to drink.

Overnight, it seems, the district has turned into *the* place to go for some of the city's best dining and drinking experiences. At least 25 restaurants, bakeries, coffeehouses, and bars have sprouted here in the last couple of years, Michelin star and James Beard Award winners among them. You may be puzzled when you arrive, though—for now, at least,

Shaw looks like what it was and still is: an old neighborhood of historic churches, modest housing, and corner shops, even amid the rising luxury condos and construction sites. The restaurants are scattered over several streets, rather than primarily along a single stretch or two (as they are in the U & 14th St. Corridors or on 8th St. SE in Barracks Row). In fact, some of the hottest spots are hidden down alleyways. You have to seek them out. Among my favorites are:

1250 9th St. NW between N and M streets: Sharing the same street address, but with separate locations right next to one another on the block, are these two different and individually owned establishments: **All Purpose Pizzeria** (www.all purposedc.com; ℂ **202/849-6174**), creating fresh takes on pizzas and classics such as eggplant Parm, and **Espita Mezcaleria** (www.espitadc.com; ℂ **202/621-9695**), with excellent southern Mexican cuisine and an awesome selection of mescals. Now look directly across Ninth Street and

the food is swell, and the prices right: *croquettas* (fritters filled with your choice of ham, chicken, or mushrooms gently blended with a bechamel sauce into a light concoction), two for $3.50; or the famous Cuban sandwich of ham, slow-roasted pork, Swiss cheese, pickles, mustard, and aioli on Cuban bread for $9.98. A dozen versions of coffee are on offer, from the Cubano (a shot of coffee sweetened with whipped sugar) to café con leche (a Cubano with hot steamed milk). And then there are the potent cocktails: daiquiris, pina coladas, mojitos, Cuba libres, and the like, each $8 to $10. Colada Shop turns this block of T Street into a party. But if you're here just to enjoy your empanadas and pastelitos, head to the back of the shop toward the kitchen and hang a right to find the quieter back room, with leather sofas, wicker chairs, and stools at high tops. Or head to the lovely rooftop garden, open daily, weather permitting, for cocktails, Caribbean tunes, and Colada's favorite bites. There's another location with even more outdoor seating at the Wharf (10 Pearl St. SW; ℂ **202/932-2980**).

1405 T St. NW (at 14th St.). www.coladashop.com. ℂ **202/332-8800.** Reservations not accepted. All items under $10. Sun 8am–10pm; Mon–Thurs 7am–9pm; Fri 7am–11pm; Sat 8am–11pm; Sun 8am–9pm. Takeout and outdoor dining available. Metro: U St./ Cardozo (13th St. exit) or take the DC Circulator.

what do you see? The convention center, right? But hiding in plain sight within that glass facade is **Unconventional Diner** (1207 9th St. NW; www.unconventional diner.com; ☎ **202/847-0122**), open for everyday brunch and dinner daily, serving the most cunning little takes on diner food (the meatloaf has a Sriracha glaze, for example) in one large room decorated with colorful pop art and including a cafe, bar, and banquette-filled dining area.

In **Blagden Alley** (more like a quaint little brick-paved village with its nookish space behind buildings on 9th and 10th sts. and M and N sts.): **The Dabney** (www.thedabney.com; ☎ **202/450-1015**), has earned a Michelin star for its Mid-Atlantic fare cooked in a wood-burning hearth; **Tiger Fork** (www.tigerforkdc; ☎ **202/733-1152**), bringing "Hong Kong's gritty, badass culinary culture" to D.C., from crab Rangoon nachos to beef buns; and the **Columbia Room** (www. columbiaroomdc.com; ☎ **202/316-9396**), the gift of Derek Brown—esteemed

mixologist, spirits historian, and perennial James Beard Award nominee—offering a robust menu of cocktails and spritzes, including artful alcohol-free options.

On O Street NW at 8th Street: Convivial (www.convivialdc.com; ☎ **202/525-2870**) is French chef Cedric Maupillier's interpretation of "an American cafe," and it's as merry an experience as the name suggests, with happy diners enjoying the steak frites with green beans followed by sticky toffee pudding or the crunchy raspberry-rhubarb tart.

1015 7th St. NW, between New York Avenue and L Street NW: Kinship and **Métier** (www.kinshipdc.com; ☎ **202/737-7700**) both serve creative contemporary American cuisine, in a casual dining room upstairs at Kinship and in the acclaimed and more intimate and formal, $200-a-person tasting room/restaurant Métier downstairs; *Washingtonian* magazine named Métier among the city's best restaurants in 2020. (Dress sharp; jackets are required for men, but ties are optional.)

ADAMS MORGAN
Expensive

Tail Up Goat ★★★ MEDITERRANEAN Fans call Tail Up Goat "Rose's Luxury with reservations." It has the same warm and whimsical vibe, as well as a menu of otherworldly combinations of tastes, similar to what you'll find at that Barracks Row restaurant (p. 93). At Tail Up Goat that means an always-changing menu that's earned it a place on Michelin's starred list. Lunch and dinner items may include plates of crispy salt cod with smoked cauliflower, corn and chickpea panisse, seared tilefish with almond skordalia and veggies, or the fairytale eggplant, with pork belly and spicy garum. If there are more than two of you, you'll want to sit at a table in the dining room, with its view of the open kitchen at the back. But if you're dining alone or with a pal, sit on a cushioned stool in the cozy bar, where you'll be coddled and amused by the charming bartenders. It's also where you can snag a seat if you haven't snagged a reservation—the bar is reserved for walk-ins.

1827 Adams Mill Rd. NW (entrance on Lanier Pl.). www.tailupgoat.com. ☎ **202/986-9600.** Reservations recommended. Small plates $13; larger plates $16–$62 (most dishes are around $16). Wed–Thurs 5:30–9pm; Fri–Sat 5–9:15pm; Sun 5–9pm. Outdoor dining available. Metro: Woodley Park–Zoo, with a walk, or take the DC Circulator.

Inexpensive

Amsterdam Falafelshop ★ MIDDLE EASTERN/DUTCH   Inspired by the falafel shops of Holland, the owners opened their own D.C. version in 2004. The shop does a steady business all day among people who just love the toasted pita sandwiches, which come stuffed with fried balls of mashed chickpeas or chicken shawarma and topped with as many garnishes as you want, from pickled turnips to hummus. The shop stays open late, closing around 4 am on weekends. There are a couple small tables where you can dine in or on the patio, but most customers carry out.

2425 18th St. NW (at Belmont Rd.). www.falafelshop.com. ℂ **202/234-1969.** Reservations not accepted. Sandwiches $7.50–$10; Dutch fries $4–$5. Sun–Mon 11am–midnight; Tues–Thurs 11am–2:30am; Fri–Sat 11am–4am. Takeout and outdoor dining available. Metro: Woodley Park–Zoo, with a walk, or take the DC Circulator.

Henry's Soul Café ★ SOUTHERN   If it looks like this counter-serve deli has been here forever, that's because it has. Henry's has been serving up comfort food like fried whitling, baked chicken, mac and cheese, and ribs in this location for more than 50 years. Not only is the food filling, you get a lot of it; each main comes with a choice of up to two generously portioned sides, plus your choice of bread (opt for the cornbread). But the dish that keeps customers coming back again and again is the sweet potato pie, The shop sells over 100,000 of these savory treats a year; it's reported that President Barack Obama was even a fan. You can order a whole pie or get it by the slice. While there are a few seats along a counter in the window, the food is served in a takeout container so it's best to take it to go. Henry's also has another location in Maryland, a short drive from National Harbor.

1704 U St. NW (at 17th St). henryssoulcafe.com. ℂ **202/265-3336.** Reservations not accepted. Mains $10–$14. Tues–Sat 11am–6pm; Sun 11am–4pm. Takeout available. Metro: Dupont Circle, then walk about 15 minutes.

Julia's Empanadas ★ LATIN   For years, I'll admit I avoided this hole-in-the-wall shop for what it looked like on the outside. But like so many things, it's what on the inside that counts. Since 1993, Julia's has baked her fresh, homemade empanadas daily, serving a steady stream of customers who keep coming back for her spiced, filled pastry. What's available changes as the day goes on, but if it's on the menu, try the Jamaican-style empanada with ground beef, potato, onions, curry, and spices, or the chorizo with black beans, white rice, onions, and spices. If you're out clubbing in the neighborhood, do what D.C.'s barhoppers do, and stop here for a late-night snack. There aren't seats inside, so grab your empanada to go or walk and eat. Other locations are in Dupont Circle (1221 Connecticut Ave. NW) and Brightwood (6235 Georgia Ave. NW).

2452 18th St. NW (at Columbia Rd.). www.juliasempanadas.com. ℂ **202/328-6232.** Reservations not accepted. $10 minimum credit card. All empanadas $6. Mon–Thurs 10am–9pm; Fri 10am–11pm; Sat 10am–midnight; Sun 10am–8pm. Takeout available. Metro: Woodley Park–Zoo, with a walk, or take the DC Circulator.

DUPONT CIRCLE

Expensive

Al Tiramisu ★★ ITALIAN   Al Tiramisu is a find, and those who have found it include George and Amal Clooney, Hillary Clinton, and Magic Johnson. I imagine celebrities like it for the same reason everyone else does: the infectious ebullience of chef/owner Luigi Diotaiuti, who bounces out from behind a curtain to greet you as you enter; the unpretentious feeling of this snug little restaurant, which is essentially one long room in the bottom of a Dupont Circle town house (you can also dine outdoors on the sidewalk in front of the restaurant); and a menu that includes excellently prepared grilled fish, house-made caciocavallo ravioli with butter and sage sauce, and grilled lamb chops. This is a place to come for romance, for cheering up, for having a good time with friends, and Tiramisu has been so obliging since it opened in 1996.

2014 P St. NW (btw. 19th and 20th sts.). www.altiramisu.com. © **202/467-4466.** Reservations recommended. Main courses $23–$33. Mon–Tues 11:30–1:30pm, 5–9pm; Wed–Thurs 11:30am–1:30pm, 5–10pm; Fri 11:30am–1:30pm, 5–10:30pm; Sat 5–10:30pm; Sun 5–9pm. Takeout and outdoor dining available. Metro: Dupont Circle (19th St./South exit).

Anju ★★ KOREAN   Fried chicken is just fried chicken, right? Unless you're dining at this Korean gastropub, helmed by chefs Danny Lee and Scott Drewno (together The Fried Rice Collective who also manage Chiko locations and I Egg You). Here, the chicken, available by the half or whole bird, is coated in a soybean powder, then dipped in a spicy *gochujang* glaze and striped with tangy white barbecue sauce. Not KFC, for sure. *Washingtonian* magazine awarded Anju the top spot in its list of very best restaurants in D.C. in 2020. It's easy to see why. Lee's mother Yesoon, who grew up in Seoul, oversees the "classic" Korean fare, including the kimchi, fermented in-house, and shredded bellflower root. Appetizers like kimchi pancakes and pan-fried dumplings are a hit. The bibimbap is cooked in hot stone making the rice on the bottom perfectly crispy. Anju is translated from Korean to mean "food consumed while drinking" and true to its name, the restaurant has a hopping happy hour daily 5pm to 7pm. Happy hour bites like a kimchi slaw dog, spicy brisket ramen and tornado potato are deliciously fun, and for $5 to $7, reasonably priced too. Order the $4 bowl of *makkoli,* a sparkling rice wine that the bar infuses with various flavors.

1805 18th St. NW (btw. Swann and S sts.). www.anjurestaurant.com. © **202/845-8935.** Reservations recommended. Appetizers $8–$25; Main courses $18–$32. Dinner Mon–Sun 5–9pm. Brunch Sat–Sun 11am–2pm. Takeout and outdoor dining available. Metro: Dupont Circle (20th St./North exit).

Iron Gate ★★ MEDITERRANEAN   This romantic restaurant lies hidden away on a quiet Dupont Circle side street. But it's no secret—just try booking a reservation. Whether you sit in the long, narrow carriageway fronting the restaurant, in the wisteria-canopied brick courtyard, or in the cozy banquette-filled and paneled main dining room, you'll be smitten. (In winter, if health restrictions permit—at this writing Iron Gate wasn't offering indoor dining, I would choose the main dining room, where the open kitchen and wood-burning hearth add a special glow.) Plates are to share or not and might include such delectable tastes as caramelized ricotta gnocchi, oak-grilled asparagus on a bed of lentil hummus, and, in season, Maryland soft-shell crab. Be sure to leave room for one of the delicious desserts, the crispy Greek yeast doughnuts with orange blossom syrup are a particular favorite.

1734 N St. NW (17th St.). www.irongaterestaurantdc.com. ✆ **202/524-5202.** Reservations recommended. Brunch/lunch a la carte dishes $6–$17; dinner a la carte $6–$75 (entrees for 2 people). Sun brunch 11am–2pm; Dinner Tues–Sun 5pm–10pm. Takeout and outdoor dining available. Metro: Dupont Circle (19th St. exit).

Pupatella ★★ PIZZA   This Neapolitan pizzeria has sat solidly on "best pizza in D.C." lists for years. The problem was, it was out in the suburbs, and you needed a car to get to it. Not anymore! In 2020, Pupatella opened its first location in Washington-proper, right next to foodie hotspot **Anju** (p. 113). The large corner outpost has a generously sized patio, plus to-go windows if you'd rather eat your pie elsewhere. The pizzas are on the smaller side; I usually order one per person. Favorites include the prosciutto and arugula pizza, the Margherita DOC, and the spicy salami–topped Diavola. They also have the best arancini in D.C.; you can get the fried risotto balls with sausage or eggplant. Finally, if you have a sweet tooth I have two words for you: dessert pizza. Try the Nutella and green apple pizza, sprinkled with powdered sugar.

1801 18th St. NW (at S St NW). www.pupatella.com. ✆ **202/506-1999.** Main courses $13–$19. Mon–Thurs 4–9pm; Fri 11:30am–10pm; Sat 11am–10pm; Sun 11am–9pm. Takeout and outdoor dining available. Metro: Dupont Circle (20th St./North exit).

Tabard Inn ★★ AMERICAN   Locals head to the Tabard for the freshly made doughnuts and whipped cream served at weekend brunch. (Actually, the doughnuts are available daily for breakfast, too, but that will be our little secret.) Other items also prove a potent lure, such as bacon-wrapped quail, shrimp ravioli with seaweed salad, and seared scallops with rice noodles, basil pesto and shiitake mushrooms. The fact that all of this is served in an absolutely charming, sky-lit room (just past the comfy old wood-paneled lounge) and adjoining covered courtyard doesn't hurt. If you can't get in for a meal, do stop for a cocktail, just so you can experience the inn's lovely ambience (it's also a hotel; see p. 78).

1739 N St. NW (at 17th St., in the Hotel Tabard Inn). www.tabardinn.com/dining. ✆ **202/785-1277.** Reservations recommended. Main courses $2–$33 breakfast, $16–$28 lunch and brunch, $28–$45 dinner. Daily 8am–3pm, 5–9pm. Takeout and outdoor dining available. Metro: Dupont Circle (19th St./South exit).

Inexpensive

Pizzeria Paradiso ★ PIZZA/ITALIAN   Another pizza spot? Hear me out. Pizzeria Paradiso has been around since before the gourmet pizza trend was born. It's 30 years old and remains a favorite among a wide field of contenders. Paradiso cooks its pizzas in a domed, wood-burning stone oven that can withstand 650-degree heat, which gives the pizza a light but doughier crust than its rivals. The pies come in 9- and 12-inch sizes, and the 44-item toppings list includes everything imaginable, from shrimp to vegan mozzarella. Paninis and salads

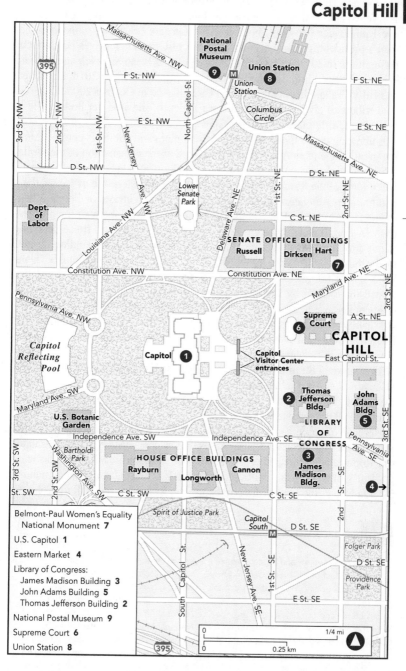

Belmont-Paul Women's Equality
National Monument 7

U.S. Capitol 1

Eastern Market 4

Library of Congress:
James Madison Building 3
John Adams Building 5
Thomas Jefferson Building 2

National Postal Museum 9

Supreme Court 6

Union Station 8

oomful of Calders, many small and toylike, some swaying mobiles suspended from skylights, all colorful whimsies.

Okay, now you're good to go explore on your own, back through the galleries of minimalist art, or on to pop art, photography, Picasso, American art from the first half of the 20th century, and French paintings from the last half of the 19th century and first half of the 20th.

If you make your way back to the West Building and exit onto 7th Street, you are directly across from the **Sculpture Garden.** Go! Positioned throughout its lushly landscaped 6 acres you'll find a stalking *Spider* by Louise Bourgeois, a tall, blue sculpture of five stacked chairs made of patinated bronze by Lucas Samaras, and 18 other modern sculptures. In the northwest corner is a delightful, large (10×17 ft.) glass and stone mosaic by Marc Chagall.

At the center of the Sculpture Garden is an expansive fountain, which turns into an ice rink in winter. The garden is famous for its summer Sculpture Garden concerts, which are free and draw a crowd.

The National Gallery also mounts killer special exhibits and offers a robust year-round schedule of films, tours, and talks, monthly after-hours events from October to April, and concert series and performing art series—all free, let me emphasize.

There are five dining options, the best of which are the **Garden Café** and the Sculpture Garden's **Pavilion Café.**

We have Andrew W. Mellon to thank for the museum. The financier/philanthropist, who served as ambassador to England from 1932 to 1933, was so inspired by London's National Gallery that he decided to give such a gift to his own country. The West Building opened in Washington, D.C., in 1941, the East Building in 1978, and the Sculpture Garden in 1999.

Constitution Ave. NW, btw. 3rd and 7th sts. NW (on the north side of the Mall). www.nga.gov. ✆ 202/737-4215. Free admission. Gallery: Daily 10am–5pm. Sculpture Garden: Daily, hours change based on programming so check the gallery's website. Ice rink: Mid-Nov to mid-Mar Mon–Thurs 10am–9pm, Fri 10am–11pm, Sat 11am–11pm Sun 11am–9pm. Rink fees: $9 adults under 50 and children 13 and older, $8 adults 50 and over and children 12 and under, plus $4 skate rental, 50¢ locker rental ($5 deposit required). Closed Dec 25 and Jan 1. Metro: Archives–Navy Memorial, Judiciary Square (either exit), or Gallery Place/Chinatown (Arena/7th and F sts. exit). DC Circulator stop.

National Mall ★★★ ICON

As part of his vision for Washington, Pierre L'Enfant conceived of the National Mall as a bustling ceremonial avenue of distinguished buildings. Today's 2-mile, 700-acre stretch of land extending westward from the base of the Capitol to the Potomac River, just behind the Lincoln Memorial, fulfills that dream. Eleven Smithsonian buildings, plus the National Gallery of Art and its Sculpture Garden, and a stray government building (Department of Agriculture), stake out the Mall's northern border along Constitution Avenue and its southern border along Independence Avenue. More than 2,000 American elm trees shade the pebbled walkways paralleling Jefferson and Madison drives. In a single year, more than 35 million tourists and locals crisscross the Mall as they visit the Smithsonians, hustle to work, exercise, participate in whatever festival, event, or demonstration is

If you're short on time or simply overwhelmed, there are two things you shouldn't miss. The **Sky Lab Orbital Workshop ★★★**, in the Space Race gallery on the first floor (you enter the spaceship on the second floor), allows you to walk through the country's first space station. You're actually *inside* the astronauts' living quarters; if you look up, you'll see that most of the rocket's construction lies overhead. And be sure to visit the second-floor **Wright Brothers** exhibit, where the Wright brothers' **1903 Flyer ★★★**, the world's first successful airplane, is on display.

Amateur astronomers should head outside to the museum's east terrace to peer through the telescopes in the **Phoebe Waterman Haas Public Observatory.** The observatory, when it's in service, is free and open to the public for daytime sightings of moon craters and sunspots, and once or twice a month for nighttime observations (more info on the website). At press time, the museum's popular **Albert Einstein Planetarium** was closed as part of the museum's ongoing renovations; check the website for updates on its scheduled return.

Wonder where the museum has put all of the aircraft and equipment that used to occupy the west wing? Much of it now resides temporarily in the National Air and Space Museum's companion location, the **Steven F. Udvar-Hazy Center,** adjacent to Washington Dulles International Airport. If you're hungry to see more aviation artifacts and spacecraft, or if you've got a flight leaving from Dulles Airport and have time to kill, drive the 25 miles out to the satellite museum. Here you can explore one huge hangar filled with aviation objects and another with space objects, each arranged by subject (Commercial Aviation, Korea and Vietnam Aviation, Sport Aviation, and so on). Perhaps the center's most notable artifact is the enormous **space shuttle** *Discovery* that retired in 2011. A Lockhead SR-71 Blackbird, the world's fastest-jet-propelled aircraft, is also here, along with the Concorde, the first supersonic airliner. IMAX movies and simulator rides also are options. *Note:* Admission is free at Udvar-Hazy, but there is a $15 fee for parking before 4pm.

Mall museum: Independence Ave. SW, btw. 4th and 7th sts. (on south side of Mall, with two entrances, one on Jefferson Dr. and the other on Independence Ave; Thurs–Mon 10am–5:30pm). Metro: L'Enfant Plaza (Smithsonian Museums/Maryland Ave. exit) or Smithsonian (Mall/Jefferson Dr. exit). DC Circulator stop. **Udvar-Hazy Center:** 14390 Air and Space Museum Pkwy., Chantilly, VA. www.airandspace.si.edu.✆ 202/633-2214 (Mall location), or 703/572-4118 (Virginia location). Free admission. Daily 10am–5:30pm. Closed Dec 25.

National Archives Museum ★★ MUSEUM

The **Rotunda** of the National Archives displays the country's most important original documents: the Declaration of Independence, the Constitution of the United States, and the Bill of Rights (collectively known as the **Charters of Freedom**). Fourteen document cases trace the story of the creation of the Charters and the ongoing influence these fundamental documents have had on the nation and the world.

It proves to be an unexpectedly thrilling experience to stand among people from all over the world and peer in this dimly lit chamber at page after page of manuscript covered top to bottom in tiny, graceful script, whose forthright declarations founded our country and changed the world. It is gratifying, too, to see the documents given context within the exhibit. For example, one panel points to the role of "founding mothers" like Abigail Adams, who cautioned her husband in a letter, "If perticular [sic] care is not paid to the Ladies, we are determined to foment a Rebelion, [sic] and will not hold ourselves bound by any Laws in which we have no voice or Representation."

But the wonders don't end there: On display in the **David M. Rubenstein Gallery** is the original 1297 Magna Carta, one of only four known to exist in the world, and the only original version on public display in the United States. The Magna Carta anchors the permanent exhibit, **Records of Rights,** which presents hundreds of other landmark documents, as well as photographs, videos, and interactive items that help visitors trace the evolution of rights in the U.S. from its founding to the present day.

Beyond famous documents are the **Public Vaults,** an area that, when open to the public, introduces visitors to the heart of the Archives: its 10 billion records, covering 2 centuries worth of documents, from patent searches to genealogical records to copies of George Washington's handwritten inaugural address, to census records, governmental records, and more. (Check before you visit to see if the vaults are open.)

Using the very latest in interactive museum design—listening booths, computer terminals, videos, you name it—the curators have mined the material for drama (and often presented it in a very kid-friendly fashion). In an area on patents, for example, the process is turned into a game: You read the patent application and then try to guess what well-known gadget it was for. A section on immigration presents the search for genealogical data as a cliffhanger mystery, detailing the steps and missteps of past Archives' users. President Nixon makes several eerie appearances: You read his resignation letter and listen to disturbing excerpts from the Watergate tapes.

Beyond its exhibits, the Archives are a vital resource for researchers. Anyone 16 and over is welcome to use the National Archives center for genealogical research. Call for details.

The National Archives building itself is worth an admiring glance. The neoclassical structure, designed by John Russell Pope (also architect of the National Gallery of Art and the Jefferson Memorial) in the 1930s, is an impressive example of the Beaux Arts style. Seventy-two columns create a Corinthian colonnade on each of the four facades. Great bronze doors mark the Constitution Avenue entrance, and four large sculptures representing the Future, the Past, Heritage, and Guardianship sit on pedestals near the entrances. Huge pediments crown both the Pennsylvania Avenue and Constitution Avenue entrances to the building.

Admission is always free, but you'll pay a $1 convenience fee when you reserve your timed ticket online at www.recreation.gov/ticket/facility/234645.

701 Constitution Ave NW (btw. 7th and 9th sts. NW). Tourists enter on Constitution Ave., researchers on Pennsylvania Ave. museum.archives.gov. ℂ **202/357-5000.** Free admission. Daily 10am–5:30pm. Call for research hours. Closed Dec 25. Metro: Archives–Navy Memorial. DC Circulator stop.

National Gallery of Art ★★★ ART MUSEUM   Best. Ar[t] Ever. That's my opinion; but let me quickly say that world-renown[ed] also consider the over 80-year-old National Gallery of Art to be a[mong the] best museums in the world. Its base collection of more than 150,0[00 paint]ings, drawings, prints, photographs, sculpture, decorative arts, and [...] trace the development of Western art from the Middle Ages to the p[resent in] a manner that's both informative and rapturously beautiful.

The National Gallery's design and programs make the artworks [and the] museum itself accessible to the ordinary visitor. Architect John Russ[ell Pope] (of Jefferson Memorial fame; see p. 142) modeled his design of the [...] West Building after the Pantheon in Rome, anchoring the main floor's [...] with a domed rotunda, and then centered a colonnaded fountain bene[ath the] dome. The overall feeling is of spaciousness and grace, especially wh[en the] huge fountain is encircled with flowers, as it often is. Extending east an[d west] are long and wide, light-filled, high-ceilinged halls, off which the ind[ividual] **paintings galleries** lie, nearly 100 in all, leading eventually to lovely [...] courts and more places to sit.

One hundred galleries? Yes, but the 1,000-some paintings are arranged i[n an easy]to-understand order, in separate rooms by age and nationality: 13th-c[entury] Italian to 18th-century Italian, Spanish, and French artists on the wes[t side;] 18th- and 19th-century Spanish, French, British, and American masters [on the] east side. You may recognize some names: Leonardo da Vinci (whose e[xquisite] portrait, *Ginevra de' Benci,* which hangs here, is the only da Vinci pain[ting on] public view in the Americas), Rubens, Raphael, Cassatt, El Greco, Br[...] Poussin, Vermeer, van Dyck, Gilbert Stuart, Winslow Homer, Turner, and[...]

Down the sweep of marble stairway to the ground floor lie the West Bu[ilding's] remaining galleries. The light-filled, vaulted-ceilinged sculpture galleries [hold] standouts by Bernini, Rodin, Degas, and Honoré Daumier, whose 36 smal[l bronze] busts of French government administrators are highly amusing cari[catures.] Other galleries display decorative arts, prints and drawings, and photo[graphs.]

Across the street from the West Building is a Sculpture Garden that [holds] 22 sculptures created by an international roster of artists in the [past few] decades, including a stunning Chagall mosaic.

The I. M. Pei–designed East Building showcases modern and contem[porary] art in galleries that lie off a dazzling atrium and includes three skyli[t rooms] and an outdoor sculpture terrace with a grand view of the city. In [the East] Building another world opens up, as graceful as the West Building, [though] it's angular, airy, and capricious. An immense and colorful Calde[r mobile] floats overhead, but where are the galleries? You're meant to wander[, so you] might miss something without a strategy. So here goes:

After arriving via the underground walkway from the West Build[ing, take] the elevator that will take you to the rooftop and its two towers. T[he first] two-gallery space presents a study in contrasts, one gallery devoted t[o a group] of mesmerizing color-block Rothkos, the other displaying Barnett N[ewman's] abstract, muted depictions of the Stations of the Cross. Tower 2 holds[...]

No Vaccine? No Party. How Covid-19 May Impact D.C. Nightlife

As of this writing, many D.C. bars, theaters, and other entertainment venues are requiring patrons to prove they're fully vaccinated against Covid-19 before entering indoor performances and events, a move that has been widely praised and accepted by the local community. These requirements are hopefully will have been lifted by the time you travel. But just in case, be prepared to show either your physical Covid-19 Vaccination Record Card, a photo of your card, or your vaccination records via a digital pass; several states are currently using My IR Mobile (www.myir mobile.com) for instance.

new voices. There's even a theater dedicated to all-things Shakespeare. Don't assume that these venues present only classic renditions from a performing arts hit list; each is wildly creative in its choices and presentations. For the most avant-garde theater, seek out smaller stages like the **Woolly Mammoth Theatre Company** and **Studio Acting Conservatory.**

Seasons for both The Kennedy Center and Arena Stage run year-round; normally, the Shakespeare Theatre's season (and that of other smaller theaters) is nearly year-round, taking a 4- to 6-week break July into August. While the Kennedy Center often has performances going on throughout the day, all theaters hold their major productions at 7:30 or 8pm nightly, with Saturday and Sunday matinée performances at 2pm and occasional midweek matinée performances on the schedule, especially at Arena Stage.

The bad news is that ticket prices have gone through the roof in the past couple of years. A lot of locals subscribe to the big three (the Kennedy Center, Shakespeare Theatre, and Arena Stage), which leaves fewer one-off tickets available to the general public. Expect to pay $75 to $100-plus—unless you're able to obtain a discounted ticket; see the "Getting Tickets" box, p. 226.

Major Theaters & Companies

Arena Stage ★★★ Founded in 1950, Arena Stage has long been about "putting the American spirit in the spotlight," as the company tagline phrases it. What that means is that the theater produces the works of American artists, choosing plays that explore themes of American diversity, challenges, and passions. A typical season features an American classic or two, a musical or two, new plays by emerging playwrights, world premieres, and, because Arena Stage is in the nation's capital, a play of political topicality. Many Arena Stage productions go on to win Tony Awards on Broadway, as did *Dear Evan Hansen,* the 2017 Tony winner for best new musical.

The theater is D.C.'s second-largest after The Kennedy Center. Officially called "The Mead Center for American Theater," the venue's three staging areas are the theater-in-the-round **Fichandler,** the fan-shaped **Kreeger,** and the intimate (202-seat), oval-shaped **Kogod Cradle.** Locals love Arena Stage's productions, which draw more than 300,000 annually. Expect a mix of

Old Town Alexandria

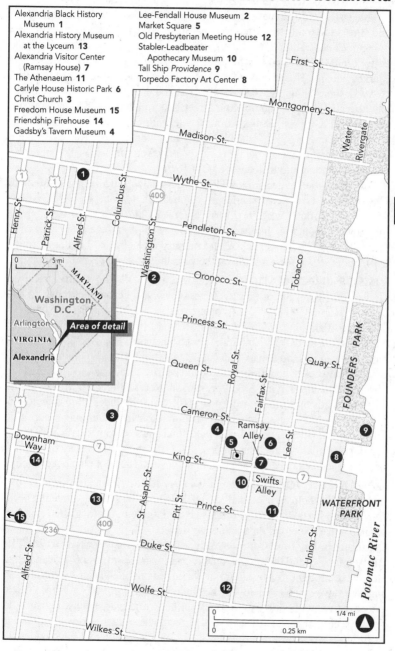

Alexandria Black History Museum 1
Alexandria History Museum at the Lyceum 13
Alexandria Visitor Center (Ramsay House) 7
The Athenaeum 11
Carlyle House Historic Park 6
Christ Church 3
Freedom House Museum 15
Friendship Firehouse 14
Gadsby's Tavern Museum 4

Lee-Fendall House Museum 2
Market Square 5
Old Presbyterian Meeting House 12
Stabler-Leadbeater Apothecary Museum 10
Tall Ship Providence 9
Torpedo Factory Art Center 8

First St.

Montgomery St.

Water Rivergate

Madison St.

Wythe St.

Columbus St.

1

Henry St.

Patrick St.

Alfred St.

400

Washington St.

Pendleton St.

Tobacco

2

Oronoco St.

MARYLAND

Washington, D.C.

Arlington

Area of detail

VIRGINIA

Alexandria

Princess St.

Royal St.

Queen St.

Fairfax St.

Quay St.

FOUNDERS PARK

Cameron St.

Ramsay Alley

3

4

5

6

Lee St.

9

Downham Way

7

King St.

St. Asaph St.

Pitt St.

10

Swifts Alley

7

8

14

13

400

15

236

Prince St.

11

WATERFRONT PARK

Alfred St.

Duke St.

Union St.

Potomac River

Wolfe St.

12

Wilkes St.

0   5 mi

0   1/4 mi

0   0.25 km

get high marks as well. Pizzeria Paradiso serves wine and also has a **Birreria,** where patrons interested in microbrews and handcrafted beers can select from 13 drafts and more than 200 bottles. Paradiso's other locations include one in Georgetown, at 3282 M St. NW (© **202/337-1245**), and one in Spring Valley, at 4850 Mass Ave. NW (© **202/885-9101**), which does take reservations.

2003 P St. NW (btw. 20th and 21st sts.). www.eatyourpizza.com. © **202/223-1245.** Reservations not accepted. Pizzas $12–$21; sandwiches and salads $9–$14. Mon–Thurs 4pm–9pm; Fri–Sun 11am–9 pm. Takeout and outdoor dining available. Metro: Dupont Circle (19th St./South exit).

Teaism Dupont Circle ★ ASIAN FUSION   This homegrown teahouse enterprise currently has three D.C. locations, each similar in their menus of bento boxes, aromatic teas, savory sandwiches, and sweets, though they differ in appearance. This one, in Dupont Circle, is the original, a homey, two-level restaurant and shop tucked inside a century-old building with French windows that overlook the tree-lined street. Penn Quarter's Teaism has a separate tea shop, one storefront away from the restaurant, and the largest inventory of teas. Lafayette Park's Teaism is a bit smaller but is conveniently located near the White House. No matter the Teaism, you'll find these are casual eateries, where you order from a menu that changes seasonally but might include curried chicken, udon noodle soup, Korean beef brisket sandwiches, and a constantly updated inventory of about 55 teas.

Visit **Teaism Lafayette Park,** 800 Connecticut Ave. NW (© **202/835-2233**), near the White House, and **Teaism Penn Quarter** ★, 400 8th St. NW (© **202/638-6010**).

2009 R St. NW (btw. Connecticut and 21st sts.). www.teaism.com. © **202/667-3827.** Reservations not accepted. All items $3–$14. Daily 11am–8pm. Takeout and outdoor dining available. Metro: Dupont Circle (Q St. exit).

FOGGY BOTTOM/WEST END

In addition to the restaurants below, consider **Tatte** (1200 New Hampshire Ave. NW; www.tattebakery.com), a Boston-based pastry shop known for its Israeli favorites like halloumi breakfast sandwiches and lamb hash.

Moderate

Founding Farmers ★ AMERICAN   An international clientele gathers at Founding Farmers, thanks to the fact that the restaurant is on the ground floor of the International Monetary Fund, 1 block from World Bank Headquarters, and within a short walk of the Pan American Health Organization and the State Department. But the real reason for its popularity may be that it led the charge in real restaurants opening in this neck of the woods (as opposed to fast-food joints and delis). So, expect a boisterous and busy atmosphere, especially downstairs, which holds a big bar as well as booths and tables. Upstairs tends to be quieter, with silo-shaped booths and small clusters of intimate seating. So, what to order? Fans enthuse about the fancy cocktails, the bourbon-battered French toast at brunch, and, for lunch and dinner, the crispy shrimp; signature dishes like Yankee pot roast and chicken pot pie; and the griddled farm bread topped with brie, onion jam, and sliced apples. The options include a number of meatless entrees. Founding Farmers has several popular siblings, including **Farmers Fishers Bakers** (www.farmersfishers bakers.com), on the Georgetown waterfront at 3000 K St. NW, and Farmers & Distillers (www.farmersanddistillers.com) at 600 Massachusetts Ave. NW.

1924 Pennsylvania Ave. NW (at 20th St.). www.wearefoundingfarmers.com. © **202/822-8783.** Reservations recommended. Main courses $7–$15 breakfast and brunch, $12–$35 (most under $20) lunch and dinner. Mon–Thurs 7:30am–10pm; Fri 7:30am–11pm; Sat 9am–11pm; Sun 9am–10pm. Takeout and outdoor dining available. Metro: Foggy Bottom.

Inexpensive

Beefsteak ★ VEGETARIAN   Inside the wide, window-wrapped, street-level corner room of George Washington University's Engineering Building is another José Andrés culinary revelation, this one serving cheap, freshly made-to-order vegetable dish assemblages. If you've ever been to a Chipotle, you'll have an idea how it works. You step up to the counter and order one of the suggested favorites or else give instructions to the line cooks to create your own. First you choose your desired veggies from a wide assortment; then your grain (quinoa, or rice); then your sauce (spicy tomato, black bean, cilantro, or garlic yogurt); and finally, your crunchy toppings, everything from pumpkin seeds to chopped scallions. Your vegetables are flash-cooked and all ingredients assembled in a recyclable container to eat there in the sunny room, on the patio, or take out. (Beefsteak does offer a couple of meaty add-ons, such as chicken sausage, for those who simply can't do without.) Overwhelmed by choices, on my last visit I opted for the Eden, which combined quinoa, edamame, green beans, asparagus, broccoli, cilantro, garlic yogurt sauce, romaine, scallions, toasted sesame seeds, and lemon honey dressing. A second Beefsteak is located at 1528 Connecticut Ave. NW (© **202/986-7597**), in the Dupont Circle neighborhood.

800 22nd St. NW (at I St.). www.beefsteakveggies.com. © **202/296-1439.** Reservations not accepted. All items around $10. Weekdays 11am–6pm. Takeout and outdoor dining available. Metro: Foggy Bottom.

GEORGETOWN

The closest Metro stop to Georgetown is the Foggy Bottom station on the Blue, Orange, and Silver lines; from there you can walk or catch the DC Circulator bus on Pennsylvania Avenue.

Expensive

1789 ★★ AMERICAN   One of the city's top tables, the 1789 is the standard-bearer for old-world charm. The restaurant's six dining rooms occupy a renovated Federal-period house on a back street in Georgetown. Equestrian and historical prints, tables laid with Limoges china and silver, and antique furnishings throughout add touches of elegance. Women usually dress up and, while not required anymore, men still wear jackets to dinner. Romancing couples like Nicole Kidman and Keith Urban, world leaders like President Obama and German Chancellor Angela Merkel, and locals celebrating

dessert wars: CUPCAKES VS. ICE CREAM

D.C. made a splash on the cupcake scene years ago; it's TV-show-spawning Georgetown Cupcake still sees lines wrap around the block for its designer treats, while many Washingtonians will argue that there are better cupcakes at their go-to cakery. But these days, it seems like the dessert of the moment is ice cream (it helps that the new resident of the White House has a major weakness for the treat). Whichever your weakness, here are some sweet spots you need to try.

Cupcakes: Georgetown is ground zero for cupcakes in the city. **Georgetown Cupcake** (3301 M Street NW; www.georgetowncupcake.com; © **202/333-8448**) opened by two sisters in 2008 and launched the cupcake craze in Washington with its impeccably designed cupcakes. There's often a line here, but you don't have to wait in it. Instead, just place your order online the day before, and you'll be able to bypass the queue. Nearby, **Baked and Wired** (1052 Thomas Jefferson St. NW; www.bakedandwired.com; © **703/663-8727**) is often compared (and dare I say preferred?) to Georgetown Cupcake. The homey family-run bakery whips up cakes in a variety of tempting flavor combos, like the Smurfette, a summery lemon cake with blueberries mixed into the batter, with lemon buttercream frosting.

Ice Cream: Georgetown isn't just cupcake turf; there's some longstanding ice cream cred here too. Ask any university student and they'll point you to **Thomas Sweet** (3214 P Street NW; www.thomassweet.com; © **202/337-0616**), the no-frills corner spot scooping out ice creams, fro-yo, and frosty blend-ins. A newer ice cream purveyor with a devoted fanbase, **Ice Cream Jubilee**'s (1407 T St. NW; www.icecreamjubilee.com; © **202/299-9042**) creative flavors are entirely made in Washington. Try the banana Bourbon caramel or Thai iced tea ice creams, or the mango habanero sorbet. There's a second location in Navy Yard near Nationals Park. And if you're more of a gelato fan, head to **Dolcezza**, which has multiple locations around town (www.dolcezzagelato.com). This coffee and gelato shop uses ingredients from local farms in its seasonally inspired gelatos, which are freshly made each morning here in D.C.

birthdays and anniversaries are among those who dine here for the sense of momentousness the 1789 confers upon any occasion.

The kitchen has seen chefs come and go in the past few years, but the 1789, at 61 years old, is an old hand at handling change. Its cuisine has always been and always will be American, the emphasis more and more on produce grown on local farms and meats, seafood, and poultry bought "direct from their native regions." As classically formal as the 1789 is, the menu is thoroughly modern—for instance, the spicy tuna tartare with avocado, and the roasted rack of lamb with seared polenta. One thing you can be sure of is that your meal will be luscious. The team behind 1789 also runs the newly opened **Fitzgerald's** (fitzgeraldsdc.com) next door, where the cocktail-forward bistro menu leans on modern Japanese and Korean influences.

1226 36th St. NW (at Prospect St.). www.1789restaurant.com. © **202/965-1789.** Reservations recommended. Main courses $32–$59. Wed–Sun 5:30–9pm. Takeout available.

Chez Billy Sud ★★ FRENCH   With its pale green walls and gold-framed mirrors and prints, parquet floor, and wall-length banquette, Chez Billy Sud could only be French. That's how it seems to me, anyway. (The green hue of the walls reminds me of the gift boxes used by the Parisian tearoom and macaron shop Ladurée, which coincidentally opened a location in Georgetown, at 3060 M St. NW.) The cuisine showcases the dishes of southern France, satisfying the hankerings of Francophiles with escargots, steak frites, sautéed trout with fennel puree, and a flourless *torte au chocolat.* A courtyard offers additional seating in fine weather and also leads to Chez Billy's sidekick wine bar, **Le Bar a Vin,** equally charming with its exposed brick walls, dark-stained wood floor, and copper-topped bar.

1039 31st St. NW (btw. M and K sts.). www.chezbillysud.com. © **202/965-2606.** Reservations recommended. Main courses $21–$38. Wed–Thurs and Sun 5pm–9pm; Fri–Sat 5–10pm. Takeout and outdoor dining available.

Fiola Mare ★★★ ITALIAN   Strictly speaking, the Potomac River is not *Il Mare,* but as the watery view for one of the trendiest and certainly one of the finest seafood restaurants in D.C., the river certainly will do. Fiola Mare's stiffest competition comes from its own siblings, **Fiola** (p. 99) in the Penn Quarter and **Del Mar** at the Wharf in the Southwest Waterfront. Sit at one of the many outdoor balcony tables and you'll be gazing out at Roosevelt Island, Key Bridge, and a slice of Georgetown's waterfront to your right, and the Watergate apartments and the Kennedy Center to your left. Great views are also available within. The sprawling modern interior has a front bar and a back bar, and more than one dining area in between. The quietly proficient staff serve up a slate of specialty cocktails, like the standout gin and tonic. Fabio Trabocchi shines in his mastery of Italian seafood (for Spanish takes on seafood, head to Del Mar). The menu's different every day, but may begin with a taste of Italian caviar, followed by lobster crudo, and a too-generous portion of sea scallops with summer squash and a sun-gold tomato sauce. Also done to perfection are the pastas, like the blue crab rotolo. End with the *bombolini:* half a dozen ricotta doughnuts dusted with sugar, or the s'mores inspired campfire sundae with a caramel popcorn crunch.

3050 K St. NW, Suite 101 (at 31st St. NW and the Washington Harbour waterfront). www.fiolamaredc.com. © **202/525-1402.** Reservations recommended. Main courses $32–$75 lunch, $16–$52 brunch, $30–$65 dinner. Tues 4–9pm; Wed–Thurs 11:30am–9:30pm; Fri–Sat 11:30am–10pm; Sun 11:30am–9pm. Takeout and outdoor dining available.

Le Bar à Vin at Chez Billy Sud.

Moderate

Martin's Tavern ★ AMERICAN   A neighborhood fixture for nearly 90 years, this tavern has served presidents, dignitaries, and Hollywood stars, but it's best known as the place where JFK, then a U.S. senator, proposed to Jacqueline Bouvier on June 24, 1953. Hard-backed wooden booths line the walls of the restaurant, and many bear plaques identifying the former president or famous person who dined within; #3 is the "Proposal Booth." Fourth-generation Billy Martin, Jr. works the room, mingling with the regulars who frequent the place. "Tavern" is exactly the word to describe Martin's food, which is a bit on the traditional side (just like the tavern): Shepherd's pie and eggs benedict are listed, and so is Martin's Delight, which is roasted turkey on toast, smothered in rarebit sauce. Martin's offers a bit of old-guard Washington and Georgetown you're not going to get anywhere else, and that's mostly why I recommend it.

1264 Wisconsin Ave. NW (at N St.). www.martinstavern.com. © **202/333-6198.** Reservations accepted. Main courses $10–$22 lunch/brunch; $16–$40 dinner. Sun 9am–10:30pm; Mon–Thurs 11am–10:30pm; Fri 11am–11:30pm; Sat 9am–11:30pm. Takeout and outdoor dining available.

Inexpensive

Call Your Mother Bagels ★★ BAGELS   D.C. has a handful of decent bagel bakeries; Bullfrog Bagels, Bethesda Bagels, Pearl's Bagels … plus a handful of delis and bakeries who have loyal followings. But none of them have reached cult status the way Call Your Mother has, especially since the company opened their second outpost a few blocks from Georgetown University in 2020. CYM calls itself a "Jew-ish" deli, offering creative takes on classic dishes. There's the Latin pastrami, which loads jalapeños and spicy herb mayo on a rye-based pastrami sandwich, and playfully named bagel combos like the Sun City, with bacon or pastrami, eggs, cheese, and spicy honey. Keep an eye out for schmear flavors you've never tried before, like the cacio e pepe or nectarine cream cheese. There's always a line here; order ahead of time but you still may have to wait. That's okay though; the darling pink-and-teal building itself is worth a few photos while you're standing around. There's no indoor dining here; everything is to go. Call Your Mother has other shops in Park View (3301 Georgia Ave. NW), Capitol Hill (701 8th St. SE), and pops up at farmers markets around town. If you like pizza, check out sister concept **Timber Pizza** (809 Upshur St. NW; timberpizza.com; © **202/853-9746**), which puts a similarly playful spin on pizza combos.

3428 O St. NW (at 35th St.). callyourmotherdeli.com. $2.50–$14. Daily 8am–2pm. Takeout available.

Chaia ★ VEGETARIAN   Another taco shop? Not so fast. Chaia takes the fast-casual taco concept and puts a super-fresh, locally sourced, entirely vegetarian spin on it. Everything here is veggie-focused, and many of the menu items can made vegan, too, such as the chipotle sweet potato tacos, the roasted eggplant tacos, and the braised mushroom enchiladas. The beverage menu rounds out the restaurant's eco-trendy vibe, with house-made natural sodas, iced hibiscus tea, and elderberry kombucha. The Georgetown location is tucked next to the C&O Canal; there's a small courtyard with tables along the canal where you can enjoy your tacos on a nice day. There's a second location in Chinatown (615 I St. NW; © **202/290-1019**), and one on the way in the Maryland suburb of Bethesda (7237 Woodmont Ave.).

3297 Grace St. NW (at Wisconsin Ave.). chaiatacos.com. $3.50–$13. Tues–Sat 11am–9pm, Sun–Mon 11am–5pm. Takeout available.

Sweetgreen ★ LIGHT FARE   This now global salad chain began right here, in Georgetown. Sweetgreen was the brainchild of three eco-conscious Georgetown University students who wanted to provide homegrown, healthy options for diners. The first Sweetgreen opened nearby on M Street in 2007; today, these popular eateries number more than 120 nationwide, popping up all over D.C. including in Dupont Circle (1512 Connecticut Ave. NW; © **202/387-9338**), 14th & U Street Corridor (1461 P St. NW; © **202/234-7336**), Farragut Square (888 17th St. NW; © **202/506-3079**), and Penn Quarter (624 E St. NW; © **202/804-2250**). Choose one of the 15 or so signature salads (my fave, the guacamole greens: organic mesclun, avocado, roasted chicken, red onion, tomatoes, tortilla chips, fresh lime squeeze, lime cilantro jalapeno vinaigrette), or create your own. *Tip:* Get your salad to go and walk a few blocks to the Georgetown Waterfront, where you can enjoy your food on a park bench overlooking the Potomac River.

1044 Wisconsin Ave. NW. www.sweetgreen.com. © **202/838-4300.** Salads $10–$15. Daily 10:30am–9pm, Fri 10:30am–6pm. Takeout and outdoor dining available.

WOODLEY PARK & CLEVELAND PARK

Moderate

Indique ★ INDIAN   Staff from the Indian Embassy and others who know authentic Indian cuisine consider Indique's regional dishes the real deal. Favorite dishes are too many to mention, but definitely order the Punjabi chole, the tandoori chicken, and the lamb *vindaloo.* The two-level town house offers two different dining spaces: Upstairs is a beautiful room of brightly painted marigold and lime-hued walls, with the best tables overlooking the atrium; downstairs has a lively window-fronted bar area, a good spot for watching commuters bustling in and out of the Cleveland Park subway station and all else that's happening on busy Connecticut Avenue. The weekend brunch is a steal at $25 for unlimited plates, plus the option to add on unlimited cocktails ($12).

3512–14 Connecticut Ave. NW (btw. Porter and Ordway sts.). www.indique.com. © **202/244-6600.** Reservations accepted. Main courses $15–$22. Thurs–Sun 5pm–9pm; Sat–Sun 5pm–9:30pm. Takeout and outdoor dining available. Metro: Cleveland Park (Connecticut Ave. west exit).

Medium Rare ★ AMERICAN   If you like surprises, then this American steakhouse is not for you. But if you like what you know, and what you like

BUT FIRST, coffee

Starbucks isn't the only coffee game in town anymore. Independent coffee shops are pouring into D.C. and satisfying Washingtonians' love for a great cuppa joe while also supporting local businesses. While typically open early (7am) to late (8pm), most have cut back hours and close in the afternoon (around 3–5pm). Still plenty of time to caffeinate up for the draining museum circuit!

- Two former Marines who served together in Afghanistan established the original **Compass Coffee** (1535 7th St. NW; ✆ **202/838-3139**) in 2014, and it's grown to 12 locations in the area. The coffee menu regularly rotates nine varieties/flavors, and the interiors are spacious and airy, with free Wi-Fi.

- Founded in 2008, **Peregrine Espresso** (660 Pennsylvania Ave. SE; ✆ **202/629-4381**) was one of the first to arrive on D.C.'s independent coffee scene and has since expanded to another location on in Union Market. Its espresso and flash-brewed iced coffee are some of the best in D.C.

- Just steps from Dupont Circle, **Emissary** (2032 P St. NW; ✆ **202/748-5655**) is an independent neighborhood coffeehouse, bar, and cafe. Go in the morning for almond butter toast topped with sliced strawberries and a house-brewed matcha latte. Then go again at night for the grilled cheese and craft beers. Happy hour is Monday to Friday from 4 to 7pm. There's a second location at 1726 20th St NW (at S St. NW).

- Owner Joel Finkelstein takes his brew seriously at **Qualia Coffee** (3917 Georgia Ave. NW; ✆ **202/248-6423**). The beans are carefully sourced from around the world and roasted frequently and in small batches on-site. The coffee is always fresh, served within 3 days of roasting. Grab a bite here, too, and sit outside on the patio. If you're around Union Market, there's another Qualia not far away (10 Harry Thomas Way NE)

is steak, then this is the best place for it. This casual restaurant has been serving the same thing for 9 years—and it's not changing anytime soon. The menu is always a prix-fixe selection of rustic bread, mixed green salad, and *culotte* steak (a sirloin strip) with "secret sauce" and hand-cut fries, and it's delicious. (A grilled portobello mushroom is available off-menu for vegetarians.) The only decision you have to make is whether to get the apple pie, key lime pie, hot fudge sundae, double chocolate fudge three-layer cake, or six-layer carrot cake for dessert. The prix-fixe brunch menu (with a whopping five choices) is also meat-heavy: steak and eggs with "the perfect poached egg," egg frites and sausage, and French toast and sausage. Sit outside along Connecticut Avenue; yes, it can be noisy, but it's ideal for people-watching. Other locations are in and the suburbs of Bethesda, Maryland, and Arlington, Virginia.

3500 Connecticut Ave. NW (at Ordway St.). www.mediumrarerestaurant.com. ✆ **202/237-1432.** Reservations accepted. Dinner $44 per person; brunch $28 including bottomless juices, mimosas, and Bloody Marys. Dinner: Sun–Thurs 5–10pm; Fri–Sat 5–11pm; Brunch Sat–Sun 10:30am–2:30pm. Takeout and outdoor dining available.

6

EXPLORING WASHINGTON, D.C.

by Jess Moss

I f you've never been to Washington, D.C., your mission is clear: Get thee to the National Mall and Capitol Hill. Within this roughly 2½-by-⅓-mile rectangular plot lies the lion's share of the capital's iconic attractions (see "Iconic Washington, D.C.," in chapter 3), including presidential and war memorials, the U.S. Capitol, the U.S. Supreme Court, the Library of Congress, most of the Smithsonian museums, the National Gallery of Art, and the National Archives.

In fact, even if you have traveled here before, you're likely to find yourself returning to this part of town, to pick up where you left off on that long list of sites worth seeing, to visit new ones, like the **National Law Enforcement Museum** (p. 181), and to revisit favorites, which in the interim have often enhanced and updated their exhibits in the most captivating ways.

You'll want to know about the new **Dwight D. Eisenhower Memorial,** designed by Frank Gehry and dedicated to commemorating the life and career of the 34th president. Or **Black Lives Matter Plaza,** 1 block from the White House, where giant letters in the street spell out a reminder that the fight for racial justice continues in this city and country. You'll also want to tour the **Hall of Fossils** at the **Smithsonian National Museum of Natural History,** which recently underwent a complete renovation and representation of its more than 700 specimens, including near-complete skeletons of the T-Rex, triceratops, and a saber-toothed cat.

Beyond the Mall and its attractions, iconic or otherwise, lie the city's charming neighborhoods, standalone museums, historic houses, and beautiful gardens; you don't want to miss those, either. Tour national landmarks and you'll gain a sense of what this country is about, both politically and culturally. Tour off-the-Mall attractions and neighborhoods and you'll get a taste of the vibrant, multicultural scene that is the real D.C. This chapter helps you do both.

CAPITOL HILL

The **U.S. Capitol** and flanking Senate and House office buildings dominate this residential neighborhood of tree-lined streets, 19th-century town houses, and pubs and casual eateries. Across the street from the Capitol lie the **U.S. Supreme Court** and the **Library of Congress;** close by are the community shopping hub **Eastern Market** and an off-the-Mall Smithsonian, the **National Postal Museum.** Only a half-mile or so away is **Union Station,** doing triple duty as historical attraction, shopping mall, and transportation hub. But the neighborhood itself is a pleasure.

The Capitol ★★★ GOVERNMENT BUILDING   In Washington, D.C., one catches sight of the Capitol all around town. That's no accident: When planner Pierre L'Enfant laid out the capital in 1791, he purposely placed "Congress House" upon this bluff, overlooking the city. The importance of the Capitol and of Congress is meant to be unmistakable. When you visit here, you understand, in a very visceral way, just what it means to govern a country democratically. The fights and compromises, the din of differing opinions, the necessity of creating "one from the many" (*e pluribus unum*) without trampling on the rights of that one. It's a powerful experience. And the ideals of the Congress are not just expressed in the debates on the floor of the House and Senate (though you should try to hear those if you can; see below), but in

PLANNING AHEAD & booking online

Here's a crucial piece of advice: **Call ahead or check the websites of the places you plan to tour each day before you arrive in Washington.** Many of the city's government buildings, museums, memorials, and monuments closed down to the public as a public health precaution during the height of the pandemic. As I write this book, many have reopened, but they're operating on limited schedules or partial closures and things continue to change.

The good news is most sites are keeping their websites up to date, with regular updates on hours, visitor guidelines such as mask or vaccine requirements, and even which exhibits are open or closed. You can also call, but since hours may be limited, the web is your best bet for getting the latest info.

You'll also need to go online to actually *book* tickets to many museums, historic homes, and government buildings. While Washington's sights are still

overwhelmingly free to visit, social distancing and capacity considerations have caused many buildings to require visitors to sign up for a spot in advance. This includes attractions such as the National Archives, the Library of Congress, and the National Zoo.

Because timed ticket availability can be tricky, you'll need to be a little more thoughtful in your planning; it's just not as easy to pop into any sight as time opens up in your schedule.

While docent-led tours are typically available at many sites, they may not be offered when you arrive. If you prefer not to go the self-guided route, websites, such as GetYourGuide.com, Viator.com, and ToursByLocals.com can connect you with a local tour guide at various attractions; they also sometimes offer discounts on high-volume products like bus and boat tours. For more tour options, see Chapter 11.

its masterful architecture, as well as within the many historical works of art and artifacts displayed within the massive building.

More recently, this iconic American symbol has endured a series of trying events. The building closed to visitors in early 2020 as the coronavirus pandemic took hold. Then, on January 6, 2021, a riot broke out here as a mob attacked the Capitol to overturn the election of President Joe Biden. The building was vandalized, and violence erupted, resulting in the deaths of five people. At this writing, the Capitol remained heavily secured and off limits to visitors.

It's unclear when the building will reopen to the public, but when it does, it will undoubtedly still be a necessary stop on any first-time tour of D.C. When the time comes, here's what you can expect on a visit here, though check the website before your trip, as things are subject to change:

Before entering the Capitol, stand back to admire the Capitol dome, from its base up to the pedestal of the "Statue of Freedom," the 19-foot, 6-inch bronze female figure at its crown. The Capitol dome weighs 9 million pounds, roughly the same as 20 Statues of Liberty.

The 45-minute guided tour (for procedures, see p. 127) starts in the Capitol Visitor Center, where you'll watch a 13-minute orientation film, then takes you to the Crypt, the Rotunda, National Statuary Hall, and back to the Visitor Center. Here's some of what you'll see:

The **Rotunda**—a huge 96-foot-wide circular hall capped by a 180-foot-high dome—is the hub of the Capitol. The dome was completed, at Lincoln's direction, while the Civil War was being fought: "If people see the Capitol going on, it is a sign we intend the Union shall go on," said Lincoln. Thirteen presidents have lain in state here, with former president George H. W. Bush, in 2018, the most recent; when John F. Kennedy's casket was displayed, the line

The Capitol Dome.

395

Massachusetts Ave. NW

National Postal Museum 9

M

Union Station 8

F St. NW

Union Station

F St. NE

3rd St. NW

2nd St. NW

1st St. NW

North Capitol St.

New Jersey Ave. NW

E St. NW

Columbus Circle

E St. NE

Massachusetts Ave. NE

D St. NW

D St. NE

Dept. of Labor

Lower Senate Park

Louisiana Ave. NW

Delaware Ave. NE

1st St. NE

2nd St. NE

C St. NE

SENATE OFFICE BUILDINGS

Russell   Dirksen   Hart 7

Constitution Ave. NW

Constitution Ave. NE

Maryland Ave. NE

3rd St. NE

Pennsylvania Ave. NW

Supreme Court 6

A St. NE

CAPITOL HILL

Capitol Reflecting Pool

Capitol 1

Capitol Visitor Center entrances

East Capitol St.

Maryland Ave. SW

Thomas Jefferson Bldg. 2

John Adams Bldg. 5

U.S. Botanic Garden

LIBRARY OF CONGRESS

3rd St. SE

Independence Ave. SW

Independence Ave. SE

Pennsylvania Ave. SE

3rd St. SW

2nd St. SW

Washington Ave. SW

Bartholdi Park

HOUSE OFFICE BUILDINGS

Rayburn   Longworth   Cannon

James Madison Bldg. 3

4

St. SW

C St. SW

C St. SE

2nd

Spirit of Justice Park

Capitol South

M

D St. SE

Folger Park

South Capitol St.

1st St. SE

New Jersey Ave. SE

2nd St. SE

D St. SE

Providence Park

E St. SE

395

0   1/4 mi

0   0.25 km

Belmont-Paul Women's Equality National Monument **7**

U.S. Capitol **1**

Eastern Market **4**

Library of Congress:
James Madison Building **3**
John Adams Building **5**
Thomas Jefferson Building **2**

National Postal Museum **9**

Supreme Court **6**

Union Station **8**

of mourners stretched 40 blocks. It's an honor bestowed on only 32 people in 169 years, among them Congressman John L. Lewis and Supreme Court Justice Ruth Bader Ginsberg, both in 2020. On rare occasions, someone other than a president, military hero, or member of Congress receives posthumous recognition. In 2021, U.S. Capitol Police Officers Brian Sicknick and William Evans, who were killed in the line of duty, were honored. In 2018, the Reverend Billy Graham lay in honor in the Capitol. And in October 2005, Congress paid tribute to civil rights legend Rosa Parks by allowing her body to lie in honor here, different from lying in state.

Embracing the Rotunda walls are eight immense oil paintings commemorating great moments in American history, such as the presentation of the Declaration of Independence and the surrender of Cornwallis at Yorktown. Inside the inner dome of the Rotunda is an allegorical fresco masterpiece by Constantino Brumidi, *The Apotheosis of Washington,* a symbolic portrayal of George Washington surrounded by Roman gods and goddesses watching over the progress of the nation. Beneath those painted figures is a *trompe l'oeil* frieze depicting major developments in the life of America, from Columbus's landing in 1492 to the birth of the aviation age in 1903. Don't miss the sculptures in the Rotunda, including George Washington; a pensive Abraham Lincoln (sculpted from 1866 to 1871 by Vinnie Reams, the first woman artist to receive a government commission); a dignified Rev. Dr. Martin Luther King, Jr.; a ponderous trinity of suffragists, Elizabeth Cady Stanton, Susan B. Anthony, and Lucretia Mott; and a bronze statue of President Ronald Reagan, looking characteristically genial.

The **National Statuary Hall** was originally the chamber of the House of Representatives; in 1864 it became Statuary Hall, and the states were invited to send two statues each of native sons and daughters. There are 100 state-contributed statues in all throughout the Capitol.

Because of space constraints, only 38 statues from the Statuary collection reside in the Hall, with the figures of seven presidents displayed in the Rotunda (the Rotunda holds three other presidents' statues, which are not part of the Statuary Hall Collection), 24 statues placed in the Visitor Center, and the remaining 34 standing in the Crypt (directly below the Rotunda), the Hall of Columns

Heads-Up

Security precautions and procedures are a post-9/11 fact of life everywhere in America, but especially in the nation's capital, thanks to the preponderance of federal structures and attractions that are open to the public. What that means for you as a visitor is that you may have to stand in line to enter a national museum (like one of the Smithsonians) or a government building (like the U.S. Capitol). At many tourist sites, you can expect staff to search handbags, briefcases, and backpacks, either by hand or by X-ray machine. Some sites, including the National Air and Space Museum and the National Museum of Natural History, require you to walk past metal detectors. Carry as little as possible, and certainly no sharp objects. Museums and public buildings rarely offer lockers for use by visitors.

THE CAPITOL visitor center

The enormous, 4,000-person-capacity **Capitol Visitor Center** is underground, which means that as you approach the East Front of the Capitol, you won't actually see it. Look for signs and the sloping sets of steps on each side of the Capitol's central section, leading down to the center's entrances. Once inside you'll pass through security screening and then enter the two-level chamber.

Most visitors find it works best to explore the center after touring the Capitol. You can admire the 24 Statuary Hall statues scattered throughout and tour **Exhibition Hall,** a mini-museum of historic documents; check out interactive kiosks that take you on virtual tours of the Capitol, filling you in on history, art, and architecture; and view exhibits that explain the legislative process, including some for children. **Emancipation Hall** is the large central chamber where you line up for tours; this is also where you'll find the 26 restrooms and 530-seat restaurant and two gift shops.

When open to the public, the visitor center is open Monday through Saturday year-round from 8:30am to 4:30pm, closed on Thanksgiving, Christmas, New Year's Day, and Inauguration Day. It may also be closed for special events such as the State of the Union.

(directly beneath the Hall of the House of Representatives), and throughout the corridors of the Capitol.

In slow seasons, usually fall and winter, your public tour may include a visit to the **Old Supreme Court Chamber,** which has been restored to its mid-19th-century appearance. The Supreme Court met here from 1810 to 1860. Busts of the first four chief justices are on display—John Marshall, John Rutledge, John Jay, and Oliver Ellsworth—and so are some of their desks. The justices handed down a number of noteworthy decisions here, including in 1857 *Dred Scott v. Sandford,* which denied the citizenship of blacks, whether slaves or free, and in so doing precipitated the Civil War.

You will not see them on a tour, but the **south and north wings** of the Capitol hold the House and Senate chambers, respectively. You must obtain a pass from the office of your senator or representative to visit these galleries. (See below for info on watching Senate and House sessions.) The House of Representatives chamber is the setting for the president's annual State of the Union address.

Procedures for Touring the Capitol: When they're running, tours of the Capitol are free and take place year-round. Capitol guides lead the hour-long general-public tours, which can include as few as one or two people or as many as 40 or 50, depending on the season. These guides, who are often historians in their own right, repositories of American lore, traditions, anecdotes, and, actual fact. Got a question? Ask away. These guides know their stuff.

You and everyone in your party must have a **timed pass,** which you can order online at **www.visitthecapitol.gov.** During peak spring and summer sessions, you should order tickets at least 2 weeks in advance. Same-day passes are also available daily from the "Visitors Without Reservations" walk-up line near the information desks on the lower level of the visitor center—even during peak times, the guides seem somehow to accommodate the crowds, so always try for a tour, even if the online system indicates that no passes are available. You can also contact your representative or senator in Congress and request constituent tours, which are usually limited to groups of 15 and conducted by congressional staff, who may take you to notable places in the Capitol beyond those seen on the public tour. Nevertheless, I would recommend you stick with the regular Capitol tour, since the guides are more experienced and knowledgeable.

The Capitol has quite a list of items it prohibits; you can read the list online at www.visitthecapitol.gov (and also make sure that the Capitol will be open when you visit). Items ranging from large bags of any kind to food and drink are prohibited; leave everything you can back at the hotel.

Procedures for Visiting the House Gallery or Senate Gallery: Both the Senate and House galleries may open to visitors when either body is **in session ★–★★★**, so do try to sit in if you're able to. (The experience receives a range of star ratings because a visit can prove fascinating or deadly boring, depending on whether a debate is underway and how lively it is.) Children 5 and under are not allowed in the Senate gallery. You can obtain visitor passes at the offices of your representative and senators; District of Columbia and Puerto Rico residents can get passes from the office of their delegates to Congress. To find out your member's office location, go online at www.house.gov or www.senate.gov or call the main switchboard ✆ **202/225-3121.** You must have a separate pass for each gallery. Once obtained, the passes are good through the remainder of the Congress. *Note:* International visitors can obtain both House and Senate gallery passes by presenting a passport or a valid driver's license with photo ID to staff at the House and Senate appointments desks on the upper level of the visitor center.

The main, staffed offices of congressional representatives and delegates are in House buildings on the south (Independence Ave.) side of the Capitol; senators' main, staffed offices are located in Senate buildings on the north (Constitution Ave.) side. You should be able to pick up passes to both the Senate and House galleries in one place, at either your representative's office or one of your senators' offices. Visit the website of the Architect of the Capitol (**www.aoc.gov**) or the Visitor Center website (**www.visitthecapitol.gov**) or call the office of your senator or congressperson for more exact information about obtaining passes to the House and Senate galleries.

Tip: You'll know that the House and/or the Senate is in session if you see flags flying over their respective wings of the Capitol (*Remember:* House, south side; Senate, north side), or visit their websites, **www.house.gov** and **www.senate.gov,** for schedules of bill debates in the House and Senate, committee markups, and links to your Senate or House representative's page.

Capitol and Capitol Visitor Center: E. Capitol St. (at First St. NW). www.visitthecapitol. gov, www.aoc.gov, www.house.gov, www.senate.gov. ✆ **202/225-6827** (recording), 202/593-1768 (Office of Visitor Services), or 202/225-3121 (Capitol operator). Free admission. Parking at Union Station or on the streets. Metro: Union Station (Massachusetts Ave. exit) or Capitol South, then walk to the Capitol Visitor Center, located on the East Front of the Capitol.

Belmont-Paul Women's Equality National Monument ★ MUSEUM

Note: **The monument will be closed through 2022 for renovations.** Welcome to a national park site dedicated to women's history. The National Park Service roster of 417 national park units includes only a dozen or so focused on women's stories, so this is significant. Formerly known as the Sewall-Belmont House and Museum, this unassuming Federal-style, old brick house situated next to the Senate Hart Office Building has been the home of the National Woman's Party (NWP) since 1929. Suffragist and organizer extraordinaire Alice Paul founded the NWP in 1917 to fight for women's rights, including the right to vote, granted by Congress's passage of the 19th amendment in and official adoption into the Constitution in 1920. The house is a repository of suffragist memorabilia, banners, political buttons, photos of events, and other artifacts.

144 Constitution Ave. NE (at 2nd St.). www.nps.gov/bepa and www.nationalwomansparty.org. ℂ **202/546-1210.** Free admission. Wed–Sun 9am–5pm for walk-ins, with guided tours typically available at 9:30, 11am, 2, and 3:30pm. Entrance is on 2nd St.—look for the signs. Closed Thanksgiving, Dec 25, and New Year's Day. Metro: Union Station or Capitol South.

Eastern Market ★ MARKET

A mainstay of the historic Capitol Hill neighborhood and of the city itself, Eastern Market has been operating continuously since 1873, with the exception of a short closure in 2020. Inside, vendors sell fresh produce, pasta, seafood, meats, cheeses, sweets, flowers, and pottery Tuesday through Sunday. Every Tuesday from noon to 4pm, a farmers market operates outside the main hall. Things get really lively on weekends, when more than 100 arts and crafts merchants, plus an additional 20 or so farmers and open-air food vendors, sell their wares on the outdoor plazas surrounding the market. The street is closed to traffic in front of the market, and the block teems with families and singles doing their weekly grocery shopping. For a real hometown experience, come for the blueberry buckwheat pancakes ("bluebucks") served for breakfast at Market Lunch inside the market, until 11am Tuesday through Friday, and until 1:30pm Saturday and Sunday.

225 7th St. SE (at North Carolina Ave.). www.easternmarket-dc.org. ℂ **202/698-5253.** Free admission. Indoor market: Tues–Sun 9am–5pm; outdoor markets: Tues noon–4pm, Sat and Sun 9am–3pm. Closed Thanksgiving, Dec 25, and New Year's Day. Metro: Union Station or Capitol South.

Library of Congress ★★ LIBRARY

You're inside the main public building of the Library of Congress—the magnificent, ornate, Italian Renaissance-style **Thomas Jefferson Building.** Maybe you've arrived via the tunnel that connects the Capitol and the Library of Congress, or maybe you've climbed the Grand Staircase facing First Street and entered through the main doors. In any case, you'll likely be startled—very startled—to find yourself suddenly inside a government structure that looks more like a palace. Admire the stained-glass skylights overhead; the Italian marble floors inlaid with brass and concentric medallions; the gorgeous murals, allegorical paintings, stenciling, sculptures,

The Library of Congress.

and intricately carved architectural elements. This building, more than any other in the city, is a visual treasure.

Now for the history lesson: Established in 1800 by an act of Congress, "for the purchase of such books as may be necessary for the use of Congress," the library today also serves the nation, with holdings for the visually impaired (for whom books are recorded and/or translated into Braille), scholars and researchers in every field, college students, journalists, and teachers. Its first collection was destroyed in 1814 when the British burned the Capitol (where the library was then housed) during the War of 1812. Thomas Jefferson then sold the institution his personal library of 6,487 books as a replacement for roughly $23,000 in 1815, and this became the foundation of what is today the world's largest library.

The Jefferson Building was erected between 1888 and 1897 to hold the burgeoning collection and to establish America as a cultured nation with magnificent institutions equal to anything in Europe. Originally intended to hold the fruits of at least 150 years of collecting, the Jefferson Building was filled up in a mere 13 years. It is now supplemented by the **James Madison Memorial Building** and the **John Adams Building.**

Today the collection contains a mind-boggling 170 million items, more than 24 million catalogued books; 72 million manuscripts; millions of prints and photographs, audio holdings, movies, and videotapes; musical instruments from the 1700s; and the letters and papers of everyone from George Washington to Groucho Marx. Its archives also include the letters, oral histories, photographs, and other documents of war veterans from World War I to the present, all part of its **Veterans History Project;** go to www.loc.gov/vets to listen to or read some of these stories, especially if you plan on visiting the National World War II Memorial (p. 157).

In addition to its art and architecture, the Library exhibits objects from its permanent collections. "Mapping a New Nation: From Independence to Statehood" showcases the first map of the newly independent United States and other maps of the northeastern and southeastern regions of the U.S. An ongoing show is "Shall Not Be Denied: Women Fight for the Vote." Always on view are two 1450s Bibles from Germany: the handwritten Giant Bible of Mainz and the Gutenberg Bible, the first book printed with movable metal type in Europe.

The concerts that take place in the Jefferson Building's Whittall Pavilion and in the elegant **Coolidge Auditorium** are free but require tickets, which you can obtain at www.loc.gov/events. Across Independence Avenue from the Jefferson Building is the **Madison Building,** which houses venues for author readings and other events.

Using the library: Visitors must register for a timed entry pass to access the library; you can do so at www.loc.gov/visit. At press time, only the Jefferson Building was open to the public, and on a limited basis, on Thursday, Friday, and Saturday between 10am and 3pm. Check the library's website for updated hours and tour availability, as the schedule is likely to change.

If you're looking to use the library's collections for research you will need to obtain a user card with your photo on it (see wwws.loc.gov/readerreg/remote/). Once you've registered for your user card, you'll need to make an appointment in a specific reading room by calling that room's phone number (listed on the library's website) or use the online Ask-a-Librarian service at ask.loc.gov. All books must be used on-site.

Jefferson Bldg.: 10 First St. SE, btw. Independence Ave. and E. Capitol St. Madison Bldg.: 101 Independence Ave. SE (at First St. SE). www.loc.gov. ⓒ **202/707-8000.** Free admission. Jefferson Bldg.: Thurs–Sat 10am–4pm. Stop at an information desk on the ground floor of the Jefferson Bldg. Metro: Capitol South.

National Postal Museum ★ MUSEUM   If you're at all interested in the romance and adventure of the story of U.S. mail correspondence and its delivery (that's right, I said romance and adventure!), and in the international artistry and invention of that most miniature of art forms, the postage stamp, you really need to venture into this less-visited Smithsonian museum. You'll find yourself in the elegant lobby of a historic structure designed by Daniel Burnham in 1914. The building operated as a post office until 1986; it was reborn in 1993 as the Postal Museum.

Head downstairs to tour the original part of the museum, where America's postal history from 1673 to the present is on display. In the central exhibit area called **Moving the Mail,** you'll see planes, trains, and other postal vehicles that have been used at one time or another to transport the mail. Kids delight in the sight of Owney the Dog, a replica of the scruffy pup that traveled with postal workers aboard Rail Mail Service trains in the late 19th century, becoming the unofficial mascot of the RMS.

In **Binding the Nation,** visitors can follow a path through a forest to trace the steps of mail carriers who traveled from New York to Boston in 1673, and climb into a stagecoach headed west. The exhibit introduces famous figures, like Buffalo Bill, of Pony Express renown; and founding father Benjamin Franklin in his role first as postmaster general for the British colonial post and then as postmaster general for the United Colonies.

Other exhibits cover mail's impact on city streets and rural routes (**Customers & Communities**), the journey a single letter takes through the postal system and how that process has changed over time (**Systems at Work**), and the history and current practice of getting mail delivered to and from military personnel (**Mail Call**). **Behind the Badge** reveals the work of the U.S. Postal Inspection Service: Established in 1776, the federal agency is responsible for restoring mail service after disasters, spotting and preventing mail fraud, and keeping mail safe from the likes of Unabombers and lesser criminals.

Return upstairs to explore the **William H. Gross Stamp Gallery ★★★**, the world's largest stamp gallery. On view are displayed treasures from the museum's six-million-piece **National Stamp Collection,** including its rarest U.S. acquisition, the 1868 1-cent "Z-grill" stamp, one of only two known to be pressed into a grill pattern. Interactive kiosks, videos, and activities keep even the non-stamp-collector interested, enthralled even. The **World of Stamps** permanent exhibit features a hit list of famous stamps, starting with the very first postage stamp, the 1840 Penny Black, bearing the profile of a young Queen Victoria. **Stamps Around the Globe** displays international stamps from 24 countries, which make up more than half the Postal Museum's overall collection. Viewing these miniature artworks is a thrill.

Don't miss the last gallery, the **Postmasters Suite,** housed in a gorgeous, six-sided paneled room. It's reserved for special exhibits. Sports fans will love the exhibit **"Baseball: America's Home Run,"** on view through January 2025 and featuring hundreds of U.S. and international stamps commemorating great players and historic moments.

Tip: The Postal Museum's wall of windows features replicas of 54 historic U.S. stamps; come by at nighttime and you'll see the artwork illuminated.

2 Massachusetts Ave. NE (at First St.). www.postalmuseum.si.edu. ✆ **202/633-5555.** Free admission. Daily 10am–5:30pm. Closed Dec 25. Metro: Union Station.

The Supreme Court of the United States ★★★ GOVERNMENT BUILDING   On many days, the Supreme Court is the most exciting place to be in town, though at press time, the building was closed to visitors. It's unclear when this will change, but when the court does admit the public again, here's what you can expect:

Beginning on the first Monday in October, the nine justices hear cases, later to render opinions that can dramatically affect every American. Visitors may attend these proceedings, in which lawyers representing opposing sides attempt to make a convincing case for their clients, even as the justices interrupt repeatedly and question them sharply to clarify the constitutional principles at stake. It's a grand show, fast-paced, sometimes heated, and always full of weighty import (the justices hear only about 80 of the most vital of the 7,000 to 8,000 or so petitions filed with the Court every year). The Court's rulings are final, reversible only by an Act of Congress. And you, the visitor, get a close-up seat…if you're lucky (see below for info on getting in).

But even when the court isn't in session, touring the building is a worthwhile experience. During those periods, docents offer 30-minute lectures inside the Supreme Court chamber to introduce visitors of all ages to the Court's judicial functions, the building's history, and the architecture of the courtroom. Lectures take place every hour on the half-hour, beginning at 9:30am on days when the Court is not sitting and at a later time on Court days. You can also tour the building on your own.

Getting in to see a case being argued: Starting the first Monday in October and continuing through late April, the Court "sits" for 2 weeks out of every month to hear two 1-hour arguments each day Monday through Wednesday, from 10am to noon, with occasional afternoon sessions scheduled as necessary starting at 1pm. You can find out the specific dates, names of arguments, and case descriptions on the Court's website and over the phone (see below).

Plan on arriving at the Supreme Court at least 90 minutes in advance of a scheduled argument during the fall and winter, and as early as 3 hours ahead in March and April, when students from schools on spring break lengthen the line. (Dress warmly; the stone plaza is exposed and can be witheringly cold.) Controversial cases also attract crowds; if you're not sure whether a particular case has created a stir, call the Court info line to reach someone who can tell you. The Court allots only about **150 first-come, first-served seats** to the public, but that number fluctuates, depending on the number of seats that have been reserved by the lawyers arguing the case, law clerks, special guests, and the press. The Court police officers direct you into one line initially; when the doors finally open, you form a second line if you want to attend only 3 to 5 minutes of the argument. Seating begins at 9:30am for those attending the full argument and at 10am for those who want to catch just a few minutes.

If you attend an oral argument, you may find yourself present as well for the release of a Supreme Court opinion, since the justices precede the hearing of new oral arguments with the announcement of their opinions on previously heard arguments, if any opinions are ready. If you're visiting the Court in May or June, you won't be able to attend an argument, but you might still see the justices in action, delivering an opinion, during a 10am 15-minute session in the courtroom. To attend one of these sessions, you must wait in line on the plaza, following the same procedure outlined above.

Leave cameras and recording devices at your hotel—they're not allowed in the courtroom. Small children and infants are allowed but not recommended. *Note:* Security procedures require you to leave all your belongings—outerwear, purses, books, sunglasses, cell phones, and so on—in a cloak room with complimentary lockers.

1 First St. NE (btw. E. Capitol St. and Maryland Ave. NE). www.supremecourt.gov. © **202/ 479-3000** or 202/479-3030 (recording). Free admission. Mon–Fri 9am–4:30pm. Closed all federal holidays. Metro: Capitol South or Union Station.

Union Station ★ ARCHITECTURAL ICON/MARKET   When it opened in 1907, this was the largest train station in the world. It was designed by noted architect Daniel H. Burnham, who modeled it after the Baths of Diocletian and the Arch of Constantine in Rome, so its facade has Ionic colonnades fashioned from white granite and 100 sculptured eagles. Graceful 50-foot Constantine

arches mark the entryways, above which are poised six carved figures representing Fire, Electricity, Freedom, Imagination, Agriculture, and Mechanics. Inside is the **Main Hall,** a massive rectangular room with a 96-foot barrel-vaulted ceiling, an expanse of white-marble flooring, and a balcony adorned with 36 Augustus Saint-Gaudens sculptures of Roman legionnaires. Off the Main Hall is the **East Hall,** shimmering with scagliola marble walls and columns, a gorgeous hand-stenciled skylight ceiling, and stunning murals of classical scenes inspired by ancient Pompeiian art.

Union Station.

In its time, this "temple of transport" has witnessed many important events. President Wilson welcomed General Pershing here in 1918 on his return from France. South Pole explorer Rear Admiral Richard Byrd was also feted at Union Station on his homecoming. And Franklin D. Roosevelt's funeral train, bearing his casket, was met here in 1945 by thousands of mourners.

But after the 1960s, with the decline of rail travel, the station fell on hard times. Rain caused parts of the roof to cave in, and the entire building—with floors buckling, rats running about, and mushrooms sprouting in damp rooms—was sealed in 1981. That same year, Congress enacted legislation to preserve and restore this national treasure, to the tune of $160 million. A remarkable 6-year restoration involving hundreds of European and American artisans returned the station to its original design. This also turned the station into a major shopping destination—before the pandemic there were about 100 shops and restaurants lining the halls (p. 208).

Union Station never closes, never pauses. But the slowdown in travel in recent years took its toll on the bustle that surrounds the station. Many shops and eateries have closed—you'll still have no problem finding a bite at a fast casual spot or killing time in shops before your train, but at this writing there are more empty storefronts on the station's three levels than open.

Several tour-bus companies use the station as a point of arrival and departure and operate ticket booths inside the front hall of the main concourse. (See p. 300 for info about tours.) Amtrak, the commuter MARC trains, Metrorail trains and Metrobuses, DC Circulator buses, taxis, rental cars, local drivers and pedestrians, and the DC Streetcar all converge on Union Station; see chapter 11 for details about Union Station as a transportation hub.

50 Massachusetts Ave. NE. www.unionstationdc.com. © **202/289-1908.** Free admission. Station daily 24 hr. Shops Mon–Sat 10am–9pm; Sun noon–6pm. Machines located inside the station near the exit/entrance to the parking garage will validate your ticket, allowing you these reduced rates: $5 for the first hr., $7 for 2 hr., $20 for 2–10 hr., and $24 for up to 24 hr. Metro: Union Station.

THE NATIONAL MALL & MEMORIAL PARKS

This one's the biggie, folks. More than one-third of the capital's major attractions lie within this complex of parkland that the National Park Service calls the **National Mall and Memorial Parks.** The centerpiece of this larger plot, the National Mall (p. 150) extends from the Capitol to the Potomac River, and from Constitution Avenue to down and around the cherry-tree-ringed Tidal Basin. Presidential and war memorials, the Washington Monument, the Martin Luther King, Jr. Memorial, 11 Smithsonian museums, the National Gallery of Art, the National Archives, and the U.S. Botanic Garden are all here.

The National Mall itself, and the memorials, are open 24/7 for visiting. Rangers and volunteer guides on duty from 9:30am to 10pm daily rotate and rove from memorial to memorial throughout the day to answer questions. If you don't see a ranger at, say, the FDR Memorial, you might at your next likely stop, the nearby MLK Memorial. In addition to being available to respond to queries, rangers lead history-based or themed bike tours, talks, and walks throughout National Mall and Memorial Parks. Check the National Mall and Memorial Parks calendar online (**www.nps.gov/nama/planyour visit/calendar.htm**) to see what's on tap while you're here. All set? Let's get started.

Arts and Industries Building ★ ARCHITECTURE   Completed in 1881 just in time to host President James Garfield's inaugural ball, this red-brick and sandstone structure was the first Smithsonian museum on the Mall, and the first U.S. National Museum. The building is mostly closed to the public except for special events and exhibitions. If there isn't a current show to see inside, you can always admire the building's exterior. Weather permitting, a 19th-century **carousel** operates across the street on the Mall.

900 Jefferson Dr. SW (on the south side of the Mall). www.aib.si.edu. Metro: Smithsonian (Mall exit). DC Circulator stop.

D.C. War Memorial ★ MONUMENT/MEMORIAL   This often-overlooked memorial commemorates the lives of the 499 citizens of Washington, D.C., who died in World War I. It's worth a stop on your way to grander, more famous edifices. President Herbert Hoover dedicated the memorial in 1931; John Phillip Sousa conducted the Marine band at the event. The structure is a graceful design of 12 Doric columns supporting a classical circular dome. The names of the 499 dead are inscribed in the stone base.

North side of Independence Ave. SW (btw. the National World War II and Lincoln memorials). www.nps.gov/nama/planyourvisit/dc-war-memorial.htm. Metro: Smithsonian (12th St./Independence Ave. exit), with a 25-min. walk. Near DC Circulator stop at MLK Memorial.

Enid A. Haupt Garden ★ GARDEN   Named for its donor, a noted supporter of horticultural projects, this pretty 4¼-acre garden presents elaborate flower beds and borders, plant-filled turn-of-the-20th-century urns, 1870s

Loop the National Mall Aboard the DC Circulator

Getting to the top attractions of the Mall is easy, thanks to the DC Circulator's National Mall route. This bus runs on a permanent, year-round, continuously looping National Mall circuit that begins and ends at Union Station, stopping at 15 points along the way. In winter, the Loop (my name for it, and I'm sticking with it) travels 7am to 7pm Monday to Friday, and 9am to 7pm Saturday to Sunday; in summer, the Loop operates 7am to 8pm Monday to Friday, and 9am to 8pm Saturday to Sunday. As with all the other Circulators, buses come by every 10 minutes, and you may board them at any of its stops. The National Mall route from Union Station takes you down Louisiana Avenue and around the Mall via the inside roads of Madison, Jefferson, West Basin, East Basin, and Ohio drives, as well as Constitution Avenue. Stops include the National Gallery of Art, the National Museum of American History, the Washington Monument, the Lincoln Memorial, and more—every place you'd want to go, in other words. The fare is $1 and if you pay with a SmarTrip Card, you'll be able to reboard for free within a 2-hour window. I've noted when an attraction is served by the Circulator in the listings in this section.

cast-iron furnishings, and lush baskets hung from reproduction 19th-century lampposts. The garden is planted on the rooftops of the subterranean Ripley Center and Sackler and African Art museums.

Most captivating is the **parterre** of symmetrically arranged plots whose vividly colorful and varied plantings change season by season. The ornamental garden patterns complement the Victorian architecture of the nearby Smithsonian Castle. The tranquil **Moongate Garden** near the Sackler Gallery employs water and granite in a landscape design inspired by a 15th-century Chinese temple. Two 9-foot-tall pink-granite moon gates frame a pool paved with half-rounds of granite. Benches backed by English boxwoods sit under a canopy of weeping cherry trees.

The **Fountain Garden** outside the African Art Museum replicates an Islamic garden, complete with elements of geometrical symmetry, low walls, a central fountain, and water cascading down the face of a stone wall. Five majestic linden trees shade a seating area around the **Downing Urn,** a memorial to American landscapist Andrew Jackson Downing, who designed the National Mall. Elaborate cast-iron carriage gates made according to a 19th-century design by James Renwick salute the Independence Avenue entrance. 10th St. and Independence Ave. SW. www.gardens.si.edu. ⓒ**202/633-2220.** Free admission. Daily dawn–dusk except Christmas. Metro: Smithsonian (12th St./Independence Ave. exit). DC Circulator stop.

Franklin Delano Roosevelt Memorial ★★ MONUMENT/MEMORIAL
Since it opened in 1997, the FDR Memorial has proven to be one of the most popular of the presidential memorials. Its popularity has to do as much with its design as the man it honors. This 7½-acre outdoor memorial stretches out, maze-like, rather than rising up, across the stone-paved floor. Granite walls define the four "galleries," each representing a different term in FDR's presidency, from

Great Depression sculpture at the FDR Memorial.

1933 to 1945. Architect Lawrence Halprin's design includes waterfalls, sculptures and Roosevelt's own words carved into the stone.

The many displays of cascading water can sound thunderous, as the fountains recycle an astonishing 100,000 gallons of water every minute. Their presence isn't a random choice: They reflect FDR's appreciation for the importance of H_2O. As someone afflicted with polio, he understood the rehabilitative powers of water exercises and established the Warm Springs Institute in Georgia to help others with polio. As president, FDR supported several water projects, including the creation of the Tennessee Valley Authority. A favorite time to visit the memorial is at night, when dramatic lighting reveals the waterfalls and statues against the dark parkland. (***Note:*** Fountains are shut off in cold weather.)

Conceived in 1946, the FDR Memorial had been in the works for 50 years. Part of the delay in its construction can be attributed to the president himself: FDR had told his friend, Supreme Court Justice Felix Frankfurter, "If any memorial is erected to me, I know exactly what I should like it to be. I should like it to consist of a block about the size of this (putting his hand on his desk) and placed in the center of that green plot in front of the Archives Building." In fact, such a memorial and plaque sit in front of the National Archives (Pennsylvania Ave. entrance). Friends and relatives struggled to honor Roosevelt's request to leave it at that, but Congress and national sentiment overrode them.

As with other presidential memorials, this one opened to some controversy. Advocates for people with disabilities were incensed that the memorial sculptures did not show the president in a wheelchair, which he used after he contracted polio. The National Organization on Disability raised funds for the additional statue of a wheelchair-bound FDR; it's at the very front of the memorial, to the right as you approach the first gallery. In the gift shop is a replica of Roosevelt's wheelchair, as well as a rare photograph of the president sitting in a wheelchair. The memorial is probably the most accessible tourist attraction in D.C.; as at most National Park Service locations, wheelchairs are available for free use on-site. Thirty minutes is sufficient for a visit.

On West Basin Dr., alongside the Tidal Basin in West Potomac Park (across Independence Ave. SW from the Mall). www.nps.gov/frde. ✆ **202/426-6841.** Free admission. Open 24 hr. daily. Limited parking. Metro: Smithsonian (12th St./Independence Ave. exit), with a 20-min. walk. DC Circulator stop.

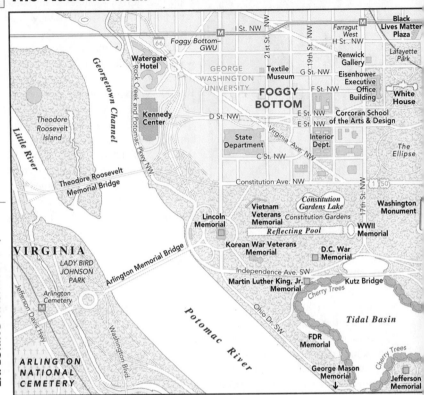

National Museum of Asian Art ★★ MUSEUM   Two major galleries, the **Freer Gallery of Art** and the **Arthur M. Sackler Gallery,** come together to form the Smithsonian's museum dedicated to the preservation and interpretation of Asian art. Together, the collection spans 44,000 objects from China, Japan, Korea, South and Southeast Asia, and the Islamic world.

While part of the same "museum" the two galleries are housed in separate buildings, a short walk apart via an underground passage:

Freer Gallery of Art: This single museum houses one of the world's finest permanent collections of Asian art as well as the most comprehensive assemblage of the works of American artist James McNeill Whistler.

The museum's namesake, Charles Lang Freer, was a self-taught connoisseur, who started out in the 1880s collecting American art, specifically living American artists, including his friend, the British-based Whistler. It was Whistler's affinity for Japanese and Chinese art that got Freer interested in collecting Asian art. (Galleries near the Peacock Room display other works by Whistler that clearly show the influence of Asian art and techniques on his own style.) Soon Freer's Asian art collection outgrew his American art collection; today,

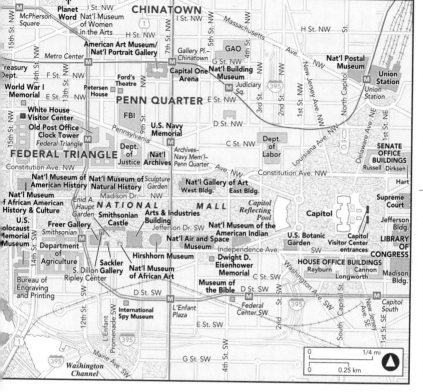

of the gallery's 25,000 objects spanning 6,000 years (from China, Japan, Korea, Syria, Iraq, Iran, India, Pakistan, Turkey, Central Asia, and Egypt), with only a small number of American works.

This Italian Renaissance–style building, unlike many of its Smithsonian sisters, is usually blessedly uncrowded, making it a wonderful place to escape D.C.'s throngs. The main galleries lie on one level and encircle a lovely, landscaped central courtyard. It's possible to stroll unhurried through the skylit rooms, which hold an astonishingly wide array of wonders, such as fine jewelry from the Chinese Liangzhu culture (which flourished during the late Neolithic and Bronze ages—we're talking 6,000 years ago); a 1760 Japanese handscroll depicting "One Hundred Old Men Gathering for a Drink Party"; 12th-century illuminated manuscripts of sacred texts created by Jain artists of western India; a monumental hammered-brass Iranian candlestick from the late 12th century; exquisite Japanese screens; a beautiful, turquoise-glazed jar from late-12th-century Syria; giant and forbidding-looking 14th-century Japanese wooden figures that stood guard outside the entrance to a temple near Osaka; and the Freer's single permanent installation, Whistler's famous (and drop-dead gorgeous) *Harmony in Blue and Gold: The Peacock Room,* conceived as a dining room for the London mansion of wealthy client F. R. Leyland.

Arthur M. Sackler Gallery: The other half of the gallery duo, the Sackler Gallery exists because primary benefactor Arthur M. Sackler gave the Smithsonian Institution 1,000 works of Asian art and $4 million to put toward museum construction. When it opened in 1987, the gallery held mostly ancient works, including early Chinese bronzes and jades, centuries-old Near East ceramics, and sculpture from South and Southeast Asia. Pieces from that stellar permanent collection continue to be on rotating view in several underground galleries, along with other precious works acquired over the years, like an assemblage of Persian book artistry and 20th-century Japanese ceramics. The collection now numbers 15,000 objects.

In the museum's street-level pavilion is a changing exhibit called **Perspectives,** always featuring captivating pieces by a contemporary Asian or Asian-diaspora artist. You'll encounter another work of contemporary art as you descend the stairs to tour the main galleries. The sculpture suspended from the skylit atrium and into the stairwell is called *Monkeys Grasp for the Moon* and was designed specifically for the gallery by Chinese artist Xu Bing. The work links 21 laminated wood pieces, each of which spells the word "monkey" in one of a dozen languages.

Freer Gallery of Art: Jefferson Dr. SW at 12th St. SW (on the south side of the Mall). ℂ **202/633-1000.** Arthur M. Sackler Gallery: 1050 Independence Ave. SW. www.asia.si.edu. ℂ **202/633-4880**). Both galleries: Free admission. Fri–Tues 10am–5:30pm. Closed Dec 25. Metro: Smithsonian (Mall/Jefferson Dr. exit). DC Circulator stop.

George Mason Memorial ★ MONUMENT/MEMORIAL George Mason's name is not famous today, but it should be: He was the Virginia politician who authored the Virginia Declaration of Rights, upon which the first part of the U.S. Declaration of Independence is based, as well as the first 10 amendments to the U.S. Constitution, known as the Bill of Rights. Dedicated in 2002, the memorial consists of a bronze statue of Mason, dressed in 18th-century garb, from buckled shoes to tricorn hat, set back in a landscaped grove of trees and flower beds. Two stone slabs are inscribed with some of Mason's words, like these, referring to Mason's rejection of slavery: THAT SLOW POISON, WHICH IS DAILY CONTAMINATING THE MINDS & MORALS OF OUR PEOPLE. An interesting stand for a slave-owner to take, wouldn't you say? *Note:* The memorial is easy to miss, because it does not lie on the Tidal Basin path. As you approach the Jefferson Memorial from the direction of the FDR Memorial, or as you approach the FDR Memorial from the direction of the Jefferson, you'll come to the bridge that arches over the inlet leading from the Tidal Basin to the Potomac River; look straight across from the bridge, and there you'll see it.

E. Basin and Ohio drs. SW (btw. the Jefferson and FDR memorials). www.nps.gov/gemm. ℂ **202/426-6841.** Free admission. Open 24 hr. daily. Limited parking. Metro: Smithsonian (12th St./Independence Ave. exit), with a 25-min. walk. DC Circulator stop.

Hirshhorn Museum and Sculpture Garden ★★ ART MUSEUM   This cylindrically shaped, concrete-and-granite building holds provocative art at its best, from de Kooning to Jeff Koons. Exhibits here focus on "art of the moment," which means they're always changing—expect to see works like Thomas Hart Benton's dizzying sprawl of figures in his 1920 painting *People of Chilmark,* Ellsworth Kelly's vivid minimalist paintings, and Damien Hirst's *The Asthmatic Escaped II, 1992,* in which one of two conjoined glass cases holds a camera on a tripod, and the other holds the clothing, inhaler, and other personal effects of "the escaped." The museum rotates works from its 12,000-piece collection, 600 at any one time, so if these artworks are not on view, others in the avant-garde family will be. Exhibitions also feature artwork on loan as well as commissions for the space, meaning you can only see it here.

You might also catch some of its newest acquisitions: the two Infinity Mirror Rooms by Yayoi Kusama and two new sculptures in the sculpture garden from Sterling Ruby and Huma Bhabha. Don't overlook the special exhibits either, which feature shows like *One with Eternity: Yayoi Kusama,* from the museum's collection, and one of the largest collections of artwork by Marcel Duchamp, the grandfather of contemporary art.

One of the most popular activations here is the "Wish Tree," by Yoko Ono. In spring and summer, visitors are asked to handwrite a wish for peace and tie it to this dogwood tree in the garden.

Speaking of the garden, the museum's 4.3-acre outdoor sculpture garden is undergoing its first renovation in almost 40 years, and at press time, an end date had not been released. The redesign, the work of Japanese artist and architect Hiroshi Sugimoto, calls for a complete redo of the formerly sunken garden. Adjacent to the National Mall, the below-ground garden was barely visible to both Mall and museum visitors. In 1974, acclaimed architect Gordon Bunshaft originally envisioned a much larger garden that traversed the entire National Mall's width and featured a substantial reflecting pool, but his ideas were never fully realized. As part of the renovation, the entrance will be enhanced, so that it's no longer below ground level. Initial concept designs also include reopening

The Hirshhorn Art Museum

the underground passage connecting the garden to the museum plaza, which has been closed for more than 30 years. During construction, visitors will find many of the sculptures throughout the museum, while others will unfortunately not be on display. *Note:* The Hirshhorn's Sculpture Garden and the **National Gallery of Art's Sculpture Garden** (p. 150), located directly across the Mall from each other **are not the same!** They offer two very different experiences.

The Hirshhorn exists thanks to a man named Joseph H. Hirshhorn, who was born in Latvia in 1899 but immigrated to the United States as a boy. In 1966, Hirshhorn donated his collection of more than 6,000 works of modern and contemporary art to the United States in gratitude for the country's welcome to him and other immigrants and bequeathed an additional 5,500 upon his death in 1981. The museum opened in 1974.

You can grab some refreshments at the coffee and gelato bar run by Dolcezza. There's also a fun store that art lovers will, well, love.

Independence Ave. at 7th St. SW (on the south side of the Mall). www.hirshhorn.si.edu. © **202/633-4674.** Free admission. Museum daily 10am–5:30pm. Sculpture Garden daily 7:30am–dusk. Closed Dec 25. Metro: L'Enfant Plaza (Smithsonian Museums/Maryland Ave. or Smithsonian exit). DC Circulator stop.

Jefferson Memorial ★★ MONUMENT/MEMORIAL   President John F. Kennedy, at a 1962 dinner honoring 29 Nobel Prize winners, told his guests that they were "the most extraordinary collection of talent, of human knowledge, that has ever been gathered together at the White House, with the possible exception of when Thomas Jefferson dined alone." Jefferson penned the Declaration of Independence and served as George Washington's secretary of state, John Adams's vice president, and America's third president. He spoke out against slavery—although, like many of his countrymen, he kept slaves himself. He also established the University of Virginia and pursued wide-ranging interests, including architecture, astronomy, anthropology, music, and farming.

Franklin Delano Roosevelt, a great admirer of Jefferson, spearheaded the effort to build him a memorial, although the site choice was problematic. The Capitol, the White House, and the Mall were already located in accordance with architect Pierre L'Enfant's master plan for the city, and there was no spot for such a project that would maintain L'Enfant's symmetry. So, the memorial was built on land reclaimed from the Potomac River, perched upon the lip of the manmade reservoir now known as the Tidal Basin. Roosevelt laid the memorial cornerstone in 1939 and had all the trees between the Jefferson Memorial and the White House cut down so that he could see the memorial every morning.

The memorial is a columned rotunda in the style of the Pantheon in Rome, whose classical architecture Jefferson himself introduced to this country (he designed his home, Monticello, and the earliest University of Virginia buildings in Charlottesville). On the Tidal Basin side, the sculptural group above the entrance depicts Jefferson with Benjamin Franklin, John Adams, Roger Sherman, and Robert Livingston, all of whom worked on drafting the Declaration of Independence. The domed interior of the memorial contains the 19-foot bronze statue of Jefferson standing on a 6-foot pedestal of black Minnesota granite. The sculpture is the work of Rudolph Evans, chosen from among more than 100 artists in a nationwide competition. Jefferson is depicted wearing a fur-collared coat given to him by his close friend, the Polish General Tadeusz Kosciuszko. If you follow Jefferson's gaze, you see that the Jefferson Memorial and the White House have an unimpeded view of each other.

Ohio Dr. SW, at the south shore of the Tidal Basin (in West Potomac Park). www.nps.gov/thje. *C* **202/426-6841.** Free admission. Open 24 hr. daily. Limited parking. Metro: Smithsonian (12th St./Independence Ave. exit), with a 20- to 30-min. walk. DC Circulator stop.

Korean War Veterans Memorial ★ MONUMENT/MEMORIAL   This privately funded memorial, founded in 1995, honors those who served in the Korean War, a 3-year conflict (1950–53) that produced almost as many casualties as Vietnam. It consists of a circular "Pool of Remembrance" in a grove of trees and a triangular "Field of Service," highlighted by lifelike statues of 19 infantrymen who appear to be trudging across fields. A 164-foot-long black granite wall depicts the array of combat and support troops that served in Korea (nurses, chaplains, airmen, mechanics, cooks, and others); engraved markers along a walkway list the 22 nations that contributed to the UN's effort; and a commemorative area honors KIAs, MIAs, and POWs. Allot 15 minutes.

Southeast of the Lincoln Memorial, on the Independence Ave. SW side of the Mall. www.nps.gov/kowa. *C* **202/426-6841.** Free admission. Open 24 hr. daily. Limited parking. Metro: Foggy Bottom, with 30-min. walk. DC Circulator stop.

Korean War Veterans Memorial.

Lincoln Memorial ★★★ MONUMENT/MEMORIAL   When famed architect Charles Follen McKim was asked to work on the 1902 McMillan Commission to reshape the overall design for the Mall, he made his views clear on what he felt would be an important addition. "As the Arc de Triomphe crowns Place de l'Étoile in Paris, so should stand a memorial erected of the memory of that one man in our history as a nation who is worthy to be joined with George Washington—Abraham Lincoln."

Location was key, but where the monument should be was not entirely obvious: Until the late 1800s, a wider Potomac River had bumped up against the western edge of the National Mall. It was only after the Army Corps of Engineers had first reclaimed land from the river and created a mile-wide westward expanse of new terrain, and then landscaped and engineered the muddy morass, that the choice was clear. The memorial for honoring the president who had saved the Union would preside at one end of the Mall on a direct axis to the Washington Monument honoring the nation's founding president, both sites linked on the same axis further still to the symbol of the country itself, the U.S. Capitol, at the eastern end of the Mall.

Construction began in 1914, and what a job it was, shoring up the unstable wetlands and creating a foundation strong enough to support the majestic memorial that architect Henry Bacon had designed. The foundation rests on concrete piles that extend from 44 to 65 feet from original grade to bedrock. The retaining wall, keeping the river at bay, measures 257 feet wide by 187 feet deep by 14 feet high. The Lincoln Memorial itself weighs 38,000 tons. The monument finally opened in 1922 after 8 years of construction.

The neoclassical templelike structure, similar in architectural design to the Parthenon in Greece, has 36 fluted Doric columns representing the states of the Union at the time of Lincoln's death, plus two at the entrance. On the attic parapet are 48 festoons symbolizing the number of states in 1922. (Hawaii and Alaska are noted in an inscription on the terrace.) Due east is the Reflecting Pool, lined with American elms and stretching 2,000 feet toward the Washington Monument and the Capitol beyond.

The memorial chamber has limestone walls inscribed with the Gettysburg Address and Lincoln's second inaugural address. Two 60-foot-high murals by Jules Guerin on the north and south walls depict, allegorically, Lincoln's principles and achievements. On the south wall, an Angel of Truth freeing a slave is flanked by groups of figures representing Justice and Immortality. The north-wall mural portrays the unity of North and South and is flanked by groups of figures symbolizing Fraternity and Charity.

Most powerful, however, is Daniel Chester French's seated statue of Lincoln. Lincoln sits, gazing down on the visitors at his feet, the burdens of guiding the Union through the Civil War etched deeply in his face. Though 19 feet tall, the figure is eerily lifelike and exudes a fatherly compassion. Some say that his hands create the sign-language shapes for A (Abraham) and L (Lincoln), as a tribute to the fact that Lincoln signed legislation giving Gallaudet University, a school for the deaf, the right to confer college degrees. The National Park Service denies the symbolism, but it should be noted that French's own son was deaf, so the sculptor *did* know sign language.

Lincoln's legacy has made his memorial the site of numerous demonstrations by those seeking justice. Most notable was a peaceful demonstration of 250,000 people on August 28, 1963, at which Martin Luther King, Jr. proclaimed, "I have a dream." Look for the words I HAVE A DREAM. MARTIN LUTHER KING, JR., THE MARCH ON WASHINGTON FOR JOBS AND FREEDOM, AUGUST 28, 1963, inscribed and centered on the 18th step down from the chamber. The inscription, which the National Park Service added in 2003, marks the precise spot where King stood to deliver his famous speech.

Thirty minutes is sufficient time for viewing this memorial.

On the western end of the Mall, at 23rd St. NW (btw. Constitution and Independence aves.). www.nps.gov/linc. (C) **202/426-6841.** Free admission. Open 24 hr. daily. Limited parking. Metro: Foggy Bottom, with a 30-min. walk. DC Circulator stop.

Martin Luther King, Jr. National Memorial ★★ MONUMENT/ MEMORIAL

Regrettably, the Martin Luther King, Jr. Memorial provides little context for King's life and work as, arguably, the United States' most important civil rights activist. (King was assassinated on April 4, 1968, at the age of 39.) Still, the very fact of its existence, here on the Mall among memorials to presidents and to those who fought in U.S. wars, affirms King's critical role in American history.

Authorized by Congress in 1996, the memorial debuted on October 16, in 2011.

The memorial's site along the northwest lip of the Tidal Basin is significant for the "visual line of leadership" it creates between the Lincoln Memorial, representing the principles of equality and civil rights as embodied in the personage of Abraham Lincoln and carried forward in King, and the Jefferson Memorial, which symbolizes the democratic ideals of the founding fathers. Set on a crescent-shaped, 4-acre parcel of land surrounded by the capital's famous cherry trees, the mammoth sculpture (created in China, a controversial decision) rests on 300 concrete piles driven into the muddy basin terrain. A 28-foot, 6-inch statue of Dr. King in a business suit, arms folded, stands front and center, representing the "Stone of Hope"; he is flanked by two enormous background pieces, representing the "Mountain of Despair." A curving boundary wall enclosing the grounds perhaps commemorates the slain civil rights leader best, with inscriptions of excerpts from his remarkable sermons and speeches. The memorial includes a bookstore and restrooms.

Adjacent to the FDR Memorial, along the northwest side of the Tidal Basin, at Independence Ave. SW, in West Potomac Park. www.nps.gov/mlkm. © **202/426-6841.** Free admission. Open 24 hr. daily. Limited parking. Metro: Smithsonian (12th St./Independence Ave. exit), with a 25-min. walk. DC Circulator stop.

National Air and Space Museum ★★ MUSEUM

Big news: The National Air and Space Museum has embarked on an enormous, multiyear, nearly $1 billion makeover that will transform the entire visitor experience and is expected to be fully completed by 2025. At press time, the museum announced it will close completely for 6 months, until the fall of 2022, to begin the first phase of renovations. Check status before going. When it reopens, expect to still see sections closed on a rolling basis. But even with renovations ongoing, rest assured that there's lots to see here. For example, the *Spirit of St. Louis,* the 1903 Wright Flyer, Bell X-1, the Apollo Lunar Module, and Skylab are all housed here, currently in a massive ground floor hall that traces the history of air transportation and explores how technology revolutionized air travel.

Based on visitation numbers (7 million annually, prior to the renovation), this is among America's favorite museums. And even in its current state, it's not hard to understand why. The National Air and Space Museum manages to tap into that most primordial of human impulses: the urge to fly. And it does so in a multi-layered fashion, mixing extraordinary artifacts with IMAX movies, videos, and hands-on exploration of displayed equipment.

The Jay I. Kislak World War II in the Air gallery at the Smithsonian National Air and Space Museum.

The seeds of this museum were planted when the Smithsonian Institution acquired its first aeronautical objects in 1876: 20 kites from the Chinese Imperial Commission. By the time the National Air and Space Museum opened on the National Mall 100 years later, the collection had grown to tens of thousands of objects. Today, the inventory of historic aircraft and spacecraft artifacts numbers more than 66,000, the world's largest such collection.

The place is huge, as is much of its collection. Enormous aircraft and spacecraft dangle from the ceiling or are placed in floor exhibits throughout both levels. Visitors of all ages, but mostly families, take pictures of each other against the backdrops of the towering Pershing II (34.8 ft.) and SS20 Pioneer (54.1 ft.) missiles, or the Hubble Space Telescope (42 ft.), or just about anything in the museum, as most of the artifacts dwarf humans. Tours and demonstrations are in constant rotation.

Our hope is that once the dust settles in 2025 (and hopefully sooner), the new visitor experience will include less time waiting in lines, which can be daunting at this always-busy museum, especially with little kids in tow. Fingers crossed that those museum designers are paying lots of attention to joy-zapping frustrations like standstill crowds and bottlenecks to see the most popular exhibits.

Currently, first-floor galleries cover the **Space Race** and the development of huge telescopes (**Explore the Universe**); the space-themed galleries upstairs highlight **Exploring the Moon** and **Time and Navigation** in space.

The central area on both floors takes a look at historic milestones and individuals in aviation and space research and development: Space and aviation artifacts in the first-floor **Boeing Milestones of Flight Hall** illustrate ways that aviation and flight transformed the world. This is where you'll see the first American jet aircraft, the *Spirit of St. Louis* ★★, flown solo by Charles Lindbergh across the Atlantic Ocean.

If you're short on time or simply overwhelmed, there are two things you shouldn't miss. The **Sky Lab Orbital Workshop ★★★**, in the Space Race gallery on the first floor (you enter the spaceship on the second floor), allows you to walk through the country's first space station. You're actually *inside* the astronauts' living quarters; if you look up, you'll see that most of the rocket's construction lies overhead. And be sure to visit the second-floor **Wright Brothers** exhibit, where the Wright brothers' **1903 Flyer ★★★**, the world's first successful airplane, is on display.

Amateur astronomers should head outside to the museum's east terrace to peer through the telescopes in the **Phoebe Waterman Haas Public Observatory.** The observatory, when it's in service, is free and open to the public for daytime sightings of moon craters and sunspots, and once or twice a month for nighttime observations (more info on the website). At press time, the museum's popular **Albert Einstein Planetarium** was closed as part of the museum's ongoing renovations; check the website for updates on its scheduled return.

Wonder where the museum has put all of the aircraft and equipment that used to occupy the west wing? Much of it now resides temporarily in the National Air and Space Museum's companion location, the **Steven F. Udvar-Hazy Center,** adjacent to Washington Dulles International Airport. If you're hungry to see more aviation artifacts and spacecraft, or if you've got a flight leaving from Dulles Airport and have time to kill, drive the 25 miles out to the satellite museum. Here you can explore one huge hangar filled with aviation objects and another with space objects, each arranged by subject (Commercial Aviation, Korea and Vietnam Aviation, Sport Aviation, and so on). Perhaps the center's most notable artifact is the enormous **space shuttle *Discovery*** that retired in 2011. A Lockhead SR-71 Blackbird, the world's fastest-jet-propelled aircraft, is also here, along with the Concorde, the first supersonic airliner. IMAX movies and simulator rides also are options. *Note:* Admission is free at Udvar-Hazy, but there is a $15 fee for parking before 4pm.

Mall museum: Independence Ave. SW, btw. 4th and 7th sts. (on south side of Mall, with two entrances, one on Jefferson Dr. and the other on Independence Ave; Thurs–Mon 10am–5:30pm). Metro: L'Enfant Plaza (Smithsonian Museums/Maryland Ave. exit) or Smithsonian (Mall/Jefferson Dr. exit). DC Circulator stop. **Udvar-Hazy Center:** 14390 Air and Space Museum Pkwy., Chantilly, VA. www.airandspace.si.edu.© **202/633-2214** (Mall location), or **703/572-4118** (Virginia location). Free admission. Daily 10am–5:30pm. Closed Dec 25.

National Archives Museum ★★ MUSEUM The **Rotunda** of the National Archives displays the country's most important original documents: the Declaration of Independence, the Constitution of the United States, and the Bill of Rights (collectively known as the **Charters of Freedom**). Fourteen document cases trace the story of the creation of the Charters and the ongoing influence these fundamental documents have had on the nation and the world.

It proves to be an unexpectedly thrilling experience to stand among people from all over the world and peer in this dimly lit chamber at page after page of manuscript covered top to bottom in tiny, graceful script, whose forthright declarations founded our country and changed the world. It is gratifying, too, to see the documents given context within the exhibit. For example, one panel points to the role of "founding mothers" like Abigail Adams, who cautioned her husband in a letter, "If perticular *[sic]* care is not paid to the Ladies, we are determined to foment a Rebellion, *[sic]* and will not hold ourselves bound by any Laws in which we have no voice or Representation."

But the wonders don't end there: On display in the **David M. Rubenstein Gallery** is the original 1297 Magna Carta, one of only four known to exist in the world, and the only original version on public display in the United States. The Magna Carta anchors the permanent exhibit, **Records of Rights,** which presents hundreds of other landmark documents, as well as photographs, videos, and interactive items that help visitors trace the evolution of rights in the U.S. from its founding to the present day.

Beyond famous documents are the **Public Vaults,** an area that, when open to the public, introduces visitors to the heart of the Archives: its 10 billion records, covering 2 centuries worth of documents, from patent searches to genealogical records to copies of George Washington's handwritten inaugural address, to census records, governmental records, and more. (Check before you visit to see if the vaults are open.)

Using the very latest in interactive museum design—listening booths, computer terminals, videos, you name it—the curators have mined the material for drama (and often presented it in a very kid-friendly fashion). In an area on patents, for example, the process is turned into a game: You read the patent application and then try to guess what well-known gadget it was for. A section on immigration presents the search for genealogical data as a cliffhanger mystery, detailing the steps and missteps of past Archives' users. President Nixon makes several eerie appearances: You read his resignation letter and listen to disturbing excerpts from the Watergate tapes.

Beyond its exhibits, the Archives are a vital resource for researchers. Anyone 16 and over is welcome to use the National Archives center for genealogical research. Call for details.

The National Archives building itself is worth an admiring glance. The neoclassical structure, designed by John Russell Pope (also architect of the National Gallery of Art and the Jefferson Memorial) in the 1930s, is an impressive example of the Beaux Arts style. Seventy-two columns create a Corinthian colonnade on each of the four facades. Great bronze doors mark the Constitution Avenue entrance, and four large sculptures representing the Future, the Past, Heritage, and Guardianship sit on pedestals near the entrances. Huge pediments crown both the Pennsylvania Avenue and Constitution Avenue entrances to the building.

Admission is always free, but you'll pay a $1 convenience fee when you reserve your timed ticket online at www.recreation.gov/ticket/facility/234645.

701 Constitution Ave NW (btw. 7th and 9th sts. NW). Tourists enter on Constitution Ave., researchers on Pennsylvania Ave. museum.archives.gov. ⓒ **202/357-5000.** Free admission. Daily 10am–5:30pm. Call for research hours. Closed Dec 25. Metro: Archives–Navy Memorial. DC Circulator stop.

National Gallery of Art ★★★ ART MUSEUM Best. Art museum. Ever. That's my opinion; but let me quickly say that world-renowned critics also consider the over 80-year-old National Gallery of Art to be among the best museums in the world. Its base collection of more than 150,000 paintings, drawings, prints, photographs, sculpture, decorative arts, and furniture trace the development of Western art from the Middle Ages to the present in a manner that's both informative and rapturously beautiful.

The National Gallery's design and programs make the artworks and the museum itself accessible to the ordinary visitor. Architect John Russell Pope (of Jefferson Memorial fame; see p. 142) modeled his design of the original West Building after the Pantheon in Rome, anchoring the main floor's interior with a domed rotunda, and then centered a colonnaded fountain beneath the dome. The overall feeling is of spaciousness and grace, especially when the huge fountain is encircled with flowers, as it often is. Extending east and west are long and wide, light-filled, high-ceilinged halls, off which the individual **paintings galleries** lie, nearly 100 in all, leading eventually to lovely garden courts and more places to sit.

One hundred galleries? Yes, but the 1,000-some paintings are arranged in easy-to-understand order, in separate rooms by age and nationality: 13th-century Italian to 18th-century Italian, Spanish, and French artists on the west side; 18th- and 19th-century Spanish, French, British, and American masters on the east side. You may recognize some names: Leonardo da Vinci (whose ethereal portrait, *Ginevra de' Benci,* which hangs here, is the only da Vinci painting on public view in the Americas), Rubens, Raphael, Cassatt, El Greco, Brueghel, Poussin, Vermeer, van Dyck, Gilbert Stuart, Winslow Homer, Turner, and so on.

Down the sweep of marble stairway to the ground floor lie the West Building's remaining galleries. The light-filled, vaulted-ceilinged sculpture galleries include standouts by Bernini, Rodin, Degas, and Honoré Daumier, whose 36 small bronze busts of French government administrators are highly amusing caricatures. Other galleries display decorative arts, prints and drawings, and photographs.

Across the street from the West Building is a Sculpture Garden that features 22 sculptures created by an international roster of artists in the last few decades, including a stunning Chagall mosaic.

The I. M. Pei–designed East Building showcases modern and contemporary art in galleries that lie off a dazzling atrium and includes three skylit towers and an outdoor sculpture terrace with a grand view of the city. In the East Building another world opens up, as graceful as the West Building, but here it's angular, airy, and capricious. An immense and colorful Calder mobile floats overhead, but where are the galleries? You're meant to wander, but you might miss something without a strategy. So here goes:

After arriving via the underground walkway from the West Building, find the elevator that will take you to the rooftop and its two towers. Tower 1's two-gallery space presents a study in contrasts, one gallery devoted to an array of mesmerizing color-block Rothkos, the other displaying Barnett Newman's abstract, muted depictions of the Stations of the Cross. Tower 2 holds an entire roomful of Calders, many small and toylike, some swaying mobiles suspended from skylights, all colorful whimsies.

Okay, now you're good to go explore on your own, back through the galleries of minimalist art, or on to pop art, photography, Picasso, American art from the first half of the 20th century, and French paintings from the last half of the 19th century and first half of the 20th.

If you make your way back to the West Building and exit onto 7th Street, you are directly across from the **Sculpture Garden.** Go! Positioned throughout its lushly landscaped 6 acres you'll find a stalking *Spider* by Louise Bourgeois, a tall, blue sculpture of five stacked chairs made of patinated bronze by Lucas Samaras, and 18 other modern sculptures. In the northwest corner is a delightful, large (10×17 ft.) glass and stone mosaic by Marc Chagall.

At the center of the Sculpture Garden is an expansive fountain, which turns into an ice rink in winter. The garden is famous for its summer Sculpture Garden concerts, which are free and draw a crowd.

The National Gallery also mounts killer special exhibits and offers a robust year-round schedule of films, tours, and talks, monthly after-hours events from October to April, and concert series and performing art series—all free, let me emphasize.

There are five dining options, the best of which are the **Garden Café** and the Sculpture Garden's **Pavilion Café.**

We have Andrew W. Mellon to thank for the museum. The financier/philanthropist, who served as ambassador to England from 1932 to 1933, was so inspired by London's National Gallery that he decided to give such a gift to his own country. The West Building opened in Washington, D.C., in 1941, the East Building in 1978, and the Sculpture Garden in 1999.

Constitution Ave. NW, btw. 3rd and 7th sts. NW (on the north side of the Mall). www. nga.gov. ✆ **202/737-4215.** Free admission. Gallery: Daily 10am–5pm. Sculpture Garden: Daily, hours change based on programming so check the gallery's website. Ice rink: Mid-Nov to mid-Mar Mon–Thurs 10am–9pm, Fri 10am–11pm, Sat 11am–11pm Sun 11am–9pm. Rink fees: $9 adults under 50 and children 13 and older, $8 adults 50 and over and children 12 and under, plus $4 skate rental, 50¢ locker rental ($5 deposit required). Closed Dec 25 and Jan 1. Metro: Archives–Navy Memorial, Judiciary Square (either exit), or Gallery Place/Chinatown (Arena/7th and F sts. exit). DC Circulator stop.

National Mall ★★★ ICON   As part of his vision for Washington, Pierre L'Enfant conceived of the National Mall as a bustling ceremonial avenue of distinguished buildings. Today's 2-mile, 700-acre stretch of land extending westward from the base of the Capitol to the Potomac River, just behind the Lincoln Memorial, fulfills that dream. Eleven Smithsonian buildings, plus the National Gallery of Art and its Sculpture Garden, and a stray government building (Department of Agriculture), stake out the Mall's northern border along Constitution Avenue and its southern border along Independence Avenue. More than 2,000 American elm trees shade the pebbled walkways paralleling Jefferson and Madison drives. In a single year, more than 35 million tourists and locals crisscross the Mall as they visit the Smithsonians, hustle to work, exercise, participate in whatever festival, event, or demonstration is taking place that day, or simply go for a stroll—just as L'Enfant envisioned, perhaps.

The National Park Service maintains the land with money from Congress and from the Trust for the National Mall (www.nationalmall.org), the Park Service's fundraising partner. A third organization of interested citizens, the National Coalition to Save Our Mall (www.savethemall.org), advocates for a public voice in Mall enhancement decisions, and for more support from Congress. While actual construction may still be years away, campaigns are underway to repair the aging Tidal Basin and prevent further flooding, and also rebuild the U.S. Park Police Horse Stables. The Mall's oldest structure, the 1835 **Lockkeeper's House,** serves as the National Mall's own small visitor center. It is located on the southwest corner of the 17th Street and Constitution Avenue NW intersection, set within a wide plaza, across 17th Street from the Washington Monument grounds.

From the foot of the Capitol to the Lincoln Memorial. www.nps.gov/nama. ℂ **202/426-6841.** Public space, open 365/24/7. Metro: Smithsonian. DC Circulator stop.

National Museum of African American History & Culture ★★★

MUSEUM   A profound and essential American experience awaits you at the Smithsonian's newest museum, which opened in 2016. Conceived as a place where visitors of all backgrounds might comprehend America's narrative through an African-American lens, the museum succeeds on every level. History exhibits, culture galleries, and the museum's architecture and design each express critical elements of the story.

Turns out, many, many people are interested in understanding that story, more people, in fact, than the museum can usually accommodate on any given day. So, a free **timed-pass system** has been instituted to control the crowds. You have two options for obtaining advance-entry passes: You can reserve them up to 30 days in advance; these timed-entry passes are released every day at 8am. Or you can try to snag same-day time-entry passes online, which go up each morning at 8:15am and last until they run out. Every visitor needs to have a timed entry ticket—even infants. You can reserve up to six tickets per reservation.

Located across from the Washington Monument, within view of the Lincoln Memorial and the White House, and next door to the National Museum of American History, the museum's very placement nudges the visitor toward a contextual appreciation. The building belongs within this panoply, but it speaks for itself, a remarkable standout in this cool landscape of white stone structures. A three-tiered shell of 3,523 bronze-colored panels, the "corona," sheaths the museum's glass-walled exterior, angling outward and upward, suggesting designs found in traditional West African sculpture and headwear. The filigreed pattern of the corona mimics the ornate ironwork crafted by slaves in 19th-century New Orleans and Charleston. (As you move along inside, you will notice cutouts in the building's bronze scrim, which allow glimpses of surrounding landmarks, including the White House, Lincoln Memorial, and Arlington Cemetery, reinforcing the museum's emphasis on viewing the American experience through the eyes of an African American.)

When you enter the museum, you are stepping inside a 400,000-square-foot space, 60% of which lies below ground. And down is where visitors go first, to the History Galleries, or "crypts"—the heart of the experience.

The museum covers more than 500 years of history, starting in the 15th century with the transatlantic slave trade and continuing to slavery in the U.S., the Civil War, Reconstruction, segregation, the Civil Rights movement, and America since 1968. Ramps lead from one exhibit area and level to the next, creating different vantage points for viewing the artifacts and for connecting the gradual progression of events in time. This bottom-to-top touring offers a symbolic converse of that in place at the United States Holocaust Memorial Museum (p. 167), where you begin at the top floor and descend (from the rise of Hitler and Nazism to the Final Solution). Exhibits at both museums reveal history through chronological storytelling that focuses on the lives of ordinary and heroic individuals. And both museums provide areas of contemplation and reflection, where visitors can sit and take everything in, from the tragic facts to celebrations of the indomitable human spirit.

Compelling, sometimes shocking, artifacts bring the history to life. These include shackles used on an enslaved child; an early 1800s weatherboard-clad slave cabin from Edisto Island, South Carolina; Harriet Tubman's shawl and hymn book; a vintage, open-cockpit biplane used at Tuskegee Institute to train African-American pilots during World War II; the Greensboro, North Carolina, Woolworth's lunch-counter stools occupied on a February day in 1960 by four black college students who refused to move after being denied service; and assorted documents and artifacts that capture more recent developments, from the presidency of Barack Obama to the Black Lives Matter movement.

On floors two and three above ground, "the Attic," are exhibits that highlight African-American stories of place, region, and migration; how African Americans carved a way for themselves in a world that denied them opportunities; and African Americans' contributions in sports and the military.

The fourth floor's Arts and Culture Galleries showcase African-American contributions in music, fashion, food, theater, and the visual arts. Artifacts displayed on these floors range from the outfit that Marian Anderson wore when she sang at the Lincoln Memorial in 1939 and Chuck Berry's red Cadillac convertible to artworks by Romare Bearden and Elizabeth Catlett.

The story of the museum itself is worth. "A Century in the Making" reveals that a group of black Civil War veterans are said to have proposed the idea for an African-American history museum in 1915. Congress took up the cause from time to time over the ensuing decades, finally enacting the NMAAHC Act in December 2003, establishing the museum within the Smithsonian Institution. A four-firm architectural unit won the design competition in 2009, groundbreaking took place in 2012. Meanwhile, staff, starting from scratch, were traveling around the country amassing artifacts. Today, more than half of the museum's collection of 37,000 objects are donations.

Given the NMAAHC's multi-layered chronicling of African-American history from its very beginnings, it is moving that President Barack Obama, the country's first black president, was the person to cut the ribbon at its opening.

This is a living museum, and it will continue to tell the ever-evolving story of African-American history and culture, which at this particular time in America is more necessary than ever.

If you have time, stop by **Sweet Home Café,** the museum's cafeteria serving African-American tastes rooted in regional cooking traditions: the agricultural south, Creole coast, north states, and the western range. Check before you arrive to current hours for both the museum and the café.

1400 Constitution Ave. NW, btw. 14th and 15th sts. NW, next to the Washington Monument, with entrances on Madison Dr. (main entrance) and Constitution Ave. www.nmaahc.si.edu. ℂ **844/750-3012.** Free admission. Daily 10am–5:30pm. Closed Dec 25. Metro: Smithsonian or Federal Triangle. DC Circulator stop.

National Museum of African Art ★ MUSEUM   This inviting little museum does not get the foot traffic of its larger, better-known sister Smithsonians, but that only makes for a happier experience for those who do visit. Find it by strolling through the Enid A. Haupt Garden, under which the subterranean museum lies, and enter via the domed pavilions, stopping first to admire the tall artwork marking the entrance, the colorful fiberglass and goldleaf "Wind Sculpture VII," evocative of a ship's sail.

Traditional and contemporary African music plays lightly in the background as you tour the dimly lit suite of rooms on three sublevels. The galleries rotate works from the museum's 12,000-piece permanent inventory of ancient and modern art, spanning art forms and geographic areas. The museum also houses a collection of some 450,000 photographs.

A tour of the museum at any time turns up diverse discoveries: a circa 13th- to 15th-century ceramic equestrian figure from Mali; face masks from Congo and Gabon; or a 15th-century Ethiopian manuscript page.

The African Art Museum was founded in 1964, joined the Smithsonian in 1979, and moved to the Mall in 1987.

950 Independence Ave. SW. www.africa.si.edu. ℂ **202/633-4600.** Free admission. Wed–Sun 10am–5:30pm. Closed Dec 25. Metro: Smithsonian. DC Circulator stop.

The National Museum of African American History & Culture.

National Museum of American History ★★★ MUSEUM   How does one museum possibly sum up the history of a nation that is 243 years old and 3.8 million square miles in size and has a population of 326 million people? And how does the museum sort through its collection of 1.8 million artifacts, which include every imaginable American object, from George Washington's uniform to an 1833 steam locomotive, from the Star-Spangled Banner to a

1960s lunch box, and choose which to display? And finally, how does the museum serve it up in such a way as to capture both the essence of American history and culture, and the attention of a diverse and international public? At nearly 60 years old, the National Museum of American History is wrapping up a massive reinvention of itself that is helping the museum meet these daunting challenges. In late 2021 a new third-floor exhibition Hall of American Culture opened in the West Wing. The exhibit showcases how and where America's great culture makers engage their audiences. A new *Entertainment Nation* exhibition explores how entertainment connects Americans and creates a forum for essential national conversations, whether that's through sports (see items from Jackie Robinson and Mia Hamm's careers), performing arts, like the Broadway hit *Hamilton* or groundbreaking movie trilogy *Star Wars*. A visit to the National Museum of American History today is a more penetrating, fun, and interesting experience than it ever was before.

In **Flag Hall** is the museum's star (or should I say "starred"?) attraction: the original Star-Spangled Banner. This 30×34-foot wool and cotton flag is the very one that Francis Scott Key spied at dawn on September 14, 1814, flying above Fort McHenry in Baltimore's harbor, signifying an American victory over the British during the War of 1812. Key memorialized that moment in a song that became the country's official National Anthem in 1931. The threadbare 208-year-old treasure is on view behind a window in an environmentally controlled chamber; terrific, interactive displays bring to life the significance and grandeur of this important artifact.

From Flag Hall, stay on the second floor to see more iconic Americana. These include objects such as Thomas Jefferson's portable desk in the exhibit **American Democracy: A Great Leap of Faith,** which explores the theme of what it takes to create a government of, by, and for the people. **Many Voices, One Nation** pulls treasures from the museum's vast collection to consider how cultural geography and identity contribute to what it means to be American—two extremely timely exhibits. One of my favorite exhibits is **Within These Walls,** which presents a partially reconstructed, two-and-a-half-level, 200+-year-old house transplanted from Ipswich, MA, and tells the stories of the five families who lived here over time, from Colonial days to the early 1960s. Displays include authentic objects from the pertinent time periods. You learn, for instance that Lucy Caldwell occupied the house in the 1830s, played that square piano you see in the parlor, and formed the Ipswich Female Anti-Slavery Society with other women in Ipswich, considering it her moral duty to "assume a public stand in favor of our oppressed sisters."

American ingenuity is celebrated in first-floor exhibits; this is also the most popular floor with young museumgoers. **Wegmans Wonderplace,** geared toward kids under age 6, is a learning playroom where kids can "cook" in a kitchen inspired by Julia Child's (on display on the first floor; see below) and find owls hidden in a miniature replica of the Smithsonian Castle. A revamped and much improved version of an old favorite attraction, the **Lemelson Center,** features **Places of Invention** and **Spark!Lab,** where interactive exhibits allow children ages 6 to 12 to learn about inventors and inventiveness hands-on.

Other first-floor exhibits display patent models of inventions by Samuel Morse, Alexander Graham Bell, and Thomas Edison, as well as the **workshop of Ralph Baer,** the progenitor of video games. An exhibit on business history, **American Enterprise,** is a kind of companion piece to the **Value of Money** exhibit here.

Vehicles including a 1903 Winton, the first car to cross the country, and a massive locomotive command a lot of space and attention in **America on the Move,** but to my mind they're not nearly as interesting as the exhibit titled **FOOD: Transforming the American Table, 1950–2000.** Its *pièce de résistance* is **Julia Child's home kitchen,** which Child donated to the museum in late 2001.

If you're interested in American wars, politics, and fashion, head to the third floor, which holds the museum's most visited exhibit: **The First Ladies** features 26 first ladies' gowns and more than 1,000 objects, which round out our perceptions about the roles and personalities of these singular women. Covering their husband's stories is **The American Presidency: A Glorious Burden,** which attempts to shine a more personal light on those who have held the office. Continue to **The Price of Freedom: Americans at War,** which explores the idea of wars as defining episodes in American history.

Note: In the same area as the children's galleries is the **Wallace H. Coulter Performance Stage and Plaza,** where cooking demonstrations, jazz concerts, and other programs frequently take place. Around the corner from this area, just inside the Constitution Avenue entrance to the museum is the **Jazz Café,** where you can power up with ice cream cones, pastries, and sandwiches. Other attractions: racecar and flight simulator rides, a large cafeteria, and a theater showing 3D American adventure movies and Hollywood films.

Constitution Ave. NW, btw. 12th and 14th sts. NW (on the north side of the Mall, with entrances on Constitution Ave. and Madison Dr.). www.americanhistory.si.edu. ℂ **202/633-1000.** Free admission. Daily 10am–5:30pm. Closed Dec 25. Metro: Smithsonian or Federal Triangle. DC Circulator stop.

National Museum of the American Indian ★ MUSEUM

This striking building, located at the Capitol end of the National Mall, stands out for the architectural contrast it makes with neighboring Smithsonian and government structures. It is the first national museum in the country dedicated exclusively to Native Americans, and Native Americans consulted on its design, both inside and out; the main architect was a member of the Canadian Blackfoot tribe. The museum's rippled exterior is clad in golden sand–colored Kasota limestone; the building stands 5 stories high within a landscape of wetland grasses, water features, and 40 large uncarved rocks and boulders known as "grandfather rocks."

Although the interior design is breathtaking (you enter a 120-ft.-high domed rotunda called "Potomac," the Piscataway word for "Where the goods are brought in"), the experience here can be bewildering, thanks to the sheer number of artifacts (some 8,500) and the variety of tribes and tribal traditions portrayed. The best way to take it all in is by joining a tour. Check at the welcome desk to see if any timed tours or events are available during your visit.

If you're exploring on your own, begin by visiting the fourth floor: where you'll find **Nation to Nation,** an exhibit exploring the history of treaty-making between the United States and American Indian nations, using more than 125 objects, such as wampum belts and peace medals, three videos, and four interactive touch-based media stations, on view until 2025.

The second floor's **Return to a Native Place** tells the more local story of the Algonquian peoples of the Chesapeake Bay region (today's Washington, D.C., Maryland, Virginia, and Delaware). **Window on the Collections** (found on both the third and fourth levels) is for art and history lovers, showcasing hundreds of objects arranged by categories, including animal-themed figurines and objects, beadwork, dolls, and peace medals.

A special ongoing exhibit worth visiting: **"Americans"** highlights the ways in which American Indian images, names, and stories infuse American history and contemporary life, and it sets the record straight about historical figures, like Pocahontas, and historical events, such as the Battle of Little Big Horn.

The recently unveiled **National Native American Veterans Memorial** honors the contributions of American Indians, Alaska Natives, and Native Hawaiians who have served in the military. The large upright stainless-steel circle sits atop a stone drum. Take a seat on any one of the benches and reflect while listening to the sounds of water, a symbol of sacred Native Indian ceremonies.

4th St. and Independence Ave. SW. www.americanindian.si.edu. ℂ **202/633-1000.** Free admission. Daily 10am–5:30pm. Closed Dec 25. Metro: Federal Center Southwest or L'Enfant Plaza (Smithsonian Museums/Maryland Ave. exit). DC Circulator stop.

National Museum of Natural History ★★ MUSEUM   Fair warning: For many visitors, this museum can be just too much. Not only is it the most visited museum in town (get ready to fight the crowds!), but there are so many exhibits, and so many items within the exhibits, that it's easy to experience sensory overload. With 146 million artifacts and specimens, 325,000 square feet of public space; and about 5 million people visit annually, this is the most visited natural history museum *in the world.*

Best advice: Use this guide and the museum's website to develop a strategy before you arrive. As the website suggests, try to visit on a Monday, Tuesday, or Wednesday, or on most weekdays September through February, when crowds are sparser (except for around Thanksgiving and Christmas—the crowds return then). And if you still find yourself feeling overwhelmed on arrival, do as I did on a recent visit to the busy museum: Go up to one of the green- or tan-vested "Visitor Concierges" you'll see roaming the museum and ask them to name the two must-see things they would recommend in the particular exhibit. A concierge I approached in the Sant Ocean Hall responded immediately with the "live coral reef" and the "shark mouth," pointing me to these in the vast hall. Perfect suggestions. The variously colored coral reef tank holds fish of brilliant blue, purple, yellow, and pink hues. The enormous jaw of a

The National Museum of Natural History rotunda.

Carcharodon megalodon, a shark that lived 5 million years ago, is enclosed in a glass case; the idea is for you to pose behind the glass case so that it appears as if you're inside the mouth—a great snapshot.

The museum has 22 different galleries, with exhibits that cover the story of natural history from the earliest beginnings of life to the present. The popular Fossil Hall is a massive 31,000-square-foot exhibition space featuring some 700 specimens, including an Alaskan palm tree, early insects, reptiles and mammals, and dramatically posed giants like the meat-and-bone-eating tyrannosaurus that stomped the earth 66 million years ago. It's not just dinosaurs, either: A mastodon, woolly mammoth, and prehistoric shark are on display, too.

Meanwhile, on the second floor, the Hope Diamond is still holding court in its own gallery within the **Geology, Gems and Minerals** area. (The deep-blue, 45.52-carat diamond has a storied past, which you can read about on p. 278, in chapter 10.) The second floor is also where you'll find a small showpiece on 3,000-year-old mummies, notable for the beautifully decorated coffins on display; and the bone hall where visitors compare the skeletons of everything from dogs and cats to flying fish and a gray whale.

What to pick? That's up to you. Good luck.

Constitution Ave. NW, btw. 9th and 12th sts. (on the north side of the Mall, with entrances on Madison Dr. and Constitution Ave.). www.naturalhistory.si.edu. ℂ **202/633-1000.** Free admission. Daily 10am–5:30pm (until 7:30pm in summer). Closed Dec 25. Metro: Smithsonian (Mall/Jefferson Dr. exit) or Federal Triangle. DC Circulator stop.

National World War II Memorial ★★ MONUMENT/MEMORIAL

When this memorial was dedicated in 2004, 150,000 people attended, among them President George W. Bush; actor Tom Hanks and now-retired news anchor Tom Brokaw, both of whom had been active in soliciting support for the memorial; and most important, thousands of World War II veterans and their families. These legions of veterans—some dressed in uniform, many wearing a cap identifying the name of their division—turned out with pride, happy to receive the nation's gratitude, 60 years in the making, expressed profoundly in this memorial.

Designed by Friedrich St. Florian and funded mostly by private donations, the memorial fits nicely into the landscape between the Washington Monument grounds to the east and the Lincoln Memorial and its Reflecting Pool to the west. St. Florian purposely situated the 7½-acre memorial so as not to obstruct this long view down the Mall. Fifty-six 17-foot-high granite pillars representing each state and territory stand to either side of a central plaza and the **Rainbow Pool.** Likewise, 24 bas-relief panels divide

The World War II Memorial.

down the middle so that 12 line each side of the walkway leading from the entrance at 17th Street. The panels to the left, as you walk toward the center of the memorial, illustrate seminal scenes from the war years as they relate to the Pacific front: Pearl Harbor, amphibious landing, jungle warfare, a field burial, and so on. The panels to the right are sculptured scenes of war moments related to the Atlantic front: Rosie the Riveter, Normandy Beach landing, the Battle of the Bulge, the Russians meeting the Americans at the Elbe River. Architect and sculptor Raymond Kaskey sculpted these panels based on archival photographs.

Large, open pavilions stake out the north and south axes of the memorial, and semicircular fountains create waterfalls on either side. Inscriptions at the base of each pavilion fountain mark key battles. Beyond the center Rainbow Pool is a wall of 4,000 gold stars, one for every 100 American soldiers who died in World War II. People often leave photos and mementos around the memorial, which the National Park Service gathers up daily for an archive. For compelling, firsthand accounts of World War II experiences, combine your tour here with an online visit to the **Library of Congress's Veterans History Project,** at www.loc.gov/vets. See p. 130 for more info.

From the 17th Street entrance, walk south around the perimeter of the memorial to reach a ranger station, where there are registry kiosks for looking up names of veterans (also at **www.wwiimemorial.com**).

17th St., near Constitution Ave. NW. www.nps.gov/nwwm. ✆ **800/639-4992** or 202/426-6841. Free admission. Limited parking. Metro: Farragut West, Federal Triangle, or Smithsonian, with a 20- to 25-min. walk. DC Circulator stop.

Smithsonian Information Center ("The Castle") ★ MUSEUM   This
1855 Medieval-style building, with its eight crenellated towers and rich red sandstone facade, lives up to its nickname, at least from the exterior. Its Great Hall interior is rather unattractive, but that doesn't matter, because you're just here for information, possibly restrooms, and perhaps a bite to eat.

There's not much else in this big building that's open to the public. The remains of Smithsonian benefactor James Smithson are buried in that big crypt in the Mall-side entrance area, which includes a small exhibit about the man. The pretty south-side entrance has been repainted to appear as it did in the early 1900s, when children's exhibits were displayed here. On the east side of the building is the **Castle Café,** which opens at 8:30am, earlier than any other building on the Mall. Coffee, pastries, sandwiches, and even beer and wine are sold. Situate yourself at a table inside, where there's free Wi-Fi, or outdoors in the lovely **Enid A. Haupt Garden,** and plot your day.

1000 Jefferson Dr. SW. www.si.edu. ⓒ **202/633-1000.** Daily 8:30am–5:30pm (info desk 9am–4pm). Closed Dec 25. Metro: Smithsonian (Mall exit). DC Circulator stop.

United States Botanic Garden ★ GARDEN   For the feel of summer in
the middle of winter and the sight of lush, breathtakingly beautiful greenery and flowers year-round, stop in at the Botanic Garden, located at the foot of the Capitol and next door to the National Museum of the American Indian. The grand conservatory devotes half of its space to exhibits that focus on the importance of plants to people, and half to exhibits that focus on ecology and the evolutionary biology of plants. But those finer points may escape you as you wander through the various chambers, outdoors and indoors, upstairs and down, gazing in stupefaction at so much flora. Throughout its 10 "garden rooms" and two courtyards, the conservatory holds about 1,300 living species, or about 25,000 plants. Individual areas include a high-walled enclosure, called "the Tropics," of palms, ferns, and vines; an **Orchid Room;** a garden of plants used for medicinal purposes; a primeval garden; and seasonal gardens created especially for children. Stairs and an elevator in the Tropics take you to a mezzanine level near the top of the greenhouse, where you can admire the jungle of greenery 24 feet below and, if condensation on the glass windows doesn't prevent it, a view of the Capitol Building. Just outside the conservatory is the **National Garden,** which includes the **First Ladies Water Garden,** a formal rose garden, a butterfly garden, an amphitheater, and a lawn terrace. Tables and benches make this a lovely spot for a picnic, though much of the garden is unshaded.

The garden annex across the street holds **Bartholdi Park.** It's about the size of a city block and features a cast-iron classical fountain created by Frédéric Auguste Bartholdi, designer of the Statue of Liberty. Flower gardens bloom amid tall ornamental grasses, benches are sheltered by vine-covered bowers, and a touch and fragrance garden contains such herbs as pineapple-scented sage. Spring through fall, this is a pleasant place to enjoy a picnic at one of the many umbrella tables.

Note: When you visit Bartholdi Park, you may notice the **American Veterans Disabled for Life Memorial** (www.nps.gov/nama/planyourvisit/american-veterans-disabled-for-life.htm or www.avdlm.org; © **877/426-6838**), located just across the street at 150 Washington Ave. SW. With its star-shaped fountain, continuously running reflecting pool, and panels of laminated glass etched with the images and quotations of injured soldiers, the memorial pays tribute to the more than 4 million soldiers injured while serving their country.

100 Maryland Ave. SW (btw. First and 3rd sts. SW, at the foot of the Capitol, bordering the National Mall). www.usbg.gov. © **202/225-8333.** Free admission. Conservatory and National Garden daily 10am–5pm (National Garden open until 7pm in summer); Bartholdi Park dawn–dusk. Metro: Federal Center SW (Smithsonian Museums/Maryland Ave. exit). DC Circulator stop.

Vietnam Veterans Memorial ★★ MONUMENT/MEMORIAL   The

Vietnam Veterans Memorial is possibly the most poignant sight in Washington: two long, black-granite walls in the shape of a V, each inscribed with the names of the men and women who gave their lives, or remain missing, in the nearly 20-year-long war. Even if no one close to you died in Vietnam, it's moving to watch visitors grimly studying the directories to find out where their loved ones are listed or rubbing pencil on paper held against a name etched into the wall. The walls list close to 60,000 people, most of whom died very young.

Because of the raging conflict over U.S. involvement in the war, Vietnam veterans had received almost no recognition of their service before the memorial was conceived by Vietnam vet Jan Scruggs. The nonprofit Vietnam Veterans Memorial Fund raised $7 million and secured a 2-acre site in tranquil Constitution Gardens to erect a memorial that would make no political statement and would harmonize with neighboring memorials. By separating the issue of the wartime service of individuals from the issue of U.S. policy in Vietnam, the VVMF hoped to begin a process of national reconciliation.

The design by Yale senior Maya Lin was chosen in a national competition open to all citizens ages 18 and over. Erected in 1982, the memorial's two walls

The Vietnam Veterans Memorial.

are angled at 125 degrees to point to the Washington Monument and the Lincoln Memorial. The walls' mirrorlike surfaces reflect surrounding trees, lawns, and monuments. The names are inscribed in chronological order, documenting an epoch in American history as a series of individual sacrifices from the date of the first casualty in 1959. The National Park Service continues to add names as Vietnam veterans die eventually of injuries sustained during the war. Catalogs near the entrances to the memorial list names alphabetically and the panel and row number for each name that is inscribed in the wall. Elsewhere on the grounds of the Vietnam Veterans Memorial, though not part of Maya Lin's design, are two other sculptures honoring the efforts of particular servicemen and women: the **Three Servicemen Statue** and the **Vietnam Women's Memorial.**

Northeast of the Lincoln Memorial, east of Henry Bacon Dr. (btw. 21st and 22nd sts. NW, on the Constitution Ave. NW side of the Mall). www.nps.gov/vive. © **202/426-6841.** Free admission. Limited parking. Metro: Foggy Bottom, with 20-min. walk. DC Circulator stop.

Washington Monument ★★★

MONUMENT/MEMORIAL Step inside the Washington Monument and onto the elevator that whisks visitors to the 500-foot observation deck of this towering obelisk with views for miles in all directions. Or gaze up at the monument's exterior—it's hard not to; it stands out. And while you're gazing, keep this history in mind:

The idea of a tribute to George Washington was first broached 16 years before his death, by the Continental Congress of 1783. But the new nation had more pressing problems, and funds were not readily available. It wasn't until the early 1830s, with the 100th anniversary of Washington's birth approaching, that any action was taken.

First there were several fiascos. A mausoleum under the Capitol

The Washington Monument, with the U.S. Capitol in the distance.

Rotunda was provided for Washington's remains, but a grandnephew, citing Washington's will, refused to allow the body to be moved from Mount Vernon. In 1830, Horatio Greenough was commissioned to create a memorial statue for the Rotunda. He came up with a bare-chested Washington, draped in classical Greek garb. A shocked public claimed he looked as if he were "entering or leaving a bath," and so the statue was relegated to the Smithsonian. Finally, in 1833, prominent citizens organized the Washington National Monument Society. The design of Treasury Building architect Robert Mills was accepted.

The cornerstone was laid in and construction continued for 6 years, until declining contributions and the Civil War brought work to a halt at an

How did the Smithsonian Institution come to be? It's rather an unlikely story, concerning the largesse of a wealthy English scientist named James Smithson (1765–1829), the illegitimate son of the Duke of Northumberland. Smithson willed his vast fortune to the United States, to found "at Washington, under the name of the Smithsonian Institution, an establishment for the increase and diffusion of knowledge." Smithson never explained why he left this handsome bequest to the United States, a country he had never visited. Speculation is that he felt the new nation, lacking established cultural institutions, most needed his funds.

Smithson died in Genoa, Italy, in 1829. Congress accepted his gift in 1836; 2 years later, half a million dollars' worth of gold sovereigns (a considerable sum in the 19th c.) arrived at the U.S. Mint in Philadelphia. For the next 8 years, Congress debated the best possible use for these funds. Finally, in 1846, President James Polk signed an act into law establishing the Smithsonian Institution and authorizing a board to receive "all objects of art and of foreign and curious research, and all objects of natural history, plants, and geological and mineralogical specimens…for research and museum purposes." In 1855, the first Smithsonian building opened on the Mall, not as a museum, but as the home of the Smithsonian Institution. The red sandstone structure today serves as the Smithsonian Information Center, known by all as "the Castle." Smithson's remains are interred in the crypt located inside the north vestibule (National Mall side).

Today, the Smithsonian Institution's 19 museums and galleries (D.C. has 17), nine research centers, and the National Zoological Park comprise the world's largest museum complex. Millions of people visit the Smithsonians annually—more than 22 million visitors toured the museums in 2019. The Smithsonian's collection of 155 million objects spans the entire world and all its history, its peoples and animals (past and present), and our attempts to probe into the future.

So vast is the collection that Smithsonian museums display only about 1% or 2% of the collection's holdings at any given time. Thousands of scientific expeditions sponsored by the Smithsonian have pushed into remote frontiers in the deserts, mountains, polar regions, and jungles of the world.

Individually, each museum is a powerhouse in its own field. The **National Museum of Natural History,** with 5 million annual visitors, is the most visited museum in the world. The **National Air and Space Museum** maintains the world's largest collection of historic aircraft and spacecraft. The **Freer** and **Sackler Galleries** house the largest Asian art research library in the United States. The **Smithsonian American Art Museum** is the nation's first-established collection of American art and one of the largest in the world.

To find out information about any of the Smithsonian museums and check for current hours, go to **www.si.edu**, which directs you to their individual home pages.

awkward 153 feet (you can still see a change in the color of the stone about one-third of the way up). It took until 1876 for sufficient funds to become available, thanks to President Grant's authorization for use of federal monies to complete the project, and another 4 years after that for work to resume on the unsightly stump. The monument finally opened to the public in 1888.

In August 2011, a large earthquake struck the D.C. area and severely damaged the landmark's structure.

Visiting the Washington Monument: Even though admission is free, you'll need a ticket; see below for details. Travel light and definitely don't bring large backpacks, strollers, or open containers of food or drink, none of which are allowed inside the Monument. When you arrive, stand in line to pass through the new permanent security screening facility, and from there into the Monument's large elevator, which takes you upward for 70 seconds.

You won't arrive at the pinnacle of the 555-foot, 5⅛-inch-tall obelisk, but close to it: the 500-foot level of the world's tallest freestanding work of masonry. At this height, it's clear to see that the Washington Monument lies at the very heart of Washington, D.C., landmarks—and its 360-degree views are spectacular. Due east are the Capitol and Smithsonian buildings; due north is the White House; due west are the World War II and Lincoln memorials (with Arlington National Cemetery beyond); due south are the Martin Luther King, Jr. and Jefferson memorials, overlooking the Tidal Basin and the Potomac River. On a clear day, it's said you can see 20 miles in any direction.

Once you've gotten your fill of the views, head down the steps to the small museum (at level 490 ft.), where you can peer at bent lightning rods removed from the top of the Monument after it had been struck; discover that Pierre L'Enfant had hoped to honor George Washington with an equestrian statue; and read the prophetic quote by Sen. Robert Winthrop, at the 1885 dedication of the Washington Monument: THE LIGHTENING OF HEAVEN MAY SCAR AND BLACKEN IT. AN EARTHQUAKE MAY SHAKE ITS FOUNDATIONS…BUT THE CHARACTER WHICH IT COMMEMORATES AND ILLUSTRATES IS SECURE.

Ticket information: Admission to the Washington Monument is free, but you will need a ticket to get in. While walk-up tickets have previously been distributed from the ticket booth in the Monument Lodge, at the bottom of the hill from the monument, on 15th Street NW between Madison and Jefferson drives, visitors are now required to reserve all tickets in advance online or call the **National Park Reservation Service** (✆ **877/444-6777**). To do so, go to www.recreation.gov and search "Washington Monument." Tickets for the next day are released each day at 10am (so, log on at 10am Aug. 20 for an Aug. 21 ticket). You'll pay a $1 service fee per ticket, and you'll need to print them or show a digital copy on your phone when you arrive. You can order up to six (6) tickets. (Check before you visit to see if the same-day ticket offering has come back.) Strollers and bulky items not permitted. There are public restrooms in the Monument Lodge at the base of the building.

15th St. NW, directly south of the White House (btw. Madison Dr. and Constitution Ave. NW). www.nps.gov/wamo. ✆ **202/426-6841.** Daily 9am–5pm, last tour at 4pm. Metro: Smithsonian (Mall/Jefferson Dr. exit), with a 10-min. walk. DC Circulator stop.

SOUTHWEST OF THE MALL

A few top attractions are located across Independence Avenue from the National Mall. These sites are not National Park Service properties, and it can be a bit of a walk to reach some of them, so I've separated them from other attractions located nearby in the southwest section of the National Mall and Memorial Parks category.

Bureau of Engraving and Printing ★ GOVERNMENT BUILDING

This is where they literally show you the money: A staff of about 1,172 works round-the-clock Monday through Friday churning it out at the rate of about $300 million a day. Everyone's eyes pop as they walk past rooms overflowing with new greenbacks. The bureau also prints security documents for other federal government agencies, including military IDs and passport pages.

A 40-minute guided tour begins with a short introductory film. Large windows allow you to see what goes into making paper money: designing, inking, engraving, stacking of bills, cutting, and examining for defects. The process combines traditional, old-world printing techniques with the latest technology to create counterfeit-proof currency. Additional exhibits display bills no longer in circulation and a $100,000 bill designed for official transactions. (Since 1969 the largest-denomination bill issued for the general public is $100.)

After you finish the tour, allow time to explore the **visitor center,** open from March to September 8:30am to 6pm and until 2:45pm September to March with additional exhibits and a gift shop, where you can buy bags of shredded money, uncut sheets of currency in different denominations, and copies of historic documents, such as a hand-engraved replica ($200) of the Declaration of Independence.

Ticket tips: Many people line up each day to get a peek at all the moolah, so arrive early, especially during the peak tourist season. To avoid a line, consider securing VIP, also called "congressional," tour tickets from one of your senators or congresspersons; e-mail or call at least 3 months in advance. Tours take place April through August at 8:15 and 8:45am, and between 4 and 4:45pm.

Tickets for general-public tours are generally not required from September to February; simply find the visitors' entrance at 14th and C streets. March through August, however, every person taking the tour must have a ticket. To obtain one, go to the ticket booth on the Raoul Wallenberg (formerly 15th St.) side of the building. You'll receive a ticket specifying a tour time for that same day and be directed to the 14th Street entrance. You're allowed as many as four tickets per person. The ticket booth opens at 8am and closes when all tickets are dispersed for the day.

14th and C sts. SW. www.moneyfactory.gov. ✆ **866/874-2330.** Free admission. Mon–Fri 9am–2pm Sept to mid-March; 9am–6pm mid-March through Aug. Closed Sat–Sun, federal holidays, and Dec 25–Jan 1. Metro: Smithsonian (Independence Ave. exit). DC Circulator stop.

Dwight D. Eisenhower Memorial ★ MEMORIAL

This Frank Gehry–designed park just south of the Air and Space Museum honors the life and career of the 34th president and leader of the Allied forces during World War II.

The monument is straightforward yet powerful, a nod to the man it represents. As a five-star general during WWII, Eisenhower commanded the Allied invasion of Normandy on D-Day and helped ultimately defeat the Nazis.

From there, he served two terms as president, promoting peace and diplomacy and bolstering American infrastructure. (The memorial's location is significant, as it's set in a plaza surrounded by the Department of Education, the Federal Aviation Administration, the Department of Health and Human Services, and Voice of America—all of which Eisenhower had an impact on.) Yet despite his grand stature in U.S. history, "Ike," as he was known, never lost sight of his humility and sense of diplomacy. The new memorial captures these characteristics of the man it celebrates: Most features here are larger than life, but they blend into the surrounding cityscape and don't dominate the skyline like some of the more prominent Washington monuments.

Start at the northwest corner of the 4-acre park, where you'll see a statue of "Ike" as a youth in Kansas, sitting on a wall and staring off at the rest of the memorial, as if imagining his future. From there you'll follow the pink limestone plaza to see highlights from Eisenhower's career: a scene of him addressing the 101st Airborne Division before D-Day, which was designed based on a photograph of the event; and an Oval Office scene from his presidency. In this portrayal, Eisenhower stands in front of a bas relief map of the world, symbolizing his global diplomacy. Figures representing the military and civilians surround the president, a nod to his role of bridging and creating balance between the two groups after multiple wars. Behind all this is a massive, 450-foot long by 80-foot-tall screen that depicts a sketched relief of the cliffs of Normandy.

You can walk through the park in just a few minutes, but I recommend pulling up the audio guide on your phone (available at the park's website or via QR code prompts at the site). Sit on the wide stone benches and listen to the stories of Ike's life, including an interview with architect Frank Gehry about how the design came to life. A small visitor center onsite contains a gift shop, info booth, and restroom.

Independence Ave. SW (btw. 4th and 6th St. SW). www.nps.gov/ddem. ✆ **202/426-6841.** Free admission. Daily 24 hours. Metro: L'Enfant Plaza (Maryland Ave. and 7th St. exit).

International Spy Museum ★★ MUSEUM   It's not hard to believe the claim made in the museum's 5-minute introductory film that Washington, D.C., has more spies than any other city in the world. Yikes. Well, if you can't flee them, join 'em. This museum gives you the chance to do just that, learning the tricks of the trade in interactive exhibits that allow you to take on a new identity and test your powers of observation. (Is that a lipstick tube in your purse or a gun?) Turns out, the most unlikely of people have acted as spies in their time. Would you believe George Washington? Julia Child? Coco Chanel?

The Spy Museum moved to its current location in 2019, doubling the floor space of the original facility and incorporating cool features in its design like the "glass veil suspended in front of an enclosed black box exhibition space," which allows the movement of people to be visible from both inside and outside. Its inventory of international-espionage artifacts numbers more than 7,000, in exhibits that cover history, as noted, as well as training, equipment, the "spies among us," legendary spooks, Civil War spies, and 21st-century cyber-spying. Explore Communist Berlin, including a Stasi office with all original artifacts, a border checkpoint, and original segments of the Berlin Wall. Or immerse yourself in the latest cyber-security threats and decipher possible future threats to the security of nations. It's a fascinating experience to hear about such a diverse cast, from the women whose analytical prowess facilitated the capture of Osama Bin Laden to James Lafayette, the African-American spy whose intelligence reports helped George Washington clinch victory in the American Revolution, and many others, famous, infamous, and unknown. *Note:* All ages welcome but the museum is best for kids 7 and up.

700 L'Enfant Plaza SW (at Independence Ave. SW). www.spymuseum.org. © **202/393-7798.** Admission $25 adults; $23 seniors/military/college students; $17 youths 7–12; children 6 and under free. Daily 10am–6pm. Metro: L'Enfant Plaza.

Museum of the Bible ★ MUSEUM   With 8 floors and 430,000 square feet, the Bible Museum's size indicates the epic nature of its subject—in this case, 3,500 years of history related to the Bible, and the Bible's impact on the world. There's a lot to see: Some 3,150 artifacts are on display, ranging from an illuminated manuscript from the 14th century to a copy of Elvis's personal Bible. And there's a lot to do: The center layers the traditional touring experience with immersive activities that have you walking through a re-creation of 1st-century Nazareth, complete with costumed villagers a la Williamsburg, or watching a film that flies you over the city of Washington, pointing out biblical inscriptions at capital landmarks as you go. Although the museum holds eight floors, the primary exhibits lie on floor 2 (**The Impact of the Bible on the World**), floor 3 (**The Stories of the Bible,** in entertainment form), and floor 4 (**The History of the Bible**). Visit levels B1, 1, and 5 to tour special exhibits and level 6 to take in an outstanding view of the capital. The museum is just a couple of blocks south of the National Museum of the American Indian and the National Mall.

I recommend my usual strategy for tackling a visit to an overwhelming museum: Start with a general guided tour, then ask your guide what exhibit or artifact is most meaningful to him or her. Designated top hits on the hour-long highlights tour include Julia Ward Howe's original draft of the *Battle Hymn of the Republic,* written in 1861; and a fragment of a first edition of the Gutenberg Bible, circa 1455. One tour guide's personal recommendation was the "Impact of the Bible" section on criminal justice in America, specifically its collection of personal anecdotes, including that of a man in jail for life who nevertheless has found peace within himself through his newfound understanding of the Bible, and the tale of a jury that relied on Bible verses to find a man guilty of murder and deserving of the death sentence. Provocative.

The Bible Museum is Smithsonian in size and scope, but a different animal altogether. This is a privately funded facility, whose founders and primary funders are the evangelical billionaire Green family, owners of the chain of Hobby Lobby arts and crafts stores. Buy tickets online for discounted rates.

400 4th St. SW (at D St. SW). museumofthebible.org. © **866/430-6682.** Admission $20–$25 adults; $10–$15 children 7–17; free for children 6 and under. Wed–Mon 10am–5pm. Closed Tuesday and Thanksgiving, Dec 25, and Jan 1. Metro: Federal Center SW.

United States Holocaust Memorial Museum ★★ MUSEUM The Holocaust Museum documents Nazi Germany's systematic persecution and annihilation of 6 million Jews and others between 1933 and 1945, presenting visitors with individual stories of both horror and courage in the persecuted people's struggle to survive. The museum calls itself a "living memorial to the Holocaust," the idea being for people to visit, confront the evil of which mankind is capable, and leave inspired to face down hatred and inhumanity when they come upon it in the world. A message repeated over and over is this one of Holocaust survivor and author Primo Levi: "It happened. Therefore, it can happen again. And it can happen everywhere." Since the museum opened in 1993, more than 43 million visitors have taken home that message, and another: "What you do matters."

You begin your tour of the permanent exhibit on the first floor, where you pick the identity card of an actual Holocaust victim, whose fate you learn about in stages at different points in the exhibit. Then you ride the elevator to the fourth floor, where "Nazi Assault, 1933–1939" covers events in Germany, from Hitler's appointment as chancellor in 1933 to Germany's invasion of Poland and the official start of World War II in 1939. You learn that anti-Semitism was nothing new and observe for yourself in newsreels how Germans were bowled over by Hitler's powers of persuasion and propaganda. Exhibits tell stories of desperation, like the voyage of the *St. Louis* passenger liner in May 1939, which sailed from Germany to Havana with 900 Jews, but was turned away and returned to Europe.

The middle floor of the permanent exhibit covers the years 1940 to 1945, laying bare the horrors of the Nazi machine's "Final Solution" for the Jews, including deportations, the ghetto experience, and life and death in the concentration camps. Survivors tell their stories in taped recordings. Throughout the museum are artifacts like transport rail cars, reconstructed concentration camp barracks, and photographs of "killing squad" executions. One of the most moving exhibits is the "Tower of Faces," which contains photographs of the Jewish people who lived in the small Lithuanian town of Eishishok for some 900 years, before the Nazis killed nearly all, in 2 days in September 1941.

"The Last Chapter," on the second floor, documents the stories of heroes, like the king of Denmark, who was able to save the lives of 90% of Denmark's Jewish population. Exhibits also recount the Allies' liberation of the concentration camps and aftermath events, from Jewish emigration to America and Israel to the Nuremberg trials. At exhibit's end is the hour-long film, *Testimonies,* in which Holocaust survivors tell their stories. The tour finishes in the **Hall of Remembrance,** a place for meditation and reflection and where you may light a memorial candle.

Don't overlook the first-floor and lower-level exhibits. Always on view are **"Daniel's Story: Remember the Children,"** for children 8 and older, and the **"Wall of Remembrance"** (Children's Tile Wall), which commemorates the 1.5 million children killed in the Holocaust. The lower level is also the site for special exhibits. The museum also houses a Resource Center that includes a registry of Holocaust survivors and victims, a library, and archives, all of which are available to anyone who wants to research family history or the Holocaust.

Note: The museum's permanent exhibit is not recommended for children 11 and under; for older children, it's advisable to prepare them for what they'll see.

A cafeteria and museum shop are on the premises.

100 Raoul Wallenberg Place SW (formerly 15th St. SW; near Independence Ave., just off the Mall). www.ushmm.org. © **202/488-0400.** Free admission. Closed Yom Kippur and Dec 25. Metro: Smithsonian (12th St./Independence Ave. exit). DC Circulator stop.

THE WHITE HOUSE AREA

The **White House** is the main attraction in this section of downtown and offers reason enough to come here, even if you're only able to admire it from the outside. But walk around and you'll also find an off-the-Mall Smithsonian museum, the **Renwick Gallery,** and smaller and more specialized art collections and several historic houses. Pick and choose from the offerings below or follow the walking tour of the neighborhood outlined in chapter 10.

Art Museum of the Americas ★ ART MUSEUM   Contemporary Latin American and Caribbean artworks are on display inside this picturesque, Spanish colonial–style structure. The museum rotates art from its permanent collection of 2,000 works, and sometimes collaborates with other organizations on special exhibits, often with the purpose of highlighting themes of democracy, development, and human rights. The Organization of American States opened the museum in 1976 as a gift to the U.S. in honor of its bicentennial.

201 18th St. NW (at Virginia Ave.). www.museum.oas.org. © **202/370-0147.** Free admission. Tues–Sun 10am–5pm. Closed federal holidays and Good Friday. Metro: Farragut West (18th St. exit) or Farragut North (K St. exit).

Black Lives Matter Plaza ★★★ MURAL   Many of Washington's monuments and memorials take years to come to life. This one happened nearly overnight. In the summer of 2020, D.C. mayor Muriel Bowser commissioned the massive yellow block letters to be painted, along with the D.C. flag, on the 2 blocks of 16th Street stretching north from Lafayette Park and the White House. The letters, and the official renaming of this portion of the street to Black Lives Matter Plaza, were initially seen not only as a response to the murder of George Floyd, but also a but also a rebuke to then-President Donald Trump, whose use of federal troops to block streets in D.C. and intimidate peaceful protestors after Floyd's death was sharply criticized by Bowser and other Washingtonians. (The plaza is clearly visible from the White House.)

But Black Lives Matter Plaza quickly became much more. It's a gathering place—you may find demonstrations, music, dance parties or people bringing grills out. It's a place of reflection; people stand in silence and parents bring their children here to learn about the fight for racial justice. The city council is now working to make it a permanent fixture, with traffic rerouted to create a pedestrian zone around the letters.

16h St. NW (between H St. and K St.). Metro: McPherson Sq.

Daughters of the American Revolution (DAR) Museum ★

MUSEUM   The DAR Museum gives visitors a glimpse of pre-Industrial American life through displays of folk art, quilts, furniture, silverware, samplers, and everyday objects. Its 31 **Period Rooms** reflect trends in decorative arts and furnishings from 1690s to 1930s. On display in the Americana Room are select items from the DAR archives of the paperwork of each period, from Colonial days through the Revolutionary War, up to the country's beginnings: diaries, letters, and household inventories. See p. 263 for more information.

1776 D St. NW (at 17th St.). www.dar.org/museum. © **202/628-1776.** Free admission. Museum and Period Rooms Mon–Fri 8:30am–4pm; Sat 9am–5pm. Americana Room Mon–Fri 8:30am–4pm. Closed federal holidays. Metro: Farragut West (17th St. exit) or Farragut North (K St. exit).

National Children's Museum ★★

MUSEUM   A 50-foot slide, an "immersive sandbox," interactive exploration, bubbles, blocks, lights. This sprawling 30,000-square-foot museum, opened in 2021, is designed to "spark curiosity and ignite creativity for kids and the young at heart." Highlights include a cloud-inspired climbing structure and slide spanning three floors of the museum (for kids 5 years and up); a live green screen where kids get superpowers to control the weather; life-sized bubbles and an immersive digital space focused on STEAM (science, technology, engineering, arts, and math) activities through play. A few engaging exhibits during a recent visit: a Spotify-powered dance space, box car building and racing, a "batting cage" featuring Nationals' helmets; an air-tube system that lets kids send a pom pom through and discover how everything is connected; and an air machine with inflatable balls to "shoot" a basket.

Founded in 1974 as the Capital Children's Museum, the museum operated out of an old nunnery behind Union Station for nearly 30 years before becoming a "museum without walls" for several years. Its newest location will hopefully be a more permanent home for the community-focused museum.

Advanced reservations are currently required for all tickets; you'll need to plan ahead and select one of two timed sessions to visit: either 9:30am to 12:30pm or 1:30pm to 4:30pm. The museum plans to open a cafe and coffee bar.

1300 Pennsylvania Ave. NW (at 13th St. in the Ronald Reagan Bldg. and International Trade Ctr.). www.nationalchildrensmuseum.org. © **202/844-2486.** Admission $16 adults and kids 2–17. Daily 9:30am–4:30pm. Metro: Federal Triangle.

Planet Word Museum ★★

LANGUAGE MUSEUM   "We are all born collectors of this one thing: words," according to this museum's founder Ann Friedman. We just don't always know how to use or appreciate them. That's where Planet Word's mission comes in: to inspire and renew a love of words and language. The museum, opened in 2020 and aptly located in the building where Alexander Graham Bell first tested his photophone, features multisensory and physical activities all meant for visitors to explore the power of words. The third-floor gallery "Where Do Words Come From?" includes a 20x40-foot-tall word wall. Speak into one of the gallery's four microphones and the word wall will respond to your voice and shape a story. In "Spoken World," various stations are centered on a 12-foot-tall LED globe where ambassadors will introduce visitors to their native language through tongue-twisters, songs or sports chants. Other exhibits focus on poetry and real stories on the impact of words in everyday life. Outside the museum's sound sculpture is a weeping willow tree that triggers audio in several different languages and forms when you get close. The museum encourages visitors to reserve advanced entry passes online; these are released each month on the first of the month. A limited number of walk-up passes are also offered every hour on the half-hour.

1300 I St. NW (at 13th St.). www.planetwordmuseum.org. *C* **202/931-3139.** Free, w/ suggested donation. Daily 10am–5pm. Metro: McPherson Square (14th St. and I St. exit).

Renwick Gallery of the Smithsonian American Art Museum ★★

ART MUSEUM   Long the city's go-to venue for lovers of American decorative arts, traditional and modern crafts, and architectural design, the museum in the past few years has morphed into a funhouse showcasing room-size installations of innovative, immersive artworks. A highlight is Janet Echelman's colorful fiber and lighting installation *1.8 Renwick,* which will be on view until April 2023. Hanging suspended from the Grand Salon's ceiling, the installation, inspired by the Japanese earthquake and tsunami in 2011, dynamically changes light and projects shadow drawings in vivid colors that move from wall to wall.

The Renwick's galleries also showcase **Connections,** highlighting more than 80 objects "celebrating craft as a discipline and an approach to living differently in the modern world." The artworks span 90 years and numerous media.

On view in other rooms of the museum are objects from the permanent collection, such as Wendell Castle's *Ghost Clock*. A showcase in the elegant Octagon Room uses photos, documents, and art objects to chronicle the building's history.

Designed by and named for James W. Renwick, Jr., architect of the Smithsonian Castle (p. 159), the Renwick was built in 1859, an example of French Second Empire–style architecture. A 2015 renovation restored the original 19th-century window configurations, and turned up some surprises, like long-concealed vaulted ceilings on the second floor. Located directly across the street from the White House, the Renwick originally was built to house the art collection of William Wilson Corcoran. The collection quickly outgrew the space, which led to the opening of the Corcoran Gallery of Art (currently closed to the public) just down the street, in 1874.

1661 Pennsylvania Ave. NW (at 17th St.). www.renwick.americanart.si.edu. © **202/633-7970.** Free admission. Daily 10am–5:30pm. Closed Labor Day and Dec 25. Metro: Farragut West or Farragut North.

The White House ★★★ GOVERNMENT BUILDING This house has served as residence, office, reception site, and world embassy for every U.S. president since John Adams. The White House is the only private residence of a head of state in the world that opens regularly to the public, free of charge, a practice that Thomas Jefferson inaugurated.

Many visitors to Washington never set foot inside the White House; they gaze at the building's North Portico through a tall fence on Pennsylvania Ave. or walk around to look up at the South Portico from the Ellipse. (Sometimes when there are events or security concerns access is fenced off on both sides.)

If you are lucky enough to score a tour, keep in mind that meanwhile, somewhere in this very building, the president and staff are meeting with foreign dignitaries, congressional members, and business leaders, hashing out the most urgent national and global decisions. For tour info, see box, p. 175.

An Act of Congress in 1790 established the city now known as Washington, District of Columbia, as the seat of the federal government. George Washington and city planner Pierre L'Enfant chose the site for the president's house and staged a contest to find a builder. Although Washington picked the winner—Irishman James Hoban—he was the only president never to live in the White House. The structure took 8 years to build, starting in 1792, when its cornerstone was laid. Its facade is made of the same stone used to construct the Capitol. The mansion quickly became known as the "White House," thanks to the limestone whitewashing applied to the walls to protect them, later replaced by white lead paint in 1818. In 1814, during the War of 1812, the British set fire to the White House and gutted the interior; the exterior managed to endure only because a rainstorm extinguished the fire. What you see today is Hoban's basic creation: a building modeled after an Irish country house.

Insider tip: Tours of the White House exit from the North Portico. Before you descend the front steps, look to your left to see the window whose sandstone still remains unpainted as a reminder of the 1814 fire.

Additions over the years have included the South Portico in 1824, the North Portico in 1829, and electricity in 1891, during Benjamin Harrison's presidency. In 1902, repairs and refurnishing of the White House cost nearly $500,000. No other great change took place until Harry Truman's presidency, when the interior was completely renovated after the leg of Margaret Truman's piano cut through the dining room ceiling. The Trumans lived at Blair House across the street for nearly 4 years while the White House interior was shored up with steel girders and concrete.

In 1961, First Lady Jacqueline Kennedy spearheaded the founding of the White House Historical Association and formed a Fine Arts Committee to help restore the famous rooms to their original grandeur, ensuring treatment of the White House as a museum of American history and decorative arts. "It just seemed to me such a shame when we came here to find hardly anything of the past in the house, hardly anything before 1902," Mrs. Kennedy observed.

Every president and first family put their own stamp on the White House, though at press time the Bidens hadn't yet announced any design changes. President Trump made subtle changes to the Oval Office, replacing maroon drapes with gold and swapping out camel-colored leather chairs for those covered in pale yellow fabric. The Obamas installed artworks on loan from the Hirshhorn Museum and the National Gallery of Art in their private residence and chose works to hang in the public rooms of the White House. (Changing the art in the public rooms requires approval from the White House curator and the Committee for the Preservation of the White House.) Michelle Obama planted a vegetable garden on the White House grounds, and President Obama altered the outdoor tennis court so that it could be used for both basketball and tennis.

Highlights of the public tour include the gold and white **East Room,** the scene of presidential receptions, weddings, major presidential addresses, and other dazzling events. This is where the president entertains visiting heads of state and the place where seven of the eight presidents who died in office lay in state. It's also where Nixon resigned. Note the famous Gilbert Stuart portrait of George Washington that Dolley Madison saved from the British torch during the War of 1812; the portrait is the only object to have remained continuously in the White House since 1800 (except during reconstructions).

You'll visit the **Green Room,** which was Thomas Jefferson's dining room but today is used as a sitting room. Mrs. Kennedy chose the green watered-silk wall covering. The oldest portrait in the White House hangs over the fireplace mantel, that of Benjamin Franklin, painted in 1767. In the **Oval Blue Room,** decorated in the French Empire style chosen by James Monroe in 1817, presidents and first ladies have officially received guests since the Jefferson administration. This room was also where the Reagans greeted the 52 Americans liberated after being held hostage in Iran for 444 days, and every year it's the setting for the White House Christmas tree. If you glance out the windows you'll spot the Jefferson Memorial vividly standing out in the distance.

The **Red Room,** with its red-satin-covered walls and Empire furnishings, is used as a reception room, primarily for afternoon teas. Several portraits of past

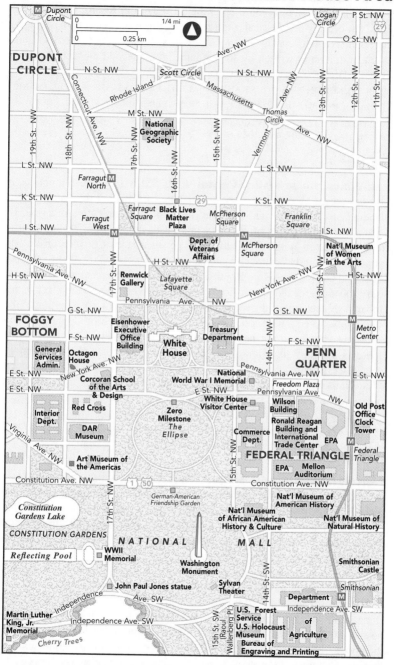

The White House Area

- Dupont Circle M
- Logan Circle
- P St. NW 29
- O St. NW
- DUPONT CIRCLE
- N St. NW
- Scott Circle
- N St. NW
- Connecticut Ave. NW
- Rhode Island
- Massachusetts Ave. NW
- 13th St. NW
- 12th St. NW
- 11th St. NW
- M St. NW
- National Geographic Society
- Thomas Circle
- Vermont Ave. NW
- L St. NW
- 19th St. NW
- 18th St. NW
- 17th St. NW
- 16th St. NW
- 15th St. NW
- L St. NW
- Farragut North M
- K St. NW
- K St. NW
- Farragut West M
- Farragut Square
- Black Lives Matter Plaza
- McPherson Square
- Franklin Square
- I St. NW
- I St. NW
- Pennsylvania Ave. NW
- Dept. of Veterans Affairs
- McPherson Square M
- Nat'l Museum of Women in the Arts
- H St. NW
- H St. NW
- Renwick Gallery
- Lafayette Square
- New York Ave. NW
- 13th St. NW
- H St. NW
- 17th St. NW
- Pennsylvania Ave. NW
- G St. NW
- G St. NW
- FOGGY BOTTOM
- Eisenhower Executive Office Building
- White House
- Treasury Department
- Metro Center M
- F St. NW
- F St. NW
- F St. NW
- PENN QUARTER
- General Services Admin.
- Octagon House
- New York Ave. NW
- Pennsylvania Ave. NW
- 14th St. NW
- E St. NW
- Corcoran School of the Arts & Design
- National World War I Memorial
- Freedom Plaza
- Pennsylvania Ave. NW
- E St. NW
- E St. NW
- Red Cross
- White House Visitor Center
- Wilson Building
- Old Post Office Clock Tower
- Interior Dept.
- Zero Milestone
- The Ellipse
- Commerce Dept.
- Ronald Reagan Building and International Trade Center
- EPA M
- Federal Triangle
- Virginia Ave. NW
- DAR Museum
- FEDERAL TRIANGLE
- Art Museum of the Americas
- EPA
- Mellon Auditorium
- Constitution Ave. NW
- 17th St. NW
- 15th St. NW
- Constitution Ave. NW
- Constitution Gardens Lake
- 1 50
- German-American Friendship Garden
- Nat'l Museum of American History
- CONSTITUTION GARDENS
- NATIONAL MALL
- Nat'l Museum of African American History & Culture
- Nat'l Museum of Natural History
- Reflecting Pool
- WWII Memorial
- Washington Monument
- Smithsonian Castle
- John Paul Jones statue
- Sylvan Theater
- 14th St. SW
- Department of Agriculture
- Smithsonian M
- Martin Luther King, Jr. Memorial
- Independence Ave. SW
- Independence Ave. SW
- U.S. Forest Service
- U.S. Holocaust Museum
- Independence Ave. SW
- Cherry Trees
- 15th St. SW (Raoul Wallenberg Pl.)
- Bureau of Engraving and Printing

0 — 1/4 mi
0 — 0.25 km

presidents and a Gilbert Stuart portrait of Dolley Madison hang here. She used the Red Room for her famous Wednesday-night receptions.

From the Red Room, you'll enter the **State Dining Room.** Modeled after late-18th-century neoclassical English houses, this room is a superb setting for state dinners and luncheons. Below G. P. A. Healy's portrait of Lincoln is a quote taken from a letter written by John Adams on his second night in the White House (FDR had it carved into the mantel): I PRAY HEAVEN TO BESTOW THE BEST OF BLESSINGS ON THIS HOUSE AND ON ALL THAT SHALL HERE-AFTER INHABIT IT. MAY NONE BUT HONEST AND WISE MEN EVER RULE UNDER THIS ROOF.

1600 Pennsylvania Ave. NW (visitor entrance gate at E St. and E. Executive Ave.). www. whitehouse.gov. ℂ **202/456-7041** or 202/208-1631. Free admission. All tours arranged only through congressional offices (see "How To's" box, above). Closed federal holidays. Metro: Federal Triangle.

The White House Visitor Center ★ MUSEUM Whether or not you're able to tour the White House, try to stop here for a behind-the-scenes understanding of the history and everyday life inside the executive mansion. Its wide range of intriguing offerings includes a 14-minute film, "White House: Reflections from Within," featuring the personal stories of the current and former First Family occupants; interactive exhibits that allow you to explore inside and outside the White House with a touch of the screen; and exhibits of some 100 artifacts, like the mahogany desk that White House architect James Hoban fashioned out of the wood scraps left over from the construction of the building. National Park Service rangers staff the information desks and hand out White House touring pamphlets that you'll find helpful for your White House visit. The White House Historical Association has a **gift shop** here (a great place to purchase mementos and presents, like the annually designed White House Christmas tree ornament). And here's a fact you might just want to know: The center has public restrooms.

1450 Pennsylvania Ave. NW (in the Department of Commerce Bldg., btw. 14th and 15th sts.). www.nps.gov/whho/planyourvisit/white-house-visitor-center.htm. ℂ **202/208-1631.** Free admission. Daily 7:30am–4pm. Closed Jan 1, Thanksgiving, and Dec 25. Metro: Federal Triangle.

World War I Memorial ★★ MONUMENT In a wide-open plaza across from the Willard Hotel you'll find Washington's newest monument. The space, known for years as Pershing Square as a tribute to General John J. Pershing, leader of the American Expeditionary Forces (AEF) during World War I, has been expanded to be inclusive of all contributors to the United States effort during the Great War.

While a small rotunda on the National Mall has commemorated Washington, D.C.'s involvement in World War I for more than 90 years, the capital city was lacking a national memorial for the conflict. After the debut of the World War II memorial in 2004, the push to create a similar tribute to the first World War heated up. At first, supporters wanted to transform the existing D.C.-centric memorial into a national one. But the bills that would do so didn't make it through Congress, so instead in a Centennial Commission was created to

THE "HOW TO'S" OF TOURING
THE white house

While specific tour logistics vary slightly with each administration, one thing's consistent: You must have a reservation to tour the White House. No fewer than 21 days and as far as 3 months in advance of your trip, contact the office of one of your senators or representatives to request the tour, provide the number of people in your group, and ask for a specific tour date. Check your rep's website first (senate.gov or house.gov), since some members instruct you to call, while others require you to submit an online request; some members do not provide this constituent service at all. The tour coordinator consults with the White House on availability, and, if your requested date is available, submits your contact details and the size of your group to the White House. The White House then sends you confirmation of receipt of your request and asks you to register for the tour by submitting the names, birth dates, Social Security numbers (for those 18 and over), and other info for each person in your party. The White House reviews the information and contacts you 2 to 3 weeks before your requested date to let you know whether your request has been approved or denied. If approved, your confirmation letter/e-mail will include a confirmation number, the list of people in your group, and the date and time of your confirmed tour. (**Note:** International visitors should contact their embassy to submit a tour request. Some countries such as Australia and Canada do not currently organize tours.)

Hours: White House tours are available to the general public year-round from 7:30 to 11:30am Tuesday through Thursday and 7:30am to 1:30pm Friday and Saturday, and at other times depending on the president's schedule. If the president is out of town, it's possible that more tours will be allowed past the usual cutoff time.

Format and timing: Tours are self-guided. Most people take no more than an hour to go through. Arrive about 15 minutes before your scheduled tour time.

Entry and ID: You'll enter at the side of East Executive Avenue, near the Southeast Gate of the White House. Bring valid, government-issued photo IDs whose information exactly matches that which you provided to your congressional member's office. Everyone in your party who is 18 or older must have an ID.

Important: On the day of your tour, call ✆ 202/456-7041 to make sure the White House is open to the public that day and that your tour hasn't been cancelled.

Do not bring the following prohibited items: Backpacks, book bags, handbags, or purses; food and beverages; strollers; video recorders; tobacco products; personal grooming items, from cosmetics to hairbrushes; any pointed objects, whether a pen or a knitting needle; aerosol containers; guns; ammunition; fireworks; electric stun guns; maces; martial arts weapons/devices; or knives of any kind. Smartphones are okay, as are small cameras. The White House does not have a coat-check facility, so there is no place for you to leave your belongings while you take the tour. There are no public restrooms or telephones in the White House. *Best advice:* Leave everything but your wallet and camera back at the hotel.

mark the 100th anniversary of the United States' involvement in the war, and ultimately Pershing Square was identified as the site of the future memorial.

To create the memorial, the commission opened up a global competition. The winning design came from sculptor Sabin Howard and architect Joseph

Weishaar, who reimagined the original design of Pershing Square to represent all 4.7 million Americans who served in the war.

At the center of the park is a circular display, with informational plaques detailing America's involvement in the war. On the ground is a medallion featuring the same Victory figured that was used on medals awarded to AEF members during the war.

In the southeast corner of the park, you'll find a statue of General Pershing, who commanded the U.S. armed forces on the Western Front from 1918–1919. Maps of the battlefields on the Western Front and the Meuse-Argonne campaign are also etched in a stone wall next to the general.

The focal point of the park is a water feature, rectangular with a reflecting pool and falling water, which is anchored by the park's signature—but unfinished—component. A large stone relief by Howard, *A Soldier's Journey,* which depicts five stages of a soldier's journey, from leaving home to scenes of battle to the return from war, will not be complete until 2024. In the meantime, a true-to-size illustration is shown so you can still get the effect.

The park is set a few feet below street level—this helps block out sounds from the surrounding streets and instead lets you focus on what's here.

Pennsylvania Ave. NW (btw. 14th and 15th sts.). Daily 24 hr. Metro: Metro Center.

PENN QUARTER

Most of this bustling downtown neighborhood's attractions congregate near the Capital One Arena, on or just off 7th Street, the main artery. The ones that aren't there, like Ford's Theatre, are just a short walk away. If you enjoy layering your touring experience with stops for delicious meals or snacks, this is your neighborhood (see chapter 5 for Penn Quarter restaurants).

Ford's Theatre National Historic Site ★★ HISTORIC SITE   On April 14, 1865, President Abraham Lincoln was in the audience at Ford's Theatre, one of the most popular playhouses in Washington. Everyone was laughing at a funny line from Tom Taylor's celebrated comedy, *Our American Cousin,* when John Wilkes Booth crept into the President's Box, shot Lincoln, and leapt to the stage, shouting, *"Sic semper tyrannis!"* ("Thus ever to tyrants!") With his left leg broken from the jump, Booth mounted his horse in the alley and galloped off. Doctors carried Lincoln across the street to the house of William Petersen, where the president died the next morning.

The theater was closed after Lincoln's assassination and used as an office by the War Department. In 1893, 22 clerks were killed when three floors of the building collapsed. It remained in disuse until the 1960s, when the National Park Service remodeled and restored Ford's to its appearance on the night of the tragedy. Grand renovations and developments completed in phases between 2009 and 2012 have since brought about a wholly new experience for visitors.

Ford's Theatre today stands as the centerpiece of the **Ford's Theatre National Historic Site,** a campus of three buildings straddling a short section of 10th Street and including the **Ford's Theatre** and its **Ford's Theatre**

Museum; **Petersen House,** where Lincoln died; and the **Aftermath Exhibits,** inside the **Center for Education and Leadership,** which debuted in 2012 and is dedicated to exploring Lincoln's legacy and promoting leadership.

I recommend visiting all four attractions if you have the time. Briefly, here's what you'll see at the Ford's Theatre National Historic Site:

The Ford's Theatre: The National Park Service ranger talks vividly recreate the events of that night, so try for an entry that includes one of these. A portrait of George Washington hangs beneath the President's Box, as it did the night Lincoln was shot. Ford's remains a working theater, so consider returning in the evening to attend a play. Ford's productions lean toward historical dramas and classic American plays and musicals; recent productions include *The Mountaintop,* which explores the night before Dr. Martin Luther King Jr.'s assassination and the world-premiere musical *Grace.* The production schedule means that the theater, and sometimes the museum, may be closed to sightseers on some days; check the online schedule before you visit.

The **Ford's Theatre Museum,** on the lower level of the theater, displays artifacts that tell the story of Lincoln's presidency, his assassination, and what life was like in Washington and in the United States during that time. Unfortunately, when the museum is crowded, as it often is, it can be hard to get close enough to (and have enough time at) each of the exhibits to properly absorb the information. An exhibit about life in the White House shines a little light on Mary Todd Lincoln; a display of artifacts—including the actual gun (a little 45 derringer) that killed Lincoln—connects the dots between the assassin and those who aided him. Other affecting artifacts: Lincoln's size-14 boots, two Lincoln life masks, and a replica of the greatcoat he wore the night of the assassination—the real coat is here but too fragile for permanent display. (The bullet that killed Lincoln was actually removed by autopsy doctors and is now in the National Museum of Health and Medicine in Silver Spring, Maryland.)

Across 10th Street from the theater and museum is **Petersen House.** The doctor attending to Lincoln and other theatergoers carried Lincoln into the street, where boarder Henry Safford, standing in the open doorway of his rooming house, gestured for them to bring the president inside. So, Lincoln died in the home of William Petersen, a German-born tailor. Now furnished with period pieces, the dark, narrow town house looks much as it did on that fateful April night. You'll see the front parlor where an anguished Mary Todd Lincoln spent the night with her son, Robert. In the back parlor, Secretary of War Edwin M. Stanton held a cabinet meeting and questioned witnesses. From this room, Stanton announced at 7:22am on April 15, 1865, "Now he belongs to the ages." Lincoln died, lying diagonally because he was so tall, on a bed the size of the one in the room. (The Chicago History Museum owns the actual bed and other items from the room.) The exit from Petersen House leads to an elevator that transports you to the fourth floor of the:

Aftermath Exhibits, in the Center for Education and Leadership, where your tour begins with the sights and sounds of the capital in the days following the assassination of Lincoln. You hear church bells tolling and horseshoes clopping and view exhibits of mourning ribbons, coffin handles, and

Albert Einstein Memorial 26
Anacostia Community
    Museum 74
African American Civil War
    Museum and Memorial 41
Anderson House 10
Arlington National Cemetery 23
Arts and Industries Building 60
Art Museum
    of the Americas 31
Belmont-Paul Woman's
    Equality National
    Monument 69
Black Lives Natter Plaza 16
Corcoran School of the Arts
    & Design 21
DAR Museum 30
DC War Memorial 29
Dumbarton House 7
Dumbarton Oaks 5
Dwight D. Eisenhower
    Memorial 64
Eastern Market 73
Enid A. Haupt Garden 58
FDR Memorial 34
Folger Shakespeare Library 71
Ford's Theatre 45

Fred. Douglass Nat'l
    Historic Site 74
Freer Gallery of Art 55
George Mason Memorial 35
Georgetown Waterfront Park 13
Hillwood Museum 2
Hirshhorn Museum 62
International Spy Museum 61
Jefferson Memorial 36
Korean War Veterans
    Memorial 28
Kreeger Museum 4
Library of Congress 72
Lincoln Memorial 25
Martin Luther King, Jr.
    Memorial 33
Mary McCleod Bethune
    Council House 11
Museum of the Bible 65
National Air and Space
    Museum 63
National Archives Museum 51
National Building Museum 47
National Children's Museum 20
National Gallery of Art 54
National Gallery of Art
    Sculpture Garden 53
National Law Enforcement
    Memorial and Museum 48
National Museum
    of African Art 59

National Museum of African American
    History & Culture 39
National Museum of American History 40
National Museum of the American Indian 66
National Museum of Natural History 52
National Museum of Women in the Arts 43
National Postal Museum 49
National Zoological Park 3
Old Post Office Clock Tower 46
Old Stone House 12
The Pentagon 24
Phillips Collection 9
Planet Word 42
Renwick Gallery 15
Sackler Gallery 56
Smithsonian Information Center 57
Smithsonian American Art Museum
    and National Portrait Gallery 44
Supreme Court 70
Textile Museum 14
Theodore Roosevelt Island 22
Tudor Place 6
Union Station 50
U.S. Botanic Garden 67
U.S. Capitol 68
U.S. Holocaust Memorial Museum 37
Vietnam Veterans Memorial 27
Washington Monument 38
Washington National Cathedral 1
White House 17
White House Visitor Center 19
Woodrow Wilson House 8
World War I Memorial 18
World War II Memorial 32

Mt .Vernon Sq./7th St.–
Convention Center

Mt. Vernon
Square

K St. NW

New York Ave. NW

CHINA-TOWN

Metro
Center

Gallery Pl.-
Chinatown

G St. NW

F St. NW

E St. NW

PENN
QUARTER

Pennsylvania

Archives-
Navy Mem'l–
Penn Quarter

Judiciary Sq.

D St. NW

C St. NW

Constitution Ave. NW

NATIONAL MALL

Madison Dr.

Jefferson Dr. SW

Smith-
sonian

Independence Ave. SW

Federal
Center SW

L'Enfant
Plaza

SOUTHWEST
WATERFRONT

Union Station

Union
Station

F St. NE

E St. NE

Massachusetts

D St. NE

C St. NE

Stanton
Square

A St. NE

East Capitol St.

U.S.
Capitol

A St. SE

Independence Ave.

Seward
Square

Capitol
South

D St. SE

Eastern Market

E St. SE

CAPITOL
HILL

CAPITOL
RIVERFRONT

G St. SE

2nd St. NE
5th St. NE
6th St. NE
7th St. NE
8th St. NE
9th St. NE
10th St. NE
11th St. NE

Maryland Ave. NE

North Carolina Ave. SE

Pennsylvania Ave.

Louisiana Ave. NW

Delaware Ave. NE

New Jersey

Washington Ave. SW

South Capitol St.

Ave. SE

179

newspaper broadsheets announcing the tragic news. Details convey the sense of piercing sorrow that prevailed: Twenty-five thousand people attended Lincoln's funeral on April 21, 1865, though not Mary Todd Lincoln, who was too overcome with grief. A staircase that winds around a sculptured tower of some 6,800 books all to do with Lincoln leads down to the center's third floor. Here, a short film, videos, and exhibits explore Lincoln's influence and legacy, including all sorts of products with Lincoln's name, from the children's building blocks to jewelry. Following the staircase another level down takes you to a gallery on real-life examples of brave individuals, such as Rosa Parks, to pose the question "What Would You Do?" in their circumstances.

The how-to: You'll need a timed ticket to tour any part of the campus. Tickets are free and tours take place daily. Visit the website, www.fords.org, for a list of offerings, which can range from a simple theater walk-through (15 min.) to a full tour encompassing the museum; the theater, including either a NPS ranger's interpretive program or a mini-play (these are great); the Petersen House; and the Aftermath Exhibits (a total of about 2 hr. and 15 min.).

A single ticket admits you to all parts of the campus, so don't lose it! Ford's really wants you to order tickets in advance online—only 20% of the daily allotment of tickets are available for same-day pickup. And even though tours are free, online tickets incur processing fees, starting at $3 per ticket. You order tickets online and print them yourself or pick them up at the theater's will-call booth. *Good to know:* When the Ford's Theatre website shows same-day tickets as unavailable, that just means they are unavailable online; go in person to the box office and you may score a same-day pass.

Spring through early fall, Ford's also sells tickets ($18 each, available online) to its popular "History on Foot" 2-hour **walking tours.** A costumed actor brings to life the events of April 14 and 15, 1865, leading tourists on a 1.6-mile traipse to about eight historically significant locations.

511 10th St. NW (btw. E and F sts.). www.fords.org. © **202/347-4833.** Daily 9am–4:30pm. Closed Thanksgiving, Christmas, and other days subject to the theatre's schedule. Timed tickets required for the free tours offered throughout the day. See above for details. Metro: Metro Center (11th and G sts. exit).

National Building Museum ★ MUSEUM The first thing you notice about the National Building Museum is the actual building, its pressed red-brick exterior and decorative terra-cotta frieze, and its *size,* 400 feet by 200 feet, big enough to hold a football field. Inside the impressive **Great Hall** is an Italian Renaissance courtyard, colossal Corinthian columns, 15-story-high ceiling, and central fountain. The structure, modeled after an Italian palazzo, was designed to house the Pension Bureau (its offices were located in those upper arcaded areas, overlooking the atrium) and to serve as a venue for grand galas. The building hosted its first event, President Grover Cleveland's inaugural ball, in 1885, even before construction was completed in 1887, and it's been the site of such balls and other events ever since.

In the 1980s, the building took on a new purpose as a museum dedicated to architecture, landscape architecture, engineering, urban planning, and historic

law enforcement MEMORIAL & MUSEUM

On E Street NW between 4th and 5th streets, directly across the street from the National Building Museum and centered in the same plaza as the entrance/exit to the Judiciary Square Metro station, is the **National Law Enforcement Memorial** (www.nleomf.org; ☏ 202/737-3400), dedicated to the federal, state, and local law enforcement officers who have died in the line of duty. The memorial is a landscaped park whose two tree-lined pathways embrace two curving, 304-foot-long blue-gray marble walls on which are inscribed the names of the more than 20,000 officers who have died protecting the nation and its people throughout U.S. history, starting in 1786. New names are added every May during National Police Week. Four sculptures of a lion protecting her cubs mark each pathway entrance; this is also where you can locate the name of a particular officer in the memorial. Adjacent to the memorial to the south is the **National Law Enforcement Museum** ★ (444 E St. NW; www.lawenforcementmuseum.org; ☏ **202/737-3400**), which opened in 2018. Built mostly underground, the 57,000-square-foot museum tells its story through high-tech interactive exhibits, a comprehensive collection of more than 25,000 artifacts, such as early law enforcement and crime-solving tools pre-dating handcuffs and mug shots, photographs of famous officers, and personal items from former FBI Director J. Edgar Hoover. A highlight of the museum is the patrol driving simulator, just like what you'd find at a police academy, which puts you behind the wheel of a police patrol and tests your ability to make rapid-fire decisions based on scenarios that pop up. To learn more about the 300-year history of law enforcement in the U.S., join a guided tour, offered daily. There are also extensive resources for research, and diverse educational programming. It's open Friday through Sunday 10am to 5pm, and admission is $22 adults, $20 seniors, military, law enforcement professionals, and college students, free for children 12 and under with purchase of adult admission.

preservation and opened to the public in 1985 as the National Building Museum. You can view the Great Hall and take a historic building tour for free, but the museum charges a fee to tour its exhibits, which are mounted in the galleries off the Great Hall on the first and second floors and change yearly. The museum's year-round **Play Work Build** exhibit is a favorite for families. Its other long-term exhibit **House & Home** examines the varying ways houses are built and what it really means to be at home in America.

If you're here in summer, you've got to stop by to experience the super-fun, interactive "Summer Block Party," which takes over the entire expanse of the Great Hall; one year it was a "beach" of nearly 1 million translucent plastic balls. Another year, it was a massive lawn, complete with hammocks and plenty of space to daydream. The museum gift shop is an especially good one (p. 182), as is the on-site eatery.

401 F St. NW (btw. 4th and 5th sts.). www.nbm.org. ☏ **202/272-2448.** Free access to the Great Hall, historic building tours, shop and café. Exhibit admission $10 adults; $7 students (with ID), children 3–17, and seniors 60 and over. Mon–Sat 10am–5pm; Sun 11am–5pm. Closed Thanksgiving and Dec 25. Metro: Gallery Place (7th and F sts. exit) or Judiciary Square (F St. exit).

Coffee Mugs & Celtic Bookends: Museum Gift Shops

Washington's museum shops hold a treasure trove of unusual gifts. I've always had a weakness for the shop at the **National Building Museum** (p. 180), which is jammed with surprising, useful, and cleverly designed housewares and interesting games, including bookends embossed with Celtic designs, Bauhaus mobiles, and collapsible strainers. And I can never visit the **National Gallery of Art** (p. 149) without lingering a little while in the store to admire captivating catalog books, notecards, posters, children's games, and a slew of other things. The Smithsonian's **National Museum of African Art** (p. 153) has unusual items from all over Africa, but I especially liked the interesting designs of the colorful dish towels, handbags, and headbands from Ghana.

Old Post Office Clock Tower ★ HISTORIC SITE   The Clock Tower offers a commanding view of the capital that's second only to that of the nearby Washington Monument. As the second-tallest structure in D.C. after the Washington Monument, it offers fabulous 360-degree views, 270 feet up, of Pennsylvania Avenue, from the Capitol to the White House, and beyond to the National Mall. The building itself was used as the city's primary post office until 1914. It was slated for demolition in 1928, but a lack of funds during the Great Depression saved the structure. It wasn't until 1977 that complete renovation on the structure began, and in 1983, it reopened as offices and retail. The bells in the tower are rung at the opening and closing of Congress and for national holidays. The National Park Service operates and maintains the building and provides interpretive programming.

To reach the clock tower, you must venture down 12th Street, to enter through the door marked "Starbucks & Clock Tower." Stride through the second set of glass doors, ignoring the Starbucks to your left, and keep going down the corridor to reach a wall-mounted exhibit of old photographs, maps, and documents that give you a little history of the building and the city. Proceed through security screening, then hop the elevator, the first of two that take you to the top (change elevators on the 9th floor).

1100 Pennsylvania Ave. NW (at 12th St.). www.nps.gov/opot. Entrance off 12th St. NW. Free admission. Daily 9am–5pm. Metro: Federal Triangle.

Smithsonian American Art Museum and National Portrait Gallery ★★★ ART MUSEUM   Walt Whitman called this historic Greek Revival structure "the noblest of Washington buildings," and if he were around today, he'd likely stick with that opinion. If you've been flitting around the Penn Quarter, you had to have noticed it, with its porticoes modeled after the Parthenon in Athens, and its monumental footprint (405×274 ft.).

The magnificent landmark, which served as the nation's patent office in the mid–19th century, now houses two distinct Smithsonian museums: the American Art Museum and the National Portrait Gallery, each occupying three levels of galleries that enclose a stunning, light-filled inner courtyard.

Whitman is here, yes he is, in portrait form, painted by John White Alexander in 1889, appearing rather old and tired, with blindingly white hair, full beard, and fluffy eyebrows, sitting at an angle and staring into the distance. Whitman's portrait hangs in the National Portrait Gallery's first-floor section, **American Origins,** a chronological arrangement of paintings of notables that tells the country's story, from Pocahontas to Harriet Beecher Stowe to Thomas Edison, in compelling fashion. Other permanent exhibits feature **20th Century Americans,** where portraits of F. Scott Fitzgerald, Michael Jackson and Douglas MacArthur among others now hang, and **America's Presidents,** home to President Obama's official portrait.

The American Art Museum's collection of American art is one of the largest in the world and the most diverse, with folk art, modern, African-American, and Latino art well represented. Standouts include Georgia O'Keeffe's take on *Manhattan;* Albert Bierstadt's idealized vision of the American West, *Among the Sierra Nevada;* a Nam June Paik video installation, *Electronic Superhighway: Continental U.S., Alaska, Hawaii;* and intriguing folk art, like James Hampton's creation of artwork out of garbage, *The Throne of the Third Heaven of the Nations' Millennium General Assembly.* You'll either love it or hate it, but you won't be able to look away from it.

In all, about 2,000 works are on display throughout both museums. You'll want to tour the top floor's two-level **Luce Foundation Center for American Art,** too, where thousands more works are stored but still on view, from walking canes to sculptures to dollhouses. In the adjacent **Lunder Conservation Center,** visitors can watch conservators work to preserve art pieces.

Women's Art, Upgraded

Unfortunately, one of the most beautiful buildings in D.C. is closed for a major renovation. When the **National Museum of Women in the Arts** (1250 New York Ave. NW [at 13th St.]; www.nmwa.org; ℂ **800/222-7270** or 202/783-5000) reopens in 2023, you can expect to find a collection of more than 5,500 works by women, 16th century to the present. The museum remains the world's only major museum dedicated to recognizing women's creative accomplishments.

Inside the white marble Renaissance Revival museum building, built as a Masonic temple in 1908, is a space so elegant it's frequently in demand as a wedding reception venue. Some of the artwork is on display in the Great Hall, but most exhibits are in upstairs galleries, accessed via the sweeping marble double stairways. Among the works from the permanent collection are those by Rosa Bonheur, Mary Cassatt, Helen Frankenthaler, Barbara Hepworth, Georgia O'Keeffe, Lilla Cabot Perry, and Elaine de Kooning. Most popular is Frida Kahlo's self-portrait, the only Kahlo on view in Washington. The museum mounts several special exhibits annually, rotating mediums from photography to painted glass and sculpture to drawings.

Also recommended is the museum's gift shop, which sells clever little items like a Dorothy Parker martini glass. And if you're hungry, have lunch in view of artworks at the **Mezzanine Café** (Mon–Fri 11am–2pm).

Note: These two museums are open later than most in D.C., so you can schedule a visit for the end of the day.

8th and F sts. NW. www.americanart.si.edu or www.npg.si.edu. © **202/633-1000.** Free admission. Daily 11:30am–7pm. Tours are offered; check online or call for schedule. Closed Dec 25. Metro: Gallery Place–Chinatown (7th and F sts. exit, or 9th and G sts. exit).

DUPONT CIRCLE

In a city of national this-and-that attractions, Dupont Circle provides a charmingly personal counterpoint. Within this lively residential neighborhood of old town houses, trendy boutiques, and bistros are mostly historic houses (such as the Christian Heurich House), embassy buildings, and beloved art galleries (such as the Phillips Collection). Follow the walking tour of Dupont Circle and Embassy Row (p. 274) for a fuller picture of the neighborhood.

Anderson House ★ HISTORIC HOME   A visit to Anderson House is about marveling over the palatial architecture and interior design (love the ballroom), and the display of artwork—from Flemish tapestries to Asian and European paintings and antiquities to Revolutionary War artifacts. A bit of background: This limestone-veneered Italianate mansion, fronted by twin arches and a Corinthian-columned portico, was built between 1902 and 1905. Its original owners were career diplomat Larz Anderson III, who served as ambassador to Japan in 1912 and 1913, and his wife, heiress and philanthropist Isabel Weld Perkins, who as a Red Cross volunteer cared for the dying and wounded in France and Belgium during World War I, and who authored at least 40 books. The couple traveled a lot and filled their home with beautiful purchases from those journeys. Upon Larz's death in 1937, Isabel donated the house to the Society of the Cincinnati, and it has served ever since as headquarters and museum for the Society, founded in 1783 for descendants of Revolutionary War army officers. Anderson's great-grandfather was a founder and George Washington the organization's first president-general. Anderson House hosts exhibits, concerts, and lectures throughout the year; all are free and open to the public.

2118 Massachusetts Ave. NW (at Q St.). www.societyofthecincinnati.org. © **202/785-2040.** Free admission. Tues–Sat 10am–4pm, Sun noon–4pm; highlights tours hourly at 15 min. past the hour. Closed most federal holidays. Metro: Dupont Circle (Q St. exit).

Heurich House Museum ★ HISTORIC HOME   Wealthy German businessman and brewer Christian Heurich built this turreted, four-story brownstone and brick Victorian castle in 1894, and lived here with his family until he died in 1945. Old Heurich was a character, as a tour of the 31-room mansion/museum reveals. Allegorical paintings cover the ceilings, silvered plaster medallions festoon the stucco walls, and a *bierstube* (tavern room) in the basement sports the brewer's favorite drinking mottos—written in German, but here's one translation: "There is room in the smallest chamber for the biggest hangover." The **Castle Garden** a good place to pause for a picnic or page through your guidebook. There's also a garden bar here, **1921,** where you can try out local D.C. beers or pick up a 6-pack of Senate beer, the brand that was originally brewed by Heurich's brewing company in the 1890s through 1950s. (It's now produced in collaboration with local brewer Right Proper.) Enter the garden through the east gate on Sunderland Place NW.

1307 New Hampshire Ave. NW (at 20th St.). www.heurichhouse.org. © **202/429-1894.** Garden free admission; house tours $10, reservations suggested. Children under 10 not allowed. Garden weekdays 11am–5pm. 1921 garden bar Thurs–Fri 5–8pm and Sat 2–6pm. Metro: Dupont Circle (19th St. exit).

National Geographic Museum ★ MUSEUM   You don't have to be an adventurer to enjoy the exhibits at the National Geographic Society headquarters. It does help, though, if you appreciate the wonders of the natural world and of human exploration. Consider the museum's permanent exhibit, "National Geographic: Exploration Starts Here," displaying excavations of shipwrecks from the bottom of the ocean and video from the top of Mount Everest. From time to time, NatGeo mounts a show that nobody can resist, like the 2019 "Queens of Egypt" exhibit, showcasing jewelry, sculpture, and artifacts from Egyptian queens like Nefertiti and Cleopatra VII. In addition to its free permanent exhibition, National Geographic always has at least one free photography show in its M Street lobby; otherwise, exhibits and most lectures, films, and performances charge admission.

1145 17th St. NW (at M St.). www.nationalgeographic.org. © **202/857-7700.** Permanent and photography exhibit admission free. Special exhibit admission $15 adults; $12 students/seniors; $10 children 5–12. Daily 10am–6pm. Closed Thanksgiving and Dec 25. Metro: Farragut North (Connecticut Ave. and L St. exit).

The Phillips Collection ★★ ART MUSEUM   The 100-year-old Phillips is beloved in Washington, mostly because of its French Impressionist and Post-Impressionist paintings by van Gogh, Bonnard, Cézanne, Picasso, Klee, and Renoir, whose *Luncheon of the Boating Party* is the most popular work on display. But as familiar and traditional as these paintings may seem now, the works and their artists were considered daring and avant-garde when Duncan Phillips opened his gallery in 1921. The Phillips Collection, indeed, was America's first official museum of modern art.

Founder Phillips's vision for "an intimate museum combined with an experiment station" is one that the museum continually renews, through programs like its *Intersections* series of contemporary art projects exploring links between old and new artistic traditions, and in exhibitions of provocative art, as well as new acquisitions from important voices in art today. The **Wolfgang Laib Wax Room** is a good example: It is the first beeswax chamber that artist Laib created for a specific museum. That's right: beeswax. You smell it before you see it, kind of a musty, faintly honey-ish, cloying scent. The artwork is the size of a powder room, with a single light bulb dangling to illuminate walls and ceiling slathered thickly with wax that has the yellow hue, flecked with bits of orangey brown.

Today the museum's nearly 6,000-work collection includes European master-pieces; treasures by American masters Dove, Homer, Hopper, Lawrence, and O'Keeffe; and works by living artists, such as Simone Leigh, Zilia Sánchez, Leonardo Drew, and Jennifer Wen Ma. The Phillips complex joins the original 1897 Georgian Revival mansion—initially both the Phillips family home and public art gallery—with a modern gallery annex that doubles the space. The elegant mansion's graceful appointments—leaded- and stained-glass windows, elliptical stairway, oak-paneled Music Room, and tiled fireplaces—provide a lovely backdrop to the art and add to the reasons that locals love the Phillips.

Also consider gallery talks, the popular "Phillips after 5" socials every first Thursday, Sunday concerts in the **Music Room** (Oct–May), and other events. The museum also has a courtyard and a small gift shop.

Timed entry tickets are required to access the museum; you can reserve these online. Some features, like the museum shop, courtyard, and first-floor galleries of the Goh Annex and Sant Building may be free and open to the public without a ticket, but this depends on capacity that day.

1600 21st St. NW (at Q St.). www.phillipscollection.org. ✆ **202/387-2151.** Admission: $16 adults; $12 seniors 62 and older; $10 students and educators (with ID); free ages 18 and under. Tues–Sat 10am–5pm (Thurs until 8:30pm); Sun noon–7pm. Closed Mon and federal holidays. Metro: Dupont Circle (Q St. exit).

Woodrow Wilson House Museum ★ HISTORIC HOME   America's 28th president's. His final residence is preserved as he left it. The story here focuses on Wilson's Washington years (1912–24), examining his public per-sona while allowing a peek behind the draperies into his and his wife Edith's personal life, much of it quite tragic. Furnishings, White House objects, per-sonal memorabilia, and elaborate gifts of state from all over the world help tell the story. A mosaic of St. Peter hangs in the drawing room, a gift from Pope Benedict XV when the Wilsons toured Europe at the conclusion of World War I. A portrait of his wife Edith hangs above the mantle. You must book a spot on a 1-hour guided tour to access the interior of the house. Some specialty tours, focusing on topics like architecture or Prohibition, are also offered by appointment only.

2340 S St. NW (at Massachusetts Ave.). www.woodrowwilsonhouse.org. ✆ **202/387-4062.** Admission $15 adults; $10 and students; free for ages 12 and under. Jan–Feb 16 Sat–Sun 11am–4pm only. Feb 17–Dec Fri–Mon 11am–4pm; Thurs 11am–7pm; closed Tues–Wed. Guided tours only. Closed federal holidays. Metro: Dupont Circle (Q St. exit).

FOGGY BOTTOM

Known primarily as the locale for the George Washington University campus, the State Department, the International Monetary Fund, and the World Bank, Foggy Bottom is home also to the George Washington Museum and the Textile Museum, and the John F. Kennedy Center for the Performing Arts (p. 223).

The George Washington Museum and the Textile Museum ★ MUSEUM   This two-museums-in-one building lies in the heart of the George

Performance at the Kennedy Center.

Washington University's urban campus. Originally located in a charming Embassy Row mansion (which Amazon founder Jeff Bezos now owns as a private residence), the nearly century-old **Textile Museum** tripled its space and was, in a sense, reborn in 2015, when it moved to this custom-designed, 46,000-square-foot gallery in Foggy Bottom. Curators pull from the museum's collection of some 20,000 textiles spanning 5,000 years and five continents to mount exhibits that in one way or another ask: How do clothes, adornments, and fabric furnishings articulate self and status within cultural, political, social, religious, and ethnic frameworks?

On the second floor of the building, is the **George Washington Museum's Albert H. Small Washingtoniana Collection,** totally unrelated to textiles but fascinating for the display of maps, prints, old photos, and rare letters that fill you in on life in the capital from the 17th to the 20th centuries.

701 21st St. NW (at G St.). https://museum.gwu.edu. © **202/994-5200.** $8 suggested donation. Mon and Fri 11am–5pm; Wed–Thurs 11am–7pm; Sat 10am–5pm; Sun 1–5pm. Metro: Foggy Bottom.

U & 14TH STREET CORRIDORS

In the old stomping grounds of Duke Ellington and his fellow Black Broadway jazz greats, the main attractions are of the nightlife and dining variety. The two museums located here reflect the neighborhood's identity as a stronghold of African-American history and heroes.

African American Civil War Memorial and Museum ★ MUSEUM
Not everyone knows that thousands of African Americans, mostly slaves, fought

Albert Einstein Memorial

In a grove of holly and elm trees at the southwest corner of the National Academy of Sciences grounds (22nd St. and Constitution Ave. NW), you'll find this dear memorial displaying the slouching figure of brilliant scientist, great thinker, and peace activist Albert Einstein. He sits slightly bent and sideways upon a granite bench, leaning on one hand and holding in the other a bronze sheet of paper on which are written mathematical equations for which he is famous. At his feet is a celestial map. His gaze looks worn and warm. The statue measures 12 feet in height and weighs 4 tons, yet children cannot resist crawling up on it and leaning against this man.

during the Civil War. This modestly sized museum displays old photographs, maps, letters, and inventories, along with ankle shackles worn by slaves and other artifacts accompanied by text to tell the stories of the United States Colored Troops and the African-American involvement in the American Civil War. Walk across the street to view the African American Civil War Memorial. A semicircular Wall of Honor curves behind the sculpture; etched into the stone are the names of the 209,145 United States Colored Troops who served in the Civil War.

1925 Vermont Ave. NW (at 10th St.; in the Grimke Bldg.). www.afroamcivilwar.org. ✆ **202/667-2667.** Free admission. Mon 10am–5pm; Tues–Fri 10am–6:30pm; Sat 10am–4pm; Sun noon–4pm. Metro: U St./Cardozo (10th St. exit).

Mary McLeod Bethune Council House National Historic Site ★ HISTORIC HOME This town house is the last D.C. residence of African-American activist/educator Bethune, who was a leading champion of blacks' and women's rights during FDR's administration. Born in South Carolina in 1875, the 15th of 17 children of former slaves, Mary McLeod grew up in poverty but learned the value of education through her schooling by missionaries. It was a lesson she passed forward. By the time she died in 1955 at the age of 79, McLeod—now Bethune, from her marriage in 1898 to Albert Bethune—had founded a school for "Negro girls" in Daytona Beach, Florida, that would later become the Bethune-Cookman College, today Bethune-Cookman University; received 11 honorary degrees; served on the National Child Welfare Commission; and acted as Special Advisor on Minority Affairs to FDR from 1935 to 1944. Bethune also established this headquarters of the National Council of Negro Women to advance the interests of African-American women and the black community. Maintained by the National Park Service, the Bethune House exhibits focus on the professional achievements of this remarkable woman.

1318 Vermont Ave. NW (at O St.). www.nps.gov/mamc. ✆ **202/673-2402.** Free admission. Thurs–Sat 9am–5pm; Sun–Wed open by appointment only. Metro: U St./Cardozo (13th St. exit).

UPPER NORTHWEST D.C.: GLOVER PARK, WOODLEY PARK & CLEVELAND PARK

These just-beyond-downtown enclaves are largely residential, but a handful of attractions also reside here.

Hillwood Estate, Museum & Gardens ★ HISTORIC HOME The magnificent estate of Post cereal heiress, businesswoman, philanthropist, and collector, Marjorie Merriweather Post encompasses the beautiful mansion where she lived from 1955 until her death in 1973, and 25 acres of gardens and woodlands. The Georgian-style manse is filled with Post's collections of art and artifacts from 18th-century France and 18th- and 19th-century Russia, from Fabergé eggs to tapestries. The spectacular grounds include a Japanese-style garden, a Russian dacha, a French *parterre,* and a dog cemetery. A rather nice conclusion to your visit here is lunch at **Hillwood's Merriweather Café.**

4155 Linnean Ave. NW (at Connecticut Ave.). www.hillwoodmuseum.org. ☎ **202/686-5807.** Admission: Suggested donation of $18 adults; $15 seniors; $10 college students; $5 children 6–18; free children under 6. $3 discount Mon–Fri and $1 Sat–Sun when you order tickets online. Tues–Sun 10am–5pm. Metro: Van Ness/UDC (east side of Connecticut Ave. exit), with a 20-min. walk.

Smithsonian's National Zoo and Conservation Biology Institute ★★ ZOO   The National Zoo was created by an act of Congress in 1889 and became part of the Smithsonian Institution in 1890. A leader in the care, breeding, and exhibition of animals, the zoo occupies 163 lushly landscaped and wooded acres and is one of the country's most delightful zoos. In all, the park is home to about 390 species—some 2,700 animals, many of them rare and/or endangered. You'll see cheetahs, zebras, gorillas, elephants, monkeys, brown pelicans, orangutans, bison, and, of course, lions, tigers, and bears. The zoo's biggest draw continues to be its **giant pandas,** Mei Xiang, Tian Tian, and their cub, Xiao Qi Ji, who was born in August 2020.

Enter the zoo at the Connecticut Avenue entrance; you'll be right by the Visitor Center, where you can pick up a map and find out about any special activities. *Note:* From this main entrance, you're headed downhill; the return uphill walk can prove trying if you have young children and/or it's a hot day. But, waiting for families at the *bottom* of the hill is the **Kids' Farm** with alpacas, chickens, goats, cows, and miniature donkeys, plus a playground. Let's face it: You might not get that far. But just in case, keep in mind that the zoo rents strollers, and snack bars and ice-cream kiosks are scattered throughout the park.

The zoo animals live in large, open enclosures—simulations of their natural habitats—along easy-to-follow paths. The **Olmsted Walk** winds from the zoo's Connecticut Avenue entrance all the way to the zoo's end, at Rock Creek Park. Off the central Olmsted Walk is the **Asia Trail,** which takes you past sloth bears, those giant pandas, fishing cats, clouded leopards, red pandas, and small-clawed otters. You can't get lost, and it's hard to miss a thing.

Across from the giant panda yard is **Elephant Trails,** the zoo's high-tech, environmentally friendly habitat for its five Asian elephants. The enclosure includes 4 acres of indoor and outdoor space, a wading pool, a walking path for exercise, a barn with soft flooring for sleeping and geothermal heating, and, a community center that offers the elephants the chance to socialize!

Moving on from there takes you to the **American Trail,** which is home to animals native to the United States and Canada that were once in danger of becoming extinct. Bald eagles, seals, sea lions, beavers, and river otters are among the creatures living here.

I also recommend **Amazonia,** where you can hang out and observe enormous 7-foot-long arapaima fish and itty-bitty red-tailed catfish and look for monkeys hiding in the 50-foot-tall trees.

Stationed in front of the **Great Cats** habitat, home to lions, tigers, and the like, is the zoo's solar-powered carousel, where you can ride 58 different species of animals. Rides are $3.50.

The zoo offers many dining options, stroller rental stations, gift shops, and several paid-parking lots, which you'll need to reserve and pay for in advance.

It's important to note, while entry to the zoo is free, all visitors must now register for entry passes in advance—even kids and babies must be registered. You can reserve up to six tickets at once; they're good for the whole day so you don't need to specify an arrival time. It's good to book ahead, though I've had luck finding same-day spaces online.

3001 Connecticut Ave. NW (adjacent to Rock Creek Park). www.nationalzoo.si.edu. ℭ **202/633-4888.** Free admission. Parking $30. Apr–Oct (weather permitting) grounds daily 8am–7pm (last admittance at 6pm), animal buildings daily 9am–6pm; Nov–Mar grounds daily 8am–5pm (last admittance at 4pm), animal buildings daily 9am–4pm. Closed Dec 25. Metro: Woodley Park–Zoo or Cleveland Park.

Washington National Cathedral ★★CATHEDRAL   Pierre L'Enfant's 1791 plan for the capital city included "a great church for national purposes."

Washington National Cathedral.

Possibly because of early America's fear of mingling church and state, more than a century elapsed before the foundation for Washington National Cathedral was laid. Its actual name is the Cathedral Church of St. Peter and St. Paul. The Church is Episcopal, but welcomes all denominations, seeking to serve the entire nation as a house of prayer for all people. It has been the setting for every kind of religious observance, from Jewish to Serbian Orthodox.

A church of this magnitude—it's the sixth-largest cathedral in the world, and the second largest in the U.S.—took a long time to build. Its principal (but not original) architect, Philip Hubert Frohman, worked on the project from 1921 until his death in 1972. The foundation stone was laid in 1907 using the mallet with which George Washington set the Capitol cornerstone. Construction was interrupted by both world wars and by periods of financial difficulty. The cathedral was finally completed with the placement of the last stone on the west front towers in 1990, 83 years after it was begun.

English Gothic in style (with several distinctly 20th-c. innovations, such as a stained-glass window commemorating the flight of *Apollo 11* and containing a piece of moon rock), the cathedral is built in the shape of a cross, complete with flying buttresses and 112 gargoyles. Along with the Capitol and the Washington Monument, it is one of the dominant structures on the Washington skyline. Frederick Law Olmsted, Jr. designed the cathedral's 59-acre

Early Risers?

Zoo grounds open daily at 8am, which might be too early for a lot of tourists, but not for families whose young children like to rise at the crack of dawn. If you know you'll need a morning activity, book your free entry passes online, then hop on the Red Line Metro, which opens at 5am weekdays, 7am Saturday, and 8am Sunday (or drive—the zoo parking lot opens at 8am, too), get off at the Cleveland Park station, and walk down the hill to the zoo. A Starbucks, which opens at 6am daily, is directly across from the zoo entrance on Connecticut Avenue. Good morning.

landscaped grounds, which include two lovely gardens (the lawn is ideal for picnicking), three schools, and two gift shops.

Among the many historic events that have taken place at the cathedral are celebrations at the end of World Wars I and II; the burial of President Wilson; funerals for presidents Eisenhower, Reagan, Ford, and George H. W. Bush; the burials of Helen Keller and her companion, Anne Sullivan; the Rev. Dr. Martin Luther King, Jr.'s final sermon; a round-the-clock prayer vigil in the Holy Spirit Chapel when Iranians held American hostages captive, and a service attended by the hostages upon their release; and President Bush's National Prayer and Remembrance service on September 14, 2001, following the cataclysm of September 11.

The best way to explore the cathedral is to take a 30-minute **guided highlights tour** (included in admission price); the tours leave continually from the west end of the nave. A behind-the-scenes tour offers visitors views of flying buttresses, stained-glass windows and other features you can't see clearly from the ground. Similarly, a gargoyle tour explores more than 200 whimsical and frightening gargoyles on the Cathedral's exterior. Can you spot Darth Vader? You can also walk through on your own, using a self-guiding brochure available in several languages. Allow additional time to tour the grounds and to visit the **Pilgrim Observation Gallery** ★, where 70 windows provide panoramic views of Washington and its surroundings. Among the most popular special-interest tours are the afternoon **Tour and Tea** events, which start with an in-depth look at the cathedral and conclude in the Observation Gallery with a lovely "high tea,"—you're sitting in the cradle of one of the highest points in Washington, gazing out, while noshing on scones and Devon cream. Call ⓒ **202/537-2228** or book online at https://tix.cathedral.org.

The cathedral hosts numerous events: organ recitals and other types of concerts; choir performances; an annual springtime **Flower Mart** (with flowers, food, and children's rides); and the playing of the 53-bell carillon.

Note: When you visit, there's a good chance you'll still see exterior renovation work. The earthquake of August 23, 2011, damaged some of the pinnacles, flying buttresses, and gargoyles at the very top of the cathedral's exterior, as well as some minor areas of the interior ceiling. Interior repair work was completed in 2015, so you'll see a fully restored nave, looking better than ever, in truth, because the restoration included cleaning clerestory windows and stones, the first time ever. Much exterior repair work remains, but the cathedral is completely safe to visit, and its programs continue as usual.

As with many sites in this chapter, the National Cathedral was still in the process of reopening when we updated this guide. Updated tour times and prices were not yet available, so check the website, cathedral.org, for opening times, admission prices, and tour info.

3101 Wisconsin Ave. NW (at Massachusetts Ave.). www.cathedral.org. © **202/537-6200.** Admission $12 adults; $8 children and seniors. Cathedral Mon–Fri 10am–5pm; Sat 10am–4pm; Sun 12:45–4pm. Gardens daily until dusk. Daily (30-min.) tours Mon–Sat 10:15am, 11, 1, 2, and 3pm; Sun as available 1–3pm. No tours on Palm Sunday, Easter, Thanksgiving, Dec 25, or during services. Check website for service times. Metro: Tenleytown, with a 20-min. walk. Bus: Any N bus up Massachusetts Ave. from Dupont Circle, or any 30-series bus along Wisconsin Ave. Parking garage $6 per hr./$22 maximum weekdays until 11pm; flat rate $7 if you arrive after 4pm; flat rate $9 on Sat; free on Sun.

GEORGETOWN

One of the oldest parts of the city has long been best known for its major shopping opportunities, but we think the better reason to come here is to experience its rich history. A walking tour in chapter 10 will lead you to centuries-old estates and dwellings, including **Tudor Place,** the **Old Stone House, Dumbarton House Museum and Gardens,** and **Dumbarton House.**

Dumbarton House ★ HISTORIC HOME   Built between 1799 and 1805, Dumbarton House is the headquarters for the National Society of Colonial Dames of America. Stop here to admire gorgeous architecture and antique decorative arts, and to glean a bit of early American history. Self-guide your way through the house, whose collection contains more than 1,000 paintings, ceramics, and furniture from the Federal period. You can reserve timed tickets in advance, but walk-up visits are also welcome.

2715 Q St. NW (at 27th St.). © **202/337-2288.** Admission $10; free for students. Feb–Dec Tues–Sun 10am–3pm. Closed federal holidays. Metro: Dupont Circle (Q St. exit), with a 20-min. walk or take the DC Circulator bus (2 routes run close by). Closed Jan.

Dumbarton Oaks ★ GARDEN & MUSEUM   One block off Wisconsin Avenue in upper Georgetown delivers you far from the madding crowds to the peaceful refuge of Dumbarton Oaks. The estate includes a museum devoted to Byzantine and pre-Columbian art, a research center and library, and 10 acres of formal and informal gardens. Many skip the museum altogether simply to wander along the garden's hedge-lined walkways, into the orangery, past the weeping cherry trees, and all around the garden plots, admiring what's in bloom as they go. If it's April, you may see bluebells. August? Dahlias. The gardens offer several pretty places to perch, and are adorned here and there with garden ornaments and artwork. ***Note:*** The gardens can get crowded in spring and early summer, when they are at their loveliest.

Do try to make time for the museum, however, whose newly renovated galleries display 1,200 Byzantine artifacts, including jewelry, lamps, icons, and

Georgetown waterfront dock.

illuminated manuscripts from the 4th to the 15th centuries; and pre-Columbian objects such as Aztec stone carvings, Inca gold ornaments, and Olmec heads. Other highlights include the Flemish tapestries and an El Greco painting, *The Visitation,* on display in the Renaissance-style **Music Room.** Like the Phillips Collection (p. 185), the museum's mansion setting adds to its charm.

The house and gardens, situated at the highest point of Georgetown, belonged to named Mildred and Robert Woods Bliss, who initiated these collections and gardens in the first half of the 20th century. Both the garden and the museum require timed tickets for entry; you can book these online at www.doaks.org.

1703 32nd St. NW (garden entrance at 31st and R sts.). www.doaks.org. ℂ **202/339-6400.** Gardens: Tues–Sun 3–6pm, $7 admission. Museum: Tues–Sun 2–5pm; admission free. Closed national holidays and Dec 24. Metrobus nos. 30N, 30S, 31, 33, D1, D2, D3, D6, and G2, plus the DC Circulator bus all have stops close to the site.

Kreeger Museum ★ ART MUSEUM   You have to make an effort to visit the Kreeger, because it's located in a residential neighborhood away from downtown, the heart of Georgetown, and public transportation. But if you don't mind driving, taking a taxi, or riding the D6 bus from Dupont Circle, then walking a half-mile up the hill to the museum, you'll be well rewarded. On view throughout this unique building designed by Philip Johnson and Richard Foster, besides the stunning architecture itself, are paintings, sculptures, prints, and drawings by 19th- and 20th-century European artists, Picasso (early and late), Kandinsky, Monet, Renoir, Munch, Pissarro, and Rodin among them. American works are on view, too, including some by Washington, D.C., artists such as Sam Gilliam and Gene Davis. Downstairs lies a small collection of traditional African masks and figures and Asian pieces. Outdoors is a sculpture terrace, where large works by Maillol and Henry Moore, and the sight of the distant Washington Monument, are some of the pleasures at hand. Situated on a summit, this 5½-acre estate opened to the public in 1994. At this writing, a timed entry pass was required to visit the collections inside.

2401 Foxhall Rd. NW (off Reservoir Rd.). www.kreegermuseum.org. © **202/337-3050.** Museum: Admission $10 adults; $8 seniors and students; free for children 12 and under; Tues–Sat 10am–4pm. Sculpture Garden: Free admission; Tues–Sat 10am–4pm. Closed federal holidays. About 2 mi. from Reservoir Rd. and Wisconsin Ave. in Georgetown (a pleasant walk on a nice day); otherwise drive, take a taxi, or ride the D6 bus from Dupont Circle.

Old Stone House ★ HISTORIC HOME   This 1766 structure is said to be the oldest in Washington. The National Park Service owns and operates the house, and NPS rangers provide information and sometimes demonstrations related to the site's pre-Revolutionary history. See p. 273.

3051 M St. NW (at Thomas Jefferson Street NW). www.nps.gov/places/old-stone-house.htm. © **202/426-6851.** Free admission. Daily 11am–7pm. Garden open during daylight hours. Closed Federal holidays. Metro: Foggy Bottom with a 15-min. walk or take the DC Circulator.

Tudor Place ★ HISTORIC HOME   Designed by Dr. William Thornton, architect of the Capitol, Tudor Place was constructed between 1796 and 1816 for Martha Parke Custis, George Washington's step-granddaughter. Family descendants lived here until 1983. Tours of the garden and house are currently self-guided, though docent-led tours of the house may be available by the time

---

MUSEUMS IN anacostia

This historic, largely black residential neighborhood located east of the Capitol and away from the center of the city is not a typical tourist destination, but two attractions do draw visitors.

The **Frederick Douglass National Historic Site** (1411 W St. SE, at 14th St. SE; www.nps.gov/frdo; © **202/426-5961**) is by far the more compelling. Born a slave in 1818, Frederick Bailey escaped his Maryland plantation, became an abolitionist and gifted orator, changed his name to Douglass to avoid capture, and fled to Britain, where he purchased his freedom. Back in the United States a free man, Douglass picked up where he had left off, fighting against slavery and for equal rights for all, including women. This house, known as Cedar Hill, was Douglass's home for the last 17 years of his life. A National Park Service ranger begins your tour on the veranda, where you can see that the house crowns one of the highest hills in

Washington. Then your guide takes you upstairs and down, filling you in on the life of the brilliant, brave, and charismatic abolitionist here at this house, and elsewhere: his love of reading, his escape from slavery, his married life, and his embrace of emancipation for all oppressed people.

See website for hours and admission, which is free, but by guided tour only. Tickets can be reserved in advanced for a $1 fee. Also see the African-American History itinerary, p. 42, in chapter 3.

The **Anacostia Community Museum** (1901 Fort Place SE, off Martin Luther King Jr. Ave.; www.anacostia.si.edu; © **202/633-4820**) is a Smithsonian museum that primarily serves the neighborhood and the local community with exhibits that resonate with area residents, focusing on social, cultural, and historical themes. As with all Smithsonians, admission is free. It's open Tuesday through Saturday from 11am to 4pm.

you visit (check the website for updates). Tudor Place is free to visit (though donations are accepted), but you'll need to reserve a ticket in advance—call or book one online. See p. 270.

1644 31st St. NW (at R St.). www.tudorplace.org. *C* **202/965-0400.** Reservations recommended. Mar–Dec: Free admission. House and Garden Feb–Dec, Tues–Sat noon–4pm; Sun noon–4pm. Closed Dec 25 and Jan. Metro: Foggy Bottom or Dupont Circle (Q St. exit), with a 20-min. walk.

NORTHERN VIRGINIA

Arlington

The land that today comprises Arlington County, Virginia, was included in the original parcel of land demarcated as the nation's capital. In 1847 the state of Virginia took its territory back, referring to it as "Alexandria County" until 1920, when Arlington at last became "Arlington," a name change made to avoid confusion with the city of Alexandria.

And where did the county pick up the name "Arlington"? From its famous estate, Arlington House, built by a descendant of Martha Washington: George Washington Parke Custis, whose daughter married Robert E. Lee. (Before that, "Arlington" was the name of the Custis family estate in Tidewater Virginia.) The Lees lived in Arlington House on and off until the onset of the Civil War in 1861. The beginnings of Arlington National Cemetery date from May 1864, when four Union soldiers were buried here, in the area now known as section 27, the oldest part of the cemetery.

The **Arlington Memorial Bridge** leads directly from the Lincoln Memorial to the Robert E. Lee Memorial at Arlington House, symbolically joining these two figures into one Union after the Civil War.

Beyond Arlington the cemetery is Arlington, a residential community from which most residents commute into Washington. In recent years, however, the suburb has come into its own, booming with businesses, restaurants, and nightlife, giving tourists more incentive to visit. Below are its worthwhile sites.

Arlington National Cemetery ★★ CEMETERY Arlington National Cemetery is, without hyperbole, the United States' most important burial ground. This shrine occupies approximately 639 acres on the high hills overlooking the capital from the west side of Memorial Bridge. More than 400,000 people are buried here, including veterans of all national wars, from the American Revolution to the Iraq and Afghanistan conflicts; Supreme Court justices; literary figures; slaves; presidents; astronauts; and assorted other national heroes. Many graves of the famous at Arlington bear nothing more than simple markers.

Upon arrival, head to the **Welcome Center,** where you can view exhibits, pick up a detailed map, and use the restrooms (there are no others until you get to Arlington House). The Welcome Center also offers kiosks where you can access the cemetery's app, **ANC Explorer,** to find locations of and directions to individual gravesites plus self-guided tours of the cemetery. (Or download the free app ahead of time at the App Store or Google Play or from the Arlington National Cemetery website.)

If you're here to visit a particular grave, you'll be gratified to know that the cemetery operates a free shuttle to individual gravesites. And if you're here as a tourist, and you've got plenty of stamina and it's a nice day, consider touring all or part of the cemetery on foot. Plenty of people do. I'd say it's worth it to spring for the narrated tour. It's a hop-on, hop-off tour that makes four stops: at the gravesites of **Pres. John F. Kennedy, Gen. John J. Pershing,** the **Memorial Amphitheater** and **Tomb of the Unknown Soldier, Arlington House.** The tour lasts an hour or more, depending on how many times you hop on and off, and how long you stay at each site. Service is continuous, and the narrated commentary is lively and informative. You can buy tickets online in advance (www.arlingtontours.com) or at the ticket counter in the Welcome Center. Tickets are $15 adults, $11 seniors, $7.25 children 4 to 12; military and active-duty personnel receive discounted prices, and disabled and active-duty military in uniform are free (with proper ID).

Remember: This is a memorial frequented not just by tourists, but also by those attending burial services or visiting the graves of beloved relatives and friends who are buried here.

Cemetery highlights include the **Tomb of the Unknown Soldier,** which contains the unidentified remains of a service member from World War I in a massive, white marble sarcophagus; just west of the sarcophagus are three white marble slabs flush with the plaza, marking the graves of unknown service members from World War II and the Korean War, as well as a crypt that honors all missing U.S. service members from the Vietnam War—but this crypt contains no remains. In 1998 the entombed remains of the unknown soldier from Vietnam were disinterred and identified as those of Air Force 1st Lt. Michael Blassie, whose A-37 was shot down in South Vietnam in 1972. The Blassie family buried Michael in his hometown of St. Louis. A 24-hour honor guard watches over the marble Tomb of the Unknowns and its companion gravesites with the changing of the guard taking place every half-hour April to September, every hour on the hour October to March, and every hour at night year-round.

Within a 20-minute walk, all uphill, from the Welcome Center is **Arlington House,** the **Robert E. Lee Memorial** (www.nps.gov/arho; © **703/235-1530**), which was begun in 1802 by Martha Washington's grandson (through her first marriage), George Washington Parke Custis, who was raised at Mount Vernon as George and Martha's adopted son. Custis's daughter, Mary Anna Randolph, inherited the estate, and she and her husband, Robert E. Lee, lived here between 1831 and 1861. When Lee headed up Virginia's army, Mary fled, and federal troops confiscated the property. The house is restored to its 1860 appearance, with detailed room displays and objects that belonged to George Washington and the Lee family, and a museum and bookstore.

It's worth visiting the Arlington House estate for the spectacular view of the capital from its hilltop location. Just below the house, look for **Pierre Charles L'Enfant's grave** at a spot that is believed to offer the best view of Washington, the city he designed.

Below Arlington House is the **gravesite of President John Fitzgerald Kennedy,** a 3-acre lawn terrace paved with irregular-sized stones of Cape Cod granite, tufts of grass growing between the stones. At the head of the gravesite is a 5-foot, circular fieldstone, with the Eternal Flame burning in the center. Embracing the terrace is a low crescent wall inscribed with quotations from President Kennedy's presidency. Slate headstones mark the actual graves for President Kennedy, Jacqueline Kennedy Onassis, and their two infant children. President Kennedy's two brothers, senators Robert Kennedy and Edward Kennedy, are buried close by. The Kennedy graves attract streams of visitors. Arrive close to 8am to contemplate the site quietly; otherwise, it's often crowded.

The **Women in Military Service for America Memorial** (www.womens memorial.org; © **800/222-2294** or 703/892-2606) is another recommended spot. It honors the nearly 3 million women who have served in the armed forces from the American Revolution to the present. The impressive memorial lies just beyond the gated entrance to the cemetery, a 3-minute walk from the visitor center. As you approach, you see a large, circular reflecting pool, perfectly placed within the curve of the granite wall rising behind it. Arched passageways within the 226-foot-long wall lead to an upper terrace and dramatic views of Arlington National Cemetery and the monuments of Washington; an arc of large glass panels contains etched quotations from famous people about contributions made by servicewomen. Behind the wall and completely underground is the **Education Center,** housing a **Hall of Honor,** a gallery of exhibits tracing the history of women in the military; a theater; and a computer register that visitors may access for the stories and information about 265,000 individual military women, past and present. Hours are 8am to 5pm. Stop at the reception desk for a brochure for a self-guided tour through the memorial. The memorial is open every day except Christmas.

Just across the Memorial Bridge from the base of the Lincoln Memorial. www.arlington cemetery.mil. © **877/907-8585.** Free admission. Daily 8am–5pm. Metro: Arlington National Cemetery. Parking $2/hr. **Note:** All visitors 16 and older (pedestrians, drivers, and passengers) must present a valid photo ID upon entering the cemetery. The cemetery is also accessible as a stop on several tour bus services, including Old Town Trolley.

The Pentagon ★ GOVERNMENT BUILDING   Completed in January 1943 after a mere 16 months of construction, the structure is the world's largest low-rise office building. The Capitol could fit inside any one of its five wedge-shaped sections. Twenty-three-thousand people work at the Pentagon, which holds 17½ miles of corridors, 19 escalators, 284 restrooms, and 691 water fountains. Tours of this headquarters for the American military establishment were suspended for a while following the September 11, 2001, attack in which terrorists hijacked American Airlines Flight 77 and crashed it into the northwest side of the Pentagon, killing 125 people working at the Pentagon and 59 people aboard the plane. In the years since, the Pentagon has been completely restored and was running tours for visitors, until the pandemic put a temporary stop to those. It's likely tours will be reinstated once public health conditions allow; here's what to expect when they're back up and running:

An active-duty staff person from the National Capital Region's ceremonial unit conducts the free, 60-minute tour that covers 1½ miles. Your tour guide is required to memorize 20 pages of informational material, outlining the mission of each military branch. It's a fascinating introduction, as is seeing the building itself, its corridors commemorating the history, people, and culture of the Air Force, Navy, Army, Marine Corps, and Coast Guard. You'll see historical photos, the Hall of Heroes for Medal of Honor recipients, an exhibit recognizing U.S. prisoners of war and those missing in action, and paintings depicting the country's founding fathers.

The tour does not include a visit to the 2-acre **Pentagon Memorial,** better known as the **9/11 Memorial,** which is located outside, on the northwest side of the building near where the plane crashed. On view are 184 granite-covered benches, each engraved with a victim's name, and arranged in order of birth date. The names are written in such a way on each bench that you must face the Pentagon to be able to read the names of those killed there and face away from the Pentagon, toward the western sky, to read the names of those who perished on the plane. *Note:* You do not need to sign up for a Pentagon tour to visit the 9/11 Memorial, which is open to the public 24 hours a day, every day. The best way to reach the memorial is to take the Metro to the Pentagon station and walk the half-mile, following the signs that lead from the station to the northwest side of the Pentagon.

You must book your tour no later than 14 days and no earlier than 90 days in advance. Request the tour online at **https://pentagontours.osd.mil**, providing the Social Security number, birth date, and other info for each member of your party. There's no public parking at the Pentagon, so it's best to arrive by Metro—the Pentagon has its own stop. Once you exit the Pentagon Metro station, look for the Pentagon Visitors Center and go to the Pentagon Tour Window.

Department of Defense, 1400 Defense Pentagon. https://pentagontours.osd.mil and www.pentagonmemorial.org. ✆ **703/697-1776.** Free admission, but reservations required; guided tours only. Check online for current tour times. Pentagon Memorial daily 24 hr. Metro: Pentagon.

PARKS

More than 27% of Washington, D.C.'s land space is national parkland. When you add in the parks and gardens maintained by the D.C. Department of Parks and Recreation, as well as private estates that are open to the public, you're talking thousands and thousands of green acres!

Potomac Park ★★★

The National Mall and Memorial Parks' individual spaces known as West and East Potomac parks are 720 riverside acres divided by the Tidal Basin. The parkland is most famous for its display of **cherry trees,** which bloom for a mere 2 weeks, tops, every spring, as they have since the city of Tokyo first gave the U.S. capital the gift of the original 3,000 trees in 1912. Today more than 3,750 cherry trees grow along the Tidal Basin in West Potomac Park, East Potomac Park, the Washington Monument grounds, and other pockets of the city.

The sight of the delicate cherry blossoms is so special that the whole city joins in cherry-blossom-related hoopla, throwing the **National Cherry Blossom Festival** (Mar 20–Apr 11, 2021). The National Park Service devotes a home page to the subject, **www.nps.gov/cherry**, and the National Cherry Blossom Festival officially has another: **www.nationalcherryblossomfestival.org**. The trees usually begin blooming sometime between March 20 and April 17; April 4 is the average date at which the blooms reach their peak, defined as the point at which 70% of the Tidal Basin–sited cherry trees have blossomed.

To get to the Tidal Basin by car (*not* recommended in cherry-blossom season—actually, let me be clear: *impossible* in cherry-blossom season unless you go before sunrise), you want to get on Independence Avenue and follow the signs posted near the Lincoln Memorial that show you where to turn to find parking. If you're walking, cross Independence Avenue where it intersects with West Basin Drive and follow the path to the Tidal Basin. There is no convenient Metro stop near here. If you don't want to walk or ride a bike, your best bet is a taxi.

West Potomac Park encompasses Constitution Gardens; the Vietnam, Korean, Lincoln, Jefferson, World War II, and FDR memorials; the D.C. World War I Memorial; the Reflecting Pool; the Tidal Basin and its paddleboats; and countless flower beds, ball fields, and trees. More than 1,500 cherry trees border the Tidal Basin, some of them Akebonos with delicate pink blossoms, but most are Yoshinos with white, cloudlike flower clusters.

East Potomac Park has 1,701 cherry trees in 10 varieties. The park also has picnic grounds, tennis courts, three golf courses, a large swimming pool, and biking and hiking paths by the water. East Potomac Park's **Hains Point** is located on a peninsula extending into the Potomac River; locals love to ride their bikes out to the point; golfers love to tee up in view of the Washington Monument. See "Outdoor Activities," p. 204, for further information.

Part of National Mall and Memorial Parks, bordering the Potomac River along the west and southwest ends. www.nps.gov/nama. ✆ **202/426-6841.** Free admission. Daily 24 hr. Metro: Smithsonian (12th St./Independence Ave. exit).

Rock Creek Park ★★★

Created in 1890, **Rock Creek Park** was purchased by Congress for its "pleasant valleys and ravines, primeval forests and open fields, its running waters, its rocks clothed with rich ferns and mosses, its repose and tranquility, its light and shade, its ever-varying shrubbery, its beautiful and extensive views," according to a Corps of Engineers officer quoted in the National Park Service's administrative history. A 1,754-acre valley within the District of Columbia, extending 12 miles from the Potomac River to the Maryland border, it's one of the biggest and finest city parks in the nation. Parts of it are still wild; coyotes have been sighted here, joining the red and gray foxes, raccoons, and beavers already resident. Most tourists encounter its southern tip, the section from the Kennedy Center to the National Zoo, but the park widens and travels much farther from there. Among the park's attractions are playgrounds, an extensive system of hiking and biking trails, sports facilities, remains of Civil War fortifications, and acres and acres of wooded parklands.

For full information on the wide range of park programs and activities, visit the **Rock Creek Nature Center and Planetarium,** 5200 Glover Rd. NW (✆ **202/895-6000**), Wednesday through Sunday from 9am to 5pm. To get to the center by public transportation, take the Metro to Friendship Heights and transfer to bus no. E4 to Military Road and Oregon Avenue/Glover Road, then walk up the hill about 100 yards.

The Nature Center and Planetarium is the scene of numerous activities, including planetarium shows, live animal demonstrations, guided nature walks, plus a mix of lectures, films, and other events. Self-guided nature trails begin here. All activities are free, but for planetarium shows you need to pick up tickets a half-hour in advance. The Nature Center is closed on federal holidays.

At Tilden Street and Beach Drive, you can see the refurbished water-powered 1820s gristmill, used until not so long ago to grind corn and wheat into flour. It's called **Peirce Mill** (a man named Isaac Peirce built it). Check the website to see if tours are running, www.nps.gov/pimi, or call ✆ **202/895-6070.**

You'll find convenient free **parking** throughout the park. In addition to the circumscribed 1,754-acre park, Rock Creek Park's charter extends to include the maintenance of other parks, gardens, and buildings throughout the city.

In Georgetown, the park's offerings include D.C.'s oldest standing structure, the 1765 **Old Stone House** (p. 194), located on busy M St. NW; the 10-acre, Potomac River–focused **Georgetown Waterfront Park** (www.georgetown waterfrontpark.org), a swath of greenways, plazas, and walkways, with benches, a labyrinth, and overlooks—you owe it to yourself to take a stroll here; and in upper Georgetown, the family-friendly **Montrose Park,** a favorite place for picnicking and playing tennis; and **Dumbarton Oaks Park,** a 27-acre preserve of naturalistic gardens. Both Montrose and Dumbarton Oaks parks adjoin one another and the Dumbarton Oaks estate and formal gardens (p. 192).

Along 16th Street NW, about 1 mile north of the White House, is **Meridian Hill Park** (www.nps.gov/mehi), 12 acres in size, and located between the Adams Morgan and Columbia Heights neighborhoods. Meridian Hill Park is worth a visit for several reasons: Its view serves up the White House, the Washington Monument, and the Jefferson Memorial in the distance; its cascading fountain is the longest in North America and planted amid its landscaped gardens are a potpourri of statues of famous people: Joan of Arc, Dante, President Buchanan. Best of all is the mix of people you'll find here, mostly from the nearby diverse neighborhoods, and the assorted activities they get up to: yoga lessons, soccer matches, and Sunday afternoon through evening, spring through fall, an African drum circle.

From the Potomac River near the Kennedy Center northwest through the city into Maryland. www.nps.gov/rocr. ✆ **202/895-6070.** Free admission. Daily during daylight hours. Metro: Access points near the stations at Dupont Circle, Foggy Bottom, Woodley Park–Zoo, and Cleveland Park.

Theodore Roosevelt Island Park ★

A serene, 88½-acre wilderness preserve, Theodore Roosevelt Island is a memorial to the nation's 26th president in recognition of his contributions to conservation. During his administration, Roosevelt, an outdoor enthusiast and expert field naturalist, set aside a total of 234 million acres of public lands for forests, national parks, wildlife and bird refuges, and monuments.

Native American tribes were here first, inhabiting the island for centuries until the arrival of English explorers in the 1600s. Over the years, the island passed through many owners before becoming what it is today—an island preserve of swamp, marsh, and upland forest that's a haven for rabbits, chipmunks, great owls, foxes, muskrats, turtles, and groundhogs. It's a complex ecosystem in which cattails, arrow arum, and pickerelweed grow in the marshes, and willow, ash, and maple trees root on the mud flats. You can observe these flora and fauna in their natural environs on 2.5 miles of foot trails.

In the northern center of the island, overlooking a terrace encircled by a water-filled moat, stands a 17-foot bronze statue of Roosevelt. Four 21-foot granite tablets are inscribed with tenets of his conservation philosophy.

To drive to the island, take the George Washington Memorial Parkway exit north from the Theodore Roosevelt Bridge. The parking area is accessible only from the northbound lane; park there and cross the pedestrian bridge that connects the lot to the island. You can also rent a canoe at Thompson Boat Center or Key Bridge Boathouse (p. 205) and paddle over, making sure to land at the north or northeast corner of the island; there is no place to secure the boat, so you'll need to stay with it. Or take the Metro to the Rosslyn Metro station, walk toward Key Bridge, and follow the short connecting trail leading downhill from the downstream side of the river and across the parkway into the parking lot. Expect bugs in summer and muddy trails after a rain.

In the Potomac River, btw. Washington and Rosslyn, VA (see above for access information). www.nps.gov/this. ✆ **703/289-2500.** Free admission. Daily 6am–10pm. Metro: Rosslyn, then follow the trail to the island.

Chesapeake & Ohio Canal National Historical Park ★★

Hidden behind the bustling streets of Georgetown is the picturesque **C&O Canal** and its unspoiled towpath, which extends 184.5 miles into Maryland. You leave urban cares and stresses behind while hiking, strolling, jogging, cycling, or boating in this lush natural setting of ancient oaks and red maples, giant sycamores, willows, and wildflowers. But the canal wasn't always just a leisure spot for city people. It was built in the 1800s, when water routes were vital to transportation. Even before it was completed, though, the canal was being rendered obsolete by the B&O Railroad, constructed at about the same time and along the same route.

You can enter the towpath in Georgetown below M Street via Thomas Jefferson Street. If you hike 14 miles, you'll reach **Great Falls,** a point where the Potomac becomes a stunning waterfall plunging 76 feet. This is also where the

National Park Service runs its **Great Falls Tavern Visitor Center,** 11710 MacArthur Blvd., Potomac, MD (📞 **301/767-3714**). At this 1831 tavern, you can see museum exhibits and a film about the canal; it also has a bookstore; check to make sure the center is open before you arrive. The park charges for entrance: $20 per car, $10 per walker or cyclist (valid for 7 days).

The C&O Canal offers many opportunities for outdoor activities (see below), but if you or your family prefer a less strenuous form of relaxation, consider a **mule-drawn 19th-century canal-boat trip.** Passengers will travel about a mile along the canal, through the locks, while being pulled by mules—the same way canal boats traditionally were propelled.

Note: Parts of the C&O Canal tow path and its locks are under ongoing construction from either storm damage or restoration. Depending on when you visit, sections of the trail may be closed altogether. Call to confirm!

Enter the towpath in Georgetown below M St. via Thomas Jefferson St. www.nps.gov/choh. 📞 **301/767-3714.** Free admission. Daily during daylight hours. Metro: Foggy Bottom, with a 20-min. walk to the towpath in Georgetown.

ESPECIALLY FOR KIDS

As far as I know, Pierre L'Enfant and his successors were not thinking of children when they incorporated the long, open stretch of the Mall into their design for the city. But they may as well have been. This 2-mile expanse of lawn running from the Lincoln Memorial to the Capitol is a playground, really, and a backyard to the Smithsonian museums and National Gallery of Art, which border it. You can visit any of these sites assured that if one of your little darlings starts to misbehave, you'll be able to head right out the door to the National Mall, where numerous distractions await. Vendors sell ice cream, soft pretzels, and sodas. Festivals of all sorts take place on a regular basis, whether it's the busy **Smithsonian Folklife Festival** for 10 days at the end of June into July (see "Washington, D.C., Calendar of Events," in chapter 2, p. 23), or the **Kite Festival** on the Washington Monument grounds in spring. Weather permitting,

Winter ice skating at the National Gallery Sculpture Garden.

Check for special children's events at museum information desks when you enter. I especially recommend a visit to the **International Spy Museum** (p. 165) for tweens and teens (and adults), for the fun interactive spy adventures; and the **National Building Museum** (p. 1810), for kids ages 3 to 11, for the assortment of hands-on building-related activities. Here's a rundown of overall kid-pleasers in town:

- **Gravelly Point:** Zzzzzooom! It's a thrill for young airplane lovers to watch jets take off and land at this park just steps from Ronald Reagan Airport's runway. It's also an ideal spot to picnic, play ball, and walk along the Potomac River.

- **National Air and Space Museum** (p. 145): Spectacular planetarium shows, missiles, rockets, and a walk-through orbital workshop.

- **National Museum of American History** (p. 153): This museum's got all your kids covered: The fabulous Wegmans Wonderplace is a playground for infants to 6-year-olds; the Lemelson Center introduces visitors of all ages to the stories of inventors and inventions (Places of Invention), and invites kids ages 6 to 12, especially, to experiment and test their curiosity with plenty of hands-on activities (Spark!Lab). There are also simulator rides where kids can practice driving a racecar or ride a roller coaster.

- **National Museum of the American Indian** (p. 155): Children, and their parents too, enjoy themselves in the museum's imagiNATIONS Activity Center, where visitors learn basket weaving, kayak balancing, and other Native American skills, and play games to discover more about American Indian culture. Check the opening status before your trip here to make sure imagiNATIONS is open to visitors.

- **National Museum of Natural History** (p. 156): This is a no-brainer: Dinosaurs, a megalodon shark jaw, mummies, a live coral reef, gemstones... nearly every exhibit here has appeal for kids of various ages.

- **National Zoological Park** (p. 189): Pandas! Cheetahs! Kids love zoos, and this is an especially good one.

- **U.S. Botanic Garden** (p. 159): Kids get their hands dirty at the seasonal digging area outside the Children's Garden.

a **19th-century carousel** operates in front of the Arts and Industries Building, on the south side of the Mall. Right across the Mall from the carousel is the child-friendly **National Gallery Sculpture Garden,** whose shallow pool is good for splashing one's feet in summer and for ice-skating in winter.

The Smithsonian's comprehensive calendar of events page (www.si.edu/events/calendar) has a daily list of family-friendly fun at all 19 locations, letting you screen for children's activities. It's a great timesaver.

The truth is that many of Washington's attractions hold various enchantments for children of all ages. It might be easier to point out which ones are *not* recommended for your youngest: the Supreme Court, the chambers of Congress, the U.S. Holocaust Memorial Museum, and the State Department Diplomatic Rooms. The International Spy Museum is now recommending that its museum is most suitable for children 10 and over. Generally speaking, the bigger and busier the museum, the better it is for kids (see box below).

For more ideas, consult the online or print version of the Friday "Weekend" section of the *Washington Post,* which lists numerous activities (mostly free) for kids: special museum events, children's theater, storytelling programs, puppet shows, video-game competitions, and so forth. View the websites for the Kennedy Center and the National Theatre to find out about children's shows; see chapter 8 for details. For outdoor fun, consider the southwest waterfront's Wharf complex, studded with oversize game boards, ice skating, a splash fountain, bocce, and waterpark activities. And see p. 36 for a family-themed tour of the capital.

OUTDOOR ACTIVITIES

For information about spectator-sports venues, see chapter 8. But if you prefer to work up your own honest sweat, Washington offers plenty of opportunities in lush surroundings. See "Parks," earlier in this chapter, for complete coverage of the city's loveliest green spaces. And look to the waterfronts: In addition to **Georgetown Waterfront Park** (p. 200), the Capitol Riverfront's **Yards Park** is a magnet for parents who let their little ones play in the fountain and canal basin, and a popular spot for outdoor festivals and concerts. Best of all is the **Wharf at the Southwest Waterfront** (www.wharfdc.com/things-to-do), which offers of outdoor recreational opportunities including boat-and bike rentals, yoga on the pier, fitness classes, sailing lessons, strolling, ice skating, you name it. East Potomac Park lies directly across the Washington Channel and a free ferry ride away from the Wharf; there you can play golf and tennis, swim, and jog (see those categories, below).

Biking

Biking is big in D.C., not just as a leisure activity but as an environmentally friendly form of transportation. Much of the city is flat, and paths are everywhere, notably around the National Mall and Memorial Parks. Rock Creek Park has a **9-mile paved bike route** ★ from the Lincoln Memorial through the park into Maryland. Or you can follow the bike path from the Lincoln Memorial over Memorial Bridge to Old Town Alexandria and on to Mount Vernon (see chapter 9). For a less-crowded ride, check out the **Anacostia Riverwalk Trail;** its 12 miles (of a planned 20-mile stretch) go from the Tidal Basin to the Capitol Riverfront neighborhood, and along the Anacostia River into other waterfront communities. *Warning:* Bike-path signage can be confusing or even missing altogether in the waterfront area and you may have to bike on neighborhood streets to pick up the path linking the Southwest Waterfront to the southeast portion of the Anacostia Riverwalk Trail.

The **C&O Canal Historical Park's towpath** (p. 201) is a popular bike path. The **Capital Crescent Trail** goes from Georgetown to the suburb of Bethesda, Maryland, following a former railroad track that parallels the Potomac River for part of the way and passes by old trestle bridges and pleasant residential neighborhoods. (*Note:* Parts of the trail nearby Bethesda may be closed due to a new train construction. Check the web site before you go.)

You can pick up the trail at the **Thompson Boat Center** in Georgetown, and at **Fletcher's Cove** along the C&O Canal; visit **www.cctrail.org** for info.

Capital BikeShare stations are located conveniently near the Tidal Basin and the National Mall; If you're here for more than a few days, consider a Capital BikeShare membership (www.capitalbikeshare.com; p. 298).

Bike rental locations include:

- The **Boat House at Fletcher's Cove,** 4940 Canal Rd. NW (www.fletchers cove.com; ✆ **202/244-0461**).

- **Bike and Roll/Bike the Sites** (www.bikeandrolldc.com; ✆ **202/842-2453**), with two locations: near the National Mall, at 955 L'Enfant Plaza SW, North Building, directly behind the new International Spy Museum location, daily tours and rentals (Metro: L'Enfant Plaza); and Old Town Alexandria, One Wales Alley, at the waterfront, self-guided tours, full-day advance-reservations rentals, and same-day walkup rentals (Metro: King St.). See p. 302 for info about their guided tours. Rates vary depending on the bike you choose but always include helmet, bike, lock, and pump; there's a 2-hour minimum.

- **Big Wheel Bikes,** 1034 33rd St. NW, near the C&O Canal just below M Street (www.bigwheelbikes.com; ✆ **202/337-0254**).

Boating & Fishing

An enterprise called **Boating in DC** (www.boatingindc.com; ✆ **202/337-9642**) operates all of the boat rental locations below. Before you access the Boating in DC website, however, it might be helpful to read my descriptions below, which provide information geared toward visitors as much as locals.

Thompson Boat Center and the **Boat House at Fletcher's Cove** both rent boats from around March to November. Thompson has canoes, kayaks, SUPs, and rowing shells (recreational and racing), and is open for boat rentals daily in season. Fletcher's is on the C&O Canal, about 2 miles from Key Bridge in Georgetown. In addition to renting bikes, canoes, rowboats, and kayaks, Fletcher's sells fishing licenses, bait, and tackle. it is accessible by car (west on M St. NW to Canal Rd. NW) and has plenty of free parking.

Key Bridge Boathouse, 3500 Water St. NW (www.boatingindc.com; ✆ **202/337-9642**), located along the Georgetown waterfront beneath Key Bridge, is open daily mid-April to November for canoe and kayak rentals. Foggy Bottom is the closest Metro station. Sister boathouses include **Ballpark Boathouse,** on the Anacostia River in the Capital Riverfront neighborhood, at Potomac Avenue SE and First Street SE; and the **Wharf Boathouse,** at 700 Water Street SW, in the Southwest Waterfront neighborhood.

Also part of the Boating in DC dynasty are **paddleboats ★**, with foot-pedals to propel the boat over the surface of the Tidal Basin. The Tidal Basin is located between Independence Ave. SW and the Jefferson Memorial. Available from 10am to 5pm daily mid-March to mid-October are four-seaters at $32 an hour, two-seaters at $20 an hour, and motorized two-seater "swan boats" at $36 an hour.

Golf

The District's best and most convenient public golf course is the historic **East Potomac Golf Course** on Hains Point, 972 Ohio Dr. SW, in East Potomac Park (www.playdcgolf.com; © 202/554-7660). Golfers use the Washington Monument to help them line up their shots. The club rents everything but shoes. In addition to its three courses, one 18-hole and two 9-hole greens, the park offers a miniature golf course. Open since 1930, it's the oldest continually operating miniature golf course in the country.

Hiking & Jogging

Washington has numerous **hiking paths.** The C&O Canal offers 184.5 miles stretching from D.C. to Cumberland, Maryland; hiking any section of the flat dirt towpath or its more rugged side paths is a pleasure (and it's free). **Hiker/ biker campsites** along the way provide a picnic table, grill, and chemical toilet. Theodore Roosevelt Island is 88½ acres of wilderness but allows hikes on only three short trails. Rock Creek Park boasts 20 miles of hiking trails (visit www.nps.gov/rocr/planyourvisit/maps.htm for maps).

Joggers can run on the National Mall, along the path in Rock Creek Park, and around the 3.5-mile roadway that loops the 327-acre **East Potomac Park** and takes you to Hains Point, the East Potomac Golf Course (see above) and tennis courts (see below).

Ice Skating

Georgetown's waterfront complex, the **Washington Harbour,** at 3050 K St. NW (www.thewashingtonharbour.com/ice-skating-rink; © 202/706-7666), operates an ice rink that, at 11,800 square feet, is the largest outdoor skating venue in the city. The season runs November to March.

For a truly memorable experience, head to the **National Gallery Sculpture Garden Ice Rink ★**, on the Mall at 7th Street and Constitution Avenue NW (www.nga.gov/visit/ice-rink.html; © 202/216-9397), where you can rent skates, twirl in view of the sculptures, and enjoy hot chocolate in the Pavilion Café next to the rink. It's also open daily, November into March.

The Capitol Riverfront neighborhood has its own figure-eight-shaped ice rink in **Canal Park** (www.capitolriverfront.org/canal-park/ice-rink), open daily from November through February.

The Wharf's ice-skating rink (www.wharfdc.com/wharf-ice-rink), located on the Transit Pier in the Southwest Waterfront neighborhood, offers a rather small rink and unprotected exposure to the wind-whipping cold, but great views of the river.

Each of these ice rinks charges for skate rentals and skating.

Swimming & Tennis

If it's summer and your hotel doesn't have a **pool,** you might consider one of the city's neighborhood pools, including a large outdoor pool at 25th and N streets NW (© 202/340-6795) and the Georgetown outdoor pool at 34th Street and Volta Place NW (© 202/645-5669). They are likely to be crowded.

Many of the same recreation centers equipped with pools also have **tennis courts,** so you'll find four courts at the 25th and N streets NW location and two courts at the Volta Place location, both cited above. In the same Georgetown neighborhood is **Montrose Park,** right next to Dumbarton Oaks (p. 192), with four courts, but no pool.

By far the best public tennis court facility is **East Potomac Park Tennis Center** at Hains Point (www.eastpotomactennis.com; ✆ **202/554-5962**), with 24 tennis courts (10 clay, 9 outdoor hard courts, and 4 indoor hard courts), including three illuminated at night; the park rents rackets as well. Fees vary with court surface and time of play.

For a list of public indoor and outdoor pools, go to **www.dpr.dc.gov** and click the "Find a Pool" link in the "Parks and Facilities" tab; for a list of public tennis courts, go to **https://dpr.dc.gov/publication/dpr-tennis-court-locations**.

SHOPPING

by Jess Moss

7

While shopping is not usually the primary reason people come to visit Washington, it's not for lack of options. The city has a rich mix of major retailers and local businesses, plus a high-income population and vigorous spending habits among residents and visitors. You can re-create your wardrobe in the latest designer styles, pick up only-in-D.C. mementos, and find arts and antiques to keep satisfying your history craving. Wherever you are in the city, shops present a variety of wares, prices, and styles. This chapter leads you to some of the best.

THE SHOPPING SCENE

The Covid-19 pandemic hit D.C.'s retail scene hard, as visitor numbers and capacity limits reduced foot traffic. Sadly, a number of longtime local favorites moved online-only or shut their doors for good. Many that did survive reduced opening hours, at least temporarily. Since this is likely to change, it's safest to check a shop's current hours before you arrive.

Sales tax on merchandise is 5.75% in the District, Maryland, and Northern Virginia. Most gift, arts, and crafts stores, including those at the Smithsonian museums, will handle shipping; clothing stores generally do not.

GREAT SHOPPING AREAS

UNION STATION It's a railroad station, a historic landmark, an architectural marvel, and a shopping mall. Yes, the beauteous Union Station offers some fine shopping opportunities, though a number of stores here closed in 2020 and 2021. Still, you'll find at least 15 shops, from eyewear at **Warby Parker** to skincare at **Blue Mercury** (see p. 211) to a few chocolatiers and souvenir shops. **Metro:** Union Station.

PENN QUARTER The area bounded east and west by 7th and 14th streets NW, and north and south by New York and Pennsylvania avenues NW, has been a hopping shopping area for years. At the northern end of the quarter, the residential/office/dining/retail complex **CityCenterDC** (www.citycenterdc.com), on H St. NW (btw. 9th and 11th sts.), beckons 1-percenters and the curious to its

An art stall in the holiday market in Penn Quarter.

high-end shops, Hermes to Salvatore Ferragamo; but local enterprises are also here, including a weekly farmers market and outdoor yoga classes. Plus, there's usually an Instagram-worthy installation strung above Palmer Alley, so check it out. Penn Quarter has plenty of national chains such as H&M and Anthropologie; international chains such as Zara; as well as one-of-a-kind stores like the museum shops at the National Building Museum, and the Smithsonian American Art Museum and Portrait Gallery. **Macy's** (formerly "Hecht's") at 12th and G streets, continues as the sole department store downtown. **Metro:** Metro Center, Gallery Place–Chinatown, or Archives–Navy Memorial.

ADAMS MORGAN   Centered on 18th Street and Columbia Road NW, Adams Morgan is known for secondhand bookshops and eclectic collectibles stores. It's a fun area for walking and shopping. **Metro:** Woodley Park–Zoo/ Adams Morgan (then walk south on Connecticut Ave. NW until you reach Calvert St., cross Connecticut Ave., and follow Calvert St. across the Duke Ellington Memorial Bridge until you reach the junction of Columbia Rd. NW and 18th St. NW) or Dupont Circle (exit at Q St. NW and walk up Connecticut Ave. NW to Columbia Rd. NW). *Best bet:* The DC Circulator bus, which runs between the McPherson Square and the Woodley Park–Zoo/Adams Morgan Metro stations, stops at the upper end of 18th Street NW.

CONNECTICUT AVENUE/DUPONT CIRCLE   Running from K Street north to S Street, Connecticut Avenue NW is the place to find clothing, from traditional business attire at Brooks Brothers to casual duds at H&M. The area closer to Dupont Circle is known for its art galleries, funky boutiques, and gift, stationery, and book shops. **Metro:** Farragut North at one end, Dupont Circle at the center.

14TH & U STREET CORRIDORS & SHAW   The number of cool shops has hit critical mass, winning the area widespread notice. If you shun brand names and box stores, you'll love the vintage boutiques and local fixtures like Miss Pixie's Furnishings and Whatnot or Salt and Sundry. National brands like Madewell, Lululemon, and West Elm have also moved into this area. 209

Metro: U Street/African American Civil War Memorial/Cardozo and Mount Vernon Square/7th Street/Convention Center.

GEORGETOWN   Home to more than 160 stores, this neighborhood has long been the city's main shopping area. Most stores sit on one of the two main, intersecting streets, Wisconsin Avenue and M Street NW. You'll find both chain and one-of-a-kind shops, chic as well as thrift. Sidewalks are almost always crowded, and parking can be tough. **Metro:** Foggy Bottom, then catch the DC Circulator bus from the stop at 22nd Street and Pennsylvania Avenue (see p. 297 for more information). Metro buses (the no. 30 series) travel through Georgetown from different parts of the city. Otherwise, consider taking a taxi or Uber.

THE WHARF   This Southwest Waterfront complex doesn't have a ton of shops—about 15 at last count—but the number is growing, and the stores on offer are pretty wonderful: offshoots of local favorites, such as the Politics and Prose bookstore, and stylish newcomers, such as and Shop Made in D.C. and A Beautiful Closet boutique. **Metro:** Waterfront.

OLD TOWN ALEXANDRIA   Old Town, in Virginia, resembles Georgetown in its picturesque location on the Potomac, streets lined with historic homes and plentiful shops, as well as in its less desirable aspects: heavy traffic, crowded sidewalks, difficult parking. Old Town extends from the Potomac River in the east to the King Street Metro station in the west, and from about 1st Street in the north to Green Street in the south, but the best shopping is in the center, where King and Washington streets intersect. Weekdays are tamer than weekends. **Metro:** King Street, then take a free King Street Trolley to reach the heart of Old Town.

SHOPPING A TO Z

Antiques

Georgetown and the 14th & U Street Corridors all have concentrations of visit-worthy antiques stores. We recommend:

Good Wood ★★   Half flea market, half antique store, this delightful shop was opened by Dan and Anna Kahoe in the early '90s. Come for the retro furniture and vintage goods as well as clothing, candles, and housewares. 1428 U St. NW (at Waverly Place NW). www.goodwooddc.com. ℂ **202/986-3640.** Metro: U St./Cardozo.

The Great Republic ★★   As its name suggests, this store celebrates all-things American, both old and new. The "old" collection features rare books, antique hand-sewn flags from the Civil War and one-of-a-kind collectables, while the "new" includes everything from American-made leather wallets and cufflinks to home décor. 973 Palmer Alley. NW (at 10th St. NW in CityCenterDC). www.great-republic.com. ℂ **202/682-1812.** Metro: Gallery Place/Chinatown.

Marston Luce Antiques ★★   This shop specializes in 18th- to 20th-century antiques and artworks, from furniture and folk art to garden items and lighting. The collection is predominantly from Sweden, Belgium, and France—the owner lives half the year in Dordogne, France, and his inventory often reflects that provenance. 1651 Wisconsin Ave. NW. www.marstonluce.com. ☎ **202/333-6800.** Metro: Foggy Bottom, then take the DC Circulator bus.

Art Galleries

Art galleries abound in the capital. The following are among the best. Check open days and hours before opening, as galleries may have irregular schedules.

Foundry Gallery ★ Established in 1971, Foundry is nonprofit and artist-owned and -operated. It features the pieces of local artists, who work in various media and styles, from abstract painting on silk to mixed-media collages. The Foundry frequently hosts talks, workshops, demonstrations, and receptions. 2118 8th St. NW (btw. U and V sts.). www.foundrygallery.org. ☎ **202/232-0203.** Metro: U St./Cardozo (10th St. exit).

IA&A at Hillyer ★ The **International Arts & Artists** center occupies a three-room gallery in a restored historic carriage house situated in an alley behind the Phillips Collection. Its shows of contemporary art fulfill its mission to "increase cross-cultural understanding and exposure to the arts internationally." 9 Hillyer Court NW (21st St.). www.athillyer.org. ☎ **202/338-0325.** Metro: Dupont Circle (Q St. exit).

Studio Gallery ★ The city's oldest and most successful cooperative gallery, in existence for 65 years. It represents local artists from the D.C., Maryland, and Virginia area, whose works are in all media: paintings, sculpture, installations, video, and mixed media. The gallery also occasionally hosts shows with national and international artists Don't miss the sculpture garden. 2108 R St. NW (20th St.). www.studiogallerydc.com. ☎ **202/232-8734.** Metro: Dupont Circle (Q St. exit).

Calloway Fine Art & Consulting ★ On display is a varied collection of contemporary and representational art by local, regional, and international artists, plus some antique prints and paintings. In addition to selling art, the gallery does conservation framing (plus shipping). 1643 Wisconsin Ave. NW (Q St.). www.callowayart.com. ☎ **202/965-4601.** Metro: Foggy Bottom, then take the DC Circulator bus.

The Fridge ★ Tucked away in an alley 2 blocks from Eastern Market, this space is equal parts art gallery, performance and music venue and classroom. Opened since 2009, it mainly showcases street art from emerging and established artists, along with special exhibitions and events. 516½ 8th St. SE (btw. 8th and 9th sts. NW). ☎ **202/664-4151.** www.thefridgedc.com. Metro: Eastern Market

Beauty

Georgetown has a high concentration of the city's premiere hair salons, cosmetic stores, and spas, but you can find places to primp all over the city.

Blue Mercury ★ Half "apothecary," half spa, this chain's five D.C. locations offer a full selection of facial, massage, waxing, and makeup treatments, as well as a smorgasbord of high-end beauty products, from Acqua di Parma fragrances to Kiehl's skincare line. www.bluemercury.com. Georgetown: 3059 M St. NW; ℂ **202/965-1300;** Metro: Foggy Bottom, then take the DC Circulator bus. Dupont Circle: 1625 Connecticut Ave. NW (ℂ **202/462-1300**); Metro: Dupont Circle (Q St. exit). Union Station: ℂ **202/289-5008;** Metro: Union Station. 14th & U St. Corridors: 1427 P St. NW; ℂ **202/238-0001;** Metro: U St./Carodozo (13th St. exit).

Debby Harper Salon & Spa ★ I have to admit, I've walked past this Dupont Circle salon hundreds of times without ever paying it much notice. But then the pandemic hit, and Debby Harper did something brilliant: They brought their nail polish stations outside. Now you can get a quick manicure or pedicure under a weather-proof but open-air roof. Indoor services are also available, as are waxing and massage. 1605 17th St NW. ℂ **202/290-1575.** www.debbyharpersalon.com. Metro: Dupont Circle.

Salon ILO ★ Gary Walker and Terry Bell (and their team of master hair and color stylists) have been delivering sleek cuts and treatments for more than 30 years. They count local politicians and known names among their clientele, but that's all I'm saying. 1637 Wisconsin Ave. NW. www.salonilo.com. ℂ **202/342-0350.** Metro: Foggy Bottom, then take the DC Circulator bus.

Take Care ★ This soothing Georgetown shop has become a community hub for the growing number of natural skincare and clean beauty advocates in D.C. The products cover skin, hair, makeup, and other wellness needs, and all are synthetic fragrance-free. The holistic spa offers a wide range of facials, reiki healing, and waxing. You can also shop a selection of crystals from shop owner Becky Waddell's brand, District Mineral. 1338 Wisconsin Ave. NW. www.takecare shopdc.com. ℂ **202/717-2600.** Metro: Foggy Bottom, then take the DC Circulator bus.

Varnish Lane ★ Cottagecore fans will feel right at home in this airy nail salon, which is lined with oversized leather recliners where all services are done. Manicures and pedicures are "waterless," which the salon claims saves up to 15 gallons of water per service. There are multiple locations around the city. www.varnishlane.com West End: 1201 24th St. NW (ℂ **202/331-7111**); Metro: Foggy Bottom. Mount Vernon Triangle: 400 K St. NW (ℂ **202/878-8222**); Metro: Gallery Place/Chinatown. Friendship Heights: 5236 44th St. NW (ℂ **202/506-5308**); Metro: Friendship Heights.

Books

Washington is a highly educated city, so it's not too surprising that there's a high concentration of bookstores here, including a broad range of specialized shops focusing on particular topic of type of book.

Amazon Books ★ Open daily, Amazon's first D.C. brick and mortar bookshop sells new releases and books that are bestsellers and/or rated 4 stars or higher on its website. E-readers, Alexa devices, toys, and games are also for sale. The two-level store includes a cafe and kids section. Forget to pack something for your trip? You can pick up Amazon orders at this store, too. 3040 M St. NW (at Thomas Jefferson St.). www.amazon.com. ℂ **202/333-2315.** Metro: Foggy Bottom, then take the DC Circulator bus.

Busboys and Poets ★   It's a bookstore, restaurant, community gathering place, theater, and political activist center. Its book inventory reflects all those angles, showcasing works by local authors, writers from diverse backgrounds, and subjects dealing with social and political struggles. The 14th St. location opened in 2005; others have followed, including a Busboys and Poets at 450 K St. NW (℗ **202/789-2227**). 2021 14th St. NW (V St.). www.busboysandpoets. com. ℗ **202/387-7368.** Metro: U St./African American Civil War Memorial/Cardozo Station (13th St. exit).

Capitol Hill Books ★   This longtime local favorite book shop has used, rare, and new books crammed into every possible bit of space throughout the three-story shop located directly across the street from Eastern Market. Look for foreign-language books in the bathroom and cookbooks in a former kitchen! 657 C St. SE. www.capitolhillbooks-dc.com. ℗ **202/544-1621.** Metro: Eastern Market.

Kramers ★★★   Opened in 1976, Kramer's (formerly known as Kramerbooks & Afterwords Café) was the first bookstore/cafe in Washington, maybe in this country, and has launched countless romances. It's often busy and noisy; stages author readings, live music, and other events; and is open past midnight on Fridays and Saturdays. Paperback fiction takes up most of its inventory, but the store carries a little of everything. 1517 Connecticut Ave. NW. www.kramers. com. ℗ **202/387-1400** or 202/387-3825 for the cafe. Metro: Dupont Circle (Q St. exit).

The Lantern ★★   Rare, used, and out-of-print books—all donated—are this store's specialty. Books on antiques and philosophy, dramatic novels, and children's books can be found, along with sheet music, vinyl, and CDs. All proceeds benefit Bryn Mawr College. 3241 P St. NW. www.lanternbookshop.org. ℗ **202/333-3222.** Metro: Foggy Bottom then walk 20 min., or take the DC Circulator Bus to the P Street stop.

Politics and Prose Bookstore ★★★   This much-cherished shop has vast offerings in literary fiction and nonfiction alike and an excellent children's department. It has expanded again and again over the years to accommodate its clientele's love of books in every genre, as well as a growing selection of greeting cards, journals, and other gifts. The shop hosts author readings nearly every night of the year, sometimes two or three in a single day. A warm, knowledgeable staff assists customers. Downstairs is a pleasant coffeehouse. Politics and Prose has another location at 70 District Square SW (℗ **202/488-3867**) at the Wharf, in the Southwest Waterfront neighborhood, and another near Union Market,

Enjoy author readings at Politics and Prose Bookstore in Cleveland Park.

at 1270 Fifth St. NE (✆ **202/544-4452**). 5015 Connecticut Ave. NW. www.politics-prose.com. ✆ **202/364-1919.** Metro: Van Ness–UDC, and walk, or transfer to an "L" bus to take you the ¾ mile from there.

Second Story Books ★   If it's old, out of print, custom bound, or a small-press publication, you'll find it here. The store also trades in used CDs and vinyl and has an interesting collection of campaign posters. 2000 P St. NW. www.secondstorybooks.com. ✆ **202/659-8884.** Metro: Dupont Circle (South/19th St. exit).

Cameras & Computers

Apple Store ★   Head to Massachusetts Avenue and Ninth Street NW in Mount Vernon Square to tour the beautifully renovated 116-year-old Carnegie Library and the Historical Society of Washington's three galleries showcasing D.C. history exhibits, and, yes, to check out Apple's D.C. flagship store. Or you can always visit the one in Georgetown, to hang out and fool around on the floor samples, study the merchandise, and get your questions answered by techy geeks roaming the room. 801 K St. NW; www.apple.com/retail/carnegielibrary; Metro: Mount Vernon Sq./7th St. Convention Center. 1229 Wisconsin Ave. NW. www.apple.com/retail/georgetown. ✆ **202/572-1460.** Metro: Foggy Bottom, then take the DC Circulator bus.

Leica Camera ★   This store is one of only eight the German company has opened in the U.S. If you know your way around cameras and don't mind spending a bit of money, this shop will likely delight. *FYI:* The store also sells used equipment and occasionally sponsors photo walks around the city. 977 F St. NW. leicacamerausa.com/pages/leica-stores/leica-store-dc.html. ✆ **202/787-5900.** Metro: Gallery Place (9th and G sts. exit).

Clothing

CHILDREN'S CLOTHING
Also consider **Macy's** at 1201 G St. NW (✆ **202/628-6661**), in Penn Quarter; and **GapKids** at 1258 Wisconsin Ave. NW (✆ **202/333-2657**) in Georgetown, and at 664 11th St. NW (✆ **202/347-0258**) in Penn Quarter.

Three Littles ★   Former nanny and District Baking Company owner Elizabeth Mahon recently opened this adorable kids' shop in Union Market, selling a curated selection of gender-neutral children's goods, heirloom pieces and toys, all sourced from companies that follow safe and fair employment practices. 1260 4th St. NE. (Union Market) www.threelittles.co. ✆ **202/753-0013.** Metro: NOMA/Gallaudet.

MEN'S & WOMEN'S CLOTHING
See the "Great Shopping Areas" (p. 208) section if you're interested in such chain stores as **Urban Outfitters, Gap, Brooks Brothers,** or **H&M.** Below are stores that speak more to the fashion zeitgeist of D.C.

Maketto ★★   It's a cafe, it's a bar, it's a store, it's an award-winning restaurant (p. 90)—it's all of that and more. Maketto the shop is primarily about menswear, its inventory of international footwear, clothing, and accessories laid out in glass display cases and on open shelving. Neighborhood, Raised by

Wolves, Vans, and Born N Raised are among the brands. 1351 H St. NE. www.maketto1351.com. ℂ **202/838-9972.** Metro: Union Station, then catch the DC Streetcar to the Atlas District.

The Outrage ★ Feeling the need to rise up in support of a cause these days? Here's a shop that allows your clothing to speak for you. Tops and tees, sweatshirts, and pants are emblazoned with messages, including RESIST and GOOD TROUBLE. The rear space of the store is a gathering place for the feminist, progressive crowd. 1811 14th St. NW, Unit B. www.the-outrage.com. ℂ **202/885-9848.** Metro: U St./Cardozo.

Proper Topper ★★ For the longest time, I thought this store was just a hat boutique. Wrong! It's a one-stop shop for stocking stuffers and bigger gifts: cozy loungewear, pretty jewelry, adorable clothes for children, stationery, all sorts of gifty things, and yes, hats. 3322 Wisconsin Ave., NW. www.propertopper.com. ℂ **202/842-3055.** Metro: Dupont Circle (19th St. exit).

Relish ★ To be blunt, you will need money—heaps of it—to shop here. But for fans of designer duds, this is your place. Dries van Noten, Calvin Klein, Marc Jacobs, and Simone Rocha are always in stock. Full-time stylists are also on hand to help you find that perfect look. 3312 Cady's Alley NW. www.relishdc.com. ℂ **202/333-5343.** Metro: Foggy Bottom, then take the DC Circulator.

Upstairs on 7th ★★ This shop is neither upstairs nor on 7th Street (that was its original location) and its Pennsylvania Avenue street address is also misleading—you enter an office building at 12th and E streets and walk through the lobby to your left to find the shop. But believe me, Washington women in the know find their way here. Judges, journalists, politicians, and other heavyweights speak truth to power through clothing they've purchased at Upstairs on 7th. Forget business-suit-oriented, though. No, mother-daughter team Ricki Peltzman and Katy Klassman sell fashionably fun and interesting apparel and accessories: crinkly and sophisticated Ray Harris dresses, edgy Rundholz designs, architecturally inspired pieces by Labo Art and whimsical Annemieke Broenink necklaces. The shop also functions as a salon, with a speaker series on timely subjects. 1299 Pennsylvania Ave. NW, Ste. 132R (enter at 12th and E sts., through the lobby of the Warner Building). www.upstairson7th.com. ℂ **301/351-8308.** Metro: Metro Center (12th and F sts. exit).

VINTAGE SHOPS

Meeps ★★ For men and women attracted to local designer wear and vintage clothes, from 1930s gabardine suits to 1950s cocktail dresses to satiny lingerie. 2104 18th St. NW. www.meepsdc.com. ℂ **202/265-6546.** Metro: U St./Cardozo (13th St. exit) or Woodley Park–Zoo, with a bit of a walk from either station.

Secondi Inc. ★ From the second floor of a building right above a Dolcezza coffee and gelato shop, this high-style consignment shop sells women's clothing and accessories, including designer suits, evening wear, and more casual items—everything from Kate Spade to Chanel. Open since 1986, Secondi is the longest-running designer consignment shop for women in D.C.

1702 Connecticut Ave. NW (btw. R St. and Florida Ave.). www.secondi.com. ✆ **202/667-1122.** Metro: Dupont Circle (Q St. exit).

Crafts

A Mano ★★   Owner Adam Mahr frequently forages in Europe and returns with unique handmade French and Italian ceramics, linens, and other decorative accessories for home and garden. 1677 Wisconsin Ave. NW. www.amano.bz. ✆ **202/298-7200.** Metro: Foggy Bottom, then take the DC Circulator bus.

Indian Craft Shop ★★   The Indian Craft Shop has represented authentic Native-American artisans since 1938, selling handwoven rugs and handcrafted baskets, jewelry, figurines, pottery, and other items. The shop is situated inside a federal government building, so you must pass through security and show photo ID to enter. It's open Tuesday to Friday and the third Saturday of each month. Department of the Interior, 1849 C St. NW, Rm. 1023. www.indiancraftshop.com. ✆ **202/208-4056.** Metro: Farragut West (17th St. exit), with a bit of a walk from the station.

The Phoenix ★   Around since 1955, this Georgetown shop sells eco- and community-conscious jewelry, clothing, and home décor. The goods here are globally inspired, from travel-ready fashions to Mexican silver bracelets to woven rugs and baskets and a line of products inspired by Maine, where third-generation owner Samantha Hays Gushner spends part of her time. 1514 Wisconsin Ave. NW. www.thephoenixdc.com. ✆ **202/338-4404.** Metro: Foggy Bottom, then take the DC Circulator bus.

Torpedo Factory Art Center ★★   Once a munitions factory, this three-story building built in 1918 now houses more than 82 working studios, 7 galleries, and the works of about 165 artists, who tend to their crafts before your very eyes, pausing to explain their techniques or to sell their pieces. Artworks include paintings, sculpture, ceramics, glasswork, and textiles. 105 N. Union St., Alexandria, VA. www.torpedofactory.org. ✆ **703/746-4570.** Metro: King St., then take the free King St. Trolley or the DASH bus (AT2, AT5) eastbound to the waterfront.

Farmers & Flea Markets

Dupont Circle FreshFarm Market ★   More than 50 local farmers sell flowers, fruits, vegetables, meat, poultry, fish, and cheeses here. The market sometimes features kids' activities, live music, and guest appearances by the chefs of some of D.C.'s best restaurants. It's open Sundays rain or shine, year-round, from 8:30am to 1:30pm. The FreshFarm Market organization stages other farmers markets on other days around town; see website. On 20th St. NW (btw. Massachusetts Ave. and Hillyer Place). www.freshfarm.org/markets/dupont-circle. ✆ **202/362-8889.** Metro: Dupont Circle (Q St. exit).

Eastern Market ★★★   Historic Eastern Market has been in operation here since 1873. Today the market's restored South Hall is a bustling bazaar, where area farmers, greengrocers, bakers, butchers, and others sell their wares Tuesday through Sunday, joined by a second line of farmers outside on Tuesdays,

Eastern Market.

1 to 7pm; on the weekend, 100 or so local artisans hawk jewelry, paintings, pottery, woodwork, and other hand-made items on the outdoor plazas and streets surrounding the market. Best of all is the Saturday morning ritual of breakfasting on blueberry buck-wheat pancakes at the Market Lunch counter. The indoor market is open Tuesday to Friday 7am to 7pm, Satur-day 7am to 6pm, and Sunday 9am to 5pm. 225 7th St. SE (North Carolina Ave.). www.easternmarket-dc.org. ✆ 202/698-5253. Metro: Eastern Market.

Old Town Alexandria Farmers Market ★   The oldest continuously operating farmers market in the country (since 1753), this market offers locally grown fruits and vegetables, along with baked goods, cut flowers, and more. It's open year-round, Saturday mornings from 7am to noon. 301 King St. (at Market Square in front of the city hall), in Alexandria, VA. www.alexandriava.gov/market. ✆ 703/258-9115. Metro: King St., then take the free King St. Trolley or the DASH bus (AT2, AT7 or AT8) eastbound to Market Square.

Union Market ★   Worth a detour from sightseeing, this year-round indoor market includes pop-up marketers hawking a particular specialty, such as small-batch pickles. At least 35 vendors set up in stalls or at counters selling fresh produce, flowers, cheeses, artworks—everything from olive oil to oysters. Stop by Salt & Sundry for lovely handcrafted gifts. Check the events calendar to join a yoga class or catch an outdoor movie. There's always something popping up. It's open daily 8am to 8pm, Thursday to Saturday 8am to 9pm. 1309 Fifth St. NE. www.unionmarketdc.com. ✆ 301/347-3998. Metro: NoMA–Gallaudet–U St.

Gifts/Souvenirs

See also "Crafts," earlier in this chapter; the Eastern Market listing above (weekend artisans sell excellent take-home gifts, such as Mary Belcher's Washington watercolors); and Hill's Kitchen under "Home Furnishings & Kitchenware," below. **Museum gift shops** (see chapter 6) are another excellent source. Also check out the **White House History Shop** (www.whitehouse history.org/our-retail-shops) at Decatur House (1610 H St. NW; ✆ 202/218-4337) and at the White House Visitor Center (1450 Pennsylvania Ave. NW; ✆ 202/208-7031); see p. 174. It sells fun memorabilia, such as the White House Christmas tree ornament (newly designed each year) and sundry items related to the White House and its history.

Chocolate Moose ★   Its website welcomes browsers with the words "Serving weirdly sophisticated Washingtonians since 1978." This translates to a shop full of quirky gifts: Think a "When Pigs Fly" tote bag; pink flamingo

UNIQUELY WASHINGTONIAN souvenirs

Step away from the T-shirt stand! Cheesy tourist gear abounds in Washington, from FBI shirts to replica White Houses, but a lot of it is cheap and can be pretty tacky. Instead, try to seek out locally loved products:

Mumbo Sauce: The unofficial condiment of D.C., this red sauce (also called mambo sauce) is a sweet-and-spicy topping for everything from fried chicken to fried rice. You'll find Capital City Mambo Sauce at supermarkets and gift shops around the city.

D.C. Flag or 51st State Gear: From statehood shirts to coasters emblazoned with the iconic three stars above two bars of D.C.'s flag you can bring home high-quality Washington goods. Shop Made in DC, Eastern Market, and Steadfast Supply are good places to start your search.

Local Liquors: Try Green Hat gin, Madam whiskey from Republic Restoratives (a nod to the first female VP by this women-run distillery), or a six-pack of DC Brau's civic-themed beers.

White House Christmas Ornament: Each year the White House unveils a new "official" commemorative Christmas ornament. You can purchase one at the White House History Shop or White House Visitor Center store.

candles; Belgian chocolate; wacky cards; hair clips; eccentric clothing; baby toys; and other funny presents like Joe Biden and Kamala Harris action figures. 1743 L St. NW. www.chocolatemoosedc.com. © **202/463-0992.** Metro: Farragut North (L St. exit).

Shop Made in DC ★★ This is the kind of shop I'm always looking for when I travel to another city. Everything in the shop, from the music playing to the to the jewelry you're eyeing, is made by D.C. artisans and is for sale. The shop is a joint venture between a local entrepreneur and a D.C. government program, and there are a growing number of outlets around the city. On a recent shopping trip here, I walked out with a Birds of D.C. print, a 202 tank top from Bailiwick Clothing, and a candle by Pose Candle Co. The shop sells hundreds of items and is happy to box and mail gifts for you. It also regularly holds classes and events, like pottery, beading or watercolor workshops. 1710 Connecticut Ave. NW (at R St.), 10 District Square SW, Wharf District and 1242 Wisconsin Ave., NW. www.shopmadeindc.com. Metro: Dupont Circle (Q St. exit), L'Enfant Plaza, then walk south or Foggy Bottom/GWU then DC Circulator or Bus 30N.

Steadfast Supply ★ What began as a temporary pop-up in 2016 has grown into a 3,000-square-foot emporium of gifts and crafts from independent designers and artisans around the world. You'll find artisanal D.C. souvenirs, pop culture–inspired prints, plants and jewelry and more. 301 Tingey Street SE. www.steadfastsupplydc.com. © **202/308-4441.** Metro: Navy Yard.

Home Furnishings & Kitchenware

Cady's Alley ★ Cady's Alley refers not to a single store, but to the southwest pocket of Georgetown, where about 20 stores reside in and around said alley, which lies south of M Street. Look for tony, big-name places such as

Waterworks and Design within Reach; European outposts, such as the hip kitchen furnishings of Bulthaup; and high-concept design stores, such as Contemporaria. 3314 M St. NW (btw. 33rd and 34th sts.). www.cadysalley.com. Metro: Foggy Bottom, then take the DC Circulator bus.

Hill's Kitchen ★★   This gourmet kitchenwares store occupies an 1884 town house adjacent to the Eastern Market Metro station on Capitol Hill. Precious take-homes include cookie cutters shaped like the Washington Monument and the Capitol dome; top-flight cooking utensils; and colorful aprons and towels. 713 D St. SE. www.hillskitchen.com. ☏ **202/543-1997.** Metro: Eastern Market.

Miss Pixie's Furnishings & Whatnot ★   The name says it all. Vintage home furnishings from armoires to old silver cram the space. The owner buys only from auctions and only things that are in good shape and ready to use. New inventory arrives every Wednesday. 1626 14th St. NW. www.misspixies.com. ☏ **202/232-8171.** Metro: U St./Cardozo (13th St. exit).

Salt and Sundry ★   This shop's stylish collection of housewares; barware, kitchen, and decor; candles and accessories feel like it's straight out of a lifestyle blogger's home. You'll see everything from French hand soap and body lotion to mugs and coaster sets. Union Market: 1309 5th St. NW (in Union Market) and 1625 14th St. NW. www.shopsaltandsundry.com. ☏ **202/556-1866.** Metro: NOMA/Gallaudet/New York Ave. 14th and U St.: 1625 14th St. NW. ☏ **202/621-6647.** Metro: U St./Cardozo.

Jewelry

You'll also find jewelry at the Phoenix, the Proper Topper, Upstairs on 7th, and Shop Made in DC, all listed above.

Tiny Jewel Box ★★   Opened and owned by the same family since 1930, this jewelry store is the first place Washingtonians go for estate and antique jewelry, engagement rings, and the finest brands of watches. Tiny Jewel Box also sells the pieces of many designers, from Alex Sepkus to Penny Preville, as well as an exclusive collection of house gifts. In the month leading up to Mother's Day, the Tiny Jewel Box holds its annual sale, where you can save up to 50% on most items in the store. 1155 Connecticut Ave. NW. www.tinyjewelbox.com. ☏ **202/393-2747.** Metro: Farragut North (L St. exit).

Shoes

Comfort One Shoes ★   This locally owned family business was founded in Old Town Alexandria in 1993. Its two D.C. stores sell a great selection of popular styles for both men and women, including Doc Martens, Birkenstocks, and Ecco. You can always find something that looks smart and actually feels comfortable. 1630 Connecticut Ave. NW. www.comfortoneshoes.com. ☏ **202/328-3141.** Metro: Dupont Circle. Also at 1329 Wisconsin Ave. NW (☏ **202/735-5332**).

Hu's Shoes ★   Fashion models in every D.C. photo shoot wear Hu's shoes, it seems. The two-level Georgetown shop sells designer ready-to-wear footwear, handbags, and accessories. Owner Marlene Hu Aldaba travels to New

York, Paris, and Milan in search of elegant specimens to suit her discriminating eye. Also here is **Hu's Wear,** a collection of designer outfits to accompany the darling shoes. 3005 M St. NW. www.husonline.com. ✆ **202/342-0202.** Metro: Foggy Bottom, then walk or take the DC Circulator bus.

Wine & Spirits

Barmy Wines & Liquors ★   Located near the White House, this family-run store sells it all, but with special emphasis on fine wines and rare cordials. 1912 L St. NW. www.barmywines.com. ✆ **202/455-6996.** Metro: Farragut North (L St. exit).

Central Liquors ★   Dating back to 1934, Central Liquors is like a clearinghouse for liquor: Its great volume allows the store to offer the best prices in town. The store specializes in small estate wines, single-malt scotches, and small-batch bourbons. 625 E St. NW. www.centralliquors.com. ✆ **202/737-2800.** Metro: Gallery Place (9th and F sts. exit).

Schneider's of Capitol Hill ★   Two blocks south of Union Station is this fourth-generation family-run liquor store, in business for more than 70 years. With a knowledgeable and enthusiastic staff, a massive inventory of wine, spirits and beer, and a selection of rare wines that draws collectors from all over, this shop is a find on Capitol Hill. 300 Massachusetts Ave. NE. www.cellar.com. ✆ **202/543-9300.** Metro: Union Station.

ENTERTAINMENT & NIGHTLIFE

by Kaeli Conforti

D.C. nightlife is rollicking and diverse. One-third of the city's population is between 21 and 35, most have jobs and are ready to party. And just about everyone in this hard-working city needs to unwind at the end of a long work week, whether that means a night out dancing in the clubs, cheering on their favorite sports team, or spending time at the theater.

The best neighborhoods for nightlife are **Adams Morgan;** the **14th St. and U St. Corridors** (14th St. btw. P and V sts. and U St. btw. 16th and 10th sts.); **Shaw** (Blagden Alley, and 7th to 10th sts. NW, btw. Massachusetts Ave. NW and U St. NW); **Dupont Circle** along Connecticut Avenue; **Penn Quarter; Georgetown;** the **H Street Corridor; Barracks Row** in Capitol Hill; **Capitol Riverfront (Navy Yard)** in southeast D.C.; **Columbia Heights,** east of Adams Morgan and north of U Street; and the **Southwest Waterfront (The Wharf).**

Most of D.C.'s clubs and bars stay open until 1 or 2am Monday through Thursday and until 3am Friday and Saturday; what time they open varies. The city also allows establishments serving alcohol to open early and stay open until 4am for certain holidays such as the 4th of July and special events like the World Cup. For current concert and club offerings, check The Washington Post's online "Going Out Guide" (www.washingtonpost.com/goingoutguide) and follow along with the Washington City Paper on social media (or check its website, www.washingtoncitypaper.com). Be sure to look closely at the calendars for all those places you visited during the day. Fun after-hours events are taking place at all sorts of unlikely venues, from the Library of Congress to the National Gallery of Art, and many of them are free or affordable to attend.

THE PERFORMING ARTS

Washington's performing arts scene has an international reputation. **The Kennedy Center** reigns supreme, staging everything from opera, dance, and classical/jazz/contemporary music performances to musicals, comedy shows, and traditional theater. **Arena Stage** is renowned for its innovative productions of American masters and new voices. There's even a theater dedicated to all-things Shakespeare. Don't assume that these venues present only classic renditions from a performing arts hit list; each is wildly creative in its choices and presentations. For the most avant-garde theater, seek out smaller stages like the **Woolly Mammoth Theatre Company** and **Studio Acting Conservatory.**

Seasons for both The Kennedy Center and Arena Stage run year-round; normally, the Shakespeare Theatre's season (and that of other smaller theaters) is nearly year-round, taking a 4- to 6-week break July into August. While the Kennedy Center often has performances going on throughout the day, all theaters hold their major productions at 7:30 or 8pm nightly, with Saturday and Sunday matinée performances at 2pm and occasional midweek matinée performances on the schedule, especially at Arena Stage.

The bad news is that ticket prices have gone through the roof in the past couple of years. A lot of locals subscribe to the big three (the Kennedy Center, Shakespeare Theatre, and Arena Stage), which leaves fewer one-off tickets available to the general public. Expect to pay $75 to $100-plus—unless you're able to obtain a discounted ticket; see the "Getting Tickets" box, p. 226.

Major Theaters & Companies

Arena Stage ★★★   Founded in 1950, Arena Stage has long been about "putting the American spirit in the spotlight," as the company tagline phrases it. What that means is that the theater produces the works of American artists, choosing plays that explore themes of American diversity, challenges, and passions. A typical season features an American classic or two, a musical or two, new plays by emerging playwrights, world premieres, and, because Arena Stage is in the nation's capital, a play of political topicality. Many Arena Stage productions go on to win Tony Awards on Broadway, as did *Dear Evan Hansen,* the 2017 Tony winner for best new musical.

The theater is D.C.'s second-largest after The Kennedy Center. Officially called "The Mead Center for American Theater," the venue's three staging areas are the theater-in-the-round **Fichandler,** the fan-shaped **Kreeger,** and the intimate (202-seat), oval-shaped **Kogod Cradle.** Locals love Arena Stage's productions, which draw more than 300,000 annually. Expect a mix of

The Arena Stage.

light-hearted musicals, shows high-lighting African music and dance, and powerful, thought-provoking productions built around historical events like the Civil Rights Movement, Cuban missile crisis, and the Cold War.

1101 6th St. SW (at Maine Ave.). www.arena stage.org. ℭ **202/488-3300** for tickets, or 202/554-9066 for general information. Tickets $40–$110; discounts available for students, those under 30 (who can pay the same amount as their age), patrons with disabilities, families, veterans, groups, and others. Metro: Waterfront.

The John F. Kennedy Center for the Performing Arts ★★★

The capital's most renowned theater covers the entire realm of performing arts: Ballet, opera, plays, musicals, modern dance, jazz, hip hop, comedy, classical and chamber music, and children's theater all take the stage at this magnificent complex overlooking the Potomac River. The setting is gorgeous, the productions superb. As a living memorial to President John F. Kennedy, the Center is committed to fulfilling his mission to make the performing arts available to everyone. The Center's 3,000 or so productions draw more than three million people annually.

Within the performing arts center's original 17-acre facility are eight different theaters and stages: the **Opera House,** the **Concert Hall,** the **Terrace Theater,** the **Eisenhower Theater,** the **Theater Lab,** the **Terrace Gallery,** the **Family Theater,** and the **Millennium Stage.** A 4-acre expansion completed in 2019 added three pavilions housing rehearsal, performance, and education spaces; a reflecting pool; a grove of trees; an outdoor performance area; and a pedestrian bridge over Rock Creek Parkway, connecting the complex to the riverfront.

Each year, the Kennedy Center offers a robust lineup of Broadway productions like "Hamilton" and "Jersey Boys," both back in 2022, as well as a range of ballet, jazz, opera, classical music, and comedy performances by nationally and internationally recognized singers, comics, musicians, and dance companies.

In 2020, The Kennedy Center also opened The Club at Studio K, designed as a more casual entertainment space showcasing artists from all genres, including comedy, contemporary music, hip hop, and jazz. It's an annual series that runs January through April, with performances on most Thursday, Friday, and Saturday evenings.

Consider stopping by The Kennedy Center for a complimentary guided tour during the day. Finish your visit by attending a free Millennium Stage performance—either musical concerts, dance, theater, comedy, and other forms of entertainment—at 6pm in the Grand Foyer, each night featuring a different act by local, up-and-coming, nationally known, or international performers.

Otherwise, expect to pay ticket prices ranging from $20 for a family concert to $300 for opera; most tickets cost between $45 and $150.

2700 F St. NW (at New Hampshire Ave. NW and Rock Creek Pkwy.). www.kennedy-center.org. ☏ **800/444-1324** or 202/467-4600. 50% discounts offered (for select performances) to students, seniors, travelers with permanent disabilities, enlisted military personnel, and persons with fixed low incomes (☏ **202/416-8340** for details). Event parking is $25; save $3 by prepaying online or via the box office (free parking for up to 2 hr. if visiting the box office or gift shop). Metro: Foggy Bottom (there's a free shuttle btw. the station and the Kennedy Center, departing every 15 min. Mon–Thurs 9:45am–11:30pm; Fri–Sat 10am–midnight; and Sun noon–11pm.) Bus: 80 from Metro Center.

National Theatre ★   Open since 1835, this is the capital's oldest continuously operating theater and the country's third oldest. In earlier days, the likes of Sarah Bernhardt, Helen Hayes, and John Barrymore took the stage, and presidents Lincoln and Fillmore were among those in the audience. These days, it's almost entirely about Broadway musicals, with past performances in the 1,676-seat theater including *Tootsie, Come from Away, Rent,* and *Hairspray,* while occasionally other types of shows are featured (Chef Alton Brown recently performed his interactive culinary variety show here). The Theatre also offers free public-service programs virtually, with children's theater (puppets, clowns, magicians, dancers, and singers) available via Facebook every other Saturday.

1321 Pennsylvania Ave. NW (at 13th and E sts.). www.thenationaldc.org. ☏ **202/628-6161** for general info or 202/783-3370 for info about free programs. Tickets $25–$150. Metro: Metro Center or Federal Triangle.

Shakespeare Theatre Company ★★★   This is one of the best Shakespeare theaters in the country, known for its accessible interpretations of plays by the Bard himself, his contemporaries, and modern masters from Oscar Wilde to Thomas Stoppard. Attend a play here and you're in for a thought-provoking, of-the-moment experience, whether it's the tweaking of a classic to address the political climate in D.C., the casting of people of color for the majority of roles, or the display of a little nudity. In its 35 years, the theater has won national and international acclaim, including a Regional Theater Tony Award and recognition by Queen Elizabeth II, who named the theater's former and longtime artistic director, Michael Kahn, an Honorary Commander of the

---

Longer Than the Washington Monument Is Tall

Most Kennedy Center performances take place in theaters that lie off the Grand Foyer. But even if the one you're attending is on the Roof Terrace level one floor up, make sure you visit the foyer anyway. Measuring 630 feet long, 40 feet wide, and 60 feet high, it's one of the largest rooms in the world—even longer than the Washington Monument is tall (555⅝ ft.). Millennium Stage hosts free performances here nightly at 6pm, while free yoga classes fill the space Saturday mornings at 10:15am. The famous Robert Berks sculpture of President John F. Kennedy is here and just beyond the Grand Foyer's glass doors is the expansive terrace, which runs its length and overlooks the Potomac.

Most Excellent Order of the British Empire for distinguished service to the arts and sciences. Washingtonians know to expect the best when they see the names of the theater's resident artists, like Edward Gero and Nancy Robinette. It also brings in renowned guest performers, like Patrick Stewart and Marsha Mason.

The Shakespeare Theatre Company has two downtown locations (literally within a stone's throw of each other), the 451-seat **Michael R. Klein Theatre,** at 450 7th St. NW, and the 774-seat **Sidney Harman Hall,** at 610 F St. NW (across the street from the Capital One Arena); both houses frequently sell out. The 2019/2020 season was the first for the Theatre's new artistic director Simon Godwin and included the lesser-performed Shakespearean tragedy *Timon of Athens,* the world premiere of Lauren Gunderson's *Peter Pan and Wendy,* and a production of James Baldwin's *The Amen Corner.* The Shakespeare Theatre also screens live performances of certain London National Theatre productions (where Godwin is associate director). Fan favorite *Much Ado About Nothing* opens in spring 2022. The theater hosts all kinds of talks, dance performances, discussions, cocktail hours, workshops, and other events, many of which target 20- to 30-somethings. The best deal for under-35s is the sale of $35 tickets, available online with a promo code.

Michael R. Klein Theatre: 450 7th St. NW (btw. D and E sts.). Sidney Harman Hall: 610 F St. NW. www.shakespearetheatre.org. © **202/547-1122.** Tickets $35–$125; discounts available for military, patrons 21–35, seniors, and groups; check the website for all options. Metro: Archives–Navy Memorial or Gallery Place–Chinatown.

Smaller Theaters

Since its founding in 1978, **Studio Theatre ★★**, 1501 14th St. NW, at P Street (www.studiotheatre.org; © **202/332-3300**), has grown in leaps and bounds into a four-theater complex, helping to revitalize its U Street neighborhood in the process. Productions are provocative and each season jam-packed, usually with four or five plays on the calendar. The Studio Theatre has had particular success in showcasing contemporary plays and nurturing local acting talent.

Ford's Theatre ★★, 511 10th St. NW, between E and F sts. NW (www.fords.org; © **202/347-4833**), is both a living museum—the site of President Abraham Lincoln's assassination in 1865—and a working theater staging multiple performances each year.

Woolly Mammoth Theatre Company ★★ (www.woollymammoth.net; © **202/393-3939**) runs up to 10 productions every year, specializing in new, offbeat, quirky plays, often world premieres. It resides in a 265-seat, state-of-the-art facility at 641 D St. NW (at 7th St. NW), in the heart of Penn Quarter.

The **Folger Theatre,** part of the **Folger Shakespeare Library ★★**, 201 E. Capitol St. SE, at 2nd Street (www.folger.edu; © **202/544-4600**), typically produces three to four plays each season, using the same fine directors (Aaron Posner is a favorite) and casting the same excellent actors (Holly Twyford is always a treat), that you'll see at the Shakespeare Theatre and other stages around town. While the Folger undergoes its multi-year building renovation, performances and programs will be staged virtually or in different spaces throughout Washington, D.C. Check the website for more information.

GETTING tickets

Most performing arts and live music venues mentioned in this chapter require tickets, which you can purchase online via the venue's website, in person at the box office, or through one of the ticket vendors listed below.

The best deals in town might be on **Goldstar** (www.goldstar.com). Sign up for a free account to get hefty discounts on admission prices to performances and venues all over the city, including museums, sent straight to your inbox.

TodayTix (www.todaytix.com) sells discounted and full-price last-minute tickets for shows in and around D.C. Purchase tickets through the website; certain features, like the use of ticket lotteries, are only available through the free app. Despite its name, the service works for tickets purchased up to a month in advance.

Live Nation Entertainment (www.livenation.com; ✆ 800/653-8000) and **Eventbrite** (www.eventbrite.com) operate in the D.C. area, selling full-price tickets for all sorts of performances. Expect to pay taxes plus a service charge, an order-processing fee, and a facility fee (if a particular venue tacks on that charge).

Three more specialized theater companies are also worth noting: **GALA Hispanic Theatre,** located at 3333 14th St. NW in Columbia Heights (www.galatheatre.org; ✆ **202/234-7174**), which presents classic and contemporary plays in Spanish and English, as well as dance, music, and other programs; **Theater J** (www.theaterj.org; ✆ **202/777-3210**), praised by the *Washington Post* as "the most influential Jewish theater company in the nation," stages provocative performances on the Jewish experience in its renovated theater at 1529 16th St. NW; and the tiny (130-seat!) **Keegan Theatre,** at 1742 Church St. NW in Dupont Circle (www.keegantheatre.com; ✆ **202/265-3767**), which often stages plays that embrace Irish writers and themes.

Concert Venues

The Anthem ★★★, 901 Wharf St. SW (www.theanthemdc.com; ✆ **202/888-0020**; Metro: Waterfront; L'Enfant Plaza, with free District Wharf Circulator shuttle), which opened in October 2017, is the much-heralded sibling of the 9:30 Club (p. 233), located at The Wharf. Expect to see rock acts, international artists, and local favorites at this "acoustically advanced" concert hall with the capacity to hold 2,500–6,000 people.

Meanwhile, headliners like John Mayer, The Killers, and Celine Dion can be seen performing at the 20,356-seat **Capital One Arena ★★★**, 601 F St. NW, at 7th Street (www.capitalonearena.com; ✆ **202/628-3200**). Situated in the center of downtown, the Capital One Arena is a hotspot for music but also Washington, D.C.'s premier indoor sports arena (p. 236).

DAR Constitution Hall ★★ 18th St. NW, between C and D sts. (www.dar.org/constitution-hall; ✆ **800/449-1776**), is housed in a beautiful turn-of-the-20th-century Beaux Arts building and seats 3,702. Its excellent acoustics have drawn an eclectic group of performers over the years, including Duke Ellington and Billy Joel. It's also a bright spot for comedy shows—Bob Hope, George Carlin, and Jim Gaffigan have all performed stand-up here.

Saxophonist Avery Dixon performs on the Millennium Stage at the John F. Kennedy Center for the Performing Arts.

Under management by the 9:30 Club (p. 233), the historic **Lincoln Theatre ★**, 1215 U St. NW, at 13th Street (www.thelincolndc.com; ℂ **202/888-0050**), showcases indie rock favorites such as Dashboard Confessional, country musicians like The Mavericks, and assorted others. Once a movie theater, vaudeville house, and nightclub featuring Black jazz mega-stars like Louis Armstrong and Cab Calloway, this "Jewel on U" closed down in the 1970s, then reopened in 1994 after a renovation restored it to its former glory.

The **Warner Theatre ★**, 513 13th St. NW, between E and F streets (www.warnertheatredc.com; ℂ **202/783-4000**), opened in 1924 as a silent movie and vaudeville palace known as the Earle Theatre and was restored to its original, neoclassical-style appearance in 1992. It's worth coming by just to ogle the ornately detailed interior. The 1,847-seat auditorium offers year-round entertainment, alternating dance performances like the Washington Ballet's Christmas performance of the *Nutcracker* with musical satirical comedy acts like Randy Rainbow and seasoned rockers like Cheap Trick and The Monkees.

And Now for Something Completely Different

Become part of the show at **ARTE-CHOUSE** (www.dc.artechouse.com), a three-level, 15,000-square-foot funhouse featuring innovative installations 7 days a week, showcasing the unique collaboration between art, science, and technology. In one 2021 exhibit, for example, D.C.'s cherry blossoms became an immersive experience, where artist Yuko Shimizu's hand-made ink illustrations were transformed digitally to follow vibrant cherry blossom flowers on an interactive journey through land, sea, and air. You really have to go and see it for yourself. Exhibits change often, so check the website for current programming. Located just southwest of the National Mall, at 1238 Maryland Ave. SW (12th St.), it's open daily 10am to 10pm. Tickets are required. General admission is $24 adults; $20 seniors, students, and military; $17 children 4–15; free for children under 4; DC, VA, and MD residents save $5 with proper ID).

THE BAR SCENE

Some of the best and most popular bars in town are in hotels, including **Off the Record** at The Hay-Adams (p. 70), **Crimson View** at Motto by Hilton Washington, D.C. City Center (p. 69), **Top of the Gate** at The Watergate Hotel (p. 79), **Summit** at The Conrad (p. 67), and the **rooftop bars** at any hotels near The Wharf (p. 65). Here's a smattering of other favorites.

Barrel ★ The upstairs is a rustic dining room, often packed with Capitol Hillers noshing on Southern fare (five-star vote for the fried chicken) and sipping craft cocktails and whiskeys. Downstairs, Rum-DMV is a—you guessed it—rum bar grooving to club sounds. 613 Pennsylvania Ave. SE (at 6th St.). www.barreldc.com. ℂ 202/543-3623. Metro: Eastern Market.

Bluejacket Brewery ★★ A Washington Nationals baseball game at Nationals Park is one reason to visit the Capitol Riverfront neighborhood. Bluejacket Brewery is another. Opened by Greg Engert and his band of master brewers, Bluejacket creates 20 unique ales and lagers daily at its three-story site, from dry-hopped ales to barley wine. You can hang out at the bar in Bluejacket's restaurant, the **Arsenal,** and sample a few homebrews, dine here, or take a tour. Bluejacket offers two options, both of which require a reservation: a $29-per-person taste-as-you-go tour on Saturday at 1pm and a $35-per-person 7pm Friday night "Beers and Bites" tour. No tours on Nationals home-game days. 300 Tingey St. SE (at 4th St. SE). www.bluejacketdc.com. ℂ 202/524-4862. Metro: Navy Yard–Ballpark.

Columbia Room ★★ Shaw's Blagden Alley is home to several dining hotspots (see "Shaw-Thing" box, p. 110) and this nationally recognized cocktail bar. Its magical concoctions and energy derive from owner Derek Brown, esteemed mixologist, spirits historian, and perennial James Beard Award nominee. Columbia Room offers three spaces, a rooftop patio punch garden, spirits library, and a new four-course tasting menu of cocktails and snacks. 124 Blagden Alley NW (behind Ninth St., btw. M and N sts.). www.columbiaroomdc.com. ℂ 202/316-9396. Metro: Mt. Vernon Square/7th St./Convention Center.

Bluejacket Brewery.

CHEAP EATS: happy hours TO WRITE HOME ABOUT

Certain restaurants around town set out tasty bites during happy hour, either free or for astonishingly low prices. The following are particularly generous:

Cheery **El Centro,** 1218 Wisconsin Ave. NW (www.eatelcentro.com; ✆ **202/333-4100**), has happy hour specials featuring $6 margaritas, $5 beer and glasses of wine, as well as $3.50 tacos and $6 quesadillas (Mon–Fri 4–7pm).

Tiki-bar **Archipelago,** 1201 U St. NW, at 12th St. (www.archipelagobardc.com; ✆ **202/627-0794**), serves up island-inspired bar bites such as Dan Dan noodles, sliders, egg rolls, and hot chicken steam buns ($3–$6 each). Drinks are a real deal:

$4 beer, $6 wine, or cocktails like pina coladas and ti punch for $8 (Mon–Sun 5–7pm).

In Shaw, **Chaplin's,** 1501 9th St. NW at P St. NW (www.chaplinsdc.com; ✆ **202/644-8806**), is known for its legendary ramen and happy hour specials, with half off glasses of wine, draft beer and draft spirit cocktails Mon–Fri 4–6pm, and Bloody Mary specials and $8 frozen monkey cocktails Sat & Sun noon–4pm. Just around the corner, its sister restaurant and sushi hotspot **Zeppelin,** 1544 9th St. NW at Q St. NW (www.zeppelindc.com; ✆ **202/506-1068**), also hosts a killer happy hour Mon–Sun 4–6pm, with half-price bubbles and draft beer.

The Green Zone ★★   The only Middle Eastern bar in D.C., The Green Zone serves up craft cocktails with a Lebanese-style twist, like the Saz'iraq and a deliciously boozy spin on Arabic mint lemonade (made with vodka or gin) with a cheeky sense of humor—it is home to the unapologetically politically named cocktail, F*ck Trump Punch after all. It's long been a favorite of locals and visitors alike, opening its current Adams Morgan space in 2018 after a 4-year stint as a pop-up bar. 2226 18th St. NW (at Kalorama Rd. NW). www.thegreenzonedc.com. ✆ **571/201-5145.** Metro: Dupont Circle (then a 15-min. walk); alternatively, U St./Cardozo or Woodley Park/Zoo/Adams Morgan, then ride the DC Circulator bus to Adams Morgan.

H Street Country Club ★   The main draw of this H Street Corridor hotspot is its assortment of activities: Skee-ball, basketball, giant Jenga, and indoor mini-golf, just to name a few. Up top is a huge rooftop deck. Shi-Queeta-Lee's Drag Bingo (Thurs 7–9pm) and Illusion Drag Brunch show (Sat noon–2pm; $55 including brunch buffet and a mimosa) are not to be missed. 1335 H St. NE (at Linden Ct NE.). www.hstreetcountryclub.com. ✆ **202/399-4722.** Metro: Union Station, then take a cab or the DC Streetcar (H/Benning Line), or walk 25 min. along H St.

Hill Country Barbecue ★★   Head to this popular Penn Quarter restaurant for awesome barbecue, strong drinks, and, downstairs, live country, rock, and blues music several nights a week. On Wednesday at 8:30pm, the HariKaraoke Band provides live backup as singers take the microphone and "rock 'n twang" their hearts out. 410 7th St. NW (at D St.). www.hillcountry.com/hill-country-live-1. ✆ **202/556-2050.** Metro: Gallery Place/Chinatown or Archives–Navy Memorial–Penn Quarter.

Jack Rose Dining Saloon ★★   Considered to be one of the best whisky bars in the country (its inventory numbers 2,700), this saloon has much going for it, including an expansive open-air (but enclosable) rooftop terrace; a subterranean, speakeasy-like cellar; and nods of approval for its comfort cooking. 2007 18th St. NW (btw. U and California sts.). www.jackrosediningsaloon.com. © **202/ 588-7388.** Metro: Dupont Circle, then a 12-min. walk.

Lucky Bar ★   Looking for a good old-fashioned bar with booths, couches, a pool table, a jukebox, cheap beer, and sticky floors? Lucky Bar is the place. It's also Soccer Central, with TV screens broadcasting soccer matches from around the globe. Lucky Bar's happy hour runs from 3–8pm Monday through Wednesday and on Friday. Look for nightly specials, like $1 tacos on Tuesday and football specials on Thursday. 1221 Connecticut Ave. NW (at N St.). www.lucky bardc.com. © **202/331-3733.** Metro: Dupont Circle or Farragut North.

Mercy Me ★★   Located inside Yours Truly D.C. (p. 80) this "Sorta South American" themed bar features a cocktail menu brought to you by Micah Wilder, the beverage guru behind Chaplin's (p. 229) and Zeppelin (p. 229), with tropical creations like the Cool Chameleon (made with cynar, pomelo, panela, mint, and club soda) and the aptly named Kick Ass Colada. For a real treat, order the South Paw Manhattan, which comes in a smoky glass and is made of a palate-pleasing blend of caramel smoke, raisin, nutty spice, mezcal reposado, vermouth, sherry, cherry cynar, and orange oil. 1143 New Hampshire Ave. NW (at M St. NW). www.mercymedc.com. © **202/828-7762.** Metro: Dupont Circle.

Never Looked Better ★★   A new arrival to Shaw's trendy Blagden Alley, this speakeasy style cocktail bar hearkens back not to the 1920s but to another time during the late-1900s when underground raves could be found in hidden places, forcing patrons to enter through alleyways, loading docks, or restaurant kitchens to brightly lit rooms of neon and blacklights. Look for the door covered in stickers and the tell-tale red glow, enter through the kitchen, and sip everything from Appletinis and Moscow Mules to Cosmopolitans, Palomas, and Penicillins, the scotch-based cure for everything. 130 Blagden Alley, NW (behind 9th St. NW). www.neverlookedbetterdc.com. Metro: Mt. Vernon Sq./7th St.–Convention Center.

Quill ★★★   Sip seasonal cocktails and nosh on plates of artisanal cheese and charcuterie Monday, Thursday, Friday, and weekends at this chicest of lounges inside the city's chicest hotel, The Jefferson. 1200 16th St. NW (at M St.). www. jeffersondc.com/dining/quill. © **202/448-2300.** Metro: Dupont Circle or Farragut North.

Swingers, The Crazy Golf Club ★★   Adulting is hard, but "crazy golf," a combination of mini-golf, craft cocktails, and gourmet street-food in an adults-only English country club setting makes it easier. Originally from London, Swingers' first U.S. outpost features lite bites (Southern fare, Neapolitan-style pizza, Mexican munchies, and other sweet treats) by neighboring restaurants and tunes spun by local DJs as you take on windmills, loop-de-loops, and other impressive obstacles at one of the 20,000-square-foot space's two indoor 9-hole courses. Not into mini-golf? Come for the food, drinks, and good vibes. A second D.C. location in Navy Yard (Capitol Riverfront) will be open in 2022. 1330 19th St. NW (at New Hampshire Ave.). www.swingers.club/us. © **202/968-1080.** Metro: Dupont Circle.

Tryst ★   Tryst is a coffeehouse bar, with plenty of coffee to charge you up in the a.m. and drinks to get you going later in the day. It's got a good loungey vibe, too. Morning, noon, and night, customers sprawl on comfy old furniture, juggling laptops and beverages. 2459 18th St. NW (at Columbia Rd.). www.trystdc. com. ℂ **202/232-5500.** Metro: U St./Cardozo or Woodley Park/Zoo/Adams Morgan, then take the DC Circulator bus to Adams Morgan.

Tune Inn Restaurant & Bar ★   In business since 1947, this Capitol Hill watering hole is a veritable institution. The divey Tune Inn is open from early morning until late at night serving police officers, Hill staffers and their bosses, and folks from the neighborhood. Sometimes they eat here, too, from a menu that includes burgers, wings, and all-day breakfast. 331 Pennsylvania Ave. SE (at 4th St.). www.tuneinndc.com. ℂ **202/543-2725.** Metro: Capitol South or Eastern Market.

THE CLUB & MUSIC SCENE
Live Music

If you're looking for a tuneful night on the town, D.C. has everything from hip jazz clubs to DJ-driven dance halls. There's something for everyone here, whether you're in the mood to sit back and listen or get up and rock out.

Prost! To D.C.'s Burgeoning Beer Garden Scene

D.C.'s fabulous Bavarian beer gardens became increasingly in 2020 and 2021 due to their natural proclivity for outdoor seating. You'll find one in nearly every neighborhood, though some offer brunch and more authentic German food (think giant pretzels, bratwurst, and chicken schnitzel) than others—the main focus here is on the beer, after all, and who you're drinking it with. **Dacha Beer Garden** (www.dachadc.com) has two locations: the original in Shaw at 1600 7th St. NW (ℂ **202/350-9888**), and another at 79 Potomac Ave. SE in Navy Yard (ℂ **202/919-3801**). Either make a great spot to catch a soccer game or other sporting event, while **Wunder Garten**, 1101 First St. NE (www.wundergartendc.com), offers burgers and empanadas through its food partners Swizzler and La Buena, and hosts other events like trivia nights, garden parties, and an epic drag bingo event on Sundays. Newcomer **Prost**, 919 5th St. NW (www.prostdc.com;

ℂ **202/290-2233**), opened in October 2020 (save room for dessert and try the *apfelstreudel!*). **Sauf Haus Bier Hall & Garden**, 1216 18th St. NW (www.sauf hausdc.com; ℂ **202/466-3355**), has been serving up German fare with a side of live music since 2014. **Garden District**, 1801 14th St. NW (www.garden districtdc.com; ℂ **202/695-2626**), offers Southern BBQ and the like in a German beer garden setting. Just north of Howard University in Parkview, **The Midlands Beer Garden**, 3333 Georgia Ave. NW (www.midlandsdc.com), offers 6,000 square-feet of indoor and outdoor space to spread out in as you nosh on casual bites and sip locally crafted and European beers. Closer to Capitol Hill, **The Brig** is a popular choice near the Capitol Riverfront at 1007 8th St. SE (www.thebrigdc.com; ℂ **202/675-1000**), while **Biergarten Haus** at 1355 H St NE (www.biergartenhaus.com; ℂ **202/388-4053**) has been operating at the end of the H Street Corridor since 2010.

JAZZ & BLUES

If you're a jazz fan, you won't want to miss the fabulous **DC Jazz Festival** (www.dcjazzfest.org), which showcases the talents of at least 100 musicians in various venues around town, including many free events, each June. Check the website for this year's exact dates; 2021's took place in September. Other times of the year, check out the following venues:

Blues Alley ★★★   An inconspicuous alley off busy Wisconsin Avenue in Georgetown delivers you to the door of Blues Alley and another world entirely. It's a showcase for jazz greats like Arturo Sandoval and Benny Golson and up-and-comers alike. The club usually offers two sets a night, at 8 and 10pm. Blues Alley is a tiny joint filled with small, candlelit tables, so tickets are a must for the first-come, first-served seating. The supper club has been around since 1965 and looks it, but that's part of its charm. Its Creole menu features dishes named after stars (try Dizzy Gillespie's Jambalaya). 1073 Wisconsin Ave. NW (in an alley below M St.). www.bluesalley.com. ✆ **202/337-4141.** Tickets $10–$35, plus a $6 surcharge. Metro: Foggy Bottom, then walk or take the DC Circulator.

The Hamilton Live ★★   Located in the heart of Penn Quarter on the subterranean level of a large restaurant, this 300-seat live-music venue stages blues, rock, jazz, R&B, and folk performances several times a week (check the website for the latest lineups). The menu of pizza sandwiches, salads, sushi, and other lite bites isn't stellar but will suffice if you haven't eaten before the show. The **Loft at The Hamilton** is the venue's cozy late-night bar on the restaurant's second floor; its late-night menu features $5 off sushi rolls Sunday through Thursday 10pm–midnight and Friday and Saturday 11pm–1am. 600 14th St. (at F St.). www.thehamiltondc.com. ✆ **202/787-1000.** Live music acts $10–$45. Metro: Metro Center.

Madam's Organ Blues Bar ★★   Although the crowd tends to be young at this Adams Morgan institution, anyone in search of a fun night out with live music, free pool, and a shot at karaoke glory (Sun, Tues, and Thurs, with a two-drink minimum) is bound to have a good time. Red heads enjoy half price drink specials all week long, while the rest of us get the same deal during happy hour Friday–Wednesday from 5–8pm (appetizers are half-price, too). Wander through four levels of music and bar scenes, enjoy rotating musical performances (everything from blues and Latin blues funk to country) and open mic nights, then venture up to the rooftop bar for some air. 2461 18th St. NW (at Columbia Road NW). www.madamsorgan.com. ✆ **202/667-5370.** Metro: U St./Cardozo or Woodley Park/Zoo/Adams Morgan, then take the DC Circulator bus to Adams Morgan.

Pearl Street Warehouse ★★   You're never more than 25 feet from the stage at this intimate Wharf venue, which only holds 150 to 300 people and showcases rock, country, roots, bluegrass, and blues artists. Some shows are seated, others are standing only, while some are a combo, so be sure to check online before arriving. All-American diner fare, craft brews, and cocktails are all available. 33 Pearl St. SW (at Maine Ave.). www.pearlstreetwarehouse.com. ✆ **202/380-9620.** Tickets $12–$40 plus $2.99 service fee. Metro: Waterfront; L'Enfant Plaza, then ride the District Wharf Circulator shuttle.

ROCK, HIP-HOP & DJS

While the following are primarily live-music clubs, there's also a sprinkling of nightclubs known for their DJs and dance floors.

Black Cat ★★★ This club is D.C.'s flagship venue for alternative music. When it opened on 14th Street in 1993, the neighborhood was a red-light district and D.C. was not a major player in the live-music scene. Today, local, national, and international groups play here, including everyone from Arcade Fire and the Foo Fighters to Childish Gambino and The Roots. 1811 14th St. NW (btw. S and T sts.). www.blackcatdc.com. ℂ **202/667-4490.** Purchase tickets ($15–$35) online or arrive with cash; the club does not accept credit cards. Metro: U St./Cardozo.

Eighteenth Street Lounge ★★ Ever the hotspot, ESL is the place to go for dressing sexy and dancing to live music and DJ-spun tunes, a range of acid jazz, hip-hop, reggae, Latin jazz, soul, and party sounds. After a 25-year stint near Dupont Circle, the nightclub moved to its new location in Shaw's hip Blagden Alley and reopened in winter 2021. 1230 9th St. NW (at Blagden Alley NW.). www.eighteenthstreetlounge.com. ℂ **202/466-3922.** Covers and hours vary; check website for the latest updates. Metro: Mt. Vernon Sq./7th St.–Convention Center.

The Howard Theatre ★ Located in the trendy Shaw neighborhood, this historic venue features a large dance floor, concert stage, and a full bar for hanging out. When it opened in 1910, it was lauded as "the largest colored theatre in the world." Restored and reopened in 2012, it's since been a hub for performances ranging from local bands to renowned solo musicians. Private VIP booths are available for some shows. 620 T St. NW (at Wiltberger St. NW). www.thehowardtheatre.com. ℂ **202/803-2899.** Ticket prices and seating options vary by show. Metro: Shaw/Howard U, then a 2-min. walk.

9:30 Club ★★★ The 9:30 Club is now a mini-dynasty, with The Lincoln Theatre (p. 227) and The Anthem (p. 226) part of the family. But this 1,200-person-capacity concert hall still rules, with excellent sightlines, a state-of-the-art sound system, four bars, and most important, an impressive concert schedule

A performance at the Black Cat.

featuring every possible star, rising or arrived, in today's varied rock world, from Finneas and Dr. Dog to GWAR and They Might Be Giants. It's frequently voted the best live-music venue, certainly in D.C., but also nationwide. Unless advertised as seated, all shows are standing room only, general admission. 815 V St. NW (at 9th St.). www.930.com. © **202/265-0930.** Tickets $20–$40. Metro: U St./Cardozo.

Comedy Clubs

Sometimes, you really just need a good laugh. In addition to **The Kennedy Center**'s growing presence on the comedy circuit, **Warner Theatre** (p. 227) sometimes features big-name comedians or troupes. Otherwise, just head to one of the venues below.

The D.C. Improv ★   Expect to see headliners on the national comedy club circuit as well as comic plays and one-person shows. Most shows are about 90–120 minutes long and generally include three comics (an emcee, a feature act, and a headliner). Showtimes vary but generally happen Wednesday through Sunday at 7, 7:30, or 8pm, with a second show at 9:30pm or later on Friday and Saturday. Acts also take place in an intimate 60-person lounge. You must be 18 and over to enter. 1140 Connecticut Ave. NW (btw. L and M sts.). www.dcimprov.com. © **202/296-7008.** Tickets $18–$55, plus a 2-item minimum per person. Metro: Farragut North.

Underground Comedy ★★   Though the main venue, **Big Hunt,** is situated in Dupont Circle (1345 Connecticut Ave. NW), Underground Comedy actually hosts a number of professional stand-up shows (in **Room 808,** located at 808 Upshur St. NW) as well as those featuring up-and-coming comics all over the capital—you'll find them at **Eaton DC** (1201 K St. NW near Penn Quarter), **Reliable Tavern** (3655 Georgia Ave. NW in Petworth), and

THE best OF D.C.'S INTERNATIONAL SCENE

Washington, D.C. is home to more than 175 embassies and international culture centers, which greatly contribute to the city's cosmopolitan flavor. Few embassies are open to the public on a walk-in basis (see p. 25 for info about embassy open houses) but many offer programs highlighting the culture of their countries. Start by checking **www.embassy.org** for a list of all the embassies, with links to their individual websites. You'll find that many, like the French Embassy's **La Maison Française** (www.franceintheus.org) and the Swedish Embassy's **House of Sweden** (www.houseofsweden.com/en/house-of-sweden/exhibitions), host events that are open to the public,

sometimes for free, sometimes at minimal cost.

You can also buy tickets for **Embassy Series** (www.embassyseries.org; © **202/625-2361**) events. These mostly classical music performances are hosted by individual embassies or the ambassador's residence. It's an intimate experience and tickets can be expensive, though they do include a hot buffet meal, cocktails, wine, and parking. In April 2020, for instance, the Embassy of Poland staged a performance by soprano Alexandra Nowakowski and pianist William Woodard at the Ambassador's Residence, along with a reception of wine and other Polish tastes, for $160 per ticket.

Wonderland Ballroom (1101 Kenyon St. NW in Columbia Heights). Ticket prices and showtimes vary by comic and location but range from free to $20 and typically happen at 8 and 10:30pm. 1345 Connecticut Ave. NW. www.undergroundcomedydc.com. © **412/436-9630.** Metro: Dupont Circle.

THE LGBTQ SCENE

With nearly 10% of the District's population identifying as LGBTQ, D.C. has one of the largest LGBTQ communities in the country. Here are three of the most popular bars favored by those 10 percenters.

A League of Her Own ★ Open Wednesday through Sunday, this self-described queer women's neighborhood bar, which also goes by "ALOHO," is open to all—except those who promote intolerance. Opened in 2018 in D.C.'s trendy Adams Morgan neighborhood, the bar hosts events like trivia, open mic, and karaoke nights, as well as new-to-DC mixers and workshops focusing on important social topics, like anti-racism and intersectionality in the workplace. 2317 18th St. NW (in Adams Morgan). www.alohodc.com/. © **202/733-2568.** Metro: Dupont Circle, then a 15-min. walk; or U St./Cardozo or Woodley Park/Zoo/Adams Morgan, then take the DC Circulator bus to Adams Morgan.

The Green Lantern ★ This premier LGBTQ bar is "attitude free" and has been around more than 10 years. Tell the bartender you're visiting, and you'll be instantly welcomed into "D.C.'s Queer Cheers." Stop by for its daily 4pm happy hour—every Thursday between 10–11pm, shirtless men drink free. The club also hosts karaoke and other popular events. 1335 Green Court NW (off 14th St. NW). www.greenlanterndc.com. © **202/347-4533.** Metro: McPherson Sq.

J.R.'s Bar ★ Opened in 1986, this friendly neighborhood bar is always packed, mostly due to its nightly specials and sing-along showtunes nights on Mondays and Saturdays. The Dupont Circle club draws an attractive crowd, here to play pool, sing along, or simply hang out. 1519 17th St. NW (btw. P and Q sts.). www.facebook.com/JRsBarDC. © **202/328-0090.** Metro: Dupont Circle.

SPECTATOR SPORTS

Washington, D.C., has professional football, basketball, baseball, ice hockey, and soccer teams, and of those five, it's a tough call on whose fans are most passionate: the **Washington Capitals** (2018 Stanley Cup champions) or the **Washington Nationals** (2019 World Series champs). During the respective season you'll see red-jersey'd devotees swarming downtown before and after matches at the Capital One Arena in Penn Quarter and around Nationals Park in Capitol Riverfront. Tickets are attainable but not always cheap.

Annual Sporting Events

Citi Open In pre-pandemic times, this U.S. Open series event attracted more than 78,000 people to watch big-time tennis pros compete. A portion of the profits benefits the Washington Tennis and Education Foundation. The 9-day tournament takes place in mid- to late-July at the **Rock Creek Park Tennis Center** at 4850 Colorado Ave. NW. www.citiopentennis.com. ✆ **202/721-9500.**

Marine Corps Marathon   Thirty thousand runners compete in this 26.2-mile race (the third-largest marathon in the United States), which winds past major memorials. The race takes place on a Sunday in late October; 2021 marks its 46th year. www.marinemarathon.com. ✆ **703/784-2225.**

General Spectator Sports

Baseball   Washington, D.C.'s Major League Baseball team and 2019 World Series champions, the **Nationals,** play at the finely designed **Nationals Park** (1500 S. Capitol St. SE; www.mlb.com/nationals; ✆ **202/675-6287**), located in southeast Washington's Capitol Riverfront). The 41,313-seat stadium is now the centerpiece of this newly vibrant waterfront locale, whose plentiful restaurants, bars, and fun activities will keep you busy if you want to arrive early for the game or amuse yourself afterward. Metro: Navy Yard–Ballpark.

Basketball   The 20,356-seat **Capital One Arena,** located in the center of downtown at 601 F St. NW (www.capitalonearena.com; ✆ **202/628-3200**), is Washington, D.C.'s premier indoor-sports arena, where the **Wizards** (NBA), **Mystics** (WNBA), and **Georgetown University Hoyas** basketball teams play. Metro: Gallery Place/Chinatown.

Football   Following several years of controversy over its previous name, The Washington Redskins, the newly branded Washington Football Team plays at the 82,000-seat **FedExField** stadium, outside D.C., in Landover, Maryland. Obtaining tickets is difficult thanks to season-ticket holders, but if you want to try, visit www.washingtonfootball.com/stadium or www.stubhub.com.

Ice Hockey   D.C. ice hockey fans rejoiced in 2018 when their beloved **Washington Capitals** brought home the Stanley Cup, winning its first NHL championship in franchise history. The team rink is inside **Capital One Arena,** 601 F St. NW (www.capitalonearena.com; ✆ **202/628-3200**). Metro: Gallery Place/Chinatown.

Soccer   The D.C. men's Major League Soccer Club team, **D.C. United** (www.dcunited.com), which has been around since 1994, finally has its own arena, the 20,000-seat capacity **Audi Field,** located at 100 Potomac Ave. SW (www.audifieldddc.com; ✆ **202/587-5000**) in the Southwest Waterfront near the Navy Yard neighborhood. The city's National Women's Soccer League team, **Washington Spirit** (www.washingtonspirit.com), also plays matches here. Metro: Navy Yard–Ballpark.

Tennis   The World Team Tennis franchise team, the **Washington Kastles** (www.washingtonkastles.com), plays at **Kastles Stadium at Union Market,** located at 1309 5th St. SE (the rooftop venue is above the market downstairs). WTT is a coed professional tennis league; the Grand Slam honor roll includes Venus Williams, Naomi Osaka, Nicole Melichar, and Martina Hingis (✆ **202/483-6647**). Metro: NOMA-Gallaudet U.

DAY TRIPS FROM D.C.

by Kaeli Conforti

You've come as far as Washington, D.C.—why not travel just a bit farther to visit Mount Vernon, the home of the man for whom the capital is named? The estate was George Washington's home for 45 years, from 1754 until his death in 1799 (as much as the American Revolution and his stints as the new republic's first president would allow). And where did Washington go to sell his produce, kick up his heels, or worship? In nearby Old Town Alexandria. Its cobblestone streets and historic churches and houses still stand, surrounded now by of-the-moment eateries and chic boutiques. Make time, if you can, for visits to both Mount Vernon and Old Town Alexandria.

MOUNT VERNON

Only 16 miles south of the capital, George Washington's former plantation dates from a 1674 land grant to the president's great-grandfather.

Essentials

GETTING THERE   If you're going by car, take any of the bridges over the Potomac River into Virginia and follow the signs pointing the way to National Airport/Mount Vernon/George Washington Memorial Parkway. Travel south on the George Washington Memorial Parkway, the river always to your left, and pass by National Airport (DCA), also on your left. Continue through Old Town Alexandria, where the parkway is renamed "Washington Street," and go another 8 miles until you reach the large circle that fronts Mount Vernon.

You might also want to take a narrated bus or boat tour from Washington, D.C., with admission to Mount Vernon as part of the ticket price. **City Tours by Loba** (www.lobatours.com; © **202/536-4664**) offers daily 5-hour tours year-round ($79 adults, $69 children) that include time in Old Town Alexandria on the way to Mount Vernon. Buses depart and return to 400 New Jersey Ave. NW near Union Station. Please plan to arrive 20 minutes prior to departure.

Note that it's important to be flexible with your travel plans, as 2020-2021 showed us that things could change at any time. Tour availability, schedules, and hours of operations at museums, restaurants, and other attractions may be affected by Virginia's Covid-19 travel restrictions and guidelines, so be prepared to wear a mask, practice social distancing, or show proof of vaccination as required. Check with your desired attraction or restaurant in advance to avoid disappointment.

The narrated Mount Vernon Sightseeing Cruise offered by **City Cruises** (www.cityexperiences.com/washington-dc; ⓒ **800/459-8105**) is a seasonal operation, cruising 75-minutes one-way to Mount Vernon on Friday, Saturday, and Sunday from March to September. The vessel leaves from the Transit Pier at The Wharf (9th St. and Wharf St. SW; about a 13-min. walk from the Green Line Metro's Waterfront station) at 9:30am, returning by 3:15pm. Tickets include admission to Mount Vernon and cost $50 adults, $45 seniors over 62, $29 children 2–11 (free for children 2 and under).

Work some exercise into your trip with **Bike and Boat** (www.bikeandrolldc.com), a self-guided tour that includes a bike rental from Bike and Roll's Old Town Alexandria location at the waterfront, admission to Mount Vernon, and a narrated return trip back to Old Town aboard The Potomac Riverboat Company's vessel, *Miss Christin*. Pedal your own merry way for 50 minutes along the Mount Vernon Trail (see box, "Biking to Old Town Alexandria & Mount Vernon," p. 248) to reach the estate, lock up your bike at Mount Vernon (where Bike and Roll staff pick it up), tour the site, then board the *Miss Christin* at 2pm to return to Old Town. Note that you must pick up your bike in Old Town no later than 11:30am; between 9–9:30am is recommended. Prices from $79 ages 13 and older, $45 ages 2–12.

If you're up for it, you can rent a bike and pedal the 18-mile round-trip distance at your own pace any time of year.

Finally, it's possible to take **public transportation** to Mount Vernon by riding DC Metro's Yellow Line to the Huntington station and catching the Fairfax Connector, bus no. 101, to Mount Vernon from the lower level. *Note:* DC Metro is always undergoing track work year-round; for details, see p. 294.

Touring the Estate

Mount Vernon Estate and Gardens ★★★

You could easily spend a full day learning about the life and times of our first president, George Washington, and his time at Mount Vernon. The 500-acre estate includes the centerpiece mansion, George and Martha Washington's home, and so much more: gardens, outbuildings, a wharf, slave quarters and burial grounds, a greenhouse, a working farm, an orientation center, education center, museum and, about 3 miles down the road, a working distillery and gristmill.

The plantation was passed down from Washington's great-grandfather, who acquired the land in 1674, to George's half-brother, and later, to George

Mount Vernon was the home of George Washington, the first president of the United States, and his wife, Martha.

himself in 1754. Washington proceeded over the next 45 years to expand and fashion it to his liking, though the American Revolution and his years as president often kept him away from his beloved estate.

What you see today is a remarkable restoration of the mansion, which dates to the 1740s. Interiors appear as they would have in 1799, with walls painted in the colors chosen by George and Martha, as well as original furnishings and objects used by the Washington family on display. Historical interpreters stationed through the house answer questions as you pass through.

Start by visiting the **Ford Orientation Center,** located inside the main entrance building, before exploring the rest of the estate. Several 25-minute films playing on a loop offer insight into Washington's character and career. If you have time after your tour, we highly recommend visiting the **Donald W. Reynolds Museum and Education Center,** which lies on the path leading to shops and the food court, making this a logical last stop at Mount Vernon. The museum's 23 galleries, theater presentations, and display of 700 original artifacts help round out the story of this heroic, larger-than-life man.

Note that those with limited time will have to choose between visiting these centers or the historic sites scattered throughout the estate. If you're at Mount Vernon April through October, when the shuttle operates and the weather is most pleasant, stick to the historic sites. Conversely, if you're visiting November through March when the weather is considerably colder, visits to the museum and education and orientation centers might be a better idea, both logistically and in terms of your personal comfort.

Fun Fact: The Parkway Is a Park

Few people realize **George Washington Memorial Parkway** is actually a national park. Constructed in 1932 to honor the bicentennial of his birth, the parkway follows the Potomac River from Mount Vernon past Old Town Alexandria and the nation's capital before ending at Great Falls in Virginia. While today it's a major commuter route leading into and out of the city, even the most impatient driver will find it hard to resist glances at the gorgeous scenery and monuments you pass along the way.

If you can, start with the **Outbuildings:** the slave quarters, spinning house, shoemaker's shop, smokehouse, wash house (where laundry was done), the "necessary" (outhouse), salt house, and a blacksmith shop with daily demonstrations. Walk or take the included seasonal shuttle service to the 4-acre **Pioneer Farm,** which includes a replicas of a slave cabin and one of Washington's 16-sided treading barns (built from his own design), as well as several kinds of animals (hogs, sheep, chicken, cattle, horses, mules, and oxen) and crops (corn, wheat, and oats) that would have been around in Washington's time. At its peak, Mount Vernon was an 8,000-acre working farm. Today, historical interpreters in period costumes demonstrate 18th-century farming methods from April to October. Nearby is the wharf, also accessible by the seasonal shuttle, where you can learn about Washington's boat building and fisheries hobbies or, in summer, take a 45-minute narrated excursion on the Potomac (Fri–Sun at 11:30am and 12:30pm; $11 adults, $7 children).

Back on land, make time to visit the **Slave Memorial,** the greenhouse, and the tombs of George and Martha Washington. Down the road from the estate are Washington's fully functioning distillery and gristmill; he was actually one of the largest whiskey producers in the U.S. by 1799. Note that it's 2.7 miles to the site and the shuttle does not go here. Admission to the distillery and gristmill is available via a separate tour ($10 per person) on Saturday and Sunday only and is not covered by regular tickets. Samplings of the whiskey produced here are available for purchase, while Mount Vernon–made whiskey and stoneground products are also sold at the Shops at Mount Vernon.

tips **FOR TOURING MOUNT VERNON**

o If you plan to visit Old Town Alexandria historic sites as well as Mount Vernon, buy a **Key to the City Attractions Pass** (www.visit alexandriava.com/things-to-do/historic-attractions-and-museums/key-to-the-city) for $20 per person online or from the Alexandria Visitor Center at Ramsay House (221 King St.) to receive 40% off the admission price for Mount Vernon (see details in the Old Town Alexandria section, below). If you're not interested in the Key to the City Pass, you can still save $2 per person by buying your Mount Vernon Grounds Passes online at least 3 days ahead of your visit.

o For $2 more per person, you can reserve a **timed entry ticket** to tour the mansion, so choose a tour time that allows you to first visit the Ford Orientation Center, where a 25-minute movie provides some good background.

o During the online ticketing process, you will have the chance to **add on specialty tours** covering areas beyond the mansion that are designed to help bring history to life. 1 hr. tours covering the lives of enslaved people at Mount Vernon, the property's gardens, immersive experiences featuring character actors, photo cruises on the Potomac River, and a look at Mount Vernon's role in the film "National Treasure," or the musical "Hamilton," are available for $10 more.

o Seasonal shuttle service is included in your admission ticket and available April through October between the Education Center, Pioneer Farm, and Wharf.

Mount Vernon belongs to the Mount Vernon Ladies' Association, which purchased the estate for $200,000 in 1858 from John Augustine Washington III, great-grandnephew of the first president. Today, more than a million people tour the property annually. The best time to visit is in the off-season; during the heavy tourist months (especially spring, when schoolchildren descend in droves), it's best to arrive in the afternoon on weekdays or anytime early Saturday or Sunday, as student groups will have departed by then.

Special Activities at Mount Vernon

Throughout the year, but especially April through October, Mount Vernon offers many special tours, demonstrations, activities, and events; some, but not all, are included with your admission ticket. Every imaginable topic is covered: 18th-century gardens, slave life, Colonial crafts, food and dining at Mount Vernon, archaeology, and, for children, hands-on history programs. Check the website for more details.

3200 Mount Vernon Memorial Hwy. Mount Vernon, Va. www.mountvernon. org. ℂ **703/780-2000.** Admission $28 adults, $14 children 6–11, free for children 5 and under and Purple Heart recipients; discounts available for military members, veterans, and medical professionals. Save $2 per ticket when you buy them online at least 3 days ahead of your visit. Apr–Oct daily 9am–5pm; Nov–Mar daily 9am–4pm. Parking is free.

Dining & Shopping

Mount Vernon's comprehensive **Shops at Mount Vernon Complex** offers a range of books, children's toys, holiday items, Mount Vernon private-label food and wine, whiskey produced at the distillery, stoneground flour made at the gristmill, and Mount Vernon–licensed furnishings. A **food court** features a menu of grilled breakfast and lunch items, pizza, salads, wraps, and other snacks. You can't **picnic** on the grounds, but just a mile north on the parkway, **Riverside Park** has tables and a lawn overlooking the Potomac. If time allows, enjoy a meal at the **Mount Vernon Inn restaurant;** lunch or dinner at the inn is an intrinsic part of the Mount Vernon experience.

Mount Vernon Inn Restaurant ★ AMERICAN TRADITIONAL   This quaint and charming Colonial-style restaurant features period furnishings and has three working fireplaces. Lunch entrées range from roasted turkey pot pies (a sort of early-American stew served with garden vegetables in an open pie shell) to club sandwiches. There's a full bar and premium wines are offered by the glass. At dinner, tablecloths and candlelight give an elegance to the setting. The menu is mostly modern with Southern flair—you'll see fried green tomatoes, jambalaya, and chicken and waffles alongside items like filet mignon and grilled sirloin. Stick around for happy hour, featuring discounted beer, wine, and spirits, along with very un-Colonial appetizers like bacon, macaroni and cheese and crab cake sliders Tuesday through Friday from 4–8pm.

Near the entrance to Mount Vernon Estate and Gardens, 3200 Mount Vernon Memorial Hwy. Mount Vernon, Va. www.mountvernon.org/inn. ℂ **703/799-5296.** Reservations recommended for dinner. Main courses $14–$29 lunch and dinner, $10–$14 brunch (Sat and Sun only). Mon 11am–5pm; Tues–Fri 11am–8pm; Sat 10am–8pm; Sun 10am–5pm.

OLD TOWN ALEXANDRIA

Old Town Alexandria is about 8 miles south of Washington, D.C.

Washington, D.C., may be named for our first president, but he never lived there—he called the other side of the Potomac his home from the tender age of 11, when he joined his half-brother Lawrence, who owned Mount Vernon. Washington came to Alexandria often, helping to map out the 60-acre town's boundaries and roads when he was 17, training his militia in Market Square, selling produce from his family's farm at Mount Vernon, worshipping at Christ Church, and dining and dancing at Gadsby's Tavern.

The town of Alexandria is actually named after John Alexander, a Scottish immigrant who purchased the land of the present-day town from an English ship captain for "six thousand pounds of Tobacco and Cask." Incorporated in 1749, it soon grew into a major trading center and port and was known for its handsome homes. Today, thanks to a multimillion-dollar urban renewal effort, some 200 structures from Alexandria's early days survive in Old Town's historic district. Market Square is where you'll find one of the oldest continuously operating farmers markets in the country, founded in 1753—catch it on Saturday from 7am–noon and you'll be participating in a 268-year-old tradition. Christ Church and Gadsby's Tavern are still open and operating. Many Alexandria streets still bear their original Colonial names (King, Queen, Prince, Princess, and Royal), while others, like Jefferson, Franklin, Lee, Patrick, and Henry, are obviously post-Revolutionary. If you have time, watch the archaeologists along King Street's waterfront as they excavate 18th-century merchant ships discovered when developers started building condos, hotels, and other commercial establishments in the area.

Twenty-first-century America thrives in Old Town's many shops, boutiques, art galleries, bars, and restaurants. But it's still easy to imagine yourself in Colonial times as you listen for the rumbling of horse-drawn vehicles over cobblestone (portions of Prince and Oronoco sts. are still paved with it), dine on Sally Lunn bread and other 18th-century grub in the centuries-old Gadsby's Tavern, and learn about the lives of the nation's forefathers during walking tours that take you in and out of their former homes.

Essentials

GETTING THERE   For spectacular views, consider biking to Old Town Alexandria (p. 248). If you're driving from the District, take the Arlington Memorial Bridge or the 14th Street Bridge to George Washington Memorial Parkway south, which becomes Washington Street in Old Town Alexandria. Washington Street intersects with King Street, Alexandria's main thoroughfare. Turn left from Washington Street onto one of the streets before or after King Street (southbound left turns are not permitted from Washington St. onto King St.), and you'll be heading toward the waterfront and the heart of Old Town. If you turn right from Washington Street onto King Street, you'll still be in Old Town, with King Street's long avenue of shops and restaurants awaiting. Parking is inexpensive at nearby garages and at street meters, but if you want to pay nothing, drive a couple of blocks off King Street, north of

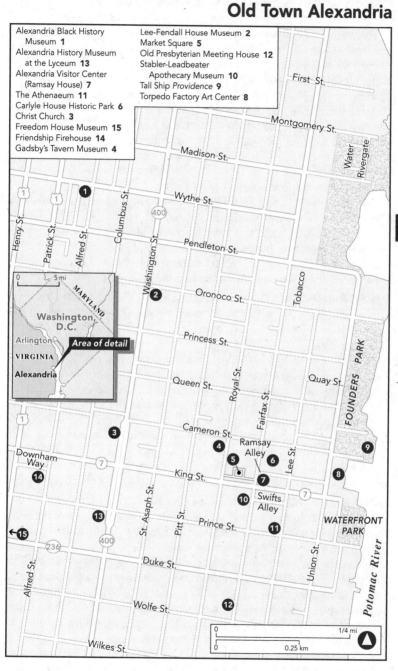

Old Town Alexandria

Alexandria Black History Museum **1**
Alexandria History Museum at the Lyceum **13**
Alexandria Visitor Center (Ramsay House) **7**
The Athenaeum **11**
Carlyle House Historic Park **6**
Christ Church **3**
Freedom House Museum **15**
Friendship Firehouse **14**
Gadsby's Tavern Museum **4**

Lee-Fendall House Museum **2**
Market Square **5**
Old Presbyterian Meeting House **12**
Stabler-Leadbeater Apothecary Museum **10**
Tall Ship *Providence* **9**
Torpedo Factory Art Center **8**

Cameron Street or south of Duke Street, where you can park for free for 2 or 3 hours. The town is compact, making it easy to get around on foot.

The easiest way to make the trip is by Metro (www.wmata.com); Yellow and Blue Line trains travel to the King Street–Old Town station. From there, you can catch the free King Street Trolley, which operates every 15 minutes daily 11am–11pm, making frequent stops between the Metro station and Market Square. The eastbound AT2, AT7, or AT8 blue-and-gold DASH bus (www.dashbus.com; © **703/746-3274**) marked OLD TOWN or BRADDOCK METRO will also take you up King Street. Ask to be dropped at the corner of Fairfax and King sts., across from the Alexandria Visitor Center at Ramsay House. The fare is $2 in cash, or free if you're transferring from Metrorail or a Metrobus and using a SmarTrip card (p. 293). You can also walk 1 mile from the Metro station into the center of Old Town.

For a memorable ride across the Potomac River, consider taking a **water taxi.** City Cruises (www.cityexperiences.com/washington-dc; © **800/459-8105**) operates year-round water taxi service between the Wharf and Georgetown, Old Town Alexandria, and National Harbor. The 35-minute ride is not cheap ($24 adults, $22 seniors over 62 and military members, $17 children, round-trip), but is scenic for sure. Check the website for schedule and reservations.

VISITOR INFORMATION The **Alexandria Visitor Center** (Ramsay House), 221 King St., at Fairfax Street (www.visitalexandriava.com; © **800/388-9119** or 703/838-5005), is open April through September, Sunday to Thursday 10am–6pm and Friday and Saturday 10am–7pm; October through March, it's open daily 10am–5pm (closed Thanksgiving, Dec 25, and Jan 1). Here you can pick up a map, self-guided walking tour, or brochures about the area and buy tickets to tours, shuttles, and nearby attractions, including Mount Vernon. Consider buying a $20-per-person **Key to the City Museum Pass** (here or in advance online, valued at $60), which includes admission to nine historic sites; 40% off coupons for admission to Mount Vernon, a tour of the Tall Ship Providence, round-trip water taxi passes from City Cruises; and discounts at many attractions, shops, and restaurants. Note that coupons can only be redeemed in person at each attraction, not when booking tickets online.

ORGANIZED TOURS Though it's easy to see Alexandria on your own and with the help of Colonial-attired guides at individual attractions, you might consider taking a comprehensive walking tour. Many guided tours are available, each focused on a particular subject.

Manumission Tour Company (www.manumissiontours.com; © **703/719-2150**) offers several 90-minute tours focusing on the stories of African people who were brought to Alexandria in bondage at the height of the slave trade, fugitive slaves who escaped via the Underground Railroad, and free African Americans and abolitionists who fought back tirelessly against injustice, all while seeing the sites around Old Town where such stories and events occurred. Tickets cost $15 for adults, $12 for children ages 12 and under and can be booked through the website or at the Alexandria Visitor Center. Check the website for scheduling as tour dates, times, and meeting places vary.

For a light-hearted look at the "G-Dubz" and some of his favorite hangouts, try a guided walk by **Alexandria the Great Tours** (www.alxtours.com; ✆ **484/680-6248**). Options include a morning stroll with coffee ($30), a trip to the Farmers Market with breakfast ($30), a 2-hour food and drink tour of Old Town ($75), and a drinking tour where you'll get to sip three Old Fashioneds.

Ghost tours are also very popular. The "Ghosts and Graveyard Tour" from **Alexandria Colonial Tours** (www.alexcolonialtours.com; ✆ **703/519-1749**) is offered Wednesday through Sunday at 7:30, 8:30, and 9pm March through November. This 1 hr. tour departs from Ramsay House and costs $15 for adults, $10 for children ages 7 to 17 (free for children 6 and under). Reservations are recommended, though not required, for these tours; or you can purchase tickets from the guide, who will be dressed in Colonial attire and standing in front of the Alexandria Visitor Center.

SELF-GUIDED TOURS   If you'd rather take your time and get to know the city at your own pace, a number of self-guided tours are available through the Alexandria Visitor Center's website (www.visitalexandriava.com). Don't miss the **African American Heritage Trail,** a 1-mile walk along the waterfront from King Street to the corner of North Royal and Montgomery sts., which takes about 45 minutes; a new extension of the trail is opening in late 2021. If you're renting a car, try **Alexandria's Black History Driving Tour,** complete with parking information so you can stop awhile and learn more at historic sites like the Edmonson Sisters Statue, African American Heritage Park, and "The Fort" community site at Fort Ward.

CITY LAYOUT   Old Town is very small and laid out in an easy grid. At the center is the intersection of Washington and King sts. Note that streets change from north to south when they cross King Street (i.e., North Alfred St. crosses King St. and becomes South Alfred St.)

OVERNIGHTING   It's not a bad idea to schedule an overnight stay in Old Town, especially if you're driving or want to plan a leisurely dinner here after a day of touring. We recommend the comfy boutique charm of the **Morrison House Old Town Alexandria, Autograph Collection ★★**, 116 S. Alfred St. (www.marriott.com/hotels/travel/wasmh-morrison-house-autograph-collection; ✆ **703/838-8000**), and the contemporary luxury of the **Kimpton Lorien Hotel & Spa ★★**, 1600 King St. (www.lorienhotelandspa.com; ✆ **703/894-3434**). **Hotel Indigo Old Town Alexandria ★** is the only waterfront hotel, with views of the Potomac (hotelindigooldtownalexandria.com; ✆ **703/721-3800**), while **The Alexandrian ★★★**, another Autograph Collection hotel (thealexandrian.com; ✆ **703/549-6080**), offers upscale comforts in the heart of Old Town.

Alexandria Calendar of Events

Visit Alexandria posts its calendar of events online at www.visitalexandriava.com, or call ✆ **800/388-9119** or 703/746-3301 for further details about the following event highlights.

FEBRUARY

George Washington's Birthday is celebrated over the course of the entire month of February, including Presidents' Weekend, which precedes the federal holiday (the third Mon in Feb). Festivities typically include a

Colonial-costume or black-tie banquet, followed by a ball at Gadsby's Tavern, special tours, "open houses" at some of Alexandria's most historic sites, a wreath-laying ceremony at the Tomb of the Unknown Soldier of the Revolution, a scavenger hunt around Alexandria, the nation's largest and oldest George Washington Birthday Parade, and a concert in Market Square. Most events, such as the parade and walking tours, are free. The **Birthnight Ball at Gadsby's Tavern** requires tickets for both the banquet and the ball. Go to www.washingtonbirthday.com.

MARCH

St. Patrick's Day Parade takes place on King Street on the first Saturday in March. Go to www.ballyshaners.org.

APRIL

Historic Garden Week in Virginia is celebrated with tours of privately owned local historic homes and gardens starting the third or fourth Saturday of the month. Check the Garden Club of Virginia's website (www.vagardenweek.org) or call (✆ **804/644-7776**) for details on tickets and admission prices for the tour.

JULY

Alexandria's birthday (its 273rd in 2022) is celebrated the Saturday following the Fourth of July with a free concert performance by the Alexandria Symphony Orchestra, fireworks, a patriotic birthday cake, and other festivities.

SEPTEMBER

The Alexandria Old Town Art Festival (www.artfestival.com/festivals/19th-annual-alexandria-old-town-art-festival) features ceramics, sculpture, photography, and other works from more than 200 juried artists. The festival is free and takes place on a Saturday and Sunday in late September.

OCTOBER

Ghost tours take place year-round but really pick up around **Halloween.** A lantern-carrying tour guide in 18th-century costume tells of Alexandria's ghosts, legends, and folklore as you tour the town and graveyards.

NOVEMBER

The Christmas Tree Lighting ceremony in Market Square usually takes place the Friday or Saturday after Thanksgiving. Festivities include a welcome by the Town Crier, musical performances, and a visit from Santa. Stick around afterward to stroll through Old Town and enjoy the thousands of tiny lights adorning the trees along King Street.

DECEMBER

The Campagna Center's Scottish Christmas Walk, typically the first weekend in December, includes kilted bagpipers, Highland dancers, a parade of Scottish clans (with horses and dogs), caroling, fashion shows, storytelling, booths (selling crafts, antiques, food, hot mulled punch, heather, fresh wreaths, and holly), and children's games. 2021 is the 51st year, organized by and benefiting the nonprofit Campagna Center, whose programs assist local families, children, and the community. Call ✆ **703/549-0111** or check www.campagnacenter.org/scottishwalkweekend for more information.

Holiday Boat Parade of Lights The water shines as dozens of lit boats cruise the Potomac River along Old Town Alexandria's historic waterfront, stretching for more than a mile. Pre-parade festivities include a beer garden, crafts, letters to Santa, and a hot chocolate bar. Look for this the first weekend in December, after the Campagna Center's Scottish Christmas Walk.

What to See & Do

Colonial and post-Revolutionary buildings like the **Carlyle House, Stabler-Leadbeater Apothecary Museum,** and **Gadsby's Tavern Museum** are most easily accessible via the King Street Metro station, combined with a ride on the free King Street Trolley to the center of Old Town. Other worthwhile historic sites are a little farther away but still worth a visit; **Alexandria Black History Museum's** closest Metro stop is the Braddock Road station, while **Fort Ward Museum & Historic Site** is a 15-minute drive or 30-minute bus ride away.

The Athenaeum in Old Town Alexandria.

Old Town is also known for its shopping scene: brand-name stores, charming boutiques, antiques shops, art galleries, and gift shops. Stop by **Bellacara,** 1000 King St. (www.bellacara.com; © **703/299-9652**), for fragrant soaps and more than 50 brands of luxe skin- and haircare products; **An American in Paris,** 1225 King St., Ste. 1 (www.anamericaninparisoldtown.com; © **703/519-8234**), where one must knock on the door to enter and sort through the beautiful, one-of-a-kind cocktail dresses and evening gowns; and **Red Barn Mercantile,** 1117 King St. (www.redbarnmercantile.com; © **703/838-0355**), a great place to buy gifts, no matter the occasion or person.

Alexandria Black History Museum ★★
In 1939, African Americans in Alexandria staged a sit-in to protest segregation at Alexandria's Barrett Branch Library, which resulted in the city building the segregated Robert Robinson Library for Black residents in the 1940s. Desegregated in the early 1960s, that building now serves as the Alexandria Black History Museum. The museum exhibits photographs, documents, and memorabilia relating to the city's Black community from the 18th century on. In addition to the permanent collection, you'll find rotating exhibits, genealogy workshops, book signings, and a host of other educational activities. *Note:* The museum is a 15-minute walk north of Old Town or a 10-minute stroll from the Braddock Road Metro Station.

902 Wythe St. (at N. Alfred St.). www.alexblackhistory.org. © **703/746-4356.** Admission $3. Tues–Sat 10am–4pm. Metro: Braddock Rd.; from the station, walk across the parking lot and bear right until you reach the corner of West and Wythe sts., where you'll proceed 5 blocks east along Wythe St.

The Athenaeum ★
This grand building, with its Greek Revival architectural style, stands out among the narrow Old Town houses on the cobblestoned street. Built in 1851, the Athenaeum has been many things: the Bank of the Old Dominion, where Robert E. Lee kept his money prior to the Civil War; a commissary for the Union Army during the Civil War; a church; a triage center where wounded Union soldiers were treated; and a medicine warehouse. 247

biking TO OLD TOWN ALEXANDRIA & MOUNT VERNON

One of the nicest ways to see the Washington, D.C. skyline is from across the river while biking in Virginia., a journey complete with stunning views of the Potomac and grand landmarks. Rent a bike at one of **Unlimited Biking's** (formerly Bike and Roll) locations near L'Enfant Plaza and the National Mall or in Old Town Alexandria (www.unlimited biking.com/washington-dc). Hop on the pathway that runs along the Potomac River and head toward the memorials and Arlington Memorial Bridge. Note that in Washington, D.C., this is called **Rock Creek Park Trail,** but when you cross Arlington Memorial Bridge near the Lincoln Memorial into Virginia, the name changes to the **Mount Vernon Trail.** Cycling is also a great way to see Old Town Alexandria and Mount Vernon. The trail carries you past Reagan National Airport via two pedestrian bridges that take you safely through the airport's roadway system. Continue to Old Town, where you should lock up your bike, have a look around, and grab a bite. If you're proceeding to Mount Vernon, note that the section from Arlington Memorial Bridge to Mount Vernon is 17 miles and takes roughly 90 minutes to cycle.

Now the hall serves as an art gallery and performance space. Pop by to admire the Athenaeum's imposing exterior, including the four soaring Doric columns and its interior hall: 24-foot-high ceilings, enormous windows, and whatever contemporary art is on display.

201 Prince St. (at S. Lee St.). www.nvfaa.org. ✆ **703/548-0035.** Free admission (donations accepted). Thurs–Sun noon–4pm. Closed major holidays.

Carlyle House Historic Park ★★   One of Virginia's most architecturally impressive 18th-century homes, Carlyle House also figured prominently in American history. A social and political center, the house was visited by the great men of the day, including George Washington. Its most important historic moment occurred in April 1755, when Major General Edward Braddock, commander-in-chief of His Majesty's forces in North America, met with five Colonial governors here and asked them to tax colonists to finance a campaign against the French. Colonial legislatures refused to comply, marking it as one of the first instances of serious friction between America and Britain.

When it was built, Carlyle House was a waterfront property with its own wharf. In 1753, Scottish merchant John Carlyle completed the mansion for his bride, Sarah Fairfax, a daughter of one of Virginia's most prominent families. Designed in the style of a Scottish/English manor house, it is lavishly furnished; a successful merchant, Carlyle had the means to import the best furnishings and appointments available abroad for his new Alexandria home.

Tours are given on the hour and half-hour and take about 45 minutes; allow another 15 minutes to tour the tiered garden of brick walks and boxed parterres. Two of the original rooms, the large parlor and the dining room, have survived intact; the former, where Braddock met the governors, still retains its original fine woodwork, paneling, and pediments. The house is furnished in period pieces, but only a few of Carlyle's possessions remain. Upstairs, an architecture exhibit depicts 18th-century building methods.

121 N. Fairfax St. (btw. Cameron and King sts.). www.novaparks.com/parks/carlyle-house-historic-park. © **703/549-2997.** Admission $5 adults; $3 children 6–12; free for children 5 and under. Thurs–Tues 10am–4pm; Sun noon–4pm. Call to reserve your tour up to 3 days ahead of time, as space is currently limited to five people due to pandemic protocols.

Christ Church ★★   This sturdy red-brick Georgian-style church would be an important national landmark even if its two most distinguished members had not been George Washington and Robert E. Lee. Continuously used since 1773—the town of Alexandria grew up around this building—it was once known as the "Church in the Woods." The building has undergone many changes since then, adding the bell tower, church bell, galleries, and organ by the early 1800s, and the "wine-glass" pulpit in 1891. Most of the original structure remains, including the hand-blown glass in the windows.

Christ Church has had its historic moments. George Washington and other early church members fomented revolution in the churchyard, while Robert E. Lee met here with Richmond representatives to discuss taking command of Virginia's military forces at the beginning of the Civil War. You can sit in the same pew where George and Martha sat with her two Custis grandchildren, or in the Lee family pew. Stroll through the churchyard, where some of the tombstones date back to the mid- to late-1700s.

World dignitaries and U.S. presidents have visited the church over the years. Shortly after Pearl Harbor, Franklin Delano Roosevelt attended services with Winston Churchill on the World Day of Prayer for Peace on January 1, 1942.

Of course, you're invited to attend a service (Sun at 8am, 10am; Wed at 12:05pm) or stop by when a guide gives brief lectures to visitors (hours listed below). A **gift shop** (121 N. Columbus St.; © **703/836-5258**) is open Thursday to Saturday 10am to 4pm and Sunday 9am to noon. Check the website before you visit; it offers a wealth of information about the history of the church and town.

118 N. Washington St. (at Cameron St.). www.historicchristchurch.org. © **703/549-1450.** Donations appreciated. Mon–Sat 9am–noon; Sun 2–4:30pm. Closed all federal holidays.

Fort Ward Museum & Historic Site ★★   A 15-minute drive (or a 30-min. bus ride) from Old Town, this 45-acre park and its museum transport you back to Alexandria during the Civil War. The action here centers, as it did in the early 1860s, on an actual Union fort that Lincoln ordered erected as part of a system of Civil War forts called the "Defenses of Washington." Most of its walls have been preserved, while six of the fort's original 36 mounted guns have been restored along its Northwest Bastion.

A model of 19th-century military engineering, the fort was never attacked by Confederate forces. Visitors can do a self-guided tour of the fort as well as replicas of the ceremonial entrance gate and an officer's hut. An onsite museum of Civil War artifacts features changing exhibits on subjects such as Union arms and equipment, medical care of the wounded, and local war history.

With picnic areas and barbecue grills in the park surrounding the fort and living-history presentations taking place throughout the year, this is a good stop if you have young children, especially if you bring a picnic.

4301 W. Braddock Rd. (btw. Rte. 7 and N. Van Dorn St.). www.fortward.org. © **703/746-4848.** Admission $3. Park daily 9am–sunset. Museum Tues–Sat 10am–5pm; Sun noon–5pm. Accessible via the AT5 DASH bus from the King Street Metro station, or by car or taxi: From Old Town, follow King St. west, go right on Kenwood Ave., then left on W. Braddock Rd.; continue for a mile to the entrance on the right.

Freedom House Museum ★★
This museum is housed in the basement of what used to be the Franklin and Armfield Slave Pen, one of the country's largest slave trading operations and part of a larger complex used to transport more than 3,750 slaves from Northern Virginia to sugar and cotton plantations in Louisiana and Mississippi between 1828 and 1836. The three-story building also served as a military prison, hospital for Black soldiers, and a holding place for slaves fleeing the south during the Civil War. Today, it's listed on the National Register of Historic Places, and reopened in fall 2021 after a series of extensive renovations.

1315 Duke St. (btw. S. Payne and S. West sts.). www.alexandriava.gov/FreedomHouse. © **703/746-4702.** Admission $5. Fri and Sat, 1–5pm.

Friendship Firehouse ★
In the early days of Alexandria's first firefighting organization, the Friendship Fire Company (founded in 1774), volunteers met in taverns and kept firefighting equipment in a member's barn. Its present Italianate-style brick building dates from 1855 and was erected after an earlier building was, ironically, destroyed by fire. Local tradition holds that George Washington was involved with the firehouse as a founding member, active firefighter, and purchaser of its first fire engine, although research does not confirm these stories. The museum displays an 1851 fire engine, old hoses, buckets, and other firefighting tools. Don't miss the annual Firehouse Festival, typically held on the first Saturday in August, featuring live music, arts and crafts, and a chance to check out antique firefighting paraphernalia.

107 S. Alfred St. (btw. King and Prince sts.). www.alexandriava.gov/friendshipfirehouse. © **703/746-3891.** Admission $3 adults, $1 children 6–17, free for children under 5. Open one Saturday per month, 11am–5pm (check the website, as dates vary).

Gadsby's Tavern Museum ★★
Alexandria commanded center stage in 18th-century America, with Gadsby's Tavern constantly in the spotlight. It's made up of two buildings—one Georgian, one Federal, dating from around 1785 and 1792, respectively. Innkeeper John Gadsby later combined them to create "a gentleman's tavern," which he operated from 1796 to 1808, and it was considered to be one of the finest in the country. George Washington was a frequent dinner guest; he and Martha danced in the second-floor ballroom, and it was here that he celebrated his last birthday. The tavern also welcomed Thomas Jefferson, James Madison, and the Marquis de Lafayette (the French soldier and statesman who served with Washington during the Revolutionary War). It was the setting of lavish parties, theatrical performances, small circuses, government meetings, and concerts. Itinerant merchants used the tavern to display their wares, while traveling doctors treated a hapless clientele on the premises.

The rooms have been restored to their 18th-century appearance. During a self-guided tour, you'll get a good look at the **Tap Room,** a small dining room; the **Assembly Room,** the ballroom; typical bedrooms; and the underground icehouse, which was filled each winter from the icy river. Cap off your visit with a meal right next door at the restored Colonial-style restaurant, **Gadsby's Tavern,** 138 N. Royal St., at Cameron Street (www.gadsbystavern restaurant.com; © **703/548-1288**).

134 N. Royal St. (at Cameron St.). www.gadsbystavern.org. © **703/746-4242.** Admission $5 adults; $3 children 5–12; free for children 4 and under. Thurs and Fri 11am–4pm, Sat 11am–5pm, Sun 1–5pm.

Lee-Fendall House Museum ★★

Thirty-seven Lees occupied this handsome Greek Revival–style house over a period of 118 years (1785–1903), and it is a veritable Lee family museum of furniture, heirlooms, and documents. While politician and Revolutionary War officer "Light-Horse Harry" Lee never actually lived here, he was a frequent visitor, as was his good friend George Washington. He did own the original lot but sold it to Philip Richard Fendall (himself a Lee on his mother's side), who built the house in 1785.

It was in this house that Harry wrote Alexandria's farewell address to George Washington, delivered when the general passed through town on his way to assume the presidency. (Harry also wrote and delivered the famous funeral oration to Washington that contained the words, "First in war, first in peace, and first in the hearts of his countrymen.") During the Civil War, the house was seized and used as a Union hospital.

Guided tours (30–45 min.) illuminate the 1850s era of the home and provide insight into Victorian family life. Much of the interior woodwork and glass is original. The Colonial garden, with its magnolia and chestnut trees, roses, and boxwood-lined paths, can be visited as part of the tour or without a ticket.

614 Oronoco St. (at Washington St.). www.leefendallhouse.org. © **703/548-1789.** Admission $7 adults; $3 children 5–17; free for children 4 and under. Wed–Sat 10am–4pm; Sun 1–4pm. Call ahead to make sure the museum is not closed for a special event or to book a private tour. Tours are open to the public on the hour 10am–3pm.

The Lyceum ★

This Greek Revival building houses a museum depicting Alexandria's history from the 17th to the 20th centuries, with changing exhibits and an ongoing series of lectures, concerts, and educational programs.

The striking brick-and-stucco Lyceum also merits a visit. Built in 1839, it was designed in the Doric temple style to serve as a lecture, meeting, and concert hall. It was an important center of Alexandria's cultural life until the Civil War, when Union forces appropriated it for use as a hospital. After the war, it became a private residence and was eventually subdivided for office space; in 1969, the city council's use of eminent domain prevented it from being demolished in favor of a parking lot.

201 S. Washington St. (off Prince St.). www.alexandriava.gov/Lyceum. © **703/746-4994.** Admission $3 adults, $1 children 6–17, free for children 4 and under. Mon–Sat 10am–5pm, Sun 1–5pm.

Old Presbyterian Meeting House ★ Presbyterian congregations have worshiped in Virginia since Reverend Alexander Whitaker baptized Pocahontas in Jamestown in 1613. The original version of this Presbyterian Meeting House was built in 1774. Although it wasn't George Washington's church, the Meeting House bell tolled continuously for 4 days after his death in December 1799, and memorial services were preached from the pulpit here by Presbyterian, Episcopal, and Methodist ministers. According to the Alexandria paper of the day, "The walking being bad to the Episcopal church, the funeral sermon of George Washington will be preached at the Presbyterian Meeting House." Two months later, on Washington's birthday, Alexandria citizens marched from Market Square to the church to pay their respects.

Many famous Alexandrians are buried in the church graveyard, including John and Sarah Carlyle; Dr. James Craik (the surgeon who treated Washington, dressed Lafayette's wounds at Brandywine, and ministered to the dying Braddock at Monongahela); and William Hunter, Jr., founder of the St. Andrew's Society of Scottish descendants, to whom bagpipers pay homage on the first Saturday of December. It's also the site of the Tomb of an Unknown Revolutionary War Soldier. Dr. James Muir, minister between 1789 and 1820, lies beneath the sanctuary in his gown and bands. The cemetery has a larger burial ground nearby that has been used since 1809.

When lightning struck and set fire to most of the original Meeting House in 1835, parishioners rebuilt the church in 1837, incorporating as much as they could from the earlier structure. This is the church you see today. The present bell, said to be recast from the metal of the old one, was hung in a newly constructed belfry in 1843, and a new organ was installed in 1849. The Meeting House closed its doors in 1889 and for 60 years was used sporadically. In 1949, it was reborn as a living Presbyterian U.S.A. church and today, the Old Meeting House looks much as it did following its first restoration. The original parsonage, or manse, is still intact.

323 S. Fairfax St. (btw. Duke and Wolfe sts.). www.opmh.org. © **703/549-6670.** Free admission. Open to the public Mon–Fri 9am–4pm (there are no guided tours). Sun services 11am.

Stabler-Leadbeater Apothecary Museum ★★ When its doors closed in 1933, this landmark drugstore was the second oldest in continuous operation in America. Run for five generations by the same Quaker family since 1792, the store counted Robert E. Lee (who purchased the paint for Arlington House here), George Mason, Henry Clay, John C. Calhoun, and George Washington among its famous patrons. Gothic Revival decorative elements and Victorian-style doors were added in the 1840s. Today the apothecary looks much as it did in Colonial times, its shelves lined with original handblown gold-leaf-labeled bottles (the most valuable collection of antique medicinal bottles in the country), old scales stamped with the royal crown, patent medicines, and equipment for bloodletting. The clock on the rear wall, the porcelain-handled mahogany drawers, and two mortars and pestles all date from about 1790. Among the shop's documentary records is this 1802 order from Mount Vernon: "Mrs. Washington desires Mr. Stabler to send by the bearer a quart bottle of his best Castor Oil and the bill for it." Self-guided tours let you explore the first floor, while for $3 more, a 45-minute guided tour provides access to both floors every hour on the quarter of the hour (:15).

105–107 S. Fairfax St. (near King St.). www.apothecarymuseum.org. © **703/746-3852.** Admission for self-guided tours of the first floor only $5 adults; $3 children 5–12; free for children under 4. Guided tours cost $8 for visitors over age 5. Apr–Oct Tues–Sat 10am–5pm, Sun–Mon 1–5pm; Nov–Mar Wed–Sat 11am–4pm, Sun 1–4pm.

The tall ship Providence sailing on the Potomac River.

Tall Ship Providence ★★

Celebrate Alexandria's maritime history and climb aboard a replica of the first 18th century tall ship to serve in the Continental Navy. 1 hr. tours are given hourly between 11am and 2pm by Captain John Paul Jones himself (i.e., a pretty convincing character actor version of the legendary Revolutionary War naval commander) and let you explore what daily life was like for those who had the pleasure of sailing with him on the high seas back in the day. The tall ship also hosts 2 hr. afternoon and sunset cruises, with complimentary non-alcoholic beverages and snacks.

1 Cameron St., Lower Level (on the waterfront). www.tallshipprovidence.org. © **703/772-8483.** Wed–Sun. Tours $16 adults; $14 seniors and military members; $12 children 5–12; free for children under 4. Admission for afternoon cruises (at 4pm) $45 per person; sunset cruises (6:30pm) $55 per person.

Torpedo Factory Art Center ★

This block-long, three-story structure was built in 1918 as a torpedo shell-case factory but now accommodates 82 artists' studios, where 160 professional artists and craftspeople create and sell their own works. Here you can see artists at work in their studios, from potters to painters, as well as those who create stained-glass windows and fiber art.

On permanent display are exhibits about the city's history from **Alexandria Archaeology** (torpedofactory.org/archaeology; © **703/746-4399**), which engages in extensive city research, including the recent excavation of three Colonial-era merchant ships uncovered at Robinson Landing in 2017 and 2018, a dig at a place City Archaeologist Eleanor Breen called "one of the most archaeologically significant sites in Virginia."

105 N. Union St. (btw. King and Cameron sts., on the waterfront). www.torpedofactory.org. © **703/746-4570.** Free admission. Daily 10am–6pm, with occasional closures at 5pm for private events. Archaeology exhibit area Tues–Fri 10am–3pm (closed Tues Nov–Mar); Sat 10am–5pm; Sun 1–5pm. Closed Jan 1, Easter, July 4, Thanksgiving, Dec 25.

Where to Eat & Play

Old Town Alexandria is in the midst of a major redevelopment centered on its waterfront. The plan calls for new restaurants, shops, bars, town houses, and a rebuilt pier. A new, expanded Waterfront Park opened in 2019 at the foot of King Street, where visitors can now enjoy broadened views of the Potomac River. In the meantime, consider these other recommended restaurants and bars.

WHERE TO EAT

The following options satisfy assorted budgets, tastes, and styles; all are easily accessible via the King Street Metro station, combined with a ride on the free King Street Trolley to the center of Old Town.

Expensive

Ada's on the River ★★★ STEAKHOUSE/AMERICAN   Named as a tribute to 19th-century mathematician Ada Lovelace and built around a wood-burning oven, chef Randall J. Matthews' waterfront restaurant serves everything from wood-fired steaks and pork chops to moule frites, wood-fired swordfish, and giant crab cakes. Vegetarian options include charred cauliflower, smoked ricotta gnocchi, and coal-fired mushroom lasagna. Save room for dessert—the chocolate soufflé takes 20 minutes to make but is well worth the wait. If you only have time for one brunch during your visit to Alexandria, make it here, if only for the Maine lobster omelet, crème brûlée French toast, and signature brunch cocktails, including three creative twists on the traditional Bloody Mary.

3 Pioneer Mill Way (at the waterfront). www.adasontheriver.com. ℂ **703/638-1400.** Reservations recommended. Main courses $16–$29 lunch, $15–$29 brunch, $19–$42 dinner. Mon–Fri 11:30am–11pm; Sat, Sun, 11am–11pm; brunch Sat, Sun 11am–3pm.

Hummingbird ★★★ SEAFOOD/AMERICAN   Owners Cathal (the chef) and Meshelle Armstrong are the married power couple behind Hummingbird, which *Washington Post* restaurant critic Tom Sietsema has called "Old Town's most appealing place to eat." (The other restaurant in the Armstrong family is the Filipino/Thai/Korean restaurant **Kaliwa,** at the Wharf in Washington, D.C.) Hummingbird debuted in 2017 inside Hotel Indigo Alexandria Old Town, scoring an early success for the city's waterfront redevelopment strategy. Come here for the wonderful views of the Potomac, both inside through the glass doors and outside on the patio, where you can dine even in winter, warmed by stoked fire pits and blankets. The theme is nautical, with a navy and white decor. The food—lobster lemon linguine, fried oyster Po'Boys, fried green tomatoes, roasted half Amish chicken, pan roasted salmon, and, naturally, Southern-style hummingbird cake—is as wonderful as the setting.

220 S. Union St. (in Hotel Indigo Old Town Alexandria, at the waterfront). www.hummingbirdva.net. ℂ **703/566-1355.** Reservations recommended. Main courses $8–$21 breakfast, $13–$21 brunch, $10–$26 lunch, $19–$35 dinner. Closed Mon. Breakfast Sat, Sun 8–10:30am; brunch Sat, Sun 11am–4:30pm; lunch Tues–Fri 11:30am–4:30pm; dinner Tues–Thurs, Sun 5–9pm, Fri and Sat 5–9:30pm.

Moderate

Blackwall Hitch ★★ AMERICAN If Hummingbird is booked, head here. The huge (seats 500), glass-enclosed restaurant and its two patios sit right on the waterfront overlooking the Potomac River and the Torpedo Factory Art Center. Inside are two dining rooms, an oyster bar, a bar and lounge where live music plays Thursday to Saturday evenings and at Sunday brunch, and the upstairs **Crow's Nest** bar, a perfect niche for boat- and people-watching. Feast on seafood items like Maryland crab cakes and shrimp and grits, or try a selection of tasty burgers, steaks, pasta, chicken, or fire-roasted flatbreads. The kids' menu has standard fare like chicken tenders, burgers, and pasta for $9 each.

5 Cameron St. (on the waterfront). www.blackwallhitchalexandria.com. ✆ **703/739-6090.** Reservations recommended. Main courses $18–$46; Sun brunch $38 adults, $15 children 12 and under, free for children under 3. Mon–Thurs 11am–11pm; Fri–Sat 11–1am; Sun 10am–10pm; Sun brunch 10am–3pm.

Mia's Italian Kitchen ★★ ITALIAN Should you need some good homemade Italian food to keep you going, head to Mia's, where you'll find housemade pasta, charcuterie, Italian sandwiches, Naples-style square pizzas, and other farm-to-table dishes inspired by Dave Nicholas' great-grandmother's homestyle Italian cooking. Take on the giant 18-oz. meatball, enjoy house-made fettuccine, rigatoni, and spaghetti, or tuck into some chargrilled branzino after a long day. The brunch menu features Italian twists on brunch classics, like meatball benedict, cinnamon-raisin Italian toast, and Bolognese baked eggs, as well as a good selection of personal-size Sicilian brick oven pizza. In a hurry? Grab a $5 margherita, Mediterranean, or pepperoni pizza and wash it down with a $4 sangria, $5 draft beer, $6 wine, or $7 cocktail during happy hour.

100 King St. (at N. Union St.). www.miasitalian.com/alexandria-va/alexandria-va. ✆ **703/997-5300.** Reservations recommended. Main courses for lunch and dinner $7–$24; brunch $7–$20; happy hour $5–$9. Mon–Thurs 11am–11pm; Fri 11am–midnight; Sat 10am–midnight; Sun 10am–11pm; Sat, Sun brunch 9am–3pm; happy hour Mon–Fri 3–7pm.

Inexpensive

Barca Pier & Wine Bar ★★ TAPAS If you're looking for some lite bites, Barca Pier & Wine Bar, which just opened in March 2021, offers Spanish and Mediterranean-style tapas like stuffed piquillo peppers, papas bravas, gambas al ajillo (jumbo shrimp), and serrano ham croquetas, as well as Spanish cheeses, montaditos (sandwiches), sangria, and cocktails, with a view of the Potomac. Choose from The Pier, a structure anchored by a freight container that serves as a bar, or the Wine Bar, situated below the Robinson Landing residences—boat owners can also pay an hourly fee to dock while they eat.

2 Pioneer Mill Way (on the waterfront). www.barcaalx.com. ✆ **703/638-1100.** Reservations recommended. Tapas and small plates for lunch and dinner $8–$14. Sun–Thurs 11:30am–11pm; Fri, Sat 11:30am–midnight.

Urbano 116 ★ MEXICAN The sights and sounds of Mexico City followed chef Alam Méndez Florián to this Oaxacan-style restaurant in the heart of Old Town. Its interior has a beamed ceiling, brick walls, cozy booths, leather bar seats, neon signs throughout, and a large mural backdrop dedicated to Mexico's theatrical professional wrestling pastime, lucha libre, with several luchador masks (traditional Mexican wrestling masks) on display. The menu is dedicated to traditional Oaxacan cuisine, with fresh takes on tacos featuring fish, carnitas, shrimp, smoked brisket, and vegetarian options. Start with some chips with guacamole or salsa, or opt for rockfish or shrimp ceviche. Entrées include roasted chicken, grilled swordfish, and smoked pork belly. Wash it down with a margarita, sangria, or another one of Urbano 116's specialty cocktails, like the Michelada, a Mexican-style Bloody Mary made with Pacifico beer.

116 King St. (btw. Union and Lee sts.). www.urbano116.com/alexandria. © **571/970-5148.** Reservations accepted. Main courses lunch and dinner $9–$28. Sun–Thurs 11am–11pm, Fri and Sat 11am–midnight.

NIGHTLIFE

The Birchmere Music Hall and Bandstand opened back in 1966, showcasing mostly bluegrass and country acts. These days, its calendar offers more range, offering performances by artists like Big Bad Voodoo Daddy and Joan Baez. Purchase tickets, which typically run between $25–$65 from the box office at 3701 Mt. Vernon Ave. (off S. Glebe Rd.) or online via Ticketmaster (www.birchmere.com; © 703/549-7500).

Otherwise, Old Town Alexandria's nightlife options center on the bar scene, which is nearly as varied as the one in Washington, D.C.

Named for St. Augustine, the patron saint of brewers, **Augie's Mussel House and Beer Garden,** located at 1106 King St. (www.eataugies.com; © **703/721-3970**), features Belgian fare and some of the best beers from around the world served indoors and on the expansive heated outdoor patio. If you're in the mood for raucous karaoke, bar trivia, DJ and local band performances, shuffleboard, and Skee-Ball, make your way to **The Light Horse,** 715 King St. (www.thelighthorserestaurant.com; © **703/549-0533**). Downstairs is the restaurant, but upstairs is where you want to be. For cocktails, live jazz, and Potomac views, snag a seat at **Blackwall Hitch** Thursday through Saturday evenings and Sunday during jazz brunch.

SELF-GUIDED WALKING TOURS

by Jess Moss

One of the greatest pleasures to be had in the nation's capital is walking. You round a corner and spy the Capitol standing proudly at the end of the avenue. You stroll a downtown street and chance to look up, and *bam*, there it is: the tip of the Washington Monument. People pass you on the sidewalk speaking a pastiche of languages. You decide to walk rather than take the Metro or a taxi back to your hotel and discover a gem of a museum. A limousine pulls up to the curb and discharges—who? A foreign ambassador? A former prez? A famous author or athlete or human-rights activist?

Beautiful sights, historic landmarks, unpredictable encounters, and multicultural experiences await you everywhere in Washington. Follow any of these three self-guided walking tours and see for yourself.

WALKING TOUR 1: STROLLING AROUND THE WHITE HOUSE

START:	**White House Visitor Center, 1450 Pennsylvania Ave. NW (Metro: Federal Triangle or Metro Center).**
FINISH:	**Penn Quarter (Metro: Federal Triangle or Metro Center).**
TIME:	**1½ hours to 2 hours (not including stops). It's a 1.6-mile trek.**
BEST TIME:	**During the day. If you want to hit all the museums, stroll on a Thursday or Friday.**
WORST TIME:	**After dark, as some streets can be deserted.**

The White House is the centerpiece of President's Park, an 18-acre national park that includes not just the house itself but also its grounds, from the Ellipse to Pennsylvania Avenue to Lafayette Square; the U.S. Treasury Building on 15th Street; and the Eisenhower Executive Office Building on 17th Street. As you wend your way from landmark to landmark, sometimes navigating a gauntlet of security fences, you'll be mingling with White House administration staff, high-powered attorneys, diplomats, and ordinary office workers. All of you are treading the same ground as early American heroes—like Stephen Decatur, whose house you'll see—and every president since George Washington (though the White House was not finished in time for him to live there).

This tour circumnavigates the White House grounds, with stops at historic sites and several noteworthy museums. The **White House Visitor Center** (p. 174) is a good place to begin and end (for one thing, it's got restrooms!).

Note: Tours of the White House require advance reservations, as do tours of the U.S. Treasury Building. For White House tour info, see p. 175. See https://home.treasury.gov/services/tours-and-library/tours-of-the-historic-treasury-building for details about registering for a Treasury Building tour.

Start: From the White House Visitor Center, stroll up 15th St. to your first stop, at 15th and F sts. NW.

---

1 U.S. Treasury Building

Lin-Manuel Miranda's brilliant musical *Hamilton* has brought the man and his times to life on Broadway and beyond. On this tour, you must settle for Hamilton, the statue. It stands outside the south end of the U.S. Treasury Building, too close to the White House for security's comfort to allow stray tourists a better look, so you must resign yourself to gazing at him from a distance through the black iron fencing. Hamilton, who devised our modern financial system, was the first secretary of the Treasury, established by Congress in 1789. Once you've caught a glimpse of Hamilton's statue, turn your attention to the Treasury's headquarters, Washington's oldest office building, initially erected in 1798 and severely damaged by fire not once, not twice, but three times (in 1801, 1814, and 1833), until reconstruction proceeded in fits and starts to completion in 1869. Its most notable architectural feature is the colonnade you see running the length of the building: 30 columns, each 36 feet tall, carved out of a single piece of granite. In its lifetime, the building has served as a Civil War barracks, a temporary home for President Andrew Johnson following the assassination of President Lincoln in 1865, and the site of President Ulysses S. Grant's inaugural reception. Today it houses offices for the U.S. treasurer, the secretary of the Treasury, its general counsel, and their staffs.

Continue north on 15th St. and turn left onto the Pennsylvania Ave. promenade, where you'll notice the statue of Albert Gallatin, the fourth secretary of the Treasury, standing accessibly on the north side of the Treasury Building. Continue along:

2 Pennsylvania Avenue

Say hello to the president, who resides in that big white house beyond the black iron fencing. Security precautions keep this 2-block section of Pennsylvania Avenue closed to traffic. But that's a good thing. You may have to dodge bicyclists, street hockey players, joggers, soapbox orators and live newscasts, but not cars. Ninety Princeton American elm trees line the 84-foot-wide promenade, which offers plenty of great photo ops as you stroll past the White House. There are benches here, too, in case you'd like to sit and people-watch. L'Enfant's original idea for Pennsylvania Avenue was that it would connect the legislative branch (Congress)

Strolling Around the White House

1 U.S. Treasury Building
2 Pennsylvania Avenue
3 Lafayette Square
4 St. John's Episcopal Church, Lafayette Square
5 Black Lives Matter Plaza
6 Decatur House
7 White House
8 Renwick Gallery
9 Eisenhower Executive Office Building
10 GCDC Grilled Cheese Bar 🖳
11 Octagon House
12 Corcoran School of the Arts & Design
13 DAR Museum and Period Rooms
14 Art Museum of the Americas
15 Ellipse

A bird's-eye view of Pennsylvania Avenue and the Capitol Building.

at one end of the avenue with the executive branch (the president's house) at the other end.

Turn your back on the White House and walk across the plaza to enter:

3 Lafayette Square

This 7-acre public park is known as a gathering spot for protesters (as I write this from a shady park bench, there's a Cuba liberation demonstration taking place in the square behind me). In its early days, the grounds held temporary shelters for the slaves building the White House, then a racetrack, zoo, graveyard, and a military encampment. The park is named for the Marquis de Lafayette, a Frenchman who served under George Washington during the Revolutionary War. But it's General Andrew Jackson's statue that centers the park. Erected in 1853, this was America's first equestrian statue. It's said that sculptor Clark Mills trained a horse to maintain a reared-up pose so that Mills could study how the horse balanced its weight. Other park statues are dedicated to foreign soldiers who fought in the War for Independence, including Lafayette; Poland's Tadeusz Kosciuszko; Prussian Baron von Steuben; and Frenchman Comte de Rochambeau.

Walk through the park and cross H St. to reach 1525 H St. NW, the site of:

4 St. John's Episcopal Church on Lafayette Square

St. John's is known as "the Church of the Presidents" because every president since James Madison has attended at least one service here. The church became an unlikely focal point during the 2020 protests after George Floyd's death. A fire was set in the basement of the church's parish house. The following day the National Guard used tear gas to clear out demonstrators here so President Trump could pose for a photo in front of the church. If you tour the church, look for pew 54, eight rows from the front, which is the one traditionally reserved for the current president and first family. Other things to notice in this 1816 church, designed by Benjamin Henry Latrobe, are the steeple bell, which was cast by Paul Revere's son and has been in continuous use since its installation in 1822, and the beautiful stained-glass windows. The Lincoln Pew, at the very back of the church, is where Lincoln would sit alone for evening services during the Civil War, slipping in after other congregants had arrived and out before they left.

Directly across the street from St. John's is the Hay-Adams Hotel, which turns 93 this year (p. 70). Look north up 16th St. to see the large yellow letters painted across the asphalt, making up:

5 Black Lives Matter Plaza

During the protests that followed the murder of George Floyd in 2020, D.C. Mayor Muriel Bowser commissioned 50-foot-tall block letters that read BLACK LIVES MATTER to be painted on the street extending from President's Park. The installation, which spans nearly 2 city blocks has become a gathering hub, place of reflection, and occasional site of street festivals—people bring grills and music and celebrate the city's Black culture.

Recross H St. to stand in front of 748 Jackson Place NW, the:

6 Decatur House

In addition to St. John's, Latrobe designed this Federal-style brick town house in 1818 for Commodore Stephen Decatur, a renowned naval hero in the War of 1812. Decatur and his wife, Susan, established themselves as gracious hosts in the 14 short months they lived here. In March 1820, 2 days after hosting a ball for President James Monroe's daughter, Marie, Decatur was killed in a gentleman's duel by his former mentor, James Barron. Barron blamed Decatur for his 5-year suspension from the Navy, following a court-martial in which Decatur had played an active role. Other distinguished occupants have included Henry Clay and Martin Van Buren, when each was serving as Secretary of State (Clay under Pres. John Quincy Adams, Van Buren under Pres. Andrew Jackson). Decatur House, which includes slave quarters, is open for free tours on a limited basis (www.whitehousehistory.org/events/tour-the-historic-decatur-house). The White House Historical Association gift shop is at the entry, at 1610 H St.

Walk back through Lafayette Sq. to return to the Pennsylvania Ave. plaza, where you'll have another chance to admire the:

7 White House

As grand as the White House is, it is at least one-fourth the size that Pierre L'Enfant had in mind when he planned a palace to house the President. George Washington and his commission went a different way and dismissed L'Enfant, though they kept L'Enfant's site proposal. An Irishman named James Hoban designed the building, having entered his architectural draft in a contest held by George Washington, beating out 52 other entries. Although Washington picked the winner, he was the only president never to live in the White House, or "President's Palace," as it was called before whitewashing brought the name "White House" into use. Construction of the White House took 8 years, beginning in 1792, when its cornerstone was laid. Its facade is made of the same stone

New mural at Black Lives Matter Plaza in front of the White House and Lafayette Park.

used to construct the Capitol. See p. 175 for in-depth info about the White House and tours.

Turn around and head toward the northwest corner of the plaza, at 17th St., to reach the:

8 Renwick Gallery

Its esteemed neighbors are the White House and, right next door, the Blair-Lee House (built in 1858), where the White House sends overnighting foreign dignitaries. The Renwick (p. 170), nevertheless, holds its own. This distinguished redbrick-and-brownstone structure was the original location for the Corcoran Gallery of Art. James Renwick designed the building (if it reminds you of the Smithsonian Castle on the Mall, it's because Renwick designed that one, too), which opened in 1874. When the collection outgrew its quarters, the Corcoran moved to its current location in 1897 (see below). Although the Renwick's mission has long focused on decorative arts and crafts from early America to the present, the gallery lately is gaining popularity for its special exhibits of ultra-inventive art by push-the-envelope contemporary artists, like Janet Echelman's colorful fiber and lighting installation show. Since 1972 the Renwick has operated as an annex of the Smithsonian American Art Museum, 8 blocks away in the Penn Quarter. By all means, head inside.

Turn to your left on 17th St., where you'll notice on your left the:

9 Eisenhower Executive Office Building

Old-timers still refer to this ornate building as the "OEOB," for "Old Executive Office Building"; the Eisenhower Executive Office Building houses the offices of people who work in or with the Executive Office of the President. When construction was completed in 1888, it was the largest office building in the world. During the Iran-Contra scandal of the Reagan presidency, the OEOB became famous as the site of document shredding by Colonel Oliver North and his secretary, Fawn Hall. Open to the public? Nope.

Keep following Pennsylvania Ave. west. See all the sandwich and coffee places? You can choose McDonald's if you'd like, but I'd rather you try a local favorite, at 1730 Pennsylvania Ave. NW:

10 GCDC Grilled Cheese Bar ☕

The standard sandwich gets a gourmet makeover here, where you'll find grilled cheeses filled with everything from mac and cheese and pulled pork with BBQ sauce ("The Carolina BBQ") to pepper jack cheese, jalapeno, and bacon jam ("The Sweet Heat"). Pair it with GCDC's homemade tomato soup "with a kick" or summer gazpacho (www.grilledcheesedc.com; ☎ 202/393-4232).

After you've satisfied your hunger, walk back to 17th St. NW, turn right, and stroll 3 blocks to New York Ave., turn right and walk 1 block, where you'll spy the unmistakable:

11 Octagon House

Count the sides of this uniquely shaped building and you'll discover that the Octagon is, in fact, a hexagon. Designed by Dr. William Thornton, first architect of the U.S. Capitol, this 1801 building apparently earned its name from interior features, though experts disagree about that. If it's open, enter the Octagon to view the round rooms; the central, oval-shaped staircase that curves gracefully to the third level; the hidden doors; and the triangular chambers. Built originally for the wealthy Tayloe family, the Octagon served as a temporary president's home for James and Dolley Madison after the British torched the White House in 1814. On February 17, 1815, President Madison sat at the circular table in the upstairs circular room and signed the Treaty of Ghent, establishing peace with Great Britain.

Cross New York Ave. and return to 17th St., where you should turn right and walk to the Corcoran Gallery. It's unlikely that the building will be open, but if it is, you should definitely try to visit.

12 Corcoran Gallery of Art

This gallery, the first art museum in Washington and one of the first in the country, has always had a penchant for playing the wild card. In 1851, gallery founder William Corcoran caused a stir when he displayed artist Hiram Powers' *The Greek Slave*, which was the first publicly exhibited, life-size American sculpture depicting a fully nude female figure. (*The Greek Slave* is currently on view at the National Gallery of Art; see p. 149.) Today the Corcoran Gallery of Art exists, but no longer as an independent entity. The George Washington University owns the building and the resident art school; the National Gallery owns 40% of the art, with the remaining 60% distributed to the American University Museum at the Katzen Arts Center (here in D.C.) and to Smithsonian museums and other institutions, including the Hirshhorn Museum and Sculpture Garden.

Walk to 17th St. and turn right, away from the White House. Follow it down to D St. and turn right, following the signs that lead to the entrance of the:

13 DAR Museum & Period Rooms

The National Headquarters of the Daughters of the American Revolution comprises three joined buildings that take up an entire block. The main entrance is in the middle building, but you'll want to make your way to the elegant Memorial Continental Hall. What you're here for is the **DAR Museum,** which rotates exhibits of items from its 33,000-object collection, and the 31 period rooms, representing interior styles from the past. The museum's collections focus on decorative arts and include furniture, ceramics, costumes, paintings, and silver. Quilters from far and wide come to admire the large collection of quilts, which you can get an up-close view of in the new study gallery. Highlights of the period rooms include the New Jersey Room, with woodwork and furnishings created from the salvaged oak timbers of the British warship *Augusta,* which sank during the Revolutionary War; an opulent Victorian Missouri parlor; and New Hampshire's "Children's Attic," filled with 19th-century toys, dolls, and children's furnishings. You can tour the museum and period rooms on your own, but if you're able to join a free docent-led tour, it'll be even more informative.

Exit the DAR, turning left and continuing along D St. to 18th St., where you'll turn left again and follow to 201 18th St. NW, the Spanish colonial–style building that houses:

14 Art Museum of the Americas

The AMA showcases the works of contemporary Latin American and Caribbean artists. You'll be on your own; a visit takes 30 minutes, tops. *Not to miss:* A stunning loggia whose tall-beamed ceiling and wall of deep-blue tiles set in patterns modeled after Aztec and Mayan art is a work of art on its own. A series of French (and usually locked) doors leads to a terrace and the museum garden, which separates the museum from the **Organization of American States (OAS) headquarters,** which owns it. When you leave the museum, you may notice the nearby sculptures of José Artigus, "Father of the Independence of Uruguay," and a large representation of liberator Simón Bolívar on horseback.

From 18th St., head back in the direction of the White House, turning right on C St. and then left on 17th St. and follow it to E St. Cross 17th St. and pick up the section of E St. that takes you between the South Lawn of the White House and the:

15 Ellipse

It's possible to bring a blanket and some food and picnic on the Ellipse, except when a White House event requires increased security and the Secret Service tell you to skedaddle. Otherwise, feel free to stroll the grounds. The Ellipse continues to be the site for the National Christmas Tree Lighting Ceremony every December, and a spot near the Zero Milestone monument remains a favored place for shooting photos against the backdrop of the White House. If you're ready to call it a day, keep walking a few more steps to return to 15th Street NW in Penn Quarter, and its many options for an end-of-stroll repast.

WALKING TOUR 2: GEORGETOWN

START:	**Kafe Leopold (DC Circulator bus; nearest Metro stop: Foggy Bottom).**
FINISH:	**Old Stone House (DC Circulator bus; nearest Metro stop: Foggy Bottom).**
TIME:	**2½ to 3 hours (not including stops). The distance is about 3½ miles.**
BEST TIME:	**Saturday and Sunday afternoon, when most buildings are open (though some still require advanced tickets).**
WORST TIME:	**Tuesday or Wednesday mornings, when many of the homes and museums are closed.**

The Georgetown famous for its shops, restaurants, and bars is not the Georgetown you'll see on this walking tour. Instead, the circuit takes you along quiet streets lined with charming houses and stately trees that remind you of the town's age and history. The original George Town, comprising 60 acres and named for the king of England, was officially established in 1751. It assumed new importance in 1790 when President George Washington, with help from his Secretary of State, Thomas Jefferson, determined that America's new capital city would be located on a site nearby, along the Potomac River. Georgetown was incorporated into the District of Columbia in 1871.

To promote social distancing, some of the stops on this tour are currently requiring timed tickets for entry. Rather than trying to coordinate multiple timed visits, my recommendation would be to pick one home or museum to enter and view the rest from the street. The walk itself is lovely even if you don't go inside.

Get your stroll off to a good start by stopping first for pastries or something more substantial at 3315 Cady's Alley NW, the charming:

1 Kafe Leopold 🍺

Through a passageway and down a flight of stairs from busy M Street NW lies a cluster of chichi shops and Leopold's Kafe (www.kafeleopolds.com; ℂ 202/965-6005), a traditional Austrian cafe that serves up classic pastries like the Sacher torte and apfelstrudel, croque madame, schnitzel and bratwurst. Also look for Viennese coffee here. Opens daily at 8am.

Return now to M St., turn left, and continue to 3350 M St. NW, where you'll find the:

2 Forrest-Marbury House

No one notices this nondescript building on the edge of Georgetown near Key Bridge. But the plaque on its pink-painted brick facade hints at reasons for giving the 1788 building a once-over. Most significant is the fact that on March 29, 1791, Revolutionary War hero Uriah Forrest hosted a dinner here for his old friend George Washington and landowners who were being asked to sell their land for the purpose of creating the federal city of Washington, District of Columbia. The meeting was a success, and America's capital was born. Forrest and his wife lived here until

Georgetown.

Federalist William Marbury bought the building in 1800. Marbury is the man whose landmark case, *Marbury v. Madison,* resulted in the recognition of the Supreme Court's power to rule on the constitutionality of laws passed by Congress and in the institutionalization of the fundamental right of judicial review. The building has served as the Ukrainian Embassy since December 31, 1992, and the interior is not open to the public.

Walk to the corner of M and 34th sts., cross M St., and walk up 34th St. 1 block to Prospect St., where you'll cross to the other side of 34th St. to view 3400 Prospect St. NW:

3 Halcyon House

Benjamin Stoddert, a Revolutionary War cavalry officer and the first secretary of the Navy, built the smaller, original version of this house in 1786 and named it for a mythical bird said to be an omen of tranquil seas. (Stoddert was also a shipping merchant.) The Georgian mansion, like its neighbor Prospect House, is situated on elevated land, the Potomac River viewable beyond. Stoddert's terraced garden—designed by Pierre Charles L'Enfant, no less—offered unobstructed views of the Potomac River nearly 230 years ago.

Sometime after 1900, an eccentric named Albert Clemons, a nephew of Mark Twain, bought the property and proceeded to transform it, creating the four-story Palladian facade and a maze of apartments and hallways between the facade and Stoddert's original structure. Clemons is said to have filled the house with religious paraphernalia, and there are numerous stories involving sightings of shadowy figures and sounds of screams and strange noises in the night. Owners of Halcyon House since Clemons' death in 1938 have included Georgetown University and noted sculptor John Dreyfuss. Today, the name "Halcyon" refers to both the house and its resident nonprofit organization "designed to seek and celebrate creativity in all forms and galvanize creative individuals aspiring to promote social good."

Strolling Around Georgetown

1 Kafe Leopold ☕
2 Forrest-Marbury House
3 Halcyon House
4 Prospect House
5 Exorcist Stairs
6 Georgetown University
7 Cox's Row
8 3307 N St.
9 St. John's Episcopal Church, Georgetown

10 Martin's Tavern ☕
11 Tudor Place
12 Dumbarton Oaks and Garden
13 Oak Hill Cemetery
14 Evermay
15 Dumbarton House
16 Mount Zion United Methodist Church
17 Old Stone House

Continue along Prospect St. to no. 3508, the site of:

4 Prospect House

This privately owned house was built in 1788 by James Maccubin Lingan, a Revolutionary War hero and wealthy tobacco merchant. He is thought to have designed the house himself. Lingan sold the house in the 1790s to a prosperous banker named John Templeman, whose guests included President John Adams and the Marquis de Lafayette. In the late 1940s, James Forrestal, the secretary of defense under President Harry Truman, bought the house and offered it to his boss as a place for entertaining visiting heads of state, because the Trumans were living in temporary digs at Blair House while the White House was being renovated. The restored Georgian-style mansion is named for its view of the Potomac River. Note the gabled roof with dormer window and the sunray fanlight over the front door; at the rear of the property (not visible from the street) is an octagonal watchtower used by 18th-century ship owners for sightings of ships returning to port.

Keep heading west on Prospect St. As you cross 36th St., take a few steps to your left to view the:

5 Exorcist Stairs

A steep staircase connects Prospect Street with Canal Street below. While the steps were constructed in 1895, it was the 1973 movie *The Exorcist* that made them famous locally. In one film scene (spoiler alert!), a priest trying to exorcise demons from a young girl falls down these stairs to his death. Running the stairs is a popular workout challenge among Georgetown University students; if you'd rather not huff and puff your way up and down you can just observe them from the top.

Continue west down Prospect St. for 1 more block. Turn right on 37th St. and follow it to its intersection with O St., where you'll see:

6 Georgetown University

Founded in 1789, Georgetown is Washington's oldest university and the nation's first Catholic university and first Jesuit-run university. Founder John Carroll, the first Catholic bishop in America and a cousin of a Maryland signer of the Declaration of Independence, opened the university to "students of every religious profession." His close friends included Benjamin Franklin and George Washington, who, along with the Marquis de Lafayette, addressed students from "Old North," the campus's oldest building. After the Civil War, students chose the school colors blue (the color of Union uniforms) and gray (the color of Confederate uniforms) to celebrate the end of the war and to honor slain students. The 104-acre campus is lovely, beginning with the stunning, spired, Romanesque-style stone building beyond the university's main entrance on 37th Street. That would be the Healy Building, named for Patrick Healy, university president from 1873 to 1882 and the first African American to head a major, predominantly white university. The irony here is that Georgetown University now is reckoning with its earlier history, when in 1838 the college president sold 272 enslaved persons to fend off financial ruin. The

University is now offering preferential consideration to descendants of these people, and a proposed plan will provide reparations and scholarships as part of a reconciliation process.

Turn right on O St. and walk 1 block to 36th St., where you'll turn right again. Continue to N St. to view Holy Trinity's parish chapel (3513 N St.). Built in 1794, the chapel is the oldest church in continuous use in the city. Continue farther on N St., strolling several blocks to nos. 3327 to 3339, collectively known as:

7 Cox's Row

Built around 1805 to 1820 and named for the owner and builder, John Cox, these five charming houses exemplify Federal-period architecture, with dormer windows, decorative facades, and handsome doorways. Besides being a master builder, Cox was also Georgetown's first elected mayor, serving 22 years. He occupied the corner house at no. 3339 and housed the Marquis de Lafayette next door at no. 3337 when he came to town in 1824.

Follow N St. to the end of the block, where you'll see:

8 3307 N St. NW

John and Jacqueline Kennedy lived in this brick town house while Kennedy served as the U.S. senator from Massachusetts. The Kennedys purchased the house shortly after the birth of their daughter Caroline. Across the street at no. 3302 is a plaque on the side wall of the brick town house inscribed by members of the press in gratitude for kindnesses received there in the days before Kennedy's presidential inauguration. Another plaque honors Stephen Bloomer Balch (1747–1833), a Revolutionary War officer who once lived here.

Turn left on 33rd St. and walk 1 block north to O St. Turn right on O St. and proceed to no. 3240, the site of:

9 St. John's Episcopal Church, Georgetown

Partially designed by Dr. William Thornton—first architect of the Capitol, who also designed the Octagon (p. 263) and Tudor Place (see below)—the church was begun in 1796 and completed in 1804. Its foundation, walls, and belltower, at least, are original. Its early congregants were the movers and shakers of their times: President Thomas Jefferson (who contributed $50 toward the building fund), Dolley Madison, Tudor Place's Thomas and Martha Peter, and Francis Scott Key. To tour the church, stop by the office, just around the corner on Potomac Street, weekdays between 9am and 4pm, or attend a service on Sunday at 9am or 11am (10am in summer). Visit www.stjohnsgeorgetown.org for more info.

Follow O St. to busy Wisconsin Ave. and turn right, walking south to reach this favorite Washington hangout. Too early for a break? Return here or to another choice restaurant later; you're never far from Wisconsin Ave. wherever you are in Georgetown.

10 Martin's Tavern 🍺

This American tavern, at 1264 Wisconsin Ave. NW (www.martinstavern.com; ☎ 202/333-7370), has been run by a string of Billy Martins since 1933. The original Billy's great-grandson runs the show today. So, it's a bar, but also very much a restaurant (bring the children—everyone does), with glass-topped white tablecloths, paneled walls, wooden booths, and an all-American menu of burgers, crab cakes, Cobb salad, and pot roast. Martin's is famous as the place where John F. Kennedy proposed to Jacqueline Bouvier in 1953—look for booth no. 3. See p. 119.

Back outside, cross Wisconsin Ave., follow it north to O St., and turn right. Walk to 31st St. and turn left; follow it until you reach the entrance to 1644 31st St. NW:

11 Tudor Place

Yet another of the architectural gems designed by the first architect of the Capitol, Dr. William Thornton, Tudor Place crowns a hill in Georgetown, set among a beautiful garden first plotted nearly 215 years ago. The 5½-acre estate belonged to Martha Washington's granddaughter, Martha Custis Peter, and her husband, Thomas Peter. Custis-Peter descendants lived here until 1983.

Free self-guided tours of the house require advance registration and reveal rooms decorated to reflect various periods of the Peter family tenancy. Exceptional architectural features include a clever floor-to-ceiling windowed wall, whose glass panes appear to curve in the domed portico (an optical illusion: It's the woodwork frame that curves, not the glass itself). On display throughout the first-floor rooms are more than 100 of George Washington's furnishings and other family items from Tudor Place's 15,000-piece collection. From a sitting-room window in this summit location, Martha Custis Peter and Anna Maria Thornton (the architect's wife) watched the Capitol burn in 1814, during the War of 1812. The Peters hosted a reception for the Marquis de Lafayette in the drawing room in 1824. Friend and family relative Robert E. Lee spent his last night in Washington in one of the upstairs bedrooms. *Tip:* Download the audio guide app from Uniguide Audio tours (uniquide.me) to listen to stories about the various rooms as you walk through.

Touring the garden is also self-guided and free; these don't require advanced tickets. A bowling green and boxwood ellipse are among the plum features. Tudor Place (www.tudorplace.org; © **202/965-0400**) is open Tuesday to Saturday to 4pm and Sunday noon to 4pm. It's closed for the entire month of January.

Continue up 31st St. half a block to R St., where you'll reach the garden entrance to Dumbarton Oaks, on 31st St. Or, if you'd prefer to visit the historic house and museum, continue around the corner to enter at 1703 32nd St. NW:

12 Dumbarton Oaks & Garden

Beyond the walls of Dumbarton Oaks is a tiered park of multiple gardens that include masses of roses, a pebble garden bordered with Mexican tiles, a wisteria-covered arbor, cherry-tree groves, overlooks, and lots of romantic, winding paths. The oldest part of Dumbarton Oaks mansion dates from 1801; since then, the house has undergone considerable change, notably at the hands of Robert and Mildred Bliss, who purchased the property in

1920. As Robert was in the Foreign Service, the Blisses lived a nomadic life, amassing collections of Byzantine and pre-Columbian art, books relating to these studies, and volumes on the history of landscape architecture. After purchasing Dumbarton Oaks, the Blisses inaugurated a grand relandscaping of the grounds and remodeling of the mansion to accommodate their collections and library, which now occupy the entire building. In 1940, the Blisses left the house, gardens, and art collections to Harvard University, Robert's alma mater. In the summer of 1944, at the height of World War II, Dumbarton Oaks served as the location for a series of diplomatic meetings that would cement the principles later incorporated into the United Nations charter. The conferences took place in the Music Room, which you should visit to admire the immense 16th-century stone chimney piece, 18th-century parquet floor, and antique Spanish, French, and Italian furniture. (See p. 192 for more info about the museum and gardens.) **Dumbarton Oaks Museum** (www.doaks.org; ℘ **202/339-6400**) is open year-round except major holidays Tuesday to Sunday 11:30am to 5:30pm, with free admission. The garden is open Tuesday to Sunday 2 to 6pm from March 15 to October 31 (admission fee $7) and Tuesday to Sunday 2 to 5pm November 1 to March 14 (free admission). Timed tickets are required for both the house and garden and can be booked online.

10

Return to R St. and take a left; follow this past Montrose Park (on your left) until you reach:

13 Oak Hill Cemetery

Founded in 1850 by banker/philanthropist/art collector William Wilson Corcoran (see Corcoran Gallery of Art; p. 263), Oak Hill is the final resting place for many of the people you've been reading about, in this chapter and in other chapters of this book. Corcoran is buried here, in a Doric temple of a mausoleum, along with the Peters of Tudor Place (see above) and the son of William Marbury of the Forrest-Marbury House (p. 265). More recently, former *Washington Post* editor Ben Bradlee was buried here (his mausoleum, which can be seen from the street, caused local drama over permits and preservation). But back to the history: Corcoran purchased the property from George Corbin Washington, a great-nephew of President Washington. The cemetery consists of 25 beautifully landscaped acres adjacent to Rock Creek Park, with winding paths shaded by ancient oaks. Look for the Gothic-style stone Renwick Chapel, designed by James Renwick, architect of the Renwick Gallery (p. 170), the Smithsonian Castle (p. 159), and New York's St. Patrick's Cathedral. The Victorian landscaping, in the Romantic tradition of its era, strives for a natural look: Iron benches have a twig motif, and many of the graves are symbolically embellished with inverted torches, draped obelisks, angels, and broken columns. Even the gatehouse is worth noting; designed in 1850 by George de la Roche, it's a beautiful brick-and-sandstone Italianate structure. Download a cemetery map (www.oakhill cemeterydc.org) or stop by the gatehouse (℘ **202/337-2835**) to pick one up. The grounds and gatehouse are open weekdays from 9am to 4:30pm;

the grounds are also open Saturday 11am to 4pm and Sunday from 1 to 4pm.

Exit Oak Hill through the main entrance and continue left on R St. until it curves and intersects 28th St. Follow this to 1623 28th St. NW, the estate of:

14 Evermay

The headquarters for a nonprofit organization, the Evermay Estate is not open to the public, unless you purchase a ticket to attend one of its concerts, which we can recommend. Otherwise, you'll have to content yourself with peering beyond the brick ramparts and thick foliage to view the impressive estate. As the plaque on the estate wall tells you, Evermay was built from 1792 to 1794 by Scottish real-estate speculator and merchant Samuel Davidson with the proceeds Davidson made from the sale of lands he owned around the city, including part of the present-day White House and Lafayette Square properties. By all accounts, Davidson was something of an eccentric misanthrope, guarding his privacy by placing menacing advertisements in the daily papers with such headlines as EVERMAY PROCLAIMS, TAKE CARE, ENTER NOT HERE, FOR PUNISHMENT IS NEAR.

Keep going downhill on 28th St., then take a left on Q St. Keep walking until you reach 2715 Q St. NW:

15 Dumbarton House

This stately redbrick mansion (www.dumbartonhouse.org; © **202/337-2288**), originally called Belle Vue, was built between 1799 and 1805. In 1915, it was moved 100 yards to its current location to accommodate the placement of nearby Dumbarton Bridge over Rock Creek. The house exemplifies Federal-period architecture, which means that its rooms are almost exactly symmetrical on all floors and centered by a large hall. Federal-period furnishings, decorative arts, and artwork fill the house; admire the dining room's late-18th-century sideboard, silver and ceramic pieces, and paintings by Charles Willson Peale. One of the original owners of Dumbarton House was Joseph Nourse, first register of the U.S. Treasury, who lived here with his family from 1805 to 1813. Dumbarton House is most famous as the place where Dolley Madison stopped for a

Visitors approaching the entrance to Dumbarton House.

cup of tea on August 24, 1814, while escaping the British, who had just set fire to the White House. It is open February to December Tuesday to Sunday from 10am to 3pm. Admission is $10, and tours are self-guided.

Exit Dumbarton House and turn right, retrace your steps along Q St., and turn left on 29th St. Follow this for about 2 blocks to 1334 29th St. NW:

16 Mount Zion United Methodist Church

This church is home to the city's oldest Black congregation, established more than 200 years ago. By 1816, African Americans, both freed slaves and the enslaved, had already been living in Georgetown for decades. But blacks were not allowed to have their own church, so they worshipped at white churches, sitting in the balcony, apart from the white worshippers. In 1816, a man named Shadrack Nugent led 125 fellow black congregants to split from the nearby Montgomery Street Church (now Dumbarton United Methodist Church) and form their own congregation. The dissidents built a church, known as the "Little Ark," at 27th and P streets, and worshipped there until a fire destroyed the meeting house in 1880. (The congregation was all black, but the times still required a white man to be their pastor!) Meanwhile, a new and larger church was already under construction, on land purchased from a freed slave and prominent businessman named Alfred Pope, whose property adjoined the churches on 29th Street. The Mount Zion United Methodist Church held its first service in 1880, in the partially completed lecture hall, and dedicated the finished redbrick edifice you see today in 1884. The church proper actually lies on the second floor, whose high tin ceiling, beautiful stained-glass windows (called "comfort" windows for the sense of tranquility their pastel tints are said to imbue), and hand-carved pews are original features. A number of families in this 200-person congregation are descendants of the church's first founders, although only one or two congregants actually live in the neighborhood now. Mount Zion United Methodist Church welcomes all who are interested to attend its Sunday services, but otherwise is not open to the general public (www.mtzionumcdc.org; ✆ **202/234-0148**).

From the front of the church, go right on 29th St. and continue downhill until you reach M St. Go right and follow the sidewalk to your final destination at 3051 M St. NW:

17 Old Stone House

Located on one of the busiest streets in Washington, the unobtrusive Old Stone House offers a quiet look at life in early America, starting in 1766, when the Layman family built this home. Originally, the structure was simply one room made of thick stone walls, oak ceiling beams, and packed dirt floors. In 1800, a man named John Suter bought the building and used it as his clock shop. The grandfather clock you see on the second floor is the only original piece remaining in the house. Acquired by the National Park Service in the 1950s, the Old Stone House today shows small rooms furnished as they would have been in the late 18th century, during the period when Georgetown was a significant tobacco and shipping port. Park rangers provide information and sometimes demonstrate

Georgetown Waterfront Park Harbour.

cooking in an open hearth, spinning, and making pomander balls. Adjacent to and behind the house is a terraced lawn and 18th-century English garden, a spot long frequented by Georgetown shop and office workers seeking a respite. Old Stone House (www.nps.gov/places/old-stone-house.htm; ☏ **202/426-6851**) is open daily 11am to 7pm; the garden is open daily dawn to dusk.

Now spend some time exploring M St. You're in the middle of Georgetown, surrounded by restaurants, shops, and bars. Go crazy! See chapters 5, 7, and 8 for recommendations.

WALKING TOUR 3: DUPONT CIRCLE/EMBASSY ROW

START:	**Dupont Circle (Metro to Dupont Circle).**
FINISH:	**Vice President's Residence/U.S. Naval Observatory (take the N2, N4, N6 buses back to either Dupont Circle or Farragut North).**
TIME:	**2 hours (not including stops). The distance is about 2 miles.**
BEST TIME:	**Any day is fine unless you want to tour the Brewmaster's Castle and/ or Anderson House, in which case you should see the descriptions for their public tour days and times, and plan accordingly.**
WORST TIME:	**Nighttime, since you won't be able to see the details on the houses.**

This is a rather lengthy walk. It's worthwhile, I think, especially because you'll see nearly the whole world—or at least its embassies—on this route. (To see more, look for the national flags of other embassies located on side streets a few steps to the left or right.)

If you feel yourself tiring, you can catch the N6 Metrobus at a number of stops along this route and it will take you back to Dupont Circle. Some of the walk is uphill, which is why I'm suggesting this precaution. You can do the walk in reverse, taking the bus to your starting point as well, though the more interesting Gilded Age sites are closer to Dupont Circle, and I want you to see those while you're still fresh.

Dupont Circle/Embassy Row

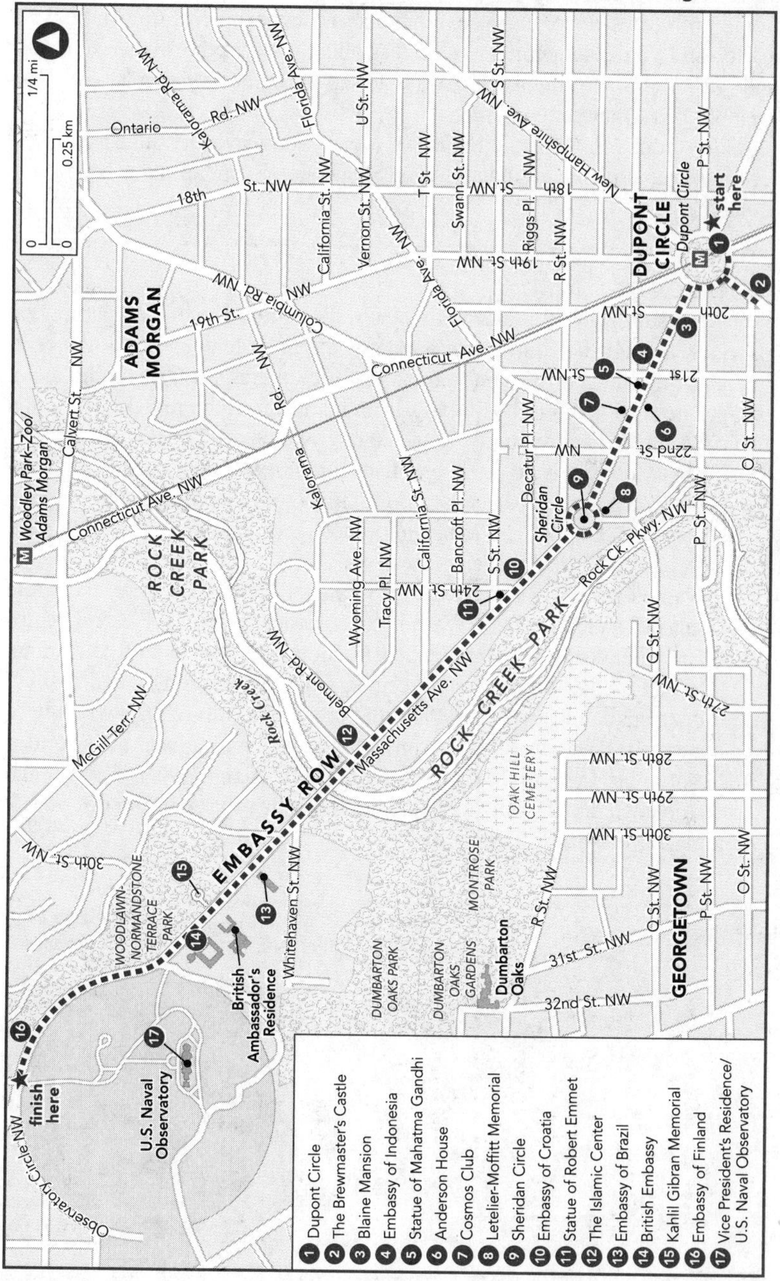

1 Dupont Circle
2 The Brewmaster's Castle
3 Blaine Mansion
4 Embassy of Indonesia
5 Statue of Mahatma Gandhi
6 Anderson House
7 Cosmos Club
8 Letelier-Moffitt Memorial
9 Sheridan Circle
10 Embassy of Croatia
11 Statue of Robert Emmet
12 The Islamic Center
13 Embassy of Brazil
14 British Embassy
15 Kahlil Gibran Memorial
16 Embassy of Finland
17 Vice President's Residence/ U.S. Naval Observatory
start here
finish here
DUPONT CIRCLE
ADAMS MORGAN
ROCK CREEK PARK
EMBASSY ROW
GEORGETOWN
U.S. Naval Observatory
British Ambassador's Residence
Dumbarton Oaks
DUMBARTON OAKS PARK
DUMBARTON OAKS GARDENS
MONTROSE PARK
OAK HILL CEMETERY
WOODLAWN-NORMANDSTONE TERRACE PARK
Sheridan Circle
Woodley Park–Zoo/ Adams Morgan
Massachusetts Ave. NW
Connecticut Ave. NW
Rock Ck. Pkwy. NW
Observatory Circle NW
New Hampshire Ave. NW
Florida Ave. NW
Columbia Rd. NW
Kalorama Rd. NW
Belmont Rd. NW
Wyoming Ave. NW
Calvert St. NW
McGill Terr. NW
Whitehaven St. NW
0.25 km
1/4 mi

Embassies are not normally open to visitors. But if you're here in May, you'll want to know about the annual embassy open-house events (p. 25). Some embassies do organize exhibitions and concerts featuring homeland artists, and you'll sometimes see notices about them in the *Washington Post* and *Washington City Paper*. For ways to tap into embassy events, see "The Best of D.C.'s International Scene" box, p. 234.

As for food, you won't find much of it once you leave Dupont Circle. Better to pick up a picnic at **Teaism** (p. 115) and stop in one of the garden areas along the way.

1 Dupont Circle

We'll start right in the center of the traffic circle so you can get a good look around. Dupont Circle is one of the most famous place names in D.C., at one and the same time a historic district, a traffic circle, and a progressive neighborhood that's been home, since the mid-1970s, to the city's LGBTQ community. In fact, every year on the Tuesday before Halloween, thousands of Washingtonians turn out to watch dozens of outrageously dressed drag queens sprint in high heels down 17th Street in the heart of the Dupont Circle neighborhood, participating in the High Heel Race, an event that's taken place since 1986.

Named for Civil War Naval hero Samuel Francis Du Pont, the circle is placed exactly where Washington's famed architect Pierre Charles L'Enfant envisioned it, though construction didn't begin until 1871, long after L'Enfant's death. For its center, Congress commissioned a small bronze statue of the Admiral, but the proud Du Pont family would have none of it. Without asking permission, they commissioned the two men behind the Lincoln Memorial—sculptor Daniel Chester French and architect Henry Bacon—to create the fountain you see in front of you. It replaced the bronze statue in 1921; on its shaft are allegorical figures

Daniel Chester French's marble fountain in the center of Dupont Circle.

representing the elements a sea captain needs to navigate and propel the boat forward. See if you can figure out which is "the stars," which is "the sea," and which is "the wind."

Cross Massachusetts Ave. to New Hampshire Ave. until you come to Sunderland Place, and stop at 1307 New Hampshire Ave:

2 The Brewmaster's Castle (the Christian Heurich House Museum)

This is the house beer built. Christian Heurich was a highly successful brewer who, in the first half of the 20th century, was Washington, D.C.'s largest landowner and employer, after the federal government. He loved his work so much that he never retired, continuing to manage his brewery until his death at the age of 102 in 1945. That wasn't just a work ethic—the man had murals celebrating the joys of beer in his breakfast room and used as the slogan for his company, "Beer recommended for family use by Physicians in General." Yup, those were the days. If you can **tour** (www.heurichhouse.org; ⓒ **202/429-1894**) it, do so—the house is notable not just for the colorful history of its owner and the people who worked here, but also for its importance architecturally. Built between 1892 and 1894, it is likely the first domestic structure framed with steel and poured concrete, an effort to make it fireproof. (The salamander symbol, at the top of the tower, was used as a superstitious shield against fire.) Many consider this Romanesque-style, 31-room structure to be one of the most intact late-Victorian structures in the country. But my favorite part is the garden; there's a bar here where you can sample local D.C. beers (Thurs–Fri 5–8pm; Sat 2–6pm).

Walk toward 20th St., turn right and continue north 2 blocks back to Massachusetts Ave. Turn left and on the corner you'll find 2000 Massachusetts Ave., which is:

3 Blaine Mansion

The last standing mansion from the early days of Dupont Circle, this imposing brick and terra-cotta structure retains the name of its first owner: James G. Blaine. Had it not been for the Mugwumps, he might well have become president instead of Grover Cleveland. As it was, charges of corruption involving illicit dealings with the railroads, ahem, derailed his campaign, and the Republican-leaning anti-corruption Mugwumps switched parties to support Cleveland, a Democrat. This, despite the fact that Blaine had a longer and more distinguished career than most, having served as secretary of state twice, congressman and senator from Maine, and speaker of the House. The vertical sweep of the house surely impresses as much as the man, though to be honest, he barely lived here. Once the home was built, he decided it would be too costly to maintain and he leased it, first to Levi Leiter (an early co-owner of Marshall Field) and then to George Westinghouse. Yes, *that* Westinghouse. The latter bought it in 1901 and lived here until his death in 1914. The building is now a mix of residential and commercial space.

Continue in the same direction on Massachusetts Ave. to our first embassy at 2020 Massachusetts Ave.:

4 Embassy of Indonesia

The ornate structure occupied today by the Embassy of Indonesia is said to have cost $835,000 when it was built by Thomas Walsh for his daughter Evalyn in 1903—the city's most expensive house at the time. Sadly, by the time the house was purchased by the Indonesians in 1951, the family fortune was so depleted that they let it go for a mere $350,000. A reminder that housing bubbles have been around for quite some time.

The man who commissioned its construction, Thomas Walsh, came to the United States from Ireland in 1869 at the age of 19. He headed west, and in 1876 struck it rich not once but twice, finding what is widely thought to be one of the richest veins of gold in the world. Suddenly a modern-day Midas, he moved to Washington, figuring a grand 60-room mansion was the way to make a splash in society. And remembering his roots, he's said to have embedded a nugget of gold ore in the porch. You'll notice that this neo-Baroque mansion is unusually curvaceous. That's because it's meant to evoke the look of an ocean liner. A grand staircase in the home itself is a direct copy of one on a White Star ocean liner.

The fortune depleter, daughter Evalyn Walsh McLean, was notable for the tragic turn her life took. Despite the jaunty title of her autobiography, *Father Struck It Rich!,* not much else went right in her life. Her son was killed at the age of 9 in a car crash, and her daughter overdosed as a young woman. Husband Edward Beale McLean, an heir to the *Post* fortune, turned out to be an alcoholic, and together they burned through some $100 million. A large chunk of it went to the purchase of the famed Hope Diamond. Those who believe the diamond is cursed claim that McLean's misfortunes started with that purchase. She died nearly penniless at the age of 58. The diamond is now on display at the Smithsonian's Natural History Museum (p. 156). The ornate white statue poised outside the embassy depicts Saraswati, the Hindu goddess of learning and wisdom. Since Indonesia is home to the world's largest Muslim population, the display of a Hindu figure is intended to express Indonesia's respect for religious freedom.

Keep walking in the same direction to a small triangular park on the opposite side of Massachusetts Ave., where you'll find the:

5 Statue of Mahatma Gandhi

Striding purposefully, the man who led India to freedom from British rule in 1947 seems to be headed (aptly) for the **Embassy of India** (2107 Massachusetts Ave.), just across the adjacent side street. His walking stick, dress, and age in the sculpture suggest that this is a portrait of him on the famed protest march when he and a number of followers walked some 200 miles to the Arabian Sea to collect salt (and evade the British tax on that condiment). A turning point in the nonviolent fight for Indian freedom, it's an apt subject for this striking portrait.

From the tip of the park where Massachusetts Ave. and Q St. intersect, look across Mass Ave. to 2118 Massachusetts Ave., the:

6 Anderson House

Larz Anderson, an American diplomat, and his wife, Isabel Weld Perkins, author and Red Cross volunteer, took advantage of their immense Boston wealth and built not just a home but a palace. Their intent? To create a space large enough to serve as a headquarters for the Society of the Cincinnati, of which Larz was a member (and to which they bequeathed the home). The membership of the society, founded in 1783, is composed of male descendants of officers in George Washington's Continental Army.

The building itself—sporting a cavernous two-story ballroom, a dining room seating 50, grand staircase, massive wall murals, acres of marble, and 23-karat gold trim—is palatial.

Head down the street to 2121 Massachusetts Ave., the:

7 Cosmos Club

A prestigious private social club, Cosmos Club was founded in 1878 as a gathering place for scientists and public-policy intellectuals. The National Geographic Society spun off from the Cosmos 10 years later. The Cosmos Club's first meeting was held in the home of John Wesley Powell, the soldier and explorer who first navigated the Colorado River through the Grand Canyon in a dory. Since then, three presidents, two vice presidents, a dozen Supreme Court justices, 36 Nobel Prize winners, 61 Pulitzer Prize winners, and 55 recipients of the Presidential Medal of Freedom have numbered among its ranks. But none of them were women until 1988, when the Washington, D.C., Human Rights Office ruled that the club's men-only policy was discriminatory and illegal and the club admitted its first women members—a group of 18 that included the then-U.S. secretary of labor, a chief judge of the U.S. Court of Appeals, and several scientists and economists.

The club is the latest occupant of a French-inspired chateau built in 1901 with the railroad wealth of Richard and Mary Scott Townsend. His fortune came from the Erie Line; hers from the Pennsylvania Railroad (no joke). They hired the famed New York architectural firm of Carrère and Hastings, which created the New York Public Library, to build a chateau designed to resemble the Petit Trianon chateau—a royal hideaway at Versailles. Somewhat superstitious, the couple had the structure built around an older one. Apparently, a gypsy had once predicted that Mrs. Townsend would die "under a new roof." Despite these precautions, Mrs. Townsend did eventually pass away. Check to see if docent-led tours of the club are offered while you're here.

Continue on Massachusetts Ave. toward Sheridan Sq., before entering the circle, walk around it to the left passing the **Embassy of Ireland** (2234 Massachusetts Ave. NW). Look down on the sidewalk to see the small round:

8 Letelier/Moffitt Memorial

On September 21, 1976, Orlando Letelier, the former foreign minister of ousted Chilean President Salvador Allende, offered his colleague Ronni

10

SELF-GUIDED WALKING TOURS | Dupont Circle/Embassy Row

279

Memorial bas-relief portraits of Orlando Letelier and Ronni K. Moffitt.

Karpen Moffitt and her husband, Michael, a ride home. A car bomb killed Letelier and Ronni Moffitt; Michael Moffitt survived. This small cylindrical monument honors the memory of Letelier and Moffitt. Thousands showed up later that week for a hastily organized protest funeral march. For years, rumors circulated that the American government was also in some way involved. But in 2016, the U.S. government released CIA documents that clearly laid the blame on Chilean dictator General Augusto Pinochet, the man who had ousted Allende in a military coup. Pinochet had sent Chilean secret police agents to the U.S. capital to carry out this terrorist act.

Turn away from the Memorial and look at:

9 Sheridan Circle

The Civil War officer mounted on his muscular horse is General Philip H. Sheridan, commander of the Union cavalry and the Army of the Shenandoah. His horse Rienzi, who carried him through 85 battles and skirmishes, became almost as famous during the war as "the steed that saved the day."

Sculpted by Gutzon Borglum, who carved the presidential faces on South Dakota's Mount Rushmore, the statue depicts Sheridan rallying his men at the Battle of Cedar Creek in northern Virginia on October 19, 1864. Sheridan was 15 miles north in the town of Winchester when a Confederate force under General Jubal A. Early surprised and drove back his army. Racing to the battle site on stout-hearted Rienzi, Sheridan led his men in a victorious counterattack.

Sheridan's wife is said to have chosen the site for the statue, which is flanked by two hidden pools. Sheridan's son, Second Lieutenant Philip H. Sheridan, Jr., served as a model for the statue. He was present at the unveiling in 1908, as was President Theodore Roosevelt. I suggest crossing (carefully) into the circle to get a close-up look.

Carefully cross the Circle to Massachusetts Ave. (or go around; traffic can be busy here) and continue going northwest to 2343 Massachusetts Ave., the:

10 Embassy of Croatia

Outside the building the muscular figure of St. Jerome the Priest (A.D. 341–420) sits hunched over a book, his head in his hand. Jerome, the pedestal of the statue informs us, was "the greatest Doctor of the Church." This is a reference to his work in translating the Bible from Hebrew into Latin, a version called the Vulgate because it was in the language of the common people of the day. Historically, it is considered the most important vernacular edition of the Bible. At times in his younger years, Jerome's religious faith declined; he became involved in numerous theological disputes, and he spent several years in the desert leading an ascetical life while fighting temptations. I get the feeling this glum statue is commemorating those troubled times. The statue initially sat on the grounds of the Franciscan Abbey near Catholic University; it was moved here when the nation of Croatia was created at the breakup of Yugoslavia.

Continue walking to the 2400 block of Massachusetts Ave. where, in a triangular park, you'll see the:

11 Statue of Robert Emmet

Within a landscaped grove of Irish yew trees, the Irish revolutionary stands in a pose that he reportedly struck in Dublin in 1803 when a British court sentenced him to death by hanging. He appears to be gazing toward the

General Philip Sheridan Memorial statue.

Embassy of Ireland 2 blocks away. Born in 1778, Emmet led a failed uprising in Dublin on July 23, 1803. The statue was presented to the Smithsonian Institution in 1917 as a gift to the American public from a group of American citizens of Irish ancestry. It was moved to its present site in 1966, marking the 50th anniversary of the Easter Uprising. In 2016, in honor of the centenary of the uprising, the Irish ambassador rededicated the statue, and the National Park Service refurbished the little park to make the bronze statue more visible.

Note the numerous embassies en route to the next stop, including the **Embassy of Japan** (2520 Massachusetts Ave.), set back behind a cobblestone courtyard. The 1932 Georgian Revival structure suggests the Far East with a subtle "rising sun" above the balcony over the door.

On the right is the **Embassy of Turkey** (2525 Massachusetts Ave.). The statue in front is of Mustafa Kemal Ataturk, the founder of modern Turkey.

Just before the bridge, head to 2551 Massachusetts Ave.:

12 The Islamic Center

The 160-foot-tall white limestone minaret, soaring above Embassy Row, makes the Islamic Center impossible to miss. From it, a loudspeaker intones the call to prayer five times daily. Built in 1949, the center does not line up directly with the street but faces Mecca. On Friday afternoons, throngs of the faithful pour into the mosque for prayer services, many of them embassy employees attired in their native dress. At times, prayer rugs are spread in the courtyard or even on the sidewalk outside the iron fence. This is when Embassy Row takes on its most dramatic multicultural look.

Try to pay a visit inside if you can (daily 10am–5pm), but be sure to remove your shoes before entering the mosque itself; leave them in one of the slots provided on the entrance wall. Men should dress neatly; no shorts. Women are not allowed to wear sleeveless clothes or short dresses and must cover their hair. The interior is filled with colorful Arabic art; Persian rugs blanket the floor, overlapping one another; 7,000 blue tiles cover the lower walls in mosaic patterns; and eight ornate pillars soar overhead, ringing a huge copper chandelier. The carved pulpit is inlaid with ivory, and stained-glass windows add more color.

Walk to the opposite side of Massachusetts Ave., cross the bridge and look down: 75 ft. below is Rock Creek Pkwy. as well as the 1,700-acre Rock Creek Park (p. 199). Walk on and take the time to look at the embassies you'll be passing until you get to 3006 Massachusetts Ave., the:

13 Embassy of Brazil

This stately, palacelike building, next door to the black, boxlike circa-1971 Brazilian Chancery, is the ambassador's residence. Derived from an Italian Renaissance palazzo, the residence was designed in 1908 by John Russell Pope, a leader of the city's early-20th-century neoclassicist movement. The Jefferson Memorial, the West Building of the National Gallery of Art, and National Archives are among Pope's other local works.

embassy row: **THE LOWDOWN**

Today, there are more than 175 foreign embassies, chanceries, or ambassadorial residences in Washington, D.C., and the majority of them are located on or near the 2-mile stretch of Massachusetts Avenue between Dupont Circle and Wisconsin Avenue NW. As a result, it's been dubbed Embassy Row.

A word on those distinctions: An embassy is the official office or residence of the ambassador. Some ambassadors live and work in the embassy; others maintain separate residences, commuting to their job like the rest of us. A *chancery* is the embassy's office; this is where you might apply for a visitor's visa. It could be located within the embassy or not. Some countries also provide separate offices for special missions, such as the military attaché's office and for cultural centers.

Continue your stroll to 3100 Massachusetts Ave., the:

14 British Embassy

Out in front and instantly recognizable in a familiar pose, **Sir Winston Churchill** stands in bronze. One foot rests on embassy property, thus British soil; the other is planted on American soil. Anglo-American unity is the symbolism, but the placement also reflects Churchill's heritage as the child of a British father and an American mother. His right hand is raised in the iconic familiar V for Victory sign he displayed in World War II. His other hand often sports a small bouquet of fresh flowers, left by admirers. The English-Speaking Union of the United States commissioned the statue, which was erected in 1965. The statue stands on a granite plinth; beneath it are blended soils from Blenheim Palace, his birthplace; the rose garden at Chartwell, his home; and his mother's home in Brooklyn, NY. Turn your back on Churchill for a moment and look directly across the street to see a smiling Nelson Mandela gazing back at you, his arm raised in a clenched fist. Churchill and Mandela appear to be communicating. Mandela stands in front of the South African Embassy, which erected this statue in 2013.

The U-shaped, redbrick structure rising behind the World War II prime minister is the main chancery, built in 1930. Sir Edwin Lutyens, one of Great Britain's leading architects of the day, designed both it and the ambassador's residence, located out of sight behind the chancery. The American Institute of Architects describes the pair as a "triumph," noting that Lutyens rejected the prevailing passion for neoclassical structures and instead created a colonial American design. Others suggest it looks like an 18th-century English country house. Whatever, it makes an impressive show. Too bad the concrete box on the right, an office building dedicated by Queen Elizabeth II in 1957, failed to match the architectural standard Lutyens set. The round glass structure, another unfortunately bland modern addition, is for conferences.

Walk a little way up Massachusetts Ave. to the stoplight in order to cross the street and double back a short ways on Mass Ave. to the:

15 Kahlil Gibran Memorial

An elaborate 2-acre garden, eight-sided star fountain, circular walkway, shaded benches, and bronze bust celebrate the life and achievements of the Lebanese-American poet and philosopher. Dedicated on May 24, 1991, it is a gift "to the people of the United States" from the Kahlil Gibran Centennial Foundation. Born in 1883 in a village near the Biblical Cedars of Lebanon, Gibran arrived in Boston as a child. Building a successful career as an artist and author, he published widely quoted books in English and Arabic. He died in New York City in 1931. Excerpts from his writings are etched into the memorial's circular wall, among them: YOU AND I ARE CHILDREN OF ONE FAITH; FINGERS OF THE LOVING HAND OF ONE SUPREME BEING; A HAND EXTENDED TO ALL. If you need to rest your feet, this lovely garden is the perfect place to do so.

Continue walking up Massachusetts Ave. On the left side of the street, you'll start to see peeks of our final stop, the U.S. Naval Observatory, but first we're heading to 3301 Massachusetts Ave., the dramatic:

16 Embassy of Finland

An abstract metal-and-glass front forms a green wall of climbing plants on a bronze, gridlike trellis. Within, huge windows in the rear look out onto a thickly forested slope, as if—to quote architectural historian William Morgan—"The Finns have brought a bit of the woods to Washington." Completed in 1994, the embassy was designed to display the life and culture of Finland. The embassy is open for tours one afternoon a month at 2pm, and you must register in advance.

From the Finnish Embassy, look across the street to the green slope behind the tall iron fence. That white Victorian-style house partially visible atop the hill is the:

17 Vice President's Residence/U.S. Naval Observatory

Number One Observatory Circle is the official residence of the U.S. vice president. The wooded estate surrounding the residence is the site of the U.S. Naval Observatory; the large white dome holding its 12-inch refracting

---

Embassies as "Open Windows"

An embassy in Washington, D.C., is different from embassies in most other capitals, where people visit them only if they have to; that is, to get a visa or to conduct official business. In Washington, D.C., embassies are expected to be much more. They need to be able to open windows on the life and culture of the countries they represent, not only for the select few, but for all Washingtonians and visitors to the capital who want to know. Many do, because Americans are curious by nature.
　　　—Jukka Valtasaari, Finnish ambassador, 1988–1996 and 2001–2005

telescope can usually be seen on the right (except in summer, when leaves may block the view). Built in 1893, the veep's house initially was assigned to the observatory's superintendent. But in 1923 the chief of naval operations took a liking to it, booted out the superintendent, and made the house his home. In 1974, Congress evicted the Navy and transformed it into the vice president's residence.

Up to that time, vice presidents occupied their own homes, as Supreme Court judges, Cabinet members, and congressional representatives and senators still do. But providing full security apparatus for the private homes of each new vice president

The telescope at the U.S. Naval Observatory.

became expensive. Nelson Rockefeller, veep in the Ford administration, was the first potential resident, but he used the house only for entertaining. So, Vice President Walter Mondale became its first official occupant, leading the way for succeeding vice presidents. If you see a big tent on the front lawn, it usually means the vice president is hosting a gala reception.

The observatory moved from Foggy Bottom to its present location in 1910. At the time, the hilltop site was rural countryside. One of the oldest scientific agencies in the country, the U.S. Naval Observatory was established in 1830. Its primary mission was to oversee the Navy's chronometers, charts, and other navigational equipment. Today it remains the preeminent authority on precise time. Scientists take observations of the sun, moon, planets, and selected stars, determine the precise time, and publish astronomical data needed for accurate navigation.

PLANNING YOUR TRIP

by Jess Moss

Washington is one of the best equipped cities in the country for visitors; it's easy to get here, get around, and have a memorable experience. But now more than ever, planning is essential to make sure you're prepared for the city's ever-evolving landscape. From shifting pandemic restrictions, to weather events, demonstrations and security considerations that may impact your visit, it's important to be equipped for whatever is going on while you're here. This chapter provides a variety of planning tools, including information on getting to D.C., tips on transportation within the city, and additional on-the-ground resources.

GETTING THERE

By Plane

Three airports serve the Washington, D.C., area. The following information should help you determine which airport is your best bet.

Ronald Reagan Washington National Airport (DCA; www. flyreagan.com; © **703/417-8000**). lies 4 miles south of D.C., across the Potomac River in Virginia, about a 10-minute trip by car in non-rush-hour traffic, and 15 to 20 minutes by Metro anytime. National's eight airlines fly nonstop to/from more than 95 destinations, nearly all domestic. Its proximity to the District and its direct access to the Metro rail system are reasons why you might want to fly into National. For Metro information, go online at **www.wmata.com**.

Washington Dulles International Airport (IAD; www.flydulles. com; © **703/572-2700**) is 26 miles outside the capital, in Chantilly, Virginia, a 35- to 45-minute ride to downtown in non-rush-hour traffic (but get ready for traffic). Of the three airports, Dulles handles more nonstop international flights (52), with about 35 airlines flying nonstop to more than 150 destinations. The airport is not as convenient to the heart of Washington as National, but it's more convenient than BWI, thanks to an uncongested airport access road that travels half the distance toward Washington.

The number one question on many travelers' minds these days is how the pandemic will impact their trip. As the situation with the virus continues to evolve, so do local guidelines.

Your best bet is to monitor the latest info before your trip. The city maintains a robust website with Covid-19 information: coronavirus.dc.gov. You'll find info on testing centers, current restrictions, and local vaccination and case data. Destination DC, Washington's tourism board, has a good resource for visitors at https://washington.org/dc-information/coronavirus-travel-update-washington-dc.

While specifics are likely to change (and change again) between this writing and when you pick up this guide, there are a few general tips to keep in mind: **Travel restrictions:** At the height of the pandemic in 2020, D.C. introduced quarantine requirements for travelers from states with high caseloads outside the local Maryland and Virginia area. At this writing, restrictions are limited to unvaccinated and all international visitors, who must have a negative test before arrival.

Local restrictions: D.C. is a very pro-mask city; even when the mayor isn't requiring masks indoors, many buildings and businesses ask customers to mask up. All federal buildings, including National Park sites, require masks when indoors. There's a growing trend toward vaccine passports in D.C., where bars, restaurants, gyms and more are requiring proof of vaccination for entry. At this time there are no capacity caps or limits on indoor dining. Again, this is all subject to change so check the above sites.

What's open: By press time, many restaurants, bars, and shops had reopened or were in the process of reopening, some with limited operating days or shorter hours. Same goes with most Smithsonian and National Park sites, though some are requiring advance tickets in order to maintain distancing. Some museums, historic sites, and government buildings (including the White House and the Capitol) have not announced a timeline for reopening or resumption of tours. Most attractions are keeping their websites up to date, even if they're currently closed, so always check before you make plans.

Last but not least, **Baltimore–Washington International Thurgood Marshall Airport (BWI;** www.bwiairport.com; ✆ **410/859-7111**) is located about 45 minutes from downtown, a few miles outside of Baltimore. One factor especially has always recommended BWI to travelers: the major presence of **Southwest Airlines** and **Spirit Airlines.** Both airlines can often offer real bargains. (Southwest also serves Dulles and National airports, but in a much smaller capacity.) BWI offers the greatest number of daily nonstop flights, 350, its 16 airlines flying to 91 domestic destinations and international destinations.

GETTING INTO TOWN FROM THE AIRPORT

All three airports could really use better signage, especially since their ground transportation desks always seem to be quite a distance from the gate at which you arrive. Keep trudging, and follow baggage claim signs, because ground transportation operations are always situated near baggage carousels.

TAXI & CAR SHARE SERVICE For a trip to downtown D.C., you can expect a taxi to cost at least $15 to $20 for the 10- to 20-minute ride from National Airport, $70 to $75 for the 35- to 45-minute ride from Dulles Airport, and about $85 for the 45-minute ride from BWI. Expect taxis to add a $3 airport pickup charge to your fee. All taxis accept cash or credit card.

Uber and Lyft are available from all three airports. National has a few pickup spots, depending on what terminal you're in. If you're arriving in tiny Terminal A, the car will meet you at the outer curb, For Terminal B and C, you'll have to select a pickup from Baggage Claim (first level) or Departures (third level). At Dulles, a new dedicated ride share curb is located outside baggage claim. Your driver will pick you up in a designated numbered zone, which is sent to you via the app. At BWI, ride shares pick up passengers on the upper Departures level. Pricing varies greatly based on demand, but you can expect to pay upwards of $20 from National, $35 from Dulles, and $60 from BWI to downtown D.C.

Public Transportation Options by Airport
FROM RONALD REAGAN WASHINGTON NATIONAL AIRPORT

If you are not too encumbered with luggage, you should take **Metrorail** into the city. Metro's Yellow and Blue Lines stop at the airport and connect via an enclosed walkway to level two, the concourse level of the main terminal, adjacent to terminals B and C. If yours is one of the airlines that still uses the smaller terminal A (Southwest, Air Canada, Frontier), you'll have a longer walk to reach the Metro. Signs pointing the way can be confusing, so ask an airport employee if you're headed in the right direction. **Metrobuses** also serve the area, should you be going somewhere off the Metro route. But Metrorail is fastest, a 15- to 20-minute non-rush-hour ride to downtown. If you haven't purchased a SmarTrip fare card online in advance (see box on SmarTrip cards, p. 293), you can do so at the Metro station. The base fare is $2 and goes up from there depending on when (fares increase during rush hours) and where you're going.

If you're renting a car from an on-site **car rental agency** (most are on-site in Terminal A), follow signs toward Terminal Parking Garage A, approximately 10 minutes from Terminals A & B and 15 minutes from Terminal C. You can also take the complimentary airport shuttle marked "Parking/Rental Car," which now stops at door 4 on the Ticketing Level/3rd Floor because of construction. Get off at the Terminal Garage A/Rental Car stop. If you've rented from an off-premises agency (such as Advantage), you'll want to take that same shuttle bus.

To get downtown by car, follow the signs out of the airport for the George Washington Parkway, headed north toward Washington. Stay on the parkway until you see signs for I-395 N. to Washington. Take the I-395 N. exit, which takes you across the 14th Street Bridge. Stay in the left lane crossing the bridge and follow the signs for Rte. 1, which will put you on 14th Street NW. (You'll see the Washington Monument off to your left.) Ask your hotel for directions from 14th Street and Constitution Avenue NW. Or take the more scenic route, always staying to the left on the GW Parkway as you follow the signs for Memorial Bridge. You'll be driving alongside the Potomac River, with the Capitol and memorials in view across the river; then, as you cross over Memorial Bridge, you're greeted by the Lincoln Memorial. Stay left coming over the bridge, swoop around to the left of the Memorial, take a left on 23rd Street NW, a right on Constitution Avenue, and then, if you want to be in the heart of downtown, left again on 15th Street NW.

FROM WASHINGTON DULLES INTERNATIONAL AIRPORT A

direct Metrorail trains connection with Dulles Airport is in the works, but until it's ready you must first catch the **Washington Flyer Silver Line Express Bus** (www.flydulles.com/iad/silver-line-express-bus-metrorail-station; ✆ **888/927-4359**) to reach the closest Metro station, the Silver Line's Wiehle Ave./Reston East depot. Find the counter at Arrivals Door no. 4 in the main terminal or, if you're in the baggage claim area, go up the ramp at the sign for Door no. 4 to purchase the $5 ticket for the bus. Buses to the Wiehle Ave./Reston East Metro station run daily, every 15 to 20 minutes; the trip takes about 15 minutes. Once you arrive at the Metro station, you can purchase a Metro SmarTrip fare card to board a Silver Line train bound for Largo Town Center, which heads into D.C.

It may be more convenient to take the **Metrobus** (no. 5A) that runs between Dulles (buses depart from curb 2E, outside the ground transportation area) and the L'Enfant Plaza Metro station, located across from the National Mall and the Smithsonian museums. The bus departs every 30 to 40 minutes weekdays, hourly on weekends. It costs $7.50 (you must use a SmarTrip card—see box, p. 293—or have exact change) and takes 45 minutes to an hour.

If you're renting a car at Dulles, head down the ramp near the baggage-claim area and walk outside through door 2 or 4 to curb 2C or 2D to wait for your rental car's shuttle bus. The buses come every 5 minutes or so en route to nearby rental lots. Almost all the major companies are represented.

To reach downtown Washington from Dulles by car, exit the airport and stay on the Dulles Access Road, keeping left as the road eventually leads right into I-66 E. Follow I-66 E., which takes you across the Theodore Roosevelt Memorial Bridge; be sure to stay in the center lane as you cross the bridge, and this will put you on Constitution Avenue (Rte. 29). Ask your hotel for directions from this point.

FROM BALTIMORE–WASHINGTON INTERNATIONAL AIRPORT

The easiest way to get downtown from BWI Airport is by train. You also have the choice of taking either an **Amtrak** (www.amtrak.com; ✆ **800/872-7245**) or the Penn line of the **Maryland Rural Commuter (MARC)** train (http://mta.maryland.gov/marc-train; ✆ **866/743-3682**) into the city. Both trains travel between the BWI Railway Station and Washington's Union Station, about a 30- to 45-minute ride. Both Amtrak (starting at $13 per person, one-way, depending on time and train type) and MARC ($7 per person, one-way) services run daily. A courtesy shuttle runs every 10 minutes or so (every 25 min. 1–5am) between the airport and the train station; stop at the desk near the baggage-claim area to check for the next departure time of both the shuttle bus and the train. Trains depart about once per hour.

BWI operates a large off-site **car rental facility.** From the ground transportation area, board a shuttle bus to the lot.

Here's how you reach Washington: Look for signs for I-195 and follow the highway west until you see signs for Washington and the Baltimore–Washington Parkway (I-295); head south on I-295. Get off when you see the signs for Rte. 50/New York Avenue, which leads into the District, via New York Avenue NE. Your hotel can provide specific directions from there.

By Car

More than one-third of visitors to Washington arrive by plane, and if that's you, don't consider renting a car. The traffic in the city and throughout the region is abysmal, parking spaces are hard to find, garage and lot and metered street parking charges are exorbitant, and hotel overnight rates are even worse. Furthermore, Washington is amazingly easy to traverse on foot, and our public transportation and taxi systems are accessible and comprehensive.

But if you are like most visitors, you're planning on driving here. No matter which road you take, there's a good chance you will have to navigate some portion of the **Capital Beltway** (I-495 and I-95) to gain entry to D.C. The Beltway girds the city, its approximately 64-mile route passing through Maryland and Virginia, with some 50 interchanges or exits leading off from it. The Beltway is nearly always congested, but especially during weekday morning and evening rush hours (roughly 5:30–9:30am and 3–7pm). Drivers can get a little crazy, weaving in and out of traffic.

The District is 240 miles from New York City, 40 miles from Baltimore, 700 miles from Chicago, 440 miles from Boston, and about 630 miles from Atlanta.

By Train

Amtrak (www.amtrak.com; ℂ **800/USA-RAIL** [872-7245]) offers daily service to Washington from New York, Boston, and Chicago. Amtrak also travels daily between Washington and points south, including Raleigh, Charlotte, Atlanta, cities in Florida, and New Orleans. Amtrak's **Acela Express** trains offer the quickest service along the "Northeast Corridor," linking Boston, New York, Philadelphia, and Washington, D.C. The trains travel as fast as 150 mph, making the trip between New York and Washington in times that range from less than 3 hours to 3 hours and 45 minutes, depending on the number of stops in the schedule. Likewise, Acela Express's Boston-Washington trip takes anywhere from 6½ hours to more than 8 hours, depending on station stops.

Amtrak runs fewer Acela trains on weekends and only honors passenger discounts (such as those for seniors or AAA members) on weekend Acela travel.

Amtrak offers a smorgasbord of rail passes and discounted fares; although not all are based on advance purchase, you often have more discount options by reserving early. Tickets for up to two children 2 to 12 cost half the price of the full adult fare when the children are accompanied by an adult. For more info, go to **www.amtrak.com**. *Note:* Most Amtrak travel requires a reservation, which means that every traveler is guaranteed, but not assigned, a seat.

Amtrak trains arrive at historic **Union Station** (p. 133), 50 Massachusetts Ave. NE (www.unionstationdc.com; ℂ **202/289-1908**), a short walk from the Capitol, near several hotels, and a short cab or Metro ride from downtown. Union Station is D.C.'s transportation hub, with its own Metrorail station, Metrobus and DC Circulator bus stops, taxi stands, bikeshare and bike rental locations, rental car facilities, intra-city bus travel operations, and connection to D.C. Streetcar service.

By Bus

Thanks to the rise of fabulously priced, clean, comfortable, and fast bus services, bus travel has become a popular and more affordable alternative to Amtrak. Quite a number of buses travel between Washington, D.C., and New York City, and a growing number travel between D.C. and cities scattered up and down the East Coast.

Megabus (www.megabus.com; © **877/462-6342**) travels between Union Station and NYC several times a day for as little as $1 and as much as $46, one-way (most fares run in the $20–$30 range); and offers cheap travel between D.C. and 28 other locations, including Boston, Pittsburgh, and Durham. **Vamoose Bus** (www.vamoosebus.com; © **212/695-6766**) travels between Rosslyn, Virginia's stop near the Rosslyn Metro station, and Bethesda, Maryland's stop near the Bethesda Metro station, and locations near NYC's Penn Station, for $20 to $60 each way, accruing one point for every dollar you've paid for your ticket. Collect 120 points and you ride one-way for free.

Greyhound (www.greyhound.com; © **800/231-2222**), the company behind BoltBus, travels all over the country for rates as cheap as the other operations here; its bus depot is also at Union Station.

GETTING AROUND

Washington is one of the easiest U.S. cities to navigate, thanks to its manageable size and easy-to-understand layout. I wish I could boast as well about the city's comprehensive public transportation system. Ours is the second-busiest rail transit network and the ninth-largest bus network in the country. It used to be swell, but 40+ years of increased usage and inadequate maintenance put the system into crisis mode in 2009, which the Washington Metropolitan Transit Authority (WMATA) has been working hard to correct ever since. And the system *is* safer and more reliable. But the effort continues, as you will surely encounter firsthand if you visit in 2022.

Here's what I recommend as you plan your trip: **Choose lodging close to where you want to be,** whether the center of the city, near the offices where you're doing business, or in a favorite neighborhood, and then consider all the transportation options in this chapter. In addition, I recommend the website **www.godcgo.com**, which has info about traversing the city, from every angle, with links to *Washington Post* articles reporting on the latest traffic and transit news. You might just find yourself shunning transportation anyway, for the pleasure of walking or bike-riding your way around the compact capital.

City Layout

Washington's appearance today pays homage to the 1791 vision of French engineer Pierre Charles L'Enfant, who created the capital's grand design of sweeping avenues intersected by spacious circles, directed that the Capitol and the White House be placed on prominent hilltops at either end of a wide stretch of avenue, and superimposed this overall plan upon a traditional street grid. The city's quadrants, grand avenues named after states, alphabetically ordered streets crossed by numerically ordered streets, and parks integrated with urban features are all ideas that started with L'Enfant. President George Washington, who had hired L'Enfant, was forced to dismiss the temperamental genius after L'Enfant apparently offended quite a number of people. But Washington recognized the brilliance of the city plan and hired surveyors Benjamin Banneker and Andrew Ellicott, who had worked with L'Enfant, to continue to implement L'Enfant's design. (For further background, see chapter 2.)

The U.S. Capitol marks the center of the city, which is divided into **northwest (NW), northeast (NE), southwest (SW),** and **southeast (SE) quadrants.** Most, but not all, areas of interest to tourists are in the northwest. The boundary demarcations are often seamless; for example, you are in the northwest quadrant at the National Museum of Natural History, but by crossing the National Mall to the other side to visit the Sackler Gallery, you put yourself in the southwest quadrant. Pay attention to the quadrant's geographic suffix; as you'll notice when you look on a map, some addresses appear in multiple quadrants (for example, the corner of G and 7th sts. appears in all four).

MAIN ARTERIES & STREETS From the Capitol, North Capitol Street and South Capitol Street run north and south, respectively. East Capitol Street divides the city north and south. The area west of the Capitol is not a street at all, but the National Mall, which is bounded on the north by Constitution Avenue and on the south by Independence Avenue.

The primary artery of Washington is **Pennsylvania Avenue,** which together with Constitution Avenue form the backdrop for parades, inaugurations, and other splashy events. Pennsylvania runs northwest in a direct line between the Capitol and the White House—if it weren't for the Treasury Building, the president would have a clear view of the Capitol—before continuing on a northwest angle to Georgetown, where it becomes M Street.

Constitution Avenue, paralleled to the south most of the way by Independence Avenue, runs east-west, flanking the Capitol and the Mall. Washington's longest avenue, **Massachusetts Avenue,** runs parallel to Pennsylvania (a few avenues north). Along the way, you'll find Union Station and then Dupont Circle, which is central to the area known as Embassy Row. Farther out are the Naval Observatory (the vice president's residence is here), the National Cathedral, American University, and, eventually, Maryland.

Connecticut Avenue, which runs more directly north (the other avenues run southeast to northwest), starts at Lafayette Square, intersects Dupont Circle, and eventually takes you to the National Zoo, on to the charming residential neighborhood known as Cleveland Park, and into Chevy Chase, Maryland, where you can pick up the Beltway to head out of town. Connecticut Avenue, with its chic-to-funky array of shops and clusters of top-dollar to good-value restaurants, is an interesting street to stroll.

Wisconsin Avenue originates in Georgetown; its intersection with M Street forms Georgetown's hub. Wisconsin Avenue basically parallels Connecticut Avenue; one of the few irritating things about the city's transportation system is that the Metro does not connect these two major arteries in the heart of the city. (Buses do, and, of course, you can always walk or take a taxi from one avenue to the other; read about the supplemental bus system, the DC Circulator, on p. 297.) Metrorail's first stop on Wisconsin Avenue is in Tenleytown, a residential area. Follow the avenue north and you land in the affluent Maryland cities of Chevy Chase and Bethesda.

FINDING AN ADDRESS   If you understand the city's layout, it's easy to find your way around. As you read this, have a map handy.

Each of the four corners of the District of Columbia is exactly the same distance from the Capitol dome. The White House and most government buildings and important monuments are west of the Capitol (in the northwest and southwest quadrants), as are major hotels and tourist facilities.

Numbered streets run north-south, beginning on either side of the Capitol with 1st Street. Lettered streets run east-west and are named alphabetically, beginning with A Street. (Don't look for J, X, Y, or Z streets, however—they don't exist.) After W Street, street names of two syllables continue in alphabetical order, followed by street names of three syllables; the more syllables in a name, the farther the street is from the Capitol.

Avenues, named for U.S. states, run at angles across the grid pattern and often intersect at traffic circles. For example, New Hampshire, Connecticut, and Massachusetts avenues intersect at Dupont Circle.

With this arrangement in mind, you can easily find an address. On lettered streets, the address tells you exactly where to go. For example, 1776 K Street NW is between 17th and 18th streets (the first two digits of 1776 tell you that) in the northwest quadrant (NW). *Note:* I Street is often written as "Eye" Street to prevent confusion with 1st Street.

Be Smart: Buy a SmarTrip Card

If you are planning on using D.C.'s Metro system while you're here, do yourself a favor and download the **SmarTrip** app (smartrip.wmata.com; ✆ **888/762-7874**) before you arrive. SmarTrip is a rechargeable card that pays your way in the subway, on Metro and DC Circulator buses, and on other area transit systems, like the DASH buses in Old Town Alexandria, VA. You can also use Apple Pay or Google pay or order a physical card by mail before your trip or purchase one while here, but the app comes with the added benefit of live transit schedules. Whatever format you have, it's easy to use: You just touch your mobile device or the card to the target on a faregate inside a Metro station, or farebox in a Metrobus. You can also purchase SmarTrip cards at vending machines in any Metro station; and the sales office at Metro Center (Tues–Thurs only 8am–noon), 12th and F streets NW. The cost of a SmarTrip card starts at $10: $2 for the card, plus $8 stored value to get you started. You can add value and special-value passes as needed online and at the SmarTrip Card Fare Vending/Passes machines in every Metro station, or even on a Metrobus, using the farebox. For more info, contact Metro.

To find an address on numbered streets, you'll probably have to use your fingers. For example, 623 8th Street SE is between F and G streets (the sixth and seventh letters of the alphabet; the first digit of 623 tells you that) in the southeast quadrant (SE). *One thing to remember:* You count B as the second letter of the alphabet even though B Street North and B Street South are now Constitution and Independence avenues, respectively, but because there's no J Street, K becomes the 10th letter, L the 11th, and so on.

By Public Transportation
METRORAIL

The Metrorail system is in the midst of long-overdue repairs and reconstruction, which means you may encounter delays and possible cancellation of service on segments of different lines during your visit. Track and platform work is ongoing and may even change day to day. Weekend service tends to be the most impacted by station closures and track work. Check Metro's website for the latest updates or do as locals do: Sign up for Metro alerts (www. metroalerts.info) to receive timely announcements of Metrorail and Metrobus service delays, disruptions, schedule changes, advisories, and enhancements.

If you do ride Metrorail, you may want to avoid traveling during rush hour (Mon–Fri 5–9:30am and 3–7pm), since trains can get overcrowded. you can expect to get a seat on the trains during off-peak hours. All cars are air-conditioned. At this writing masks were still required on all public transit, per federal law.

Metrorail's base system of 91 stations and 117 miles of track includes locations at or near almost every sightseeing attraction; it also extends to suburban Maryland and northern Virginia. There are six lines in operation—**Red, Blue, Orange, Yellow, Green,** and the new **Silver** line. At this writing, the Silver Line has five stops that snake off the Orange line in Northern Virginia, and if everything goes according to plan an extension connecting to Dulles Airport should open in 2022. The lines connect at several central points, making transfers relatively easy. All but Yellow and Green trains stop at Metro Center; all except Red Line trains stop at L'Enfant Plaza; all but Blue, Orange, and Silver Line trains stop at Gallery Place–Chinatown. See the map inside the back cover of this book.

Metro stations are indicated by discreet brown columns bearing the station's name and topped by the letter M. Below the M is a colored stripe or stripes indicating the line or lines that stop there. To reach the train platform of a Metro station, you need a computerized **SmarTrip** card or mobile app (see box above). SmarTrip card "Fare Vending" and "Add Value" machines are located inside

---

Metro Etiquette 101

To avoid risking the ire of fellow commuters, be sure to follow these guidelines: Stand to the right on the escalator so that people in a hurry can get past you on the left. And when you reach the train level, don't puddle at the bottom of the escalator, blocking the path of those coming behind you; move down the platform. Eating, drinking, and smoking are strictly prohibited on the Metro and in stations.

Metrorail doesn't go to Georgetown, and although Metro buses do (nos. 30, 31, 33, 38B, D2, D6, and G2), the public transportation I'd recommend is the **DC Circulator bus** (see box, p. 297), which travels two Georgetown routes: one that runs between the Rosslyn, VA, and Dupont Circle Metro stations, stopping at designated points in Georgetown along the way, and a second one that runs between Georgetown and Union Station. The buses come every 10 minutes from 6am to midnight Monday to Thursday; 6 or 7am to 3am Friday; 7am to 3am Saturday; and 7am to midnight Sunday. One-way fares cost $1; you'll need exact change or can use a SmarTrip card. Check www.dccirculator.com for schedule updates.

the vestibule areas of the Metro stations. The blue SmarTrip Card Fare Vending machines sell SmarTrip cards for $10 ($2 for the card and $8 in trip value), add value up to $300, and add special-value passes to your SmarTrip Card; the machines accept debit and credit cards and bills up to $20, with change up to $10 returned in coins. The black Fare Vending machines are strictly for adding value to your current SmarTrip Card; the machines accept cash only, up to $20, with change up to $10 returned in coins.

Metrorail fares are calculated on distance traveled and time of day. Base fare during **nonpeak hours** (Mon–Fri 9:30am–3pm; Mon–Thurs 7–11:30pm; Fri 7pm–1am; Sat–Sun all day) ranges from a **minimum of $2** to a **maximum of $3.85.** During **peak hours** (Mon–Fri 5–9:30am and 3–7pm), the fare ranges from a **minimum of $2.25** to a **maximum of $6.**

For best value, consider buying a $13 **1-Day Rail/Bus** pass or a $38 **7-Day short trip** pass for travel on Metrorail. You can buy these online, adding the value to the SmarTrip card you're purchasing, or at the machines in the stations. See Metro's website for details.

Up to two children ages 4 and under can ride free with a paying passenger. Seniors (65 and older) and travelers with disabilities (with valid proof) ride Metrorail and Metrobus for a reduced fare.

To get to the train platforms, enter the station through the faregates, touching your SmarTrip card to the SmarTrip logo–marked target on top of the regular faregates or on the inside of the wide faregates. When you exit a station, you touch your card again to the SmarTrip logo–marked target on the faregate at your destination. If you arrive at a destination and the exit faregate tells you that you need to add value to your SmarTrip Card to exit, use the brown Exit-fare machines near the faregate to add the necessary amount—cash only.

Most Metro stations have more than one exit. To save yourself time and confusion, try to figure out ahead of time which exit gets you closer to where you're going. In this book, I **include the appropriate exit for every venue.**

Metrorail opens at 5am weekdays, 7am Saturday, and 8am Sunday, operating until 11:30pm Monday through Thursday, 1am Friday and Saturday, and 11pm Sunday. Visit www.wmata.com for the up-to-date info on routes and schedules. Metro will stay open later for certain special events, like a baseball or hockey game. Check the web site for details.

The long-awaited **DC Streetcar** is up and running, transporting people between Union Station and points along H Street NE in the dining and nightlife-rich neighborhood known as the Atlas District. The distance between Union Station and the heart of the Atlas District is about 1 mile; the entire Union Station-to-Benning Road streetcar segment is close to 2.5 miles. All you have to do is ride the Metro to Union Station, and transfer to the streetcar from there. Here's the deal, though: When you arrive at the Union Station Metro stop, you must make your way up through the station to the bus deck level of the parking garage, then walk and walk and walk the marked pathway that leads to H Street, where you cross at the crosswalk to reach the streetcar stop. Dimly lit during the day, Union Station's garage is downright creepy at night. That's one drawback. Second, from Union Station, you're actually not that far, only a couple of blocks, from the start of the Atlas District; personally, I think it makes more sense most of the time to just walk the distance. For more information, go to www.dcstreetcar.com.

METROBUS

The Transit Authority's bus system is a comprehensive operation that encompasses 1,500 buses traveling 269 routes, making about 11,125 stops, operating within a 1,500-square-mile area that includes major arteries in D.C. and the Virginia and Maryland suburbs. The system is gradually phasing in new, sleekly designed red and silver buses that run on a combination of diesel and electric hybrid fuel.

The Transit Authority is also working to improve placement of bus stop signs. For now, look for red, white, and blue signs that tell you which buses stop at that location. Eventually, signage should tell you the routes and schedules. In the meantime, the Transit Authority has inaugurated electronic NEXT BUS signs at some bus stops that post real-time arrival information and alerts. You can also find out when the next bus is due to arrive at www.wmata.com (scroll to the NEXT BUS section on your screen and enter intersection, bus route no., or bus stop code).

Base fare in the District, using a SmarTrip card, is $2, or $4.25 for the faster express buses, which make fewer stops. There may be additional charges for travel into the Maryland and Virginia suburbs. Bus drivers are not equipped to make change, so if you have not purchased a SmarTrip card (see box, p. 293) or a pass, be sure to carry exact change.

If you'll be in Washington for a while and plan to use the buses a lot, buy a 1-week pass ($12), which loads onto a SmarTrip card.

Most buses operate daily from 4am to midnight. Service is quite frequent on weekdays, especially during peak hours, and less frequent on weekends and late at night. Up to two children 4 and under ride free with a paying passenger on Metrobus, and there are reduced fares for seniors and travelers with disabilities. If you leave something on a bus, on a train, or in a station, use the online form at www.wmata.com or call **Lost and Found** Monday through Friday 9am to 5pm at © **202/962-1195.**

By Car

If you must drive, be aware that traffic is thick during the week, parking spaces hard to find, and parking lots ruinously expensive. Expect to pay overnight rates of $25 to $60 at hotels, hourly rates starting at $8 at downtown parking lots and garages, and flat rates starting at $20 in the most popular parts of town, such as Georgetown and Penn Quarter. If you're hoping to snag one of the 18,000 metered parking spaces on the street, you can expect to pay a minimum of $2.30 per hour by coin, credit or debit card, or smartphone. To use your smartphone, you must first sign up online at www.parkmobile.com, or download the app, to register your license plate number and credit card or debit card number. Once you arrive in D.C. and park on a street that requires payment for parking, you simply call the phone number marked on the meter or nearby kiosk (or use the app) and follow the prompts to enter the location ID marked on the meter and the amount of time you're paying for. If your parking space has neither a meter nor Parkmobile number to call, pay for parking at the nearby kiosk, print a receipt, and place it against the windshield. Most street parking spaces allow up to 2 hours of parking; check signs for any time-of-day restrictions.

DC CIRCULATOR: fast, easy & cheap

Meet D.C.'s fantastic supplemental bus system. It's efficient, inexpensive, and convenient, traveling six routes in the city. These red-and-gray buses travel:

o The **Eastern Market to L'Enfant Plaza (EM-LP) route** connecting the Eastern Market Metro Station, Barracks Row, the Navy Yard Metro station in Capitol Riverfront, the Southwest Waterfront and its Wharf, and L'Enfant Plaza near the National Mall (Mon–Fri 6am–9pm, Sat–Sun 7am–9pm, with extended service on nights the Nationals or DC United has a game).

o The **Congress Heights-Union Station (CH-US) route** from Union Station to Barracks Row to Anacostia and back (Mon–Fri 6am–9pm; Sat–Sun 7am–9pm).

o The **Union Station to upper Georgetown (GT-US) track** via downtown D.C. (Mon–Thurs 6am–midnight; Fri 6am–3am; Sat 7am–3am; Sun 7am–midnight).

o The **Rosslyn to Dupont Circle route (RS-DP)** that travels between the Rosslyn Metro station in Virginia and the Dupont Circle Metro station in the District, via Georgetown (Sun–Thurs 6am–midnight; Fri–Sat 7am–3am).

o The **Woodley Park–Zoo to McPherson Square (WP-AM) route** connecting those two Metro stations via Adams Morgan and the U & 14th Street Corridors (Mon–Thurs 6am–midnight; Fri 6am–3:30am; Sat 7am–3:30am; Sun 7am–midnight).

o The **National Mall (NM)** route, which loops the National Mall from Union Station and stops at 14 other sites en route (Winter: Mon–Fri 7am–7pm, Sat–Sun 9am–7pm; summer: Mon–Fri 7am–8pm, Sat–Sun 9am–8pm).

Buses stop at designated points on their routes (look for the distinctive red-and-gold sign, often topping a regular Metro bus stop sign) every 10 minutes. The fare is $1, and transfers between Circulator routes is free within 2 hours. For easy and fast transportation in the busiest parts of town, you can't beat it. Go to www.dccirculator.com or call ℂ 202/671-2020.

D.C.'s traffic circles can be confusing to navigate. The law states that traffic already in the circle has the right of way, but you can't always depend on other drivers to obey that law. You also need to be aware of rush-hour rules: Sections of certain streets in Washington become **one-way** during rush hour: Rock Creek Parkway and Canal Road are two examples. Other streets change the direction of some of their traffic lanes during rush hour. Connecticut Avenue NW is the main one: In the morning, traffic in four of its six lanes travels south to downtown, and in late afternoon/early evening, downtown traffic in four of its six lanes heads north; between the hours of 9am and 3:30pm, traffic in both directions keeps to the normally correct side of the yellow line. Lit-up traffic signs alert you to what's going on, but pay attention. Unless a sign is posted prohibiting it, a right-on-red law is in effect.

FYI: If you don't drive to D.C. but need a car while you're here, you can rent one at the airport or at Union Station, as noted earlier in this chapter, or you can turn to a car-sharing service, such as **Zipcar** (www.zipcar.com) or **Free2Move** (www.free2move-carsharing.com).

By Taxi, Uber, or Lyft

The D.C. taxicab system charges passengers according to time- and distance-based meters. Fares may increase, but at press time, fares began at $3.50, plus $2.16 per each additional mile and $1.20 per mile per additional passenger. Other charges might apply (for example, if you telephone for a cab rather than hail one in the street, it'll cost you $2). Download the free DC Taxi app from the website www.dctaxionline.com, and order your transportation using your smartphone, à la Uber. *Note:* The big news about D.C. taxis is that they now accept credit cards.

Try **V.I.P. Cab Company** (© **202/269-9000**) or **Yellow Cab** (www.dcyellow cab.com; © **202/544-1212**).

Or download the app for **Uber** (www.uber.com) or **Lyft** (www.lyft.com), both of which operate in the District.

By Boat

The many allures of the Southwest Waterfront Wharf include assorted transportation options for getting you there. In addition to public transportation, taxi, and bike-share programs already in place, the **Potomac Riverboat Company** (www.potomacriverboatco.com; © **877/511-2628**) operates water taxi service March to December 31 between the Wharf and Georgetown, Old Town Alexandria, and National Harbor. One-way tickets for adults cost $15. A water jitney ferries passengers between the Wharf and East Potomac Park, April through November. Check **www.wharfdc.com** for details.

By Bike

Thanks to the city's robust bike-share program (**Capital BikeShare**—www. capitalbikeshare.com; © **877/430-2453**—is the city's largest, with more than 4,500 bikes and 553 bike stations), Washington, D.C., is increasingly a city where locals themselves get around by bike. The flat terrain of the National Mall and many neighborhoods make the city conducive to two wheels. Over

100 marked bike lanes traverse D.C. and bike paths through Rock Creek Park, the C&O Canal in Georgetown, along the waterfront via the Anacostia River-walk Trail, and around the National Mall. Interested? Visit www.godcgo.com and click on the "Bike" link under "Discover" to view a map that shows bike lanes and Capital BikeShare stations, which are all over. The Capital Bike-Share program, which starts at $2 per ride and is now supported by Lyft, might be a better option economically for members who use the bikes for short commutes, but be sure to consider that option, along with traditional bike-rental companies (see chapter 6, p. 205), which are also plentiful.

In addition to Capital Bikeshares, several dockless bike and electric scooter companies operate in D.C., including **Jump** (www.jump.com) and **Lime** (www.li.me), so consider those if the thought of ditching your bike or scooter where you may appeals (rather than having to return it to a rack).

GUIDED TOURS

D.C. offers a slew of guided tours, from themed jaunts to sites where famous scandals occurred to Segway tours. Beyond those in this chapter are self-guided neighborhood walking trails on the **Cultural Tourism D.C.** website, **www.culturaltourismdc.org**. If you're here in September, be sure to check out Cultural Tourism D.C.'s Walkingtown D.C. offering of 50 free tours throughout the city over the course of 8 days.

On Foot

o **DC by Foot:** These tours operate under a "name your price" model, mean-ing you pay what you think the experience is worth. Guides for **DC by Foot** (www.freetoursbyfoot.com/washington-dc-tours; ✆ **202/370-1830**) like to spin humor with history as they shepherd participants around the sites. His-tory is the emphasis on the popular National Mall tour, but other offerings cover such topics as spies and scandals or Lincoln's assassination; the outfit has expanded to include neighborhood, ghost, and Arlington National Cem-etery tours. Private tours are also available. Unlike other guided tours, DC by Foot operates year-round.

o **Washington Walks:** Excellent guides and dynamite in-depth tours of neigh-borhoods off the National Mall make **Washington Walks** (www.washington walks.com; ✆ **202/484-1565**) a long-time favorite. "Women Who Changed America" and "Memorials by Moonlight" are among the most popular tours. Public walks ($25/person) take place April through November; private and group tours year-round.

o **DC Metro Food Tours: DC Metro** (www.dcmetrofoodtours.com; ✆ **202/851-2268**) leads participants on 3½-hour-long gastronomic adventures in a particular neighborhood, serving side dishes of historical and cultural refer-ences. For example, a Georgetown tour might include a walk along the C&O Canal, a sampling of house-made pasta at a decades-old restaurant, tales of the neighborhood's famous residents (like President and Jacqueline

Kennedy), and a sweet finish with dessert at one of the city's best bakeries. Ask about pub crawls. Rates vary from about $30 to $70 per person.

o **The Guild of Professional Tour Guides of Washington, D.C.:** Would you like your tour tailored to your interest in women's history or architecture, or an evening tour of the monuments and memorials? **The Guild** (www. washingtondctourguides.com), a membership organization for licensed, professional tour guides and companies, offers a slew of set tours, but also operates a guide-for-hire service on its website (click on "For Visitors," then "Book a Custom Tour"). Complete the online request form and then choose from among the responders. The price ranges from $45 to $60 per hour, depending on the guide and subject matter. These guides are the best of the best, with many members doubling as docents at places like the Capitol Visitor Center and Smithsonian museums.

o **Segway Tours:** See the sights while riding self-propelling scooters that operate based on "dynamic stabilization" technology, which uses your body movements. **Capital Segway** (capitalsegway.com; © **202/682-1980;** ages 16 and up) offers 2-hour tours around the National Mall and White House. Tours cost $60 per person and includes training and headsets so you can hear the guide's narration even from the back of the pack.

By Bus

The three major companies that offer narrated bus tours of the city all operate out of Union Station: **Big Bus Tours** (www.bigbustours.com), **City Sights DC** (www.citysightsdc.com; © **202/650-5444**), and **Old Town Trolley Tours** (www.trolleytours.com/washington-dc/; © **202/832-9800**). Old Town Trolley Tours provides "entertainment narration" and is the only company authorized to operate the narrated tour throughout Arlington National Cemetery (p. 195). Big Bus Tours' Red Loop, National Mall route is the official sightseeing tour of National Mall and Memorial Parks. City Sights DC offers the most flexible array of add-on options, including a bike rental or boat tour. Big Bus and City Sights tour buses are double-deckers, which provide a fun point of view; and they also have air-conditioned interiors, which the trolleys do not (enclosed and heated in winter, the trolleys in summer open their windows). So, each narrated tour has its individual appeals for you to mull over.

All three tours allow you to buy your tickets ahead of time online. (City Sights DC allows you to purchase your tour online, but you must print out your voucher and redeem it at L'Enfant for the ticket that lets you board the bus.) Old Town Trolley and Big Bus Tours also have ticket stands at Union Station, and City Sights DC and Big Bus share a ticket desk at 700 L'Enfant Plaza SW (near the Spy Museum). Big Bus and City Sights tours provide hop-on, hop-off service and Old Town Trolley and Big Bus offer a night tour, which I recommend.

The basic narrated tour for each operation takes about 2 hours (if you don't get off and tour the sites, obviously), and trolleys/buses come by every 30 to 60 minutes. Rates start at $50/adult, $40/child for City Sights DC; $45/adult, $30/child for Old Town Trolley; and $49/adult, $39/child for Big Bus Tours. Check out each operation's website for full details.

By Boat

Potomac cruises offer sweeping vistas of the monuments and memorials, Georgetown, the Kennedy Center, and other Washington sights. Read the information below carefully, because not all boat cruises offer guided tours. Some of the following boats leave from Washington's waterfront, whether in Southwest or in Georgetown, and some from Old Town Alexandria. Parts of the Southwest Waterfront are still under development, so check boarding and parking information carefully online if you're booking a cruise that leaves from a D.C. dock. Consult the website, **www.wharfdc.com**, for the latest information about the Southwest Waterfront's newest cruise options.

o **Potomac Riverboat Company Monuments Tour** (Georgetown Waterfront, in front of Fiola Mare restaurant, or Alexandria City Marina, behind the Torpedo Art Factory; potomacriverboatco.com; © **877/511-2628;** Metro: Foggy Bottom, then take the D.C. Circulator bus, or King St.–Old Town, then take the AT2 or AT8 bus) offers a different way to see Washington's monuments: by water. Tours travel between Georgetown and Alexandria and take in sights like the Kennedy Center and Jefferson Memorial. The boats operate Wednesday to Sunday Memorial Day through Labor Day; you can board at either end and can ride one-way (45 min./$18) or round-trip (90 min./$32). The cruises are part of the Hornblower **City Cruises** operation (www.city experiences.com/washington-dc/city-cruises), which also runs Washington's Water Taxi and a number of dining cruises and private charters.

o **Potomac Paddle Club,** Georgetown Waterfront, in front of Nick's Riverside or Tony & Joe's Seafood restaurants (www.potomacpaddleclub.com; © **202/656-3336;** Metro: Foggy Bottom, then take the D.C. Circulator bus), puts a party spin on your tour. These booze cruises are like bikes on floats—up to 10 passengers sit around a big open-air bar and pedal to power the boat's paddlewheel and propel it down the river around the monuments. (There's also a motor in case you need to rest your legs.) Drinking is encouraged; guests can bring their own wine and beer. Tours departing from Georgetown are 90 minutes and start at $45 per person; there's a longer 2½-hour route between Alexandria and National Harbor ($75 per person).

o **Water Taxi, by Potomac Riverboat Company** ★ (www.cityexperiences. com/washington-dc/city-cruises/potomac-river/water-taxi; © **877/511-2628** or 703/684-0580) is more than just a way to get from point A to B. The transportation service runs between multiple waterfront stops and can serve as a DIY boat-based tour of the city, since it follows the same route as most other sightseeing tours, just without the guided narration. You board the taxicab-yellow boats at the Georgetown Waterfront (3100 K St. NW), The Wharf (Transit Pier, 950 Wharf St. SW), Old Town Alexandria in Virginia (behind the Torpedo Factory Art Center), or National Harbor in Maryland (45 National Plaza). At press time the boats were running Wednesday to Sunday, and passengers must book tickets (starting at $15) for specific timed boats (though you can change your ticket time as long as there's space on the boat). A concession stand sells light refreshments onboard. March through December only.

o The **Capitol River Cruise**'s *Nightingales* (www.capitolrivercruises.com; ℰ **301/460-7447**) are historic 65-foot steel riverboats that can accommodate 90 people. The *Nightingales'* narrated jaunts depart Georgetown's Washington Harbour every hour on the hour, from noon to 7pm, April through October (with an 8pm outing offered in summer months only). The 45-minute narrated tour travels past the monuments and memorials to National Airport and back. Tickets ($20/adult, $10/child) can be purchased online or when you arrive at the boat. Bring a picnic or eat from the snack bar. To get here, take the Metro to Foggy Bottom and then walk into Georgetown, following Pennsylvania Avenue, which becomes M Street. Turn left on 31st Street NW and follow to the Washington Harbour complex on the water.

By Bike

Bike and Roll DC ★★ (www.bikeandrolldc.com; ℰ **202/842-2453**) offers a more active way to see Washington, from March to December. The company has designed several biking tours, including the popular Capital Sites Ride, which takes you past museums, memorials, the White House, the Capitol, and the Supreme Court. The ride takes 3 hours, covers 7 to 8 miles, and costs $44/hour adults, $34 children 12 and under. Bike the Sites provides a hybrid bicycle fitted to your size, a helmet, water bottle, light snack, and a professional guide. Tours depart from a location near the National Mall, at 955 L'Enfant Plaza SW, North Building Suite 905 (Metro: L'Enfant Plaza), and the guide imparts historical and anecdotal information as you go. Bike and Roll also offers this tour departing from the steps of the National Museum of American History, on the Mall. Bike and Roll rents bikes as well; see p. 205 in chapter 6.

[FastFACTS] WASHINGTON, D.C.

Area Codes Within the District of Columbia, the area code is 202. In Northern Virginia it's 703, and in the Maryland suburbs, its 301. You must use the area code when dialing a phone number, whether it's a local 202, 703, or 301 phone number.

Business Hours Most museums are open daily 10am to 5:30pm; some, including several Smithsonians, stay open later in spring and summer. Most banks are open from 9am to 5pm weekdays, with some open Saturdays as well, for abbreviated hours. Stores typically open between 9 and 10am

and close between 8 and 9pm, Monday to Saturday.

Doctors Most hotels are prepared for medical emergencies and work with local doctors who are able to see ill or injured hotel guests. Also see "Hospitals," below.

Drinking Laws The legal age for purchase and consumption of alcoholic beverages is 21; proof of age is required and often requested at bars, nightclubs, and restaurants, so it's always a good idea to bring ID when you go out. Do not carry open containers of alcohol in your car or any public area that isn't zoned

for alcohol consumption. The police can fine you on the spot. Don't even think about driving while intoxicated.

Grocery stores, convenience stores, and other retailers can sell beer and wine 7 days a week. D.C. liquor stores are open on Sunday. Bars and nightclubs serve liquor until 2am Sunday through Thursday and until 3am Friday and Saturday.

Electricity Like Canada, the United States uses 110–120 volts AC (60 cycles), compared to 220–240 volts AC (50 cycles) in most of Europe, Australia, and New Zealand. Downward converters that change 220–240 volts to 110–120 volts are difficult to find in the United States, so bring one with you.

Embassies & Consulates All embassies are located here in the nation's capital. Check for yours at www.embassy.org/embassies.

Emergencies Call ℂ 911 for police, fire, and medical emergencies. This is a toll-free call.

If you encounter serious problems, contact the **Travelers Aid Society International** (www.travelersaid.org; ℂ 202/546-1127), a nationwide, nonprofit, social-service organization geared to helping travelers in difficult straits, from reuniting families separated while traveling to providing food and/or shelter to people stranded without cash. Travelers Aid operates help desks at Washington Dulles International Airport, Ronald Reagan Washington National Airport, and Union Station. At Baltimore–Washington International Thurgood Marshall Airport, a volunteer agency called **Pathfinders** (ℂ 410/859-7826) staffs the customer service desks throughout the airport.

Family Travel Field trips during the school year and family vacations during the summer keep Washington, D.C., crawling with kids all year long. More than any other city, Washington is crammed with historic sites, arts and science museums, parks, and recreational sites to interest young and old alike. Plus, the fact that so many attractions are free is a boon to the family budget.

Look for boxes on family-friendly hotels, restaurants, and attractions in their appropriate chapters.

Hospitals If you don't require immediate ambulance transportation but still need emergency-room treatment, call one of the following hospitals (and be sure to get directions): **Children's Hospital National Medical Center,** 111 Michigan Ave. NW (ℂ 888/884-2327); **George Washington University Hospital,** 900 23rd St. NW, at Washington Circle (ℂ 202/715-4000); **Medstar Georgetown University Hospital,** 3800 Reservoir Rd. NW (ℂ 202/444-2000); or **Howard University Hospital,** 2041 Georgia Ave. NW (ℂ 202/865-7677).

Internet & Wi-Fi Most hotels, resorts, cafes, and retailers now offer free Wi-Fi. Likewise, all three D.C. airports offer complimentary Wi-Fi. The city also offers Wi-Fi in some public spaces like the National Mall; check wifi.dc.gov to find a hotspot. All D.C. hotels listed in chapter 4 offer Internet access, and many offer it for free.

Legal Aid While driving, if you are pulled over for a minor infraction (such as speeding), never attempt to pay the fine directly to a police officer; this could be construed as attempted bribery, a much more serious crime. Pay fines online, by mail or directly into the hands of the clerk of the court. If accused of a more serious offense, say and do nothing before consulting a lawyer. In the U.S., the

burden is on the state to prove a person's guilt beyond a reasonable doubt, and everyone has the right to remain silent, whether he or she is suspected of a crime or is actually arrested. Once arrested, a person can make one telephone call to a party of his or her choice. The international visitor should call his or her embassy or consulate.

LGBTQ+ Travelers The nation's capital is very welcoming to the gay and lesbian community. D.C.'s LGBTQ+ population is one of the largest in the country, with an estimated 7% to 10% of residents identifying themselves as such. The capital's annual, week-long Capital Pride celebration is held in June, complete with a street fair and a parade.

Dupont Circle, once the unofficial headquarters for gay life, continues to host the annual 17th Street High Heel Drag Race on the Tuesday preceding Halloween, and is home to long-established gay bars and dance clubs (see chapter 8), but the whole city is pretty much LGBTQ+-friendly.

Mail At press time, domestic postage rates were 36¢ for a postcard and 55¢ for a letter. For international mail, a first-class letter of up to 1 ounce costs $1.20; a first-class postcard costs the same as a letter.

Mobile Phones AT&T, Verizon, Sprint, and T-Mobile are the primary cellphone networks operating in Washington, D.C., so there's a good chance you'll have

WHAT THINGS COST IN WASHINGTON, D.C.

	US$
Taxi from National Airport to downtown	18.00
Double room, moderate	250.00
Double room, inexpensive	180.00
Three-course dinner for one without wine, moderate	50.00
Glass of wine	12.00
Cup of coffee	2.75
1 gallon of regular unleaded gas	3.27
Admission to most museums	Free
1-day Metrorail pass	13.00

full and excellent coverage anywhere in the city.

International visitors should check their **GSM (Global System for Mobile Communications) wireless network** to see where GSM phones and text messaging work in the U.S.

You can **rent** a phone before you leave home from **InTouch USA** (www.intouch usa.us; ℂ **800/872-7626** in the U.S., or 703/222-7161 outside the U.S.).

You can purchase a pay-as-you-go phone from all sorts of places, from Amazon. com to any Verizon Wireless store. In D.C., Verizon has stores around the city, including at 1529 14th St. NW (ℂ **202/313-7000**), and another at 1318 F St. NW (ℂ **202/624-0072**), to name just two convenient locations.

Money & Costs If you are traveling to Washington, D.C., from outside the United States, you should consult a currency exchange website such as www.xe.com/curren-cyconverter to check up-to-the-minute exchange rates before your departure.

Anyone who travels to the nation's capital

expecting bargains is in for a rude awakening, especially when it comes to lodging. Less expensive than New York and London, Washington, D.C.'s daily hotel rate nevertheless reflects the city's popularity as a top destination among U.S. travelers, averaging $221 (according to most recent statistics). D.C.'s restaurant scene is rather more egalitarian: heavy on the fine, top-dollar establishments, where you can easily spend $100 per person, but with plenty of excellent bistros and small restaurants offering great eats at lower prices. When it comes to attractions, though, the nation's capital has the rest of the world beat, because most of its museums and tourist sites offer free admission.

In Washington, D.C., ATMs are ubiquitous, in locations ranging from the National Gallery of Art's gift shop to Union Station to grocery stores.

In addition to debit cards, credit cards are the most widely used form of payment in the United

States. Beware of hidden credit card fees while traveling internationally. Check with your credit or debit card issuer to see what fees, if any, will be charged for overseas transactions. Fees can amount to 3% or more of the purchase price.

Newspapers & Magazines The preeminent newspaper in Washington is the *Washington Post,* available online and sold in bookstores, train and subway stations, and drugstores all over town. These are also the places to buy other newspapers, such as the *New York Times,* and *Washingtonian* magazine, the city's popular monthly full of penetrating features, restaurant reviews, and nightlife calendars. The websites of these publications are www. washingtonpost.com, www. nytimes.com, and www. washingtonian.com.

Also be sure to pick up a copy of *Washington City Paper,* a weekly publication available free all over the city, at CVS drugstores, movie theaters, you name it, but also online at www. washingtoncitypaper.com.

Police The number of different police agencies in Washington is quite staggering. They include the city's own Metropolitan Police Department, the National Park Service police, the U.S. Capitol police, the Secret Service, the FBI, and the Metro Transit police. The only thing you need to know is: In an emergency, dial ℂ **911.**

Safety In the years following the September 11, 2001, terrorist attack on the Pentagon, the federal and D.C. governments, along with agencies such as the National Park Service, have continued to work together to increase security, not just at airports but also around the city, including at tourist attractions, and in the subway.

Despite what some news reports may suggest, D.C.'s protest culture is overwhelmingly peaceful. You can find people protesting something almost every day, and the city is generally equipped to handle large, peaceful demonstrations.

The most noticeable and, honestly, most irksome aspect of increased security at tourist attractions can be summed up in three little words: **waiting in line.** You can expect to pass through metal detectors and have your purse or bag checked when you enter federal buildings and some museums.

Besides lines, you will notice the intense amount of security in place around the White House and the Capitol, as well as a profusion of vehicle barriers.

Just because so many police are around, you shouldn't let your guard down. Washington, like any urban area, has a criminal element, so it's important to stay alert and take normal safety precautions. See "The Neighborhoods in Brief" in chapter 3 to get a better idea of where you might feel most comfortable.

Avoid deserted areas, especially at night, and don't go into public parks at night unless there's a concert or a similar occasion attracting a crowd.

Avoid carrying valuables with you on the street, and don't display expensive cameras or electronic equipment. If you're using a map, consult it inconspicuously—or better yet, try to study it before you leave your room. In general, the more you look like a tourist, the more likely someone will try to take advantage of you. If you're walking, pay attention to who is near you as you walk. If you're attending a convention or event where you wear a name tag, remove it before venturing outside. Hold on to your purse and place your wallet in an inside pocket. In theaters, restaurants, and other public places, keep your possessions in sight. Also remember that hotels are open to the public, and in a large hotel, security may not be able to screen everyone entering. Always lock your room door.

Senior Travel Members of **AARP** (www.aarp.org; ℂ **888/687-2277**) get

discounts on hotels, airfares, and car rentals. Anyone over 50 can join.

With or without AARP membership, seniors often find that discounts are available to them at hotels, so be sure to inquire when you book your reservation. Venues in Washington that grant discounts to seniors include the Metro; certain theaters, such as the Shakespeare Theatre; and those few museums, such as the Phillips Collection, that charge for entry. Each place has its own eligibility rules, including designated "senior" ages: The Shakespeare Theatre's is 60 and over, the Phillips Collection's is 62 and over, and the Metro discounts seniors 65 and over.

Smoking The District is smoke-free, meaning that the city bans smoking in restaurants, bars, and other public buildings. Smoking is permitted outdoors, unless otherwise noted.

Taxes The United States has no value-added tax (VAT) or other indirect tax at the national level. The sales tax on merchandise is 6% in the District and Maryland, and 5.3% in most parts of Virginia. Restaurant tax is 10% in the District, 6% in Maryland, and varied in Virginia, depending on the city and county. Hotel tax is 14.95% in the District, and averages 6% in Maryland and 4.3% in Virginia.

Telephones Most long-distance and international calls can be dialed directly from any phone. **To make calls within the United**

States and to Canada, dial 1 followed by the area code and the seven-digit number. **For other international calls,** dial 011 followed by the country code, the city code, and the number you are calling.

Calls to area codes **800, 888, 877,** and **866** are toll free. However, calls to area codes **700** and **900** (chat lines, bulletin boards, "dating" services, and so on) can be expensive—charges of 95¢ to $3 or more per minute. Some numbers have minimum charges that can run $15 or more.

For **directory assistance** ("Information"), dial **411** for local numbers and national numbers in the U.S. and Canada. For dedicated long-distance information, dial 1, then the appropriate area code, plus 555-1212.

Time The continental United States is divided into **four time zones:** Eastern Standard Time (EST)—this is Washington, D.C.'s time zone—Central Standard Time (CST), Mountain Standard Time (MST), and Pacific Standard Time (PST). Alaska and Hawaii have their own zones. For example, when it's 9am in Los Angeles (PST), it's noon in Washington, D.C. (EST), 5pm in London (GMT), and 2am the next day in Sydney.

Daylight saving time is in effect from 2am on the second Sunday in March to 2am on the first Sunday in November. Daylight saving time moves the clock 1 hour ahead of standard time, so come that first Sunday in November, the clock is turned back 1 hour.

Tipping In hotels, tip **bellhops** at least $1 per bag ($2–$3 if you have a lot of luggage) and tip the **chamber staff** $1 to $2 per day (more if you've left a big mess). Tip the **doorman** or **concierge** only if he or she has provided you with some specific service (for example, getting you a cab or obtaining difficult-to-get theater tickets). Tip the **valet-parking attendant** $1 every time you get your car.

In restaurants, bars, and nightclubs, tip **service staff** and **bartenders** 15% to 20% of the check, tip **checkroom attendants** $1 per garment, and tip **valet-parking attendants** $1 per vehicle.

As for other service personnel, tip **cab drivers** 15% of the fare; tip **skycaps** at airports at least $1 per bag ($2–$3 if you have a lot of luggage); and tip **hairdressers** and **barbers** 15% to 20%.

Toilets You won't find many public toilets or "restrooms" on the streets of D.C. (other than in The Wharf), but they can be found in hotel lobbies, bars, restaurants, museums, service stations, and at many sightseeing attractions. Starbucks and fast-food restaurants abound in D.C., and these might be your most reliable option. If you're on the Mall, there's a restroom at the base of the Washington Monument. Restaurants and bars may reserve their restrooms for patrons.

Travelers with Disabilities Although Washington, D.C., is one of the most accessible cities in the world, it is not perfect—especially when it comes to historic buildings, as well as some restaurants and shops. Theaters, museums, and government buildings are generally well-equipped. Still, for the least hassle, call ahead to places you hope to visit to find out specific accessibility features. In the case of restaurants and bars, I'm afraid you'll have to work to pin them down—no one wants to discourage a potential customer. Several sources might help. Destination: D.C.'s website offers some helpful, though hardly comprehensive, info, http://washington.org/DC-information/washington-dc-disability-information, including links to the **Washington Metropolitan Transit Authority,** which publishes accessibility information on its website, www.wmata.com.

Visas The U.S. State Department has a Visa Waiver Program (VWP) allowing citizens of the following countries to enter the United States without a visa for stays of up to 90 days: Andorra, Australia, Austria, Belgium, Brunei, Chile, Czech Republic, Denmark, Estonia, Finland, France, Germany, Greece, Hungary, Iceland, Ireland, Italy, Japan, Latvia, Liechtenstein, Lithuania, Luxembourg, Malta, Monaco, the Netherlands, New Zealand, Norway, Portugal, San Marino, Singapore, Slovakia, Slovenia, South Korea, Spain, Sweden, Switzerland, Taiwan, and the United

Kingdom. (**Note:** This list was accurate at press time; for the most up-to-date list of countries in the VWP, consult https://travel.state.gov/content/travel/en/us-visas/tourism-visit/visa-waiver-program.html.)

Even though a visa isn't necessary, in an effort to help U.S. officials check travelers against terror watch lists before they arrive at U.S. borders, visitors from VWP countries must register online through the Electronic System for Travel Authorization (ESTA) before boarding a plane or a boat to the U.S. Travelers must complete an electronic application providing basic personal and travel eligibility information. Authorizations will be valid for up to 2 years or until the traveler's passport expires, whichever comes first. Currently, there is one $14 fee for the online application. Existing ESTA registrations remain valid through their expiration dates. **Note:** As of April 1, 2016, travelers from VWP countries must have an e-Passport to be eligible to enter the U.S. without a visa. E-Passports contain computer chips capable of storing biometric information, such as the required digital photograph of the holder.

Furthermore, the State Department states that "Under the Visa Waiver Program Improvement and Terrorist Travel Prevention Act of 2015, travelers in the following categories are no longer eligible to travel or be admitted to the United States under the Visa Waiver Program (VWP):

Nationals of VWP countries who have traveled to or been present in Iran, Iraq, Libya, Somalia, Sudan, Syria, or Yemen after March 1, 2011 (with limited exceptions for travel for diplomatic or military purposes in the service of a VWP country), and Nationals of VWP countries who are also nationals of Iran, Iraq, Sudan, or Syria.

These individuals will still be able to apply for a visa using the regular appointment process at a U.S. Embassy or Consulate."

Canadian citizens may enter the United States without visas but will need to show passports and proof of residence.

Citizens of all other countries must have (1) a valid passport that expires at least 6 months later than the scheduled end of their visit to the U.S., and (2) a tourist visa.

For more information about U.S. visas, go to **www.travel.state.gov** and click "Visas."

Visitor Information

Destination D.C. is the official tourism and convention corporation for Washington, D.C. (www.washington.org; ℂ **202/789-7000**). Call staff "visitor services specialists" for answers to any specific questions about the city. Destination D.C.'s website is a good source for the latest travel information, including upcoming exhibits at the museums and anticipated opening or closing status of tourist attractions.

National Park Service information kiosks are located inside or near the Jefferson, Lincoln, FDR, Vietnam Veterans, Korean War, and World War II memorials, and at the Washington Monument (www.nps.gov/nama for National Mall and Memorial Parks sites; ℂ **202/426-6841** or 619-7222).

The **White House Visitor Center,** on the first floor of the Herbert Hoover Building, Department of Commerce, 1450 Pennsylvania Ave. NW (btw. 14th and 15th sts.; ℂ **202/208-1631,** or 202/456-7041 for recorded information), is open daily (except New Year's Day, Christmas Day, and Thanksgiving) from 7:30am to 4pm.

The **Smithsonian Information Center,** in the Castle, 1000 Jefferson Dr. SW (www.si.edu; ℂ **202/633-1000,** or TTY [text telephone] 633-5285), is open every day but Christmas from 8:30am to 5:30pm; knowledgeable staff answer questions and dispense maps and brochures.

Visit the D.C. government's website, **www.dc.gov**, and that of the nonprofit organization Cultural Tourism DC, **www.culturaltourismdc.org**, for more information about the city. The latter site in particular provides helpful and interesting background knowledge of D.C.'s historic and cultural landmarks, especially in neighborhoods or parts of neighborhoods not usually visited by tourists.

Index

See also Accommodations and Restaurant indexes, below.

General Index

14th and U Street neighborhood, 50
  accommodations, 83–85
  attractions, 187–188
  dining, 106–110
  nightlife, 221
  shopping, 209–210
17th Street NW, 91
9:30 Club, 233–234
1903 Flyer, 147
3307 N St. NW, 269

A

Abraham Lincoln's Birthday, 24
Accommodations, See also Accommodations Index
  best, 9
  Covid-19, 55
  deals, 54–57
  discounts, 55, 57
  extended stays, 72
  family-friendly, 67
  guest amenity fees, 56
  hostels, 56
  house swapping, 56
  Internet booking, 57
  Old Town Alexandria, 245
  taxes, 56
  vacation rentals, 56
Adams Morgan neighborhood, 50
  accommodations, 72–74
  dining, 111–112
  nightlife, 221
  shopping, 209
Addresses, 293–294
African American Civil War Memorial and Museum, 47, 110, 187–188
African American Heritage Trail, 245
Air travel, 286–287
Albert Einstein Memorial, 187
Albert Einstein Planetarium, 147
Alexandria, see Old Town Alexandria
Alexandria Black History Museum, 246–247
Alexandria Colonial Tours, 245
Alexandria the Great Tours, 245
Alexandria's birthday, 246
Alexandria's Black History Driving Tour, 245
Alexandria Visitor Center, 244
A Mano, 216
Amazon Books, 212
Anacostia neighborhood, 50, 194
Anacostia Community Museum, 194
Anderson House, 184, 279

An American in Paris, 247
The Anthem, 8, 226
Antiques, shopping, 210–211
Apple Store, 214
Archipelago, 229
Area codes, 302
Arena Stage, 221–223
Arlington House, 196
Arlington Memorial Bridge, 195
Arlington National Cemetery, 26–27, 195–197
Arlington, Virginia, 195–198
Around the World Embassy Tour, 25
Art galleries, 211
Art Museum of the Americas, 168, 264
ARTECHOUSE, 227
Arthur M. Sackler Gallery, 140
Arts and Industries Building, 135
The Athenaeum, 247–248
Audi Field, 96
Augie's Mussel House and Beer Garden, 256

B

Baked and Wired, 117
Baltimore–Washington International Thurgood Marshall Airport, 287, 289
Barbie Pond on Ave. Q, 10
Barmy Wines & Liquors, 220
Barracks Row, 50
  dining, 93–95
  nightlife, 221
Barrel, 228
Bars, 228–231
Baseball, 236
Basketball, 236
Beauty, shopping, 211–212
Beer gardens, 231
Bellacara, 247
Belmont-Paul Women's Equality National Monument, 25, 129
Biden, Joe, 21
Biergarten Haus, 231
Big Bus Tours, 300
Bike and Boat, 238
Bike and Roll DC, 302
Bike tours, 302
Biking, 204–205, 248, 298–299
The Birchmere Music Hall and Bandstand, 256
Birthnight Ball at Gadsby's Tavern, 246
The Black Cat, 8, 233
Black History Month, 24
Black Lives Matter Plaza, 47, 122, 168, 261
Blackwall Hitch, 256
Blaine Mansion, 277
Blue Mercury, 211–212
Bluejacket Brewery, 228
Blues Alley, 8, 232
Blues, 232
Boat tours, 301–302
Boat transportation, 298
Boating, 205

Boeing Milestones of Flight Hall, 146
Books, shopping, 212–214
The Brewmaster's Castle, 277
The Brig, 231
British Embassy, 283
Bureau of Engraving and Printing, 164
Bus tours, 300
Bus travel, 291
Busboys and Poets, 213
Business hours, 302

C

Cady's Alley, 218–219
Calendar of Events, 23–27
Calloway Fine Art & Consulting, 211
Cameras, shopping, 214
Campagna Center's Scottish Christmas Walk, 246
Capital Beltway, 290
Capital Fringe Festival, 26
Capital One Arena, 226
Capital Pride, 26
Capital Segway, 300
Capitol Hill, 7, 50
  accommodations, 57–59
  attractions, 123–134
  dining, 93–95
Capitol Hill Books, 213
Capitol River Cruise, 302
Capitol Riverfront/Navy Yard neighborhood, 50
  accommodations, 62–64
  dining, 95–96
  nightlife, 221
Capitol Visitor Center, 127
Car sharing, 287–288, 298
Car travel, 290, 297–298
Carlyle House, 246, 248–249
The Castle, see Smithsonian Information Center
Center for Education and Leadership, 24
Central Liquors, 220
Chaplin's, 229
Chesapeake & Ohio Canal National Historical Park, 201–202
Chinese New Year Celebration, 24
Chocolate Moose, 217–218
Christ Church, 249
Christian Heurich House Museum, 277
Churchill, Winston, 283
Citi Open, 26, 235–236
City Cruises, 238, 301
City layout, 291–294
City Sights DC, 300
City Tours by Loba, 237
Cleveland Park, 50–51
  attractions, 188–192
  dining, 120–121
Clothing, shopping, 214–216
Clubs, 7–8, 231–235
Coffee, 121

Columbia Heights, 51
    dining, 105–106
    nightlife, 221
Columbia Room, 228
Comedy clubs, 234–235
Comfort One Shoes, 219
Computers, shopping, 214
Congress Heights, 297
Connecticut Avenue, 209, 292
Conservation Biology Institute,
    189–190
Constitution Avenue, 26, 292
Constitution, 3
Consulates, 303
Coolidge Auditorium, 131
Corcoran Gallery of Art, 263
Cosmos Club, 279
Costs, 304
Covid-19, 55, 208, 222, 238, 287
Cox's Row, 269
Crafts, shopping, 216
Crimson View, Motto by
    Hilton, 228
Cupcakes, 117

D
Dacha Beer Garden, 231
DAR Constitution Hall, 226
Daughters of the American
    Revolution (DAR) Museum, 169,
    263–264
DC Circulator, 136, 295, 297
D.C. Fashion Week, 24
DC by Foot, 299
The D.C. Improv, 234
DC Jazz Festival, 26
DC Metro Food Tours, 299–300
DC Streetcar, 296
D.C. War Memorial, 135
Decatur House, 261
Debby Harper Salon & Spa, 212
Destination DC website, 55
Dickey, J. D., 16
Dining, see also Restaurants Index
    17th Street NW, 91
    best, 4–5
    coffee, 121
    cupcakes, 117
    family-friendly, 104
    ice cream, 117
    Mount Vernon, 241
    Old Town Alexandria, 254–256
    outdoor cafes, 9
    outdoor dining, 91
Disabilities, 306
Discounts, accommodations,
    54–57
District Cutlery, 92
DJs, 233–234
Doctors, 302
Dolcezza, 117
Donald W. Reynolds Museum and
    Education Center, 239
Downtown, 51
    accommodations, 70–72
    dining, 99–105
Drinking laws, 302
Drum circle, 10

Dumbarton House, 192, 272–273
Dumbarton Oaks, 192–193,
    270–271
Dumbarton Oaks Park, 200
Dupont Circle, 6–7, 36, 51, 297
    accommodations, 74–78
    attractions, 184–186
    dining, 113–115
    nightlife, 221
    shopping, 209
    walking tour, 274–285
Dupont Circle FreshFarm
    Market, 216
Dwight D. Eisenhower Memorial,
    122, 164–165

E
East Potomac Park, 66, 199
Eastern Market, 7, 123, 129,
    216–217, 297
Eighteenth Street Lounge, 233
Eisenhower Executive Office
    Building, 262–263
El Centro, 229
Electricity, 302–303
Ellipse, 27, 264
Emancipation Day, 25
Emancipation Hall, 127
Embassies, 21, 284, 303
Embassy of Brazil, 282
Embassy of Croatia, 281
Embassy of Finland, 284
Embassy of Indonesia, 278
Embassy of Japan, 282
Embassy Open Houses, 25
Embassy Row, 36, 283
    walking tour, 274–285
Embassy of Turkey, 282
Emergencies, 303
*Empire of Mud: The Secret
    History of Washington, D.C.*
    (J. D. Dickey), 16
Enid A. Haupt Garden, 135–136
EU Open House, 25
Eventbrite, 226
Everymay, 272
Exhibition Hall, 127
The Exorcist stairs, 268

F
Fall, 22
Family travel, 303
    accommodations, 67
    attractions for kids, 202–204
    dining, 104
    experiences, 3–4, 36–39
Farmers markets, 216–217
Fishing, 205
Flea markets, 216–217
Foggy Bottom neighborhood, 51
    accommodations, 78–81
    attractions, 186–187
    dining, 115–116
Folger Shakespeare Library, 225
Folger Theatre, 225
Foot tours, 299–300
Football, 236

Ford's Theatre, 2, 24,
    176–180, 225
Forrest-Marbury House, 265–266
Fort Ward Museum & Historic
    Site, 246, 249–250
Foundry Gallery, 211
Franklin Delano Roosevelt
    Memorial, 136–137
Frederick Douglass House, 24
Frederick Douglass National
    Historic Site, 43–46, 194
Free activities, 6–7
Freedom House Museum, 250
Freer Gallery of Art,
    138–140, 162
The Fridge, 211
Friendship Firehouse, 250

G
Gadsby's Tavern Museum, 246,
    250–251
GALA Hispanic Theatre, 226
Garden District, 231
George Mason Memorial, 140
George Washington Memorial
    Parkway, 239
George Washington Museum,
    186–187
George Washington's Birthday,
    24, 245–246
Georgetown, 7, 35, 51–52,
    295, 297
    3307 N St. NW, 269
    accommodations, 81–83
    attractions, 192–195
    Cox's Row, 269
    dining, 116–120
    Dumbarton House, 272–273
    Dumbarton Oaks, 270–271
    Everymay, 272
    The Exorcist stairs, 268
    Forrest-Marbury House,
        265–266
    Halcyon House, 266
    Mount Zion United Methodist
        Church, 273
    nightlife, 221
    Oak Hill Cemetery, 271–272
    Old Stone House, 273–274
    Prospect House, 268
    shopping, 210
    St. John's Episcopal
        Church, 269
    Tudor Place, 270
    walking tour, 265–274
Georgetown Cupcake, 117
Georgetown University, 268–269
Georgetown Waterfront Park,
    200, 204
Ghost tours, Old Town
    Alexandria, 246
Gifts, shopping, 217–218
Glover Park, 52, 188–192
Goldstar, 226
Golf, 206
Good Wood, 210
Gravelly Point, 6, 203

The Great Decision: Jefferson, Adams, Marshall and the Battle for the Supreme Court (Cliff Sloan and David McKean), 16
The Great Republic, 210
The Green Lantern, 235
The Green Zone, 229
Guest amenity fees, 56
The Guild of Professional Tour Guides of Washington, D.C., 300

H

H Street, 87–92, 221, 296
H Street Country Club, 229
H Street Festival, 27
Hains Point, 199
Halcyon House, 266
Hall of Fossils, 122
Hamilton, 8, 232
The Hamilton Live, 232
Happy hours, 229
Heurich House Museum, 184–185
Hiking, 206
Hill's Kitchen, 219
Hillwood Estate, Museum, and Gardens, 188–189
Hip-hop, 233–234
Hirshhorn Museum and Sculpture Garden, 141–142
Historic Garden Week in Virginia, 246
Historical Washington, D.C., 14–22
    beautification program, 17–18
    birth of the capital, 15–16
    Black Broadway, 18
    civil rights, 18–20
    Civil War, 16–17
    early 1800s, 16
    early history, 14–15
    Presidential Commission of Fine Arts, 18
    Reconstruction, 16–17
    Works Progress Administration (WPA), 18
Holiday Boat Parade of Lights, Old Town Alexandria, 246
Holidays, 23
Home furnishings, shopping, 218–219
Hospitals, 303
Hostels, 56
Hotels, *see also* Accommodations Index
House Gallery, 128
House swapping, 56
The Howard Theatre, 233
Hu's Shoes, 219–220

I

IA&A at Hillyer, 211
Ice cream, 117
Ice Cream Jubilee, 117
Ice hockey, 236
Ice skating, 206
Independence Day, 26

Indian Craft Shop, 216
International entertainment, 234
International Spy Museum, 165–166, 203
Internet, 303
The Islamic Center, 282
Itineraries, 28–36
    one-day, 29–33
    three-day, 35–36
    two-day, 33–35

J

Jack Rose Dining Saloon, 229–230
James Madison Memorial Building, 130
Jazz, 232
Jefferson Memorial, 142–143
Jewelry, shopping, 219
Jogging, 8, 206
John Adams Building, 130
John F. Kennedy Center for the Performing Arts, 223–224
J.R.s Bar, 235

K

Kahlil Gibran Memorial, 284
Keegan Theatre, 226
Kennedy Center, 6, 24, 36, 221, 234
Kennedy, John F., 20, 196
Key to the City Attractions Pass, 240
Kids, *see* Family travel
King, Martin Luther, Jr., 19
Kitchenware, shopping, 218–219
Kite Festival, 202
Korean War Veterans Memorial, 143
Kramers, 213
Kreeger Museum, 193–194

L

La Cosecha, 92
Labor Day, 27
Lafayette Square, 260
Landmarks
    measurements, 21
    by moonlight, 2
The Lantern, 213
A League of Her Own, 235
Lee-Fendall House Museum, 251
Legal aid, 303
Leica Camera, 214
L'Enfant, Pierre Charles, 196
L'Enfant Plaza, 297
Letelier/Moffitt Memorial, 279–280
LGBTQ travelers, 235, 303
Library of Congress, 27, 123, 129–131
Lincoln, Abraham, 17
Lincoln Memorial, 2, 24, 33, 143–144
Lincoln Theatre, 47, 227
Live Nation Entertainment, 226
Local experiences, 7–9
Lucky Bar, 230

The Lyceum, 251
Lyft, 298

M

Madam's Organ Blues Bar, 232
Madison Building, 131
Magazines, 304
Mahatma Gandhi, statue, 278
Mail, 303
Maketto, 214–215
Manumission Tour Company, 244
Marine Corps Marathon, 27, 236
Marston Luce Antiques, 210–211
Martin Luther King, Jr. National Memorial, 24, 46, 145
Mary McLeod Bethune Council House National Historic Site, 40, 110, 188
Massachusetts Avenue, 292
McKean, David, 16
McPherson Square, 297
Meeps, 215
Memorial Day, 26
Mercy Me, 230
Meridian Hill Park, 10, 200
Metrobus, 296
Metrorail, 294–295
The Midlands Beer Garden, 231
Miss Pixie's Furnishings & Whatnot, 219
Mobile phones, 303–304
Modern Washington, D.C., 11–14, 20–22
Money, 304
Montrose Park, 200
Mount Vernon, 237–241
    Bike and Boat, 238
    biking, 248
    City Cruises, 238
    City Tours by Loba, 237
    dining, 241
    Donald W. Reynolds Museum and Education Center, 239
    George Washington Memorial Parkway, 239
    Mount Vernon Estate and Garden, 238–241
    public transportation, 238
    shopping, 241
    touring, 240
Mount Vernon Estate and Garden, 238–241
Mount Vernon Trail, 248
Mount Vernon Triangle, 52
Mount Zion United Methodist Church, 43, 273
Mumbo sauce, 218
Museum of the Bible, 166
Museum gift shops, 182
Music, live, 8, 231–235

N

Name of city, 21
National Air and Space Museum, 4, 6, 42, 145–147, 162, 203
National Archives Museum, 32, 147–148

National Book Festival, 27
National Building Museum, 180–182, 203
National Cherry Blossom Festival, 25, 199
National Children's Museum, 169
National Christmas Tree Lighting, 27
National Gallery of Art, 6, 32, 149–150, 182
National Gallery, 3, 203
National Geographic Museum, 185
National Law Enforcement Memorial, 181
National Law Enforcement Museum, 122, 181
National Mall, 6–8, 29-32, 38, 52, 297
    accommodations, 64–65
    attractions, 135–163
National Mall and Memorial Parks, 135–163
National Museum of African American History & Culture, 6, 24, 29, 40, 46, 151–153
National Museum of African Art, 153, 182
National Museum of American History, 4, 34, 38, 42, 153–155, 203
National Museum of the American Indian, 155–156, 203
National Museum of Asian Art, 24, 138–140
National Museum of Natural History, 156–157, 162, 203
National Museum of Women in the Arts, 183
National parkland, 21
National Park Reservation Service, 163
National Park Service, 24
National Postal Museum, 123, 131–132
National Statuary Hall, 126
National Symphony Orchestra, 26
National Theatre, 224
National Trust for Historic Preservation, 55
National World War II Memorial, 26, 157–158
National Zoo, 3, 38, 189–191, 297
National Zoological Park, 203
Nationals Park, 8
Neighborhoods, 7, 50–53
    14th and U Street, 50
    Adams Morgan, 50
    Anacostia, 50
    Barracks Row, 50
    Capitol Hill, 7, 50
    Capitol Riverfront/Navy Yard, 50
    Cleveland Park, 50–51
    Columbia Heights, 51
    Downtown, 51
    Dupont Circle, 7, 51
    Foggy Bottom, 51

    Georgetown, 7, 51–52
    Glover Park, 52
    Mount Vernon Triangle, 52
    National Mall, 52
    NoMa, 52
    Northern Virginia, 52
    Old Town Alexandria, 7
    Penn Quarter, 52
    Shaw, 52
    Southwest Waterfront, 53
    West End, 51
    Woodley Park, 53
Never Looked Better, 230
Newspapers, 304
Nightlife, 221–236
    bars, 228–231
    clubs, 231–235
    LGBTQ, 235
    music scene, 231–235
    Old Town Alexandria, 256
    performing arts, 221–227
    spectator sports, 235–236
NoMa neighborhood, 52
Northern Virginia, 52, 195–198

O

Oak Hill Cemetery, 10, 271–272
Obama, Barrack, 20
Octagon House, 263
Off-beat experiences, 10
Off the Record, The Hay-Adams, 228
Old Post Office Clock Tower, 182
Old Presbyterian Meeting House, 252
Old Stone House, 15, 194, 200, 273–274
Old Supreme Court Chamber, 127
Old Town Alexandria, 7, 24, 210, 242–256
    accommodations, 245
    African American Heritage Trail, 245
    Alexandria Black History Museum, 246–247
    Alexandria Colonial Tours, 245
    Alexandria the Great Tours, 245
    Alexandria's birthday, 246
    Alexandria's Black History Driving Tour, 245
    Alexandria Visitor Center, 244
    An American in Paris, 247
    The Athenaeum, 247–248
    attractions, 246–253
    Bellacara, 247
    biking, 248
    Birthnight Ball at Gadsby's Tavern, 246
    calendar of events, 245–246
    Campagna Center's Scottish Christmas Walk, 246
    Carlyle House, 246, 248–249
    Christ Church, 249
    Christmas tree lighting, 246
    dining, 254–256
    Fort Ward Museum & Historic Site, 246, 249–250
    Freedom House Museum, 250

    Friendship Firehouse, 250
    Gadsby's Tavern Museum, 246, 250–251
    George Washington's Birthday, 245–246
    ghost tours, 246
    Historic Garden Week in Virginia, 246
    Holiday Boat Parade of Lights, 246
    Lee-Fendall House Museum, 251
    The Lyceum, 251
    Manumission Tour Company, 244
    nightlife, 256
    Old Presbyterian Meeting House, 252
    Red Barn Mercantile, 247
    St. Patrick's Day Parade, 246
    Stabler-Leadbeater Apothecary Museum, 246, 252–253
    Tall Ship Providence, 253
    Torpedo Factory Art Center, 253
    tours, 244–245
    visitor information, 244
Old Town Alexandria Farmers Market, 217
Old Town Trolley Tours, 300
One-day itinerary, 29–33
Online booking, 123
Outdoor activities, 204–206
Outdoor cafes, 9
Outdoor dining, 91
The Outrage, 215

P

Parks, 198–202
Pearl Street Warehouse, 232
Peirce Mill, 200
Penn Quarter, 34, 52
    accommodations, 66–69
    attractions, 176–184
    dining, 99–105
    nightlife, 221
    shopping, 208–209
Pennsylvania Avenue, 258–260, 292
Pentagon, 197–198
Performing arts, 221–227
Phillips Collection, 36, 185–186
Phoebe Waterman Haas Public Observatory, 147
The Phoenix, 216
Planet Word Museum, 169–170
Planning trip, 22–27, 29, 286–299
Police, 305
Politics and Prose Bookstore, 213–214
Potomac Paddle Club, 301
Potomac Park, 198–199
Potomac Riverboat Company, 298, 301
Presidents' Day, 24
Professional sports teams, 8
Proper Topper, 215
Prospect House, 268

Publication transportation, 288–289, 294–296
Pubs, 7–8

Q

Quill, 230

R

Rainfall, 23
Red Barn Mercantile, 247
Relish, 215
Renwick Gallery of the Smithsonian American Art Museum, 170–171, 262
Residence Act of 1790, 15
Restaurant Week, 24
Restaurants, see also Restaurants Index
Robert E. Lee Memorial, 196
Robert Emmet statue, 281–282
Rock Creek Nature Center and Planetarium, 200
Rock Creek Park, 3, 6, 199–200
Rock music, 233–234
Ronald Reagan Washington National Airport, 286, 288
Rosslyn, 297
Rotunda, U.S. Capitol, 124

S

Sackler Gallery, 162
Safety, 305
Salon ILO, 212
Salt & Sundry, 92, 219
Sauf Haus Bier Hall & Garden, 231
Schneider's of Capitol Hill, 220
Sculpture Garden, National Gallery of Art, 6
Second Story Books, 214
Secondi Inc., 215–216
Security, 126
Segway tours, 300
Senate Gallery, 128
Senior travel, 305
Shakespeare Theatre Company, 224–225
Shaw neighborhood, 52
    accommodations, 83–85
    dining, 110–111
    drinks, 110–111
    nightlife, 221
    shopping, 209–210
Sheridan Circle, 280–281
Shoes, shopping, 219–220
Shop Made in DC, 218
Shopping, 208–220
    14th and U Street, 209–210
    Adams Morgan, 209
    antiques, 210–211
    art galleries, 211
    beauty, 211–212
    books, 212–214
    cameras, 214
    clothing, 214–216
    computers, 214
    Connecticut Avenue, 209

Covid-19, 208
    crafts, 216
    Dupont Circle, 209
    farmers markets, 216–217
    flea markets, 216–217
    Georgetown, 210
    gifts, 217–218
    home furnishings, 218–219
    jewelry, 219
    kitchenware, 218–219
    Mount Vernon, 241
    Old Town Alexandria, 210
    Penn Quarter, 208–209
    Shaw, 209–210
    shoes, 219–220
    souvenirs, 217–218
    spirits, 220
    Union Station, 208
    Wharf, 210
    wine, 220
Sky Lab Orbital Workshop, 147
Sloan, Cliff, 16
SmarTrip card, 293–295
Smithson, James, 162
The Smithsonian, 4, 6, 38, 162
Smithsonian American Art Museum & National Portrait Gallery, 35, 162, 182–184
Smithsonian Conservation Biology Institute, 189–190
Smithsonian Craft Show, 25
Smithsonian Folklife Festival, 26, 202
Smithsonian Information Center, 159
Smithsonian National Museum of Natural History, 122
Smithsonian National Zoo, 189–190
Smoking, 305
Snallygaster, 27
Soccer, 236
Southwest of Mall, 163–168
Southwest Waterfront, 53
    accommodations, 65–66
    attractions,
    dining, 97–98
Souvenirs, 217–218
Spectator sports, 235–236
Spirit of St. Louis, 146
Spring, 23
Stabler-Leadbeater Apothecary Museum, 246, 252–253
Steadfast Supply, 218
St. John's Episcopal Church, 70, 260–261, 269
St. Patrick's Day Parade, 25, 246
Street hockey, 10
Studio Acting Conservatory, 222
Studio Gallery, 211
Studio Theatre, 225
Summer, 23
Summit, The Conrad, 228
Supreme Court, 3, 132–133
Swimming, 206–207
Swingers, The Crazy Golf Club, 230

T

Take Care, 212
Tall Ship Providence, 253
Taxes, 305
Taxis, 287–288, 298
Telephones, 305–306
Temperatures, 23
Tennis, 206–207, 236
Textile Museum, 186–187
Theater J, 226
Theodore Roosevelt Island Park, 201
Thomas Jefferson Building, 129
Thomas Sweet, 117
Three Littles, 92, 214
Three-day itinerary, 35–36
Tickets, purchasing, 226
Tidal Basin, 39
Time, 306
Tiny Jewel box, 219
Tipping, 306
TodayTix, 226
Toilets, 306
Tomb of the Unknown Soldier, 26–27, 196
Top of the Gate, Watergate Hotel, 228
Torpedo Factory Art Center, 216, 253
Tourism board, 55, 57
Tours, 299–302
    African-American history, 42–47
    Arlington National Cemetery, 196
    Big Bus Tours, 300
    Bike and Roll DC, 302
    bike tours, 302
    boat tours, 301–302
    bus tours, 300
    Capital Segway, 300
    Capitol River Cruise, 302
    City Cruises, 301
    City Sights DC, 300
    DC by Foot, 299
    DC Metro Food Tours, 299–300
    Dupont Circle/Embassy Row, walking tour, 274–285
    foot tours, 299–300
    Georgetown, walking tour, 265–274
    ghost tours, Old Town Alexandria, 246
    The Guild of Professional Tour Guides of Washington, D.C., 300
    Mount Vernon, 240
    Old Town Alexandria, 244–245
    Old Town Trolley Tours, 300
    Potomac Paddle Club, 301
    Potomac Riverboat Company Monuments Tour, 301
    Segway tours, 300
    U.S. Capitol, 124, 127
    walking tours, 257–285
    Washington Walks, 299
    Water Taxi, Potomac Riverboat Company, 301
    White House, walking tour, 257–264
    women's history, 40–42

Train travel, 290
Trollope, Anthony, 16
Tryst, 231
Tudor Place, 194–195, 270
Tune Inn Restaurant & Bar, 231
Two-day itinerary, 33–35

U

Uber, 298
Underground Comedy, 234-235
Union Market, 92, 217
Union Station, 123, 133–134, 208, 290, 297
United States Botanic Garden, 159–160
United States Holocaust Memorial Museum, 167–168
Upper Northwest D.C., attractions, 188–192
Upstairs on 7th, 215
U.S. Botanic Garden, 6, 203
U.S. Capitol, 3, 17, 29, 35, 123–128
U.S. Naval Observatory, 284–285
U.S. Supreme Court, 123
U.S. Treasury Building, 258

V

Vacation rentals, 56
Valtasaari, Jukka, 284
Varnish Lane, 212
Veterans Day, 27
Veterans History Project, 130
Vice President's Residence, 284–285
Vietnam Veterans Memorial, 26, 160–161
Vintage shops, 215–216
Visas, 306–307
Visitor information
    Old Town Alexandria, 244
    Washington, D.C., 307

W

Walking tours, 257–285
    Dupont Circle/Embassy Row, 274–285
    Georgetown, 265–274
    White House, 257–264
Warner Theatre, 227, 234
Washington Capitals, 8, 235–236
Washington Dulles International Airport, 286, 289
Washington Kastles, 236
Washington Monument, 24, 29, 32–33, 161–163
Washington Mystics, 8
Washington National Cathedral Annual Flower Mart, 25–26, 191
Washington National Cathedral, 190–192
Washington Nationals, 8, 235
Washington Walks, 299
Washington Wizards, 8

Water Taxi, Potomac Riverboat Company, 301
Waterfront, 53; see Southwest Waterfront
Weather, 22–23
West End, 51
    accommodations, 78–81
    dining, 115–116
West Potomac Park, 199
The Wharf, 42, 65, 91, 204, 210, 221, 228
The Wharf Spa by L'Occitane Spa, 66
White House, 2, 10, 34, 168, 171–174
    area attractions, 168–176
    Art Museum of the Americas, 264
    Black Lives Matter Plaza, 261
    Corcoran Gallery of Art, 263
    DAR Museum, 263–264
    Decatur House, 261
    Eisenhower Executive Office Building, 262–263
    Ellipse, 264
    Lafayette Square, 260
    Octagon House, 263
    Pennsylvania Avenue, 258–260
    Renwick Gallery, 262
    St. John's Episcopal Church on Lafayette Square, 260–261
    tour, 29, 174–175
    U.S. Treasury Building, 258
    visitor center, 174, 258
    walking tour, 257–264
White House Easter Egg Roll, 25
White House History Shop, 217
Wi-Fi, 303
Wine, shopping, 220
Winter, 22
Wisconsin Avenue, 292
Women's History Month, 24–25
Women in Military Service for America Memorial, 197
Woodley Park, 53, 297
    accommodations, 85–86
    attractions, 188–192
    dining, 120–121
Woodrow Wilson House Museum, 186
Woolly Mammoth Theatre Company, 222, 225
World War I Memorial, 174–176
Wunder Garten, 231

Y

Yards Park, 204

Z

Zeppelin, 229

Accommodations

AKA White House, 72
The Alexandrian, Old Town Alexandria, 245
Cambria Hotel Washington, D.C., Capitol Riverfront, 62

Cambria Hotel Washington, D.C., Convention Center, 84
Canopy by Hilton Washington, D.C./The Wharf, 66
Capitol Hill Hotel, 54, 58
CitizenM, 64–65
Conrad Washington, D.C., 67, 228
Courtyard Washington Capitol Hill/Navy Yard, 66
Fairfield Inn & Suites Washington, D.C./Downtown, 68–69
Generator Hotel Washington, D.C., 78
The Georgetown Inn, 82–83
The Graham Georgetown, 81–82
Hampton Inn & Suites Washington DC-Navy Yard, 54, 63
Hay-Adams, 9, 54, 70, 228
HighRoad Hotel Washington, D.C., 74
Hilton Washington, D.C., National Mall The Wharf, 64
Hotel Hive, 81
Hotel Indigo Old Town Alexandria, 245
Hotel Madera, 75
Hotel Zena Washington, D.C., 83–84
Hyatt Regency Washington on Capitol Hill, 58–59
InterContinental Washington, D.C.— The Wharf, 9, 66
The Jefferson, 9, 74–75
Kalorama Guest House, 86
Kimpton Banneker Hotel, 67, 75–76
Kimpton George Hotel, 59
Kimpton Hotel Monaco Washington, D.C., 68
Kimpton Lorien Hotel & Spa, Old Town Alexandria, 245
The Line Hotel D.C., 72–73, 92
The Lyle D.C., 76
Mob Hotel, 54
Morrison House Old Town Alexandria, Autograph Collection, 245
Motto by Hilton Washington, D.C., City Center, 69, 228
The Normandy Hotel, 72–73
Omni Shoreham Hotel, 67, 85
Residence Inn Washington, DC/Capitol, 9, 65
Riggs Washington, D.C., 67–68
River Inn, 9, 80
Rosewood Washington, D.C., 82
Royal Sonesta Washington, D.C. Dupont Circle, 77
The Tabard Inn, 78
Thompson Washington, D.C., 63–64
U Street Hostel, 84–85
The Ven at Embassy Row, 54, 77
Watergate Hotel, 9, 79, 228
Willard InterContinental, 9, 70–71
Woodley Park Guest House, 86
Yotel Washington, D.C., 9, 59
Yours Truly D.C., 80–81

Restaurants

1310 Kitchen & Bar, 83
1789 Restaurant, 4, 116–117
2Amy's, 104
&Pizza, 81
Ada's on the River, Old Town Alexandria, 254
Agora, 91
Al Tiramisu, 113
Al Volo, 92
Alex Craft Cocktail Cellar & Speakeasy, 82
All Purpose Pizzeria, 91, 110
Amsterdam Falafelshop, 112
Anchovy Social, 64
Anju, 113
Arsenal, 228
Article One American Grill, 58
Article One Lounge & Bar, 58
Bad Saint, 105
Barca Pier & Wine Bar, Old Town Alexandria, 255
Beefsteak, 5, 101, 116
Belga Café, 9, 93
Ben's Chili Bowl, 5, 47, 109
Blackwall Hitch, Old Town Alexandria, 255
Blue Bottle Coffee, 92
Bombay Club, 5, 100
Boots Bar, 100
Café du Parc, 9, 99
Café Riggs, 68
Café Unido, 92
Call Your Mother Bagels, 119
Cane, 87–90
CanteenM, 65
Central Michel Richard, 99
Certo!, 77
Chaia, 119–120
Chercher Ethiopian Restaurant, 107
Chez Billy Sud, 117–118
CHIKO, 94
China Chilcano, 101
Chloe, 95
Chopsmith, 98
CloudM, 65
Colada Shop, 9, 109–110
Columbia Room, 111
Compass Coffee, 121
Convivial, 111
Cork Wine Bar & Market, 108
Crimson Diner and Coffee Bar, 69
Crimson View, 69
Crimson Whiskey Bar, 69
CUT by Wolfgang Puck, 82
The Dabney, 111
Daikaya, 104–105
Del Mar, 118
Dirty Habit DC, 68
District Winery, 91
Duke's Counter, 38, 104

El Cielo, 92
Emissary, 121
Espita Mezcaleria, 110
Estadio, 106–107
Fancy Radish, 5, 90
Farmers Fishers Bakers, 116
Figleaf Bar & Lounge, 84
Fiola Mare, 9, 99, 118
Fiola, 99, 118
Firefly, 75
Fitzgerald's, 117
Five Guys Burgers and Fries, 105
Floriana Restaurant, 91
Founding Farmers, 72, 115–116
Fred & Stilla, 77
Garden Café, 150
GCDC Grilled Cheese Bar, 263
Good Stuff Eatery, 4, 95
Greenhouse, 75
Hank's Oyster Bar, 91, 97
Henry's Soul Café, 5, 112
Hill Country Barbecue Market, 4, 100, 229
Hillwood's Merriweather Café, 189
Hummingbird, Old Town Alexandria, 254
Indique, 120
Irish Channel Restaurant and Pub, 69
Iron Gate, 113–114
Jaleo, 5, 34, 101
Jazz Café, 155
Julia's Empanadas, 112
Kafe Leopold, 265
Kinship, 111
Kirwin's on the Wharf, 91
Kramers, 36
Lady Bird, 76
La Vie, 4, 91, 97
The Lafayette, 70
Las Gemelas, 92
Lauriol Plaza, 91
Le Bar a Vin, 118
Le Diplomate, 9, 107
Le Sel, 76
Little Pearl, 93
Lucky Buns, 92
Lupo Pizzeria, 108
Lupo Verde Cucina and Bar, 108
Lyle's, 76
Maialino Mare, 63, 95–96
Makan, 106
Maketto, 90–92
Market Lunch, 93
Martin's Tavern, 9, 119, 269–270
Masseria, 92
Matchbox, 101
Maydan, 108–109
Medium Rare, 120–121
Mercy Me, 80
Métier, 111
Mezzanine Café, 183

Mia's Italian Kitchen, Old Town Alexandria, 255
Mi Cuba Café, 105
Mi Vida, 91
minibar by José Andrés, 101
Moon Rabbit, 66
Mount Vernon Inn Restaurant, 241
No Goodbyes, 72
Off the Record, 70
Old Ebbitt Grill, 39, 102, 104
Oyamel, 101
Pavilion Café, National Gallery Sculpture Garden, 32, 150
Perch SW, 62
Peregrine Espresso, 121
Pete's Diner and Carryout, 93
Pineapple and Pearls, 93
Pinstripes, 4, 104
Pizzeria Paradiso, 4, 114–115
Pluma by Bluebird, 92
Plume, 75
The Point D.C., 4, 91, 96
The Pool Bar, 85
Punjab Grill, 99–100
Pupatella, 114
Qualia Coffee, 121
Quill, 74–75
Rappahannock Oyster Bar, 4–5, 98
Rasika, 5, 100–102
Robert's Restaurant, 85
Rooster and Owl, 105–106
Rose's Luxury, 4, 93
Round Robin Bar, 71
RowHouse Restaurant & Bar, 62
Sakura Club, 67
The Salt Line, 91, 96
Serenata, 92
Shouk, 92
Silver Lyan, 68
The Smith, 102–103
Social Circle, 84
Spanish Diner, 101
Succotash, 68
Summit, 67
Sweetgreen, 98, 120
Sweet Home Café, 153
Tabard Inn, 114
Tail Up Goat, 111
Tatte, 115
Teaism Dupont Circle, 115
Teaism Lafayette Park, 115
Teaism Penn Quarter, 115
Ted's Bulletin, 4, 94, 104
Thip Khao, 105
Tiger Fork, 5, 111
Top of the Yard, 63
Unconventional Diner, 111
Urbano 116, Old Town Alexandria, 255–256
We, The Pizza, 95
Zaytinya, 5, 101, 103

Photo Credits

Map List

MAP LIST

Iconic Washington, D.C.   30
Washington, D.C., for Families   37
A Women's History Tour of
    Washington, D.C.   41
An African-American History Tour of
    Washington, D.C.   44
Washington, D.C., at a Glance   48
Washington, D.C., Hotels   60
Washington, D.C., Restaurants   88

Capitol Hill   125
The National Mall   138
The White House Area   173
Exploring Washington, D.C.   178
Old Town Alexandria   243
Strolling Around the White House   259
Strolling Around Georgetown   267
Dupont Circle/Embassy Row   275

Frommer's EasyGuide to Washington, D.C., 8th edition

Published by
FROMMER MEDIA LLC

ISBN 978-1-62887-527-0 (paper), 978-1-62887-528-7 (e-book)

Editorial Director: Pauline Frommer
Editor: Elizabeth Heath
Production Editor: Heather Wilcox
Cartographer: Roberta Stockwell
Photo Editor: Meghan Lamb
Cover Design: Dave Riedy

For information on our other products or services, see www.frommers.com.

Frommer Media LLC also publishes its books in a variety of electronic formats. Some content that appears in print may not be available in electronic formats.

Manufactured in the United States of America

5 4 3 2 1

ABOUT THE AUTHORS

Jess Moss is a travel writer, editor, and photographer who has lived in Washington, D.C., for more than a decade. Her work has appeared in Conde Nast Traveler, AOL Travel, US News Travel, as well as a number of travel guides. In her spare time, you can find Jess running on the National Mall, hiking in Rock Creek Park, cheering on Georgetown at basketball games, and wandering the city's neighborhoods with her camera in tow.

Originally from New York City, **Kaeli Conforti** grew up in Hawaii and Florida and then moved to Washington, D.C., following an epic 2-year Working Holiday Visa adventure in Australia and New Zealand. A seasoned travel writer and editor, her work has been featured in Budget Travel, Forbes, Business Insider, CNBC Select, Thrillist, TripSavvy, Mental Floss, and The Points Guy, among other sites. Kaeli has thoroughly enjoyed learning about D.C.'s many diverse neighborhoods, going for long walks in Rock Creek Park, and checking out as many bars and restaurants as possible near her place in Shaw.

ABOUT THE FROMMER TRAVEL GUIDES

For most of the past 50 years, Frommer's has been the leading series of travel guides in North America, accounting for as many as 24% of all guidebooks sold. I think I know why.

Though we hope our books are entertaining, we nevertheless deal with travel in a serious fashion. Our guidebooks have never looked on such journeys as a mere recreation, but as a far more important human function, a time of learning and introspection, an essential part of a civilized life. We stress the culture, lifestyle, history, and beliefs of the destinations we cover, and urge our readers to seek out people and new ideas as the chief rewards of travel.

We have never shied from controversy. We have, from the beginning, encouraged our authors to be intensely judgmental, critical—both pro and con—in their comments, and wholly independent. Our only clients are our readers, and we have triggered the ire of countless prominent sorts, from a tourist newspaper we called "practically worthless" (it unsuccessfully sued us) to the many rip-offs we've condemned.

And because we believe that travel should be available to everyone regardless of their incomes, we have always been cost-conscious at every level of expenditure. Though we have broadened our recommendations beyond the budget category, we insist that every lodging we include be sensibly priced. We use every form of media to assist our readers, and are particularly proud of our feisty daily website, the award-winning Frommers.com.

I have high hopes for the future of Frommer's. May these guidebooks, in all the years ahead, continue to reflect the joy of travel and the freedom that travel represents. May they always pursue a cost-conscious path, so that people of all incomes can enjoy the rewards of travel. And may they create, for both the traveler and the persons among whom we travel, a community of friends, where all human beings live in harmony and peace.

Arthur Frommer